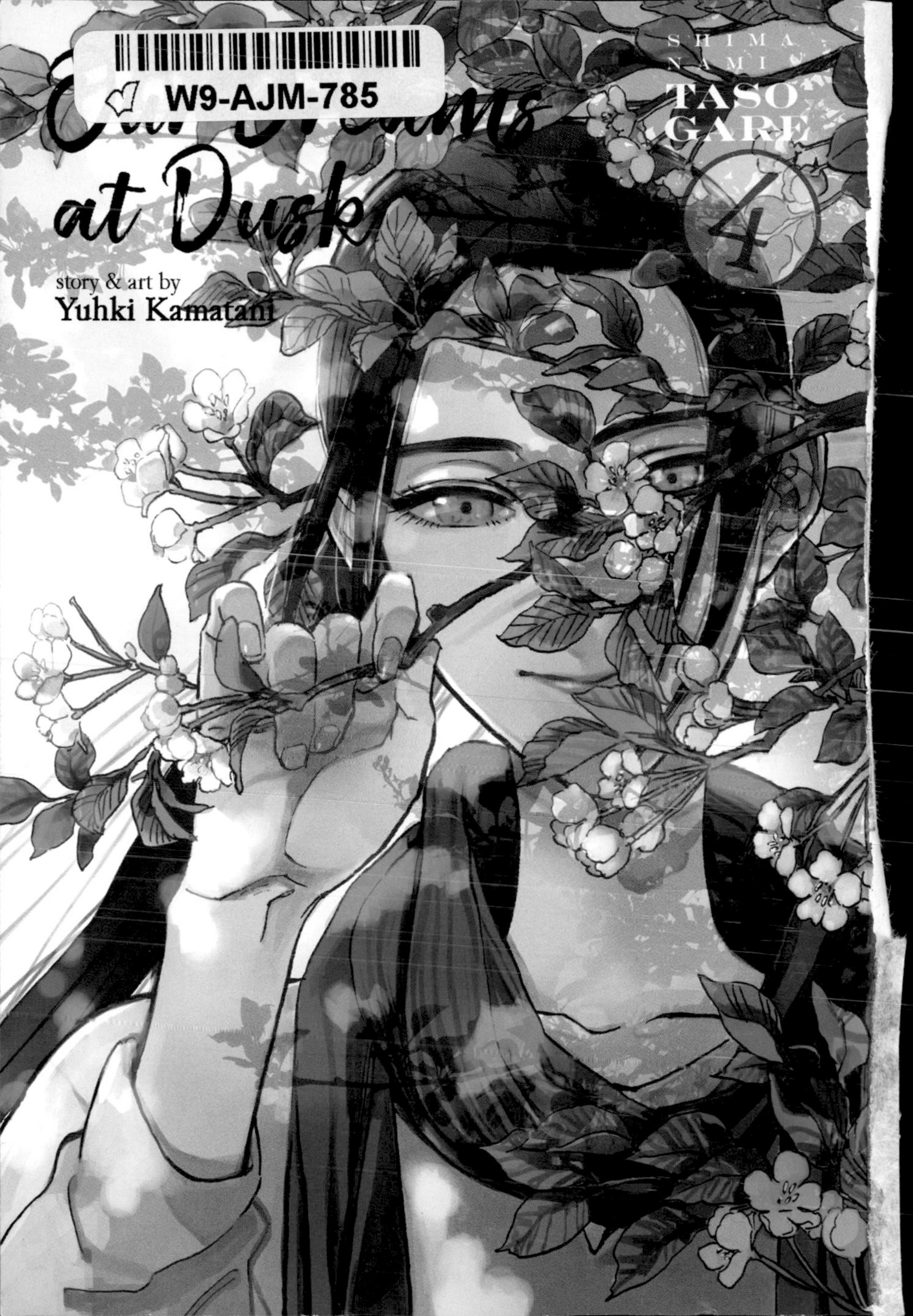

at Dusk
story & art by
Yuhki Kamatani
SHIMA NAMI
TASO GARE
4

CONTENTS

Chapter 16

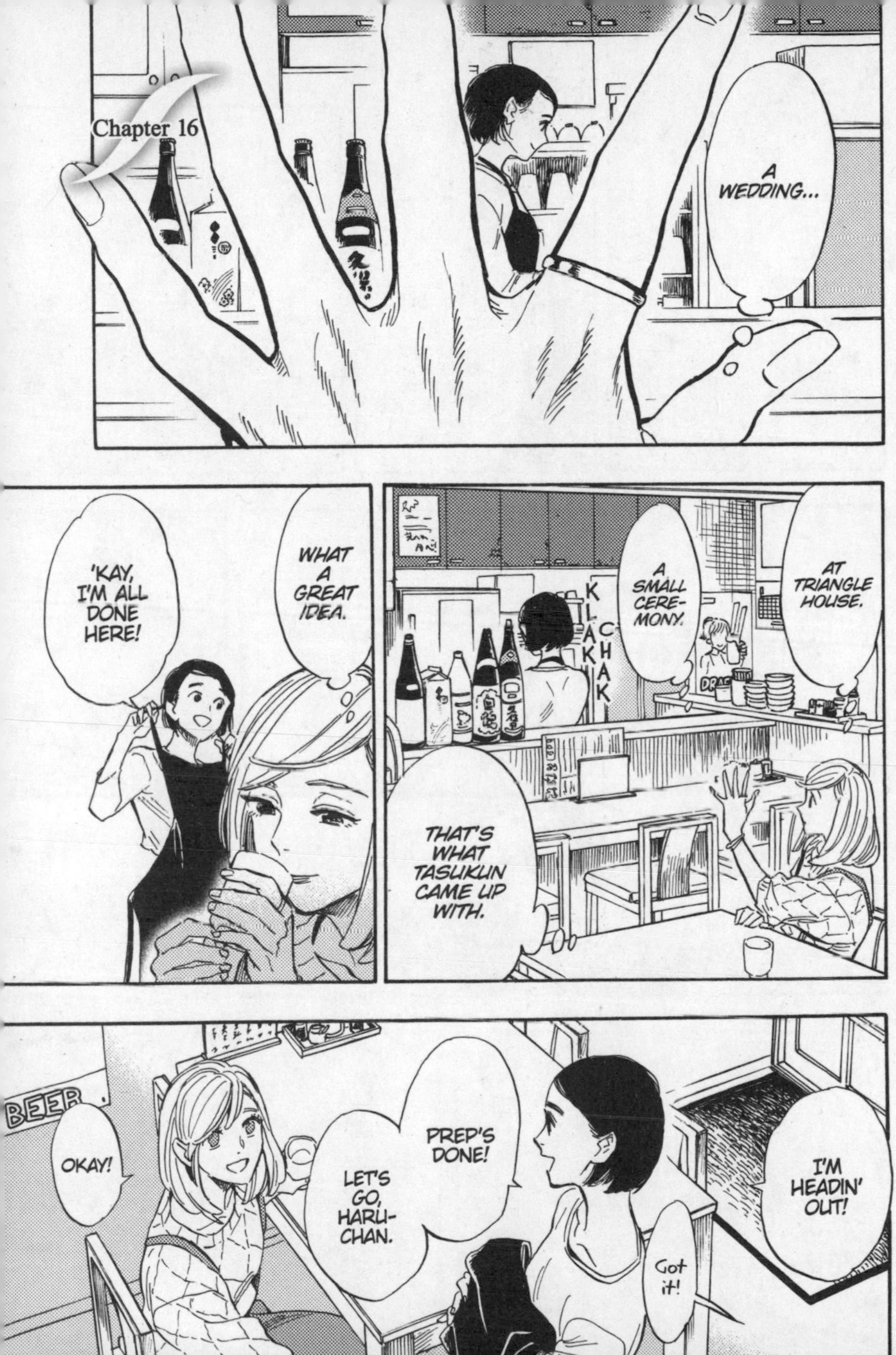
A WEDDING...
AT TRIANGLE HOUSE.
A SMALL CEREMONY.
KLAK KLAK
CHAK CHAK
THAT'S WHAT TASUKUN CAME UP WITH.
WHAT A GREAT IDEA.
'KAY, I'M ALL DONE HERE!
I'M HEADIN' OUT!
Got it!
PREP'S DONE!
LET'S GO, HARU-CHAN.
BEER
OKAY!

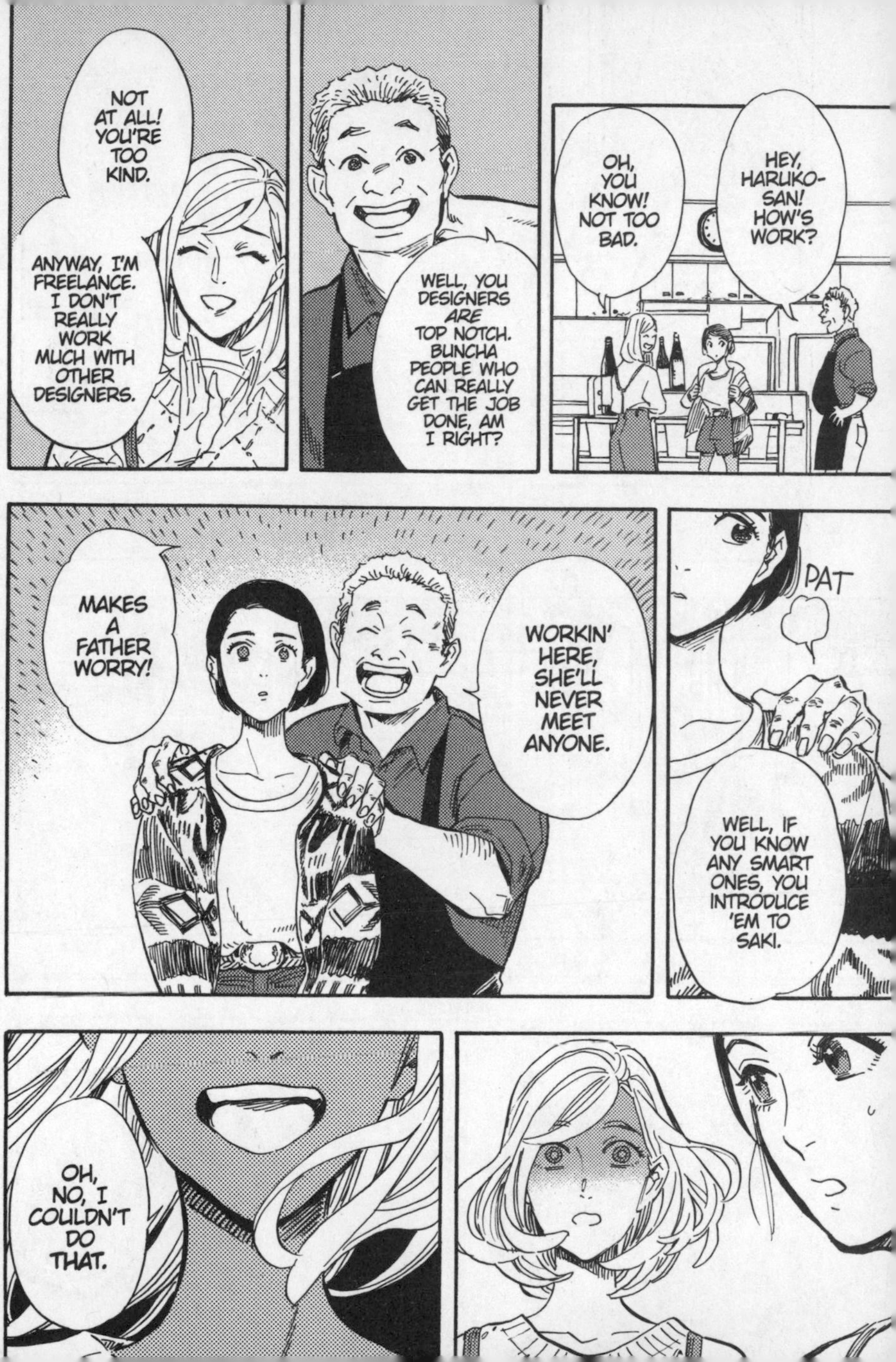
HEY, HARUKO-SAN! HOW'S WORK?
OH, YOU KNOW! NOT TOO BAD.
WELL, YOU DESIGNERS *ARE* TOP NOTCH. BUNCHA PEOPLE WHO CAN REALLY GET THE JOB DONE, AM I RIGHT?
NOT AT ALL! YOU'RE TOO KIND.
ANYWAY, I'M FREELANCE. I DON'T REALLY WORK MUCH WITH OTHER DESIGNERS.
PAT
WELL, IF YOU KNOW ANY SMART ONES, YOU INTRODUCE 'EM TO SAKI.
WORKIN' HERE, SHE'LL NEVER MEET ANYONE.
MAKES A FATHER WORRY!
OH, NO, I COULDN'T DO THAT.

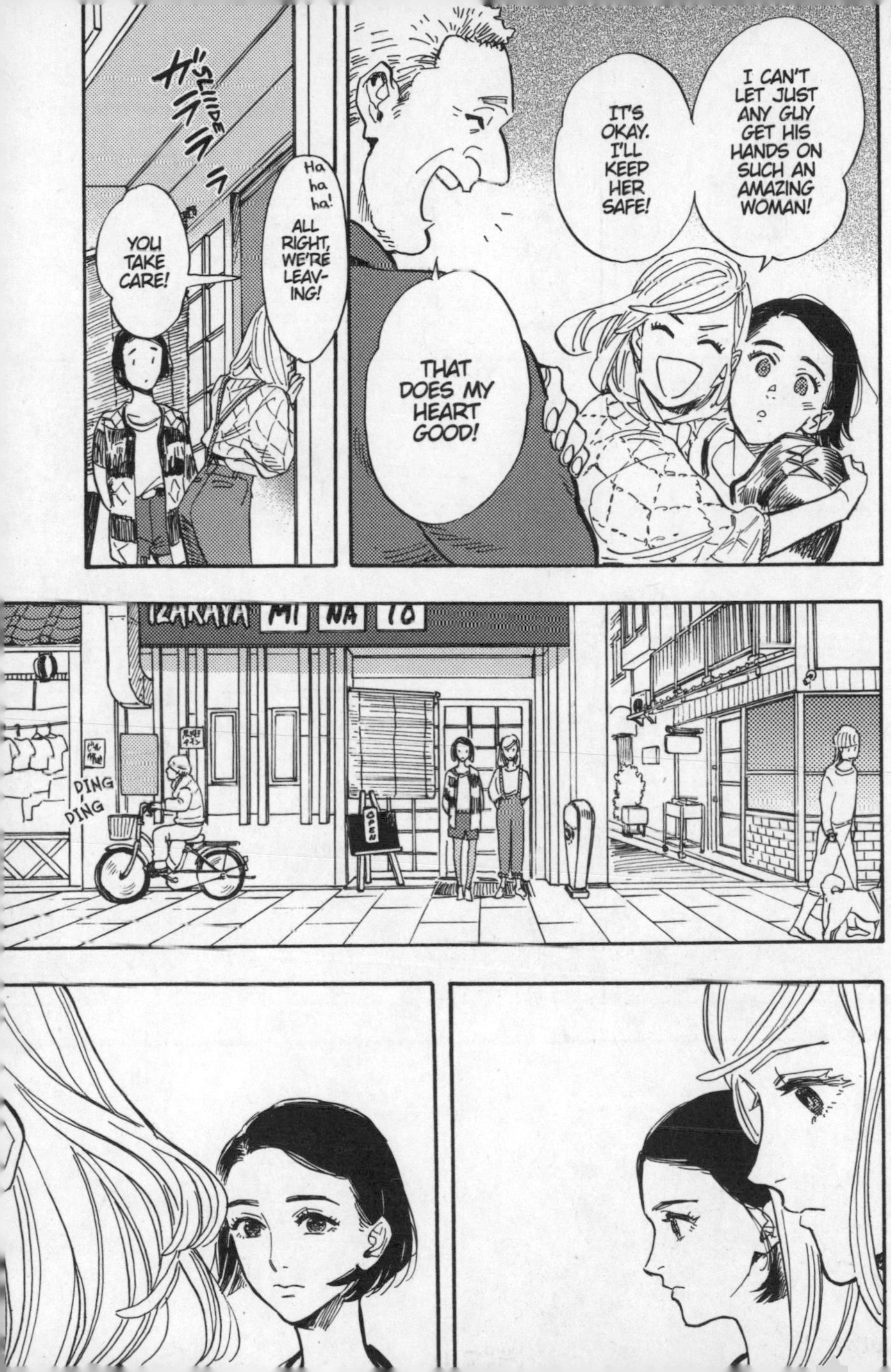
I CAN'T LET JUST ANY GUY GET HIS HANDS ON SUCH AN AMAZING WOMAN!
IT'S OKAY. I'LL KEEP HER SAFE!
THAT DOES MY HEART GOOD!
Ha ha ha! ALL RIGHT, WE'RE LEAV-ING!
YOU TAKE CARE!
SLIIIDE
IZAKAYA MI NA TO
DING DING
OPEN

MARRIAGE.

SOMEDAY, RIGHT?

WE'LL GET MARRIED SOMEDAY.

BUT WHEN WILL "SOMEDAY" GET HERE?

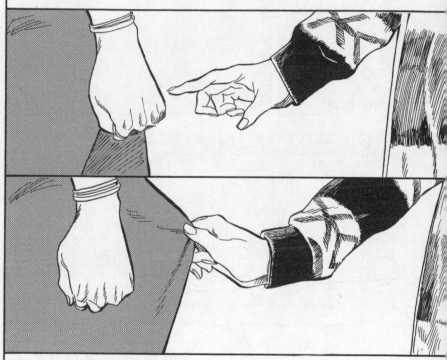

I WANT THE FORMALITIES.

Chapter 16

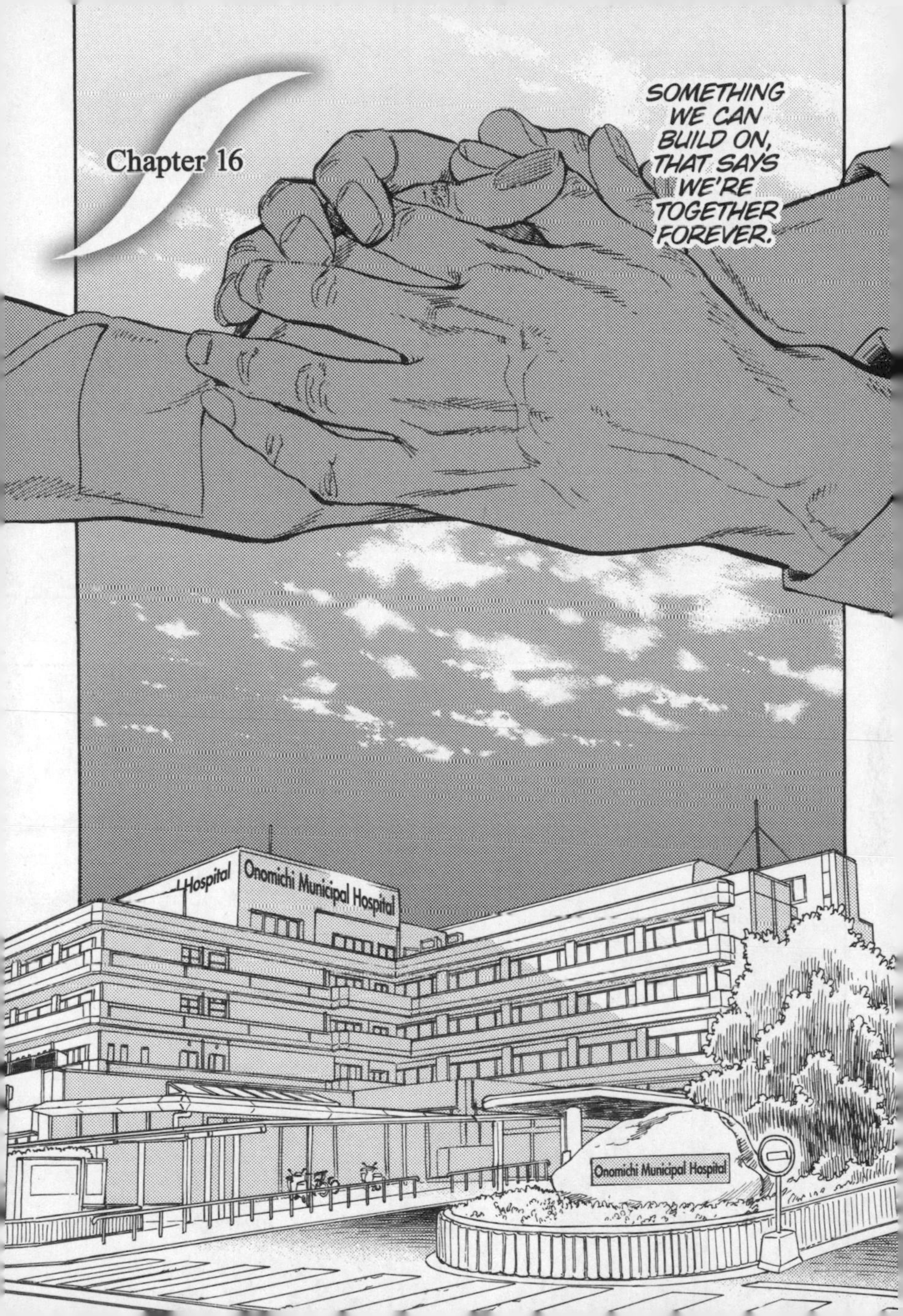
SOMETHING WE CAN BUILD ON, THAT SAYS WE'RE TOGETHER FOREVER.
Onomichi Municipal Hospital
Hospital
Onomichi Municipal Hospital

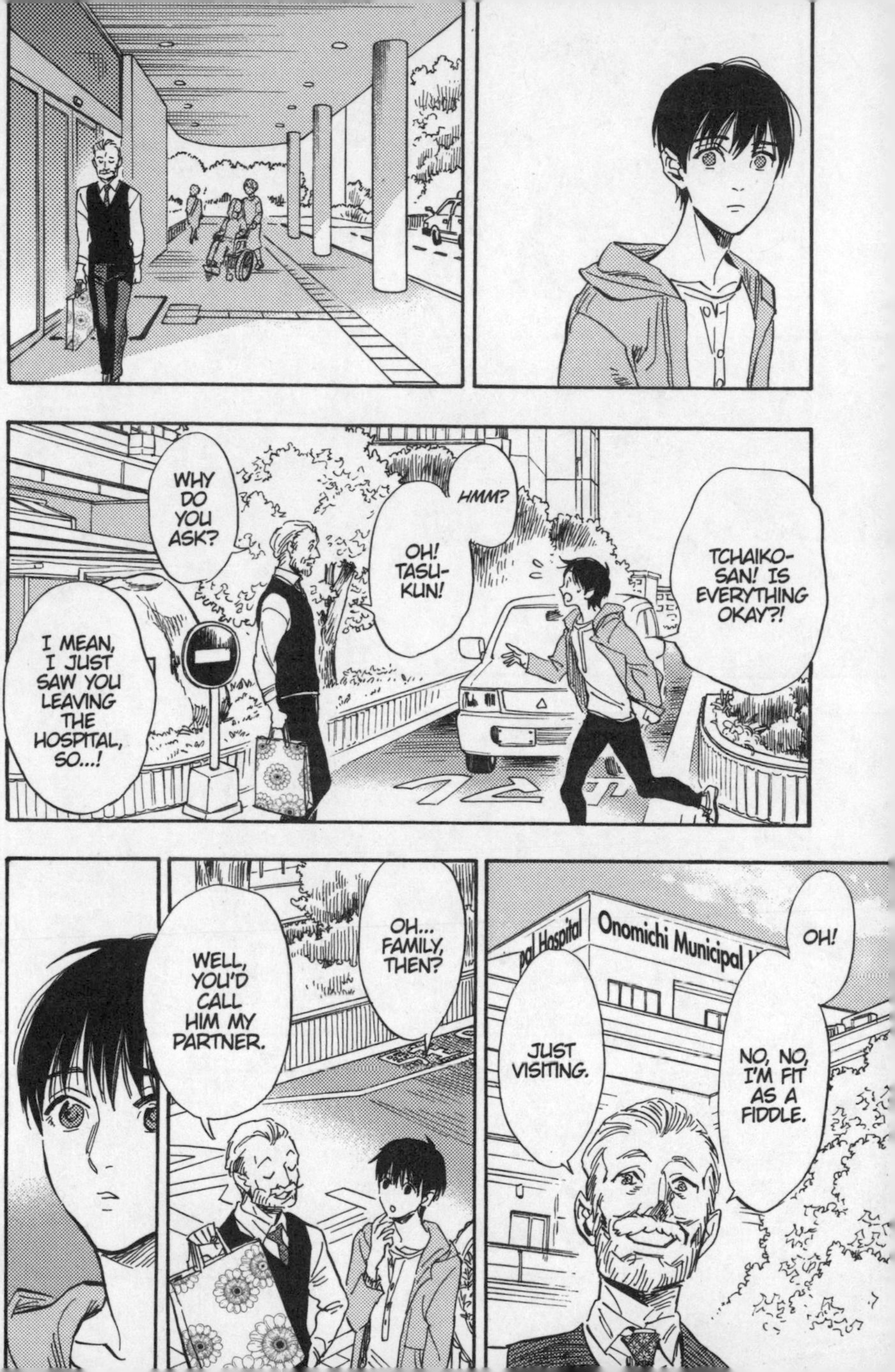
TCHAIKO-SAN! IS EVERYTHING OKAY?!
HMM?
OH! TASU-KUN!
WHY DO YOU ASK?
I MEAN, I JUST SAW YOU LEAVING THE HOSPITAL, SO...!
Onomichi Municipal
OH!
NO, NO, I'M FIT AS A FIDDLE.
JUST VISITING.
OH... FAMILY, THEN?
WELL, YOU'D CALL HIM MY PARTNER.

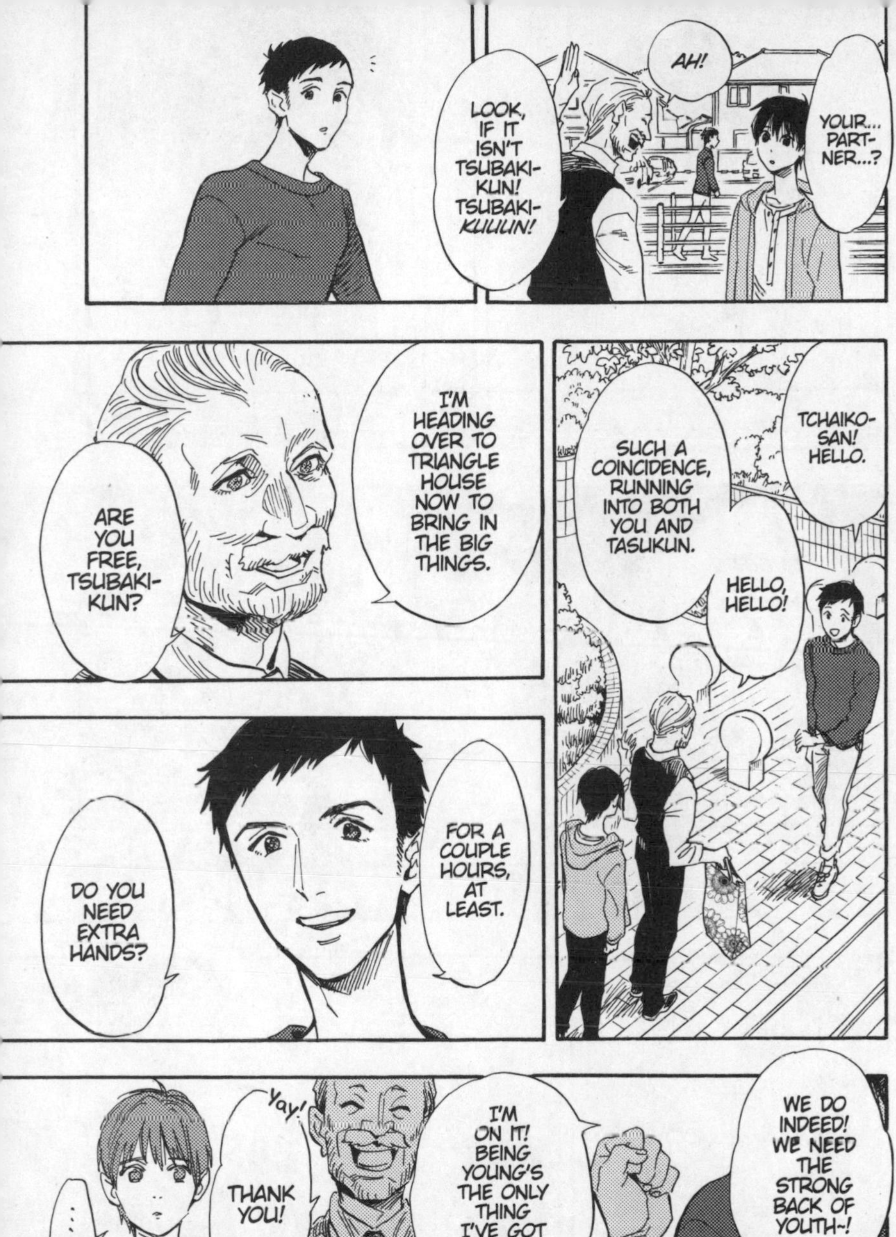
YOUR... PARTNER...?
AH!
LOOK, IF IT ISN'T TSUBAKI-KUN! TSUBAKI-KUUUN!
TCHAIKO-SAN! HELLO.
SUCH A COINCIDENCE, RUNNING INTO BOTH YOU AND TASUKUN.
HELLO, HELLO!
I'M HEADING OVER TO TRIANGLE HOUSE NOW TO BRING IN THE BIG THINGS.
ARE YOU FREE, TSUBAKI-KUN?
FOR A COUPLE HOURS, AT LEAST.
DO YOU NEED EXTRA HANDS?
WE DO INDEED! WE NEED THE STRONG BACK OF YOUTH~!
I'M ON IT! BEING YOUNG'S THE ONLY THING I'VE GOT GOING FOR ME.
Yay!
THANK YOU!
......

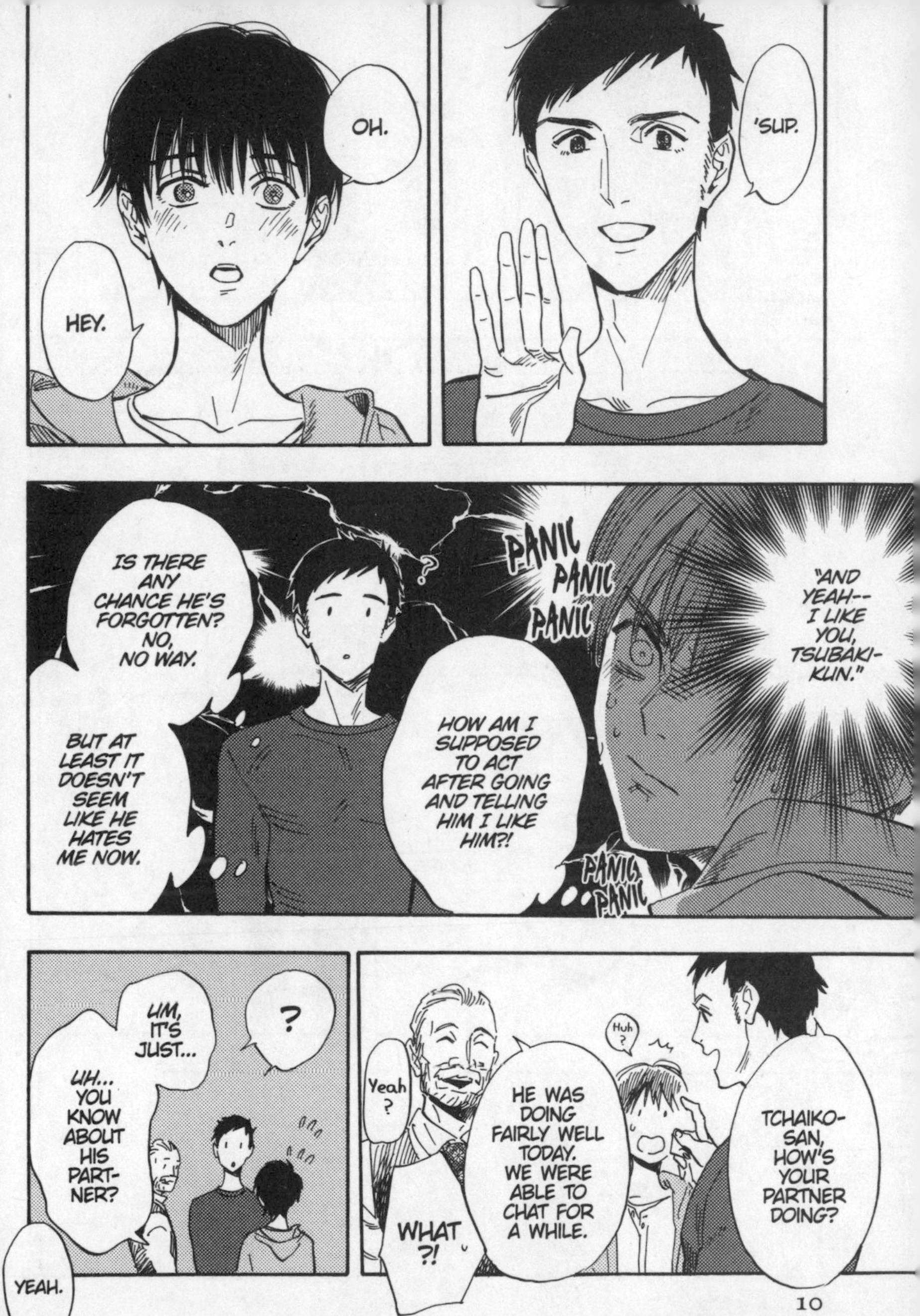
'SUP.
OH.
HEY.
"AND YEAH-- I LIKE YOU, TSUBAKI-KUN."
PANIC PANIC PANIC
HOW AM I SUPPOSED TO ACT AFTER GOING AND TELLING HIM I LIKE HIM?!
IS THERE ANY CHANCE HE'S FORGOTTEN? NO, NO WAY.
BUT AT LEAST IT DOESN'T SEEM LIKE HE HATES ME NOW.
PANIC PANIC
TCHAIKO-SAN, HOW'S YOUR PARTNER DOING?
Huh?
HE WAS DOING FAIRLY WELL TODAY. WE WERE ABLE TO CHAT FOR A WHILE.
Yeah?
WHAT?!
?
UM, IT'S JUST...
UH... YOU KNOW ABOUT HIS PARTNER?
YEAH.

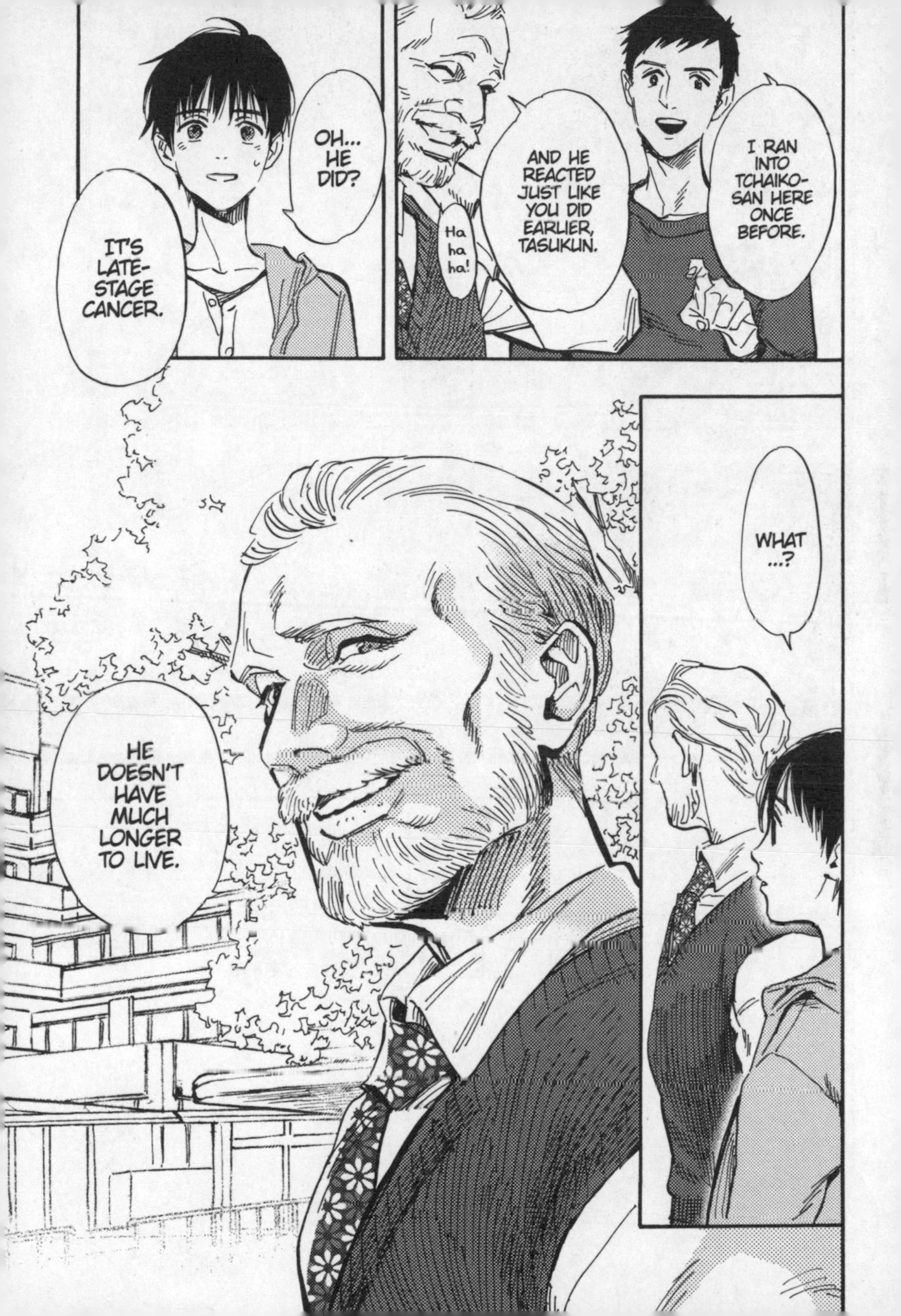
I RAN INTO TCHAIKO-SAN HERE ONCE BEFORE.
AND HE REACTED JUST LIKE YOU DID EARLIER, TASUKUN.
Ha ha ha!
OH... HE DID?
IT'S LATE-STAGE CANCER.
WHAT ...?
HE DOESN'T HAVE MUCH LONGER TO LIVE.

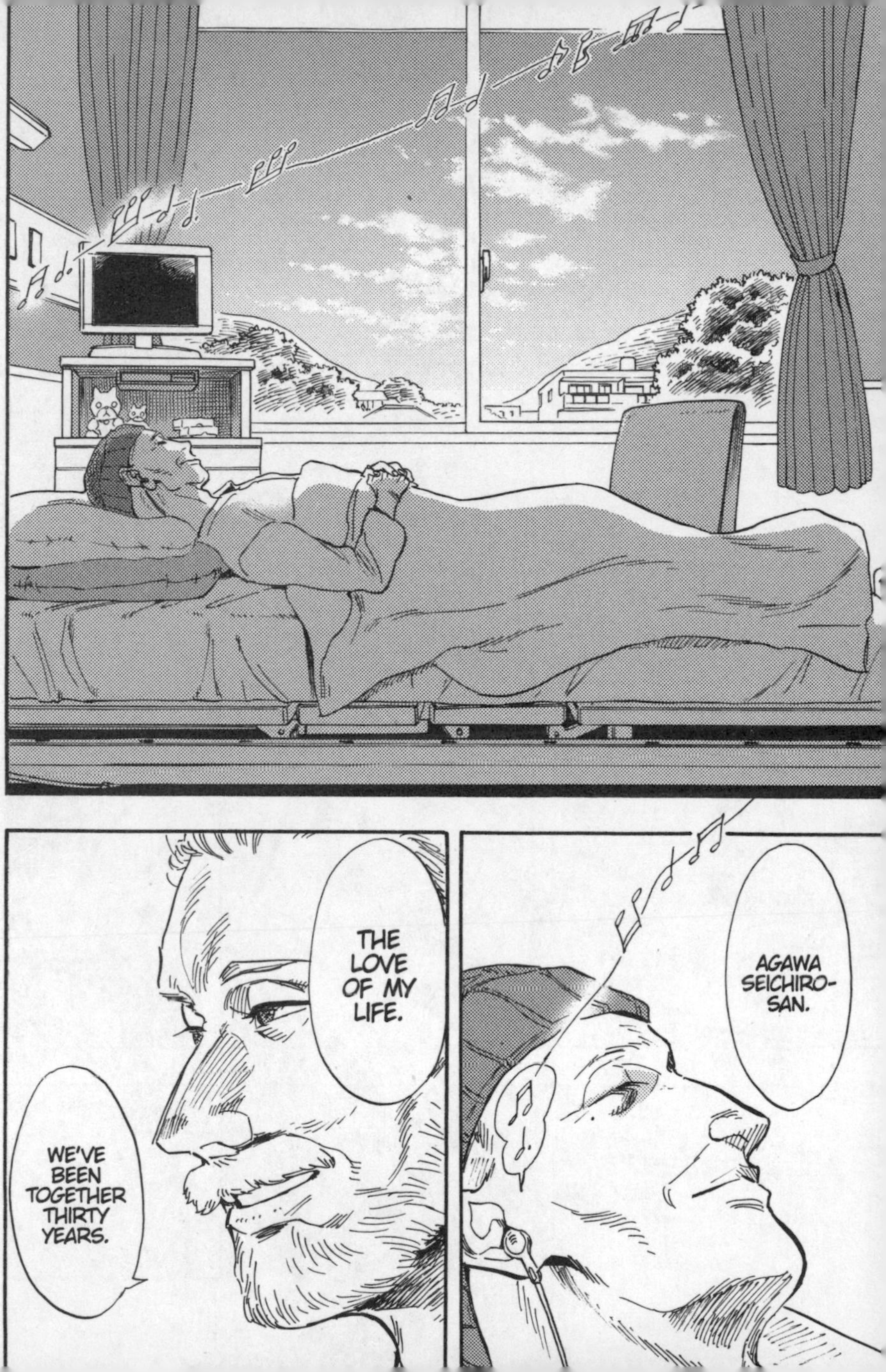
AGAWA SEICHIRO-SAN.
THE LOVE OF MY LIFE.
WE'VE BEEN TOGETHER THIRTY YEARS.

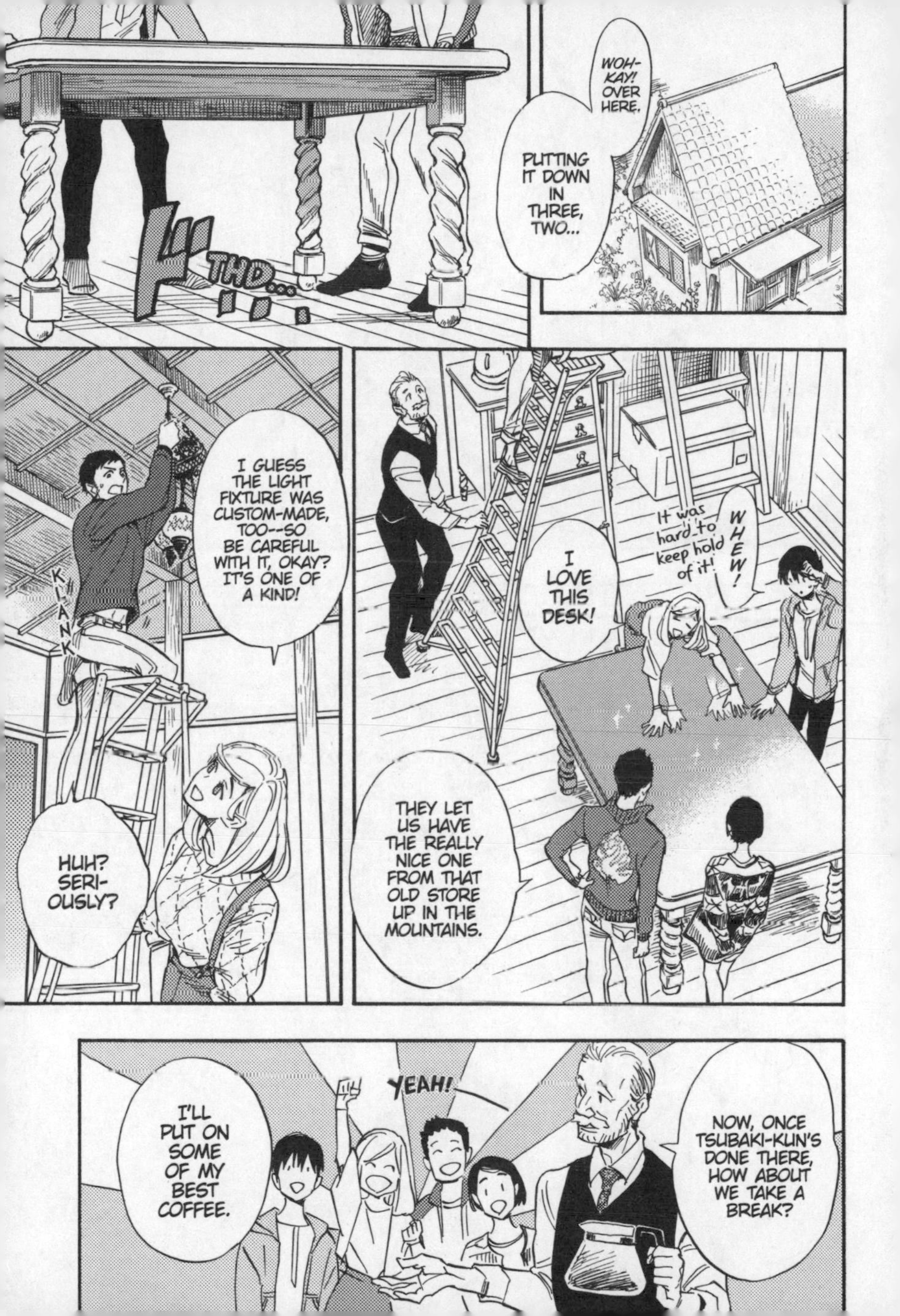
WOH-KAY! OVER HERE.
PUTTING IT DOWN IN THREE, TWO...
THD...
WHEW!
It was hard to keep hold of it!
I LOVE THIS DESK!
THEY LET US HAVE THE REALLY NICE ONE FROM THAT OLD STORE UP IN THE MOUNTAINS.
I GUESS THE LIGHT FIXTURE WAS CUSTOM-MADE, TOO--SO BE CAREFUL WITH IT, OKAY? IT'S ONE OF A KIND!
KLANK
HUH? SERI-OUSLY?
NOW, ONCE TSUBAKI-KUN'S DONE THERE, HOW ABOUT WE TAKE A BREAK?
YEAH!
I'LL PUT ON SOME OF MY BEST COFFEE.

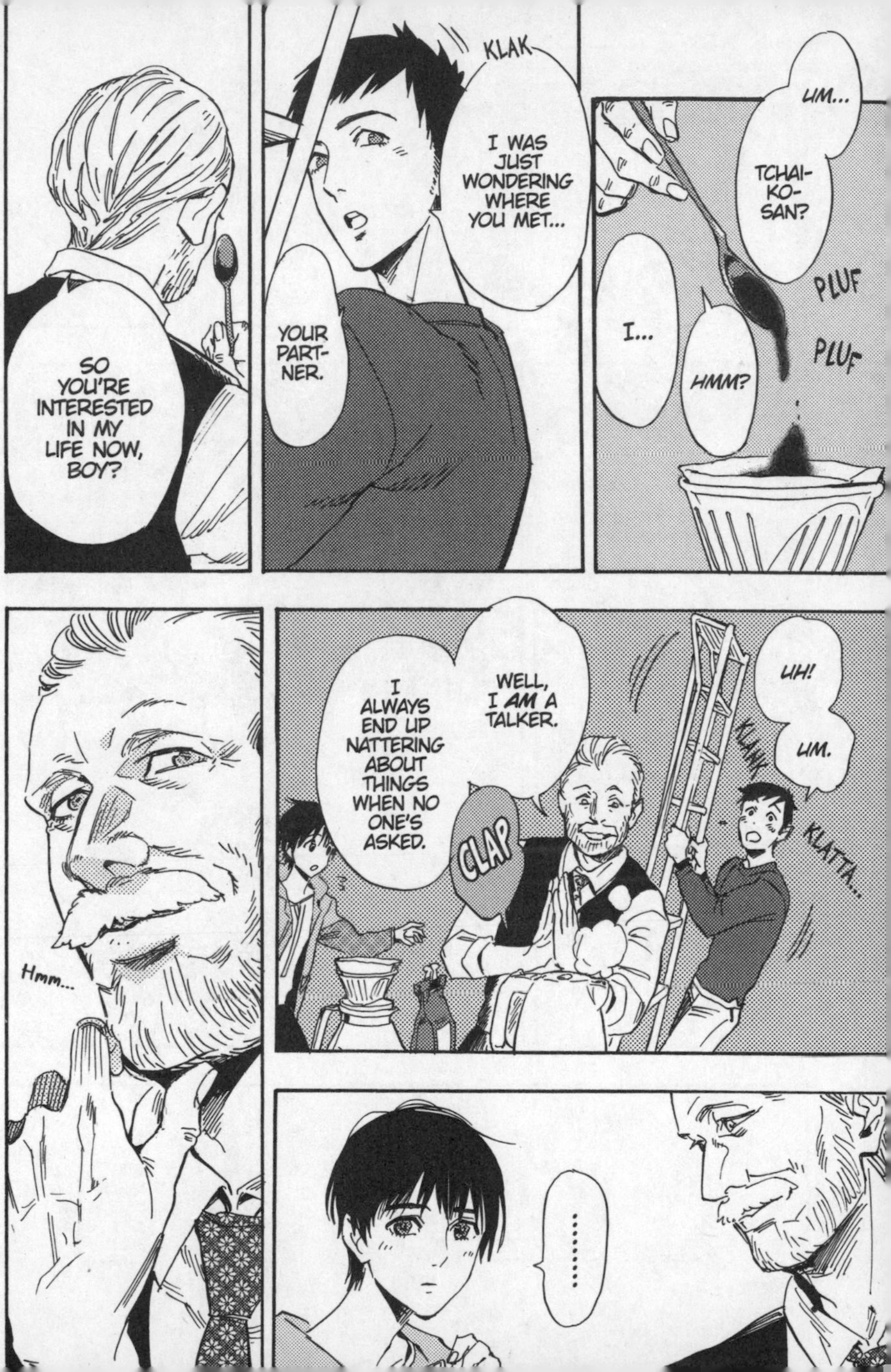
UM... TCHAI-KO-SAN?
PLUF
PLUF
I...
HMM?
KLAK
I WAS JUST WONDERING WHERE YOU MET...
YOUR PART-NER.
SO YOU'RE INTERESTED IN MY LIFE NOW, BOY?
UH!
UM.
KLANK
KLATTA...
WELL, I *AM* A TALKER.
I ALWAYS END UP NATTERING ABOUT THINGS WHEN NO ONE'S ASKED.
CLAP
Hmm...
......

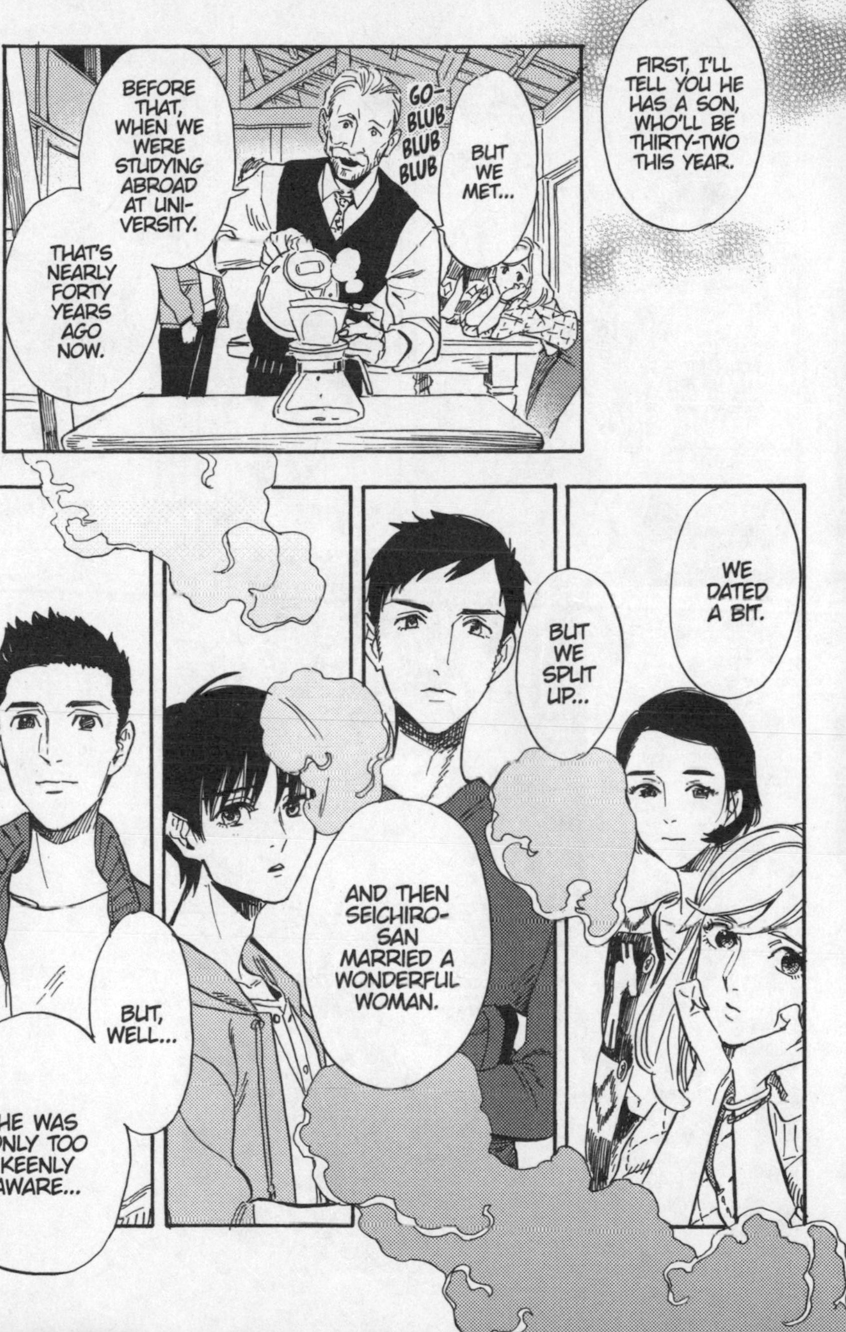
FIRST, I'LL TELL YOU HE HAS A SON, WHO'LL BE THIRTY-TWO THIS YEAR.
BUT WE MET...
GO-BLUB BLUB BLUB
BEFORE THAT, WHEN WE WERE STUDYING ABROAD AT UNI-VERSITY.
THAT'S NEARLY FORTY YEARS AGO NOW.
WE DATED A BIT.
BUT WE SPLIT UP...
AND THEN SEICHIRO-SAN MARRIED A WONDERFUL WOMAN.
BUT, WELL...
HE WAS ONLY TOO KEENLY AWARE...

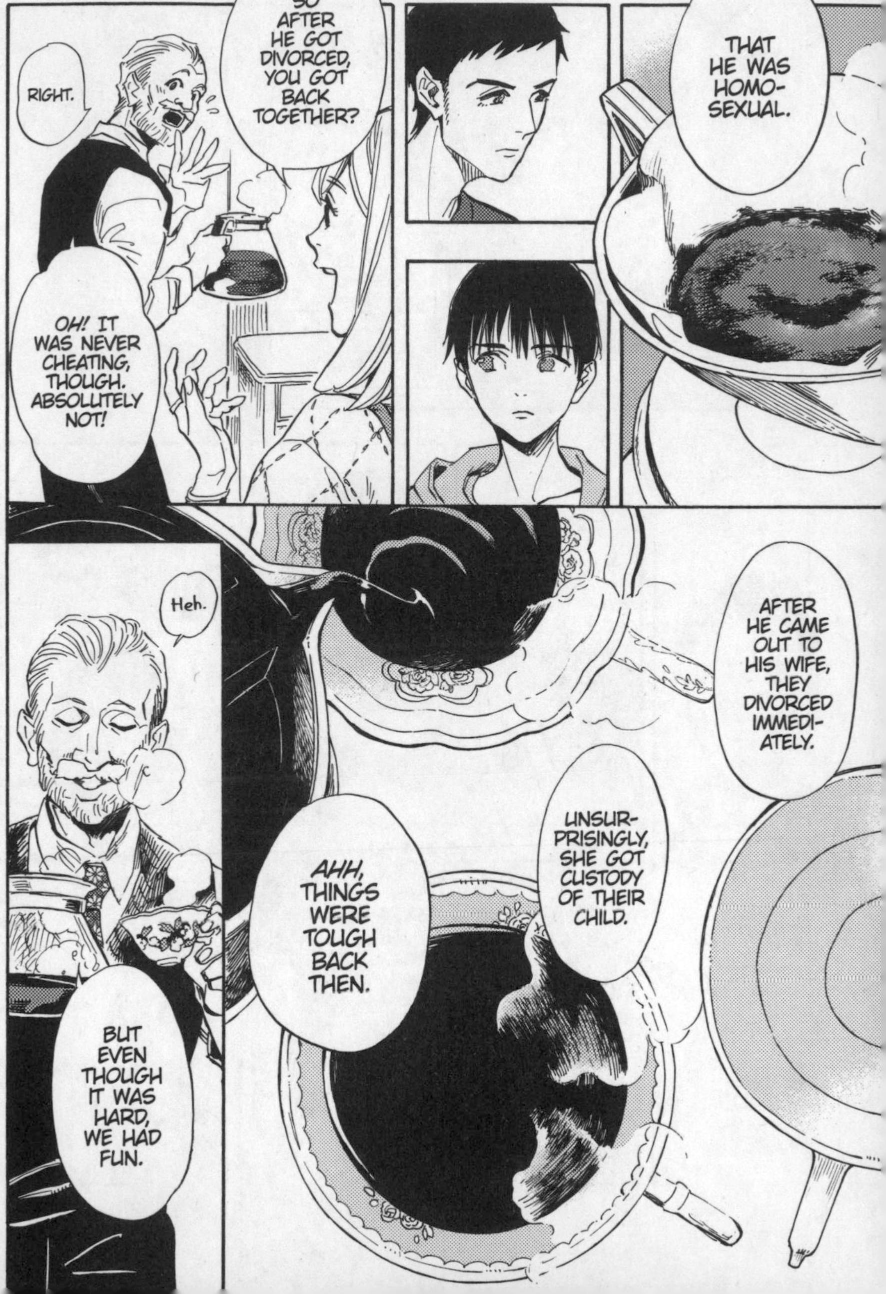
THAT HE WAS HOMO-SEXUAL.
SO AFTER HE GOT DIVORCED, YOU GOT BACK TOGETHER?
RIGHT.
OH! IT WAS NEVER CHEATING, THOUGH. ABSOLUTELY NOT!
AFTER HE CAME OUT TO HIS WIFE, THEY DIVORCED IMMEDI-ATELY.
UNSUR-PRISINGLY, SHE GOT CUSTODY OF THEIR CHILD.
AHH, THINGS WERE TOUGH BACK THEN.
Heh.
BUT EVEN THOUGH IT WAS HARD, WE HAD FUN.

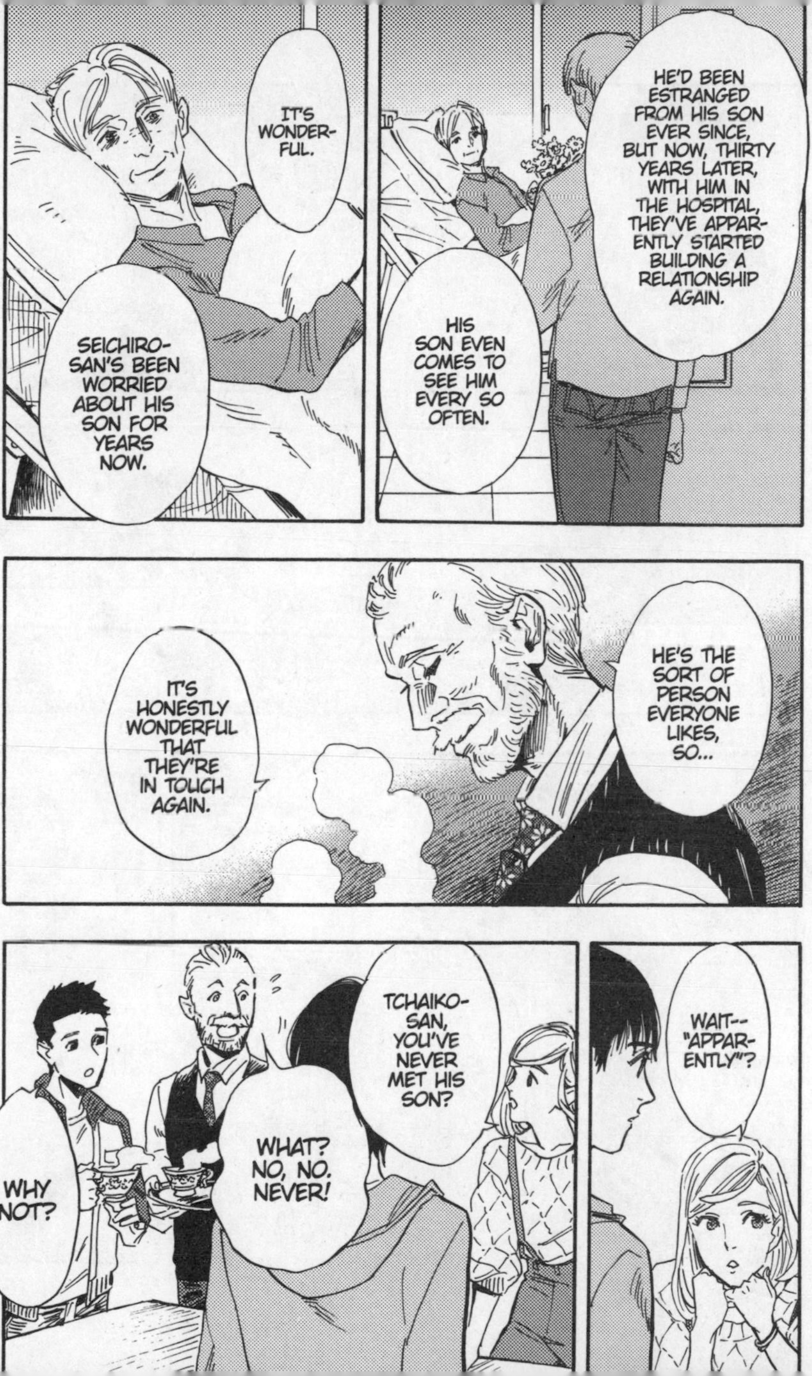
HE'D BEEN ESTRANGED FROM HIS SON EVER SINCE, BUT NOW, THIRTY YEARS LATER, WITH HIM IN THE HOSPITAL, THEY'VE APPARENTLY STARTED BUILDING A RELATIONSHIP AGAIN.
HIS SON EVEN COMES TO SEE HIM EVERY SO OFTEN.
IT'S WONDERFUL.
SEICHIRO-SAN'S BEEN WORRIED ABOUT HIS SON FOR YEARS NOW.
HE'S THE SORT OF PERSON EVERYONE LIKES, SO...
IT'S HONESTLY WONDERFUL THAT THEY'RE IN TOUCH AGAIN.
WAIT-- "APPARENTLY"?
TCHAIKO-SAN, YOU'VE NEVER MET HIS SON?
WHAT? NO, NO. NEVER!
WHY NOT?

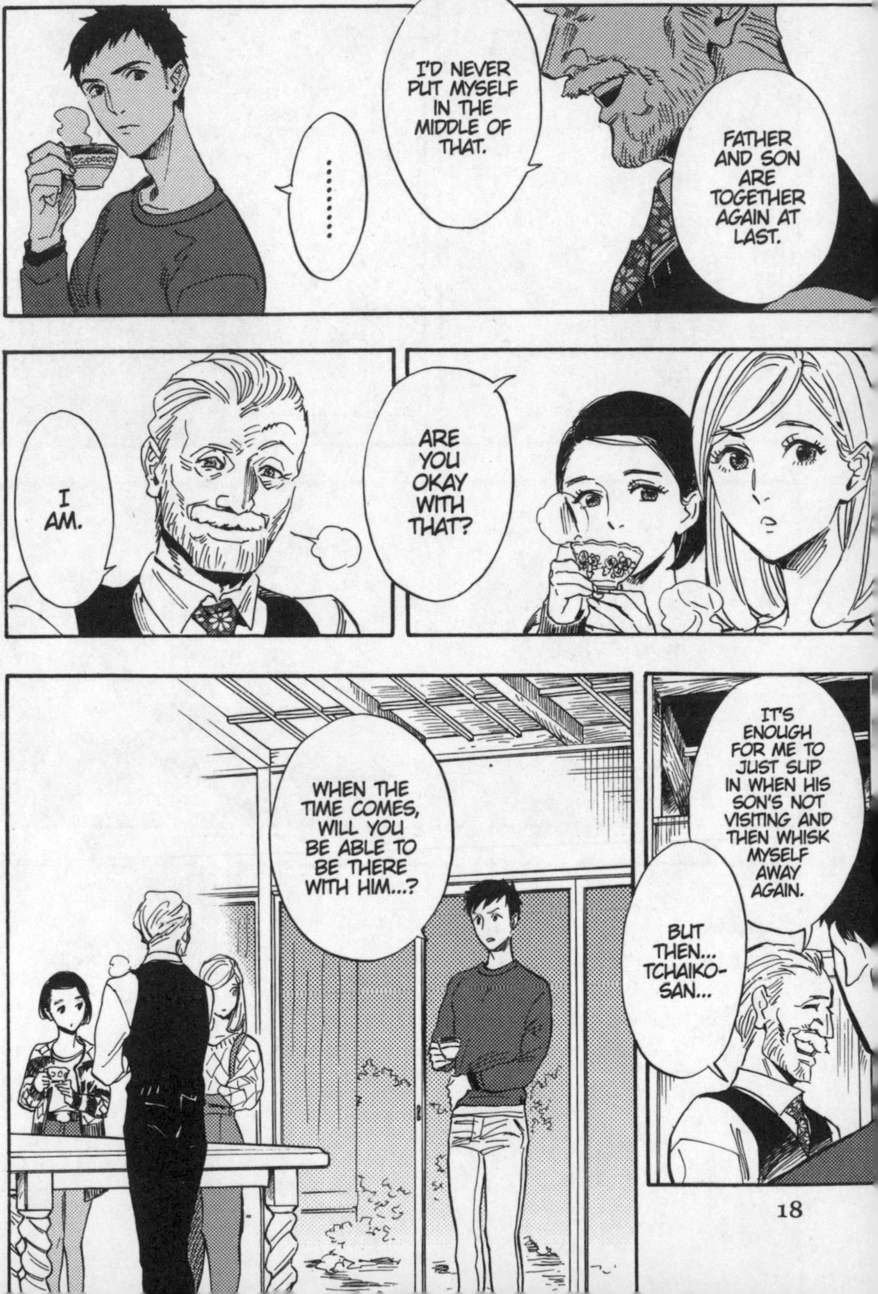
FATHER AND SON ARE TOGETHER AGAIN AT LAST.
I'D NEVER PUT MYSELF IN THE MIDDLE OF THAT.
......
ARE YOU OKAY WITH THAT?
I AM.
IT'S ENOUGH FOR ME TO JUST SLIP IN WHEN HIS SON'S NOT VISITING AND THEN WHISK MYSELF AWAY AGAIN.
BUT THEN... TCHAIKO-SAN...
WHEN THE TIME COMES, WILL YOU BE ABLE TO BE THERE WITH HIM...?

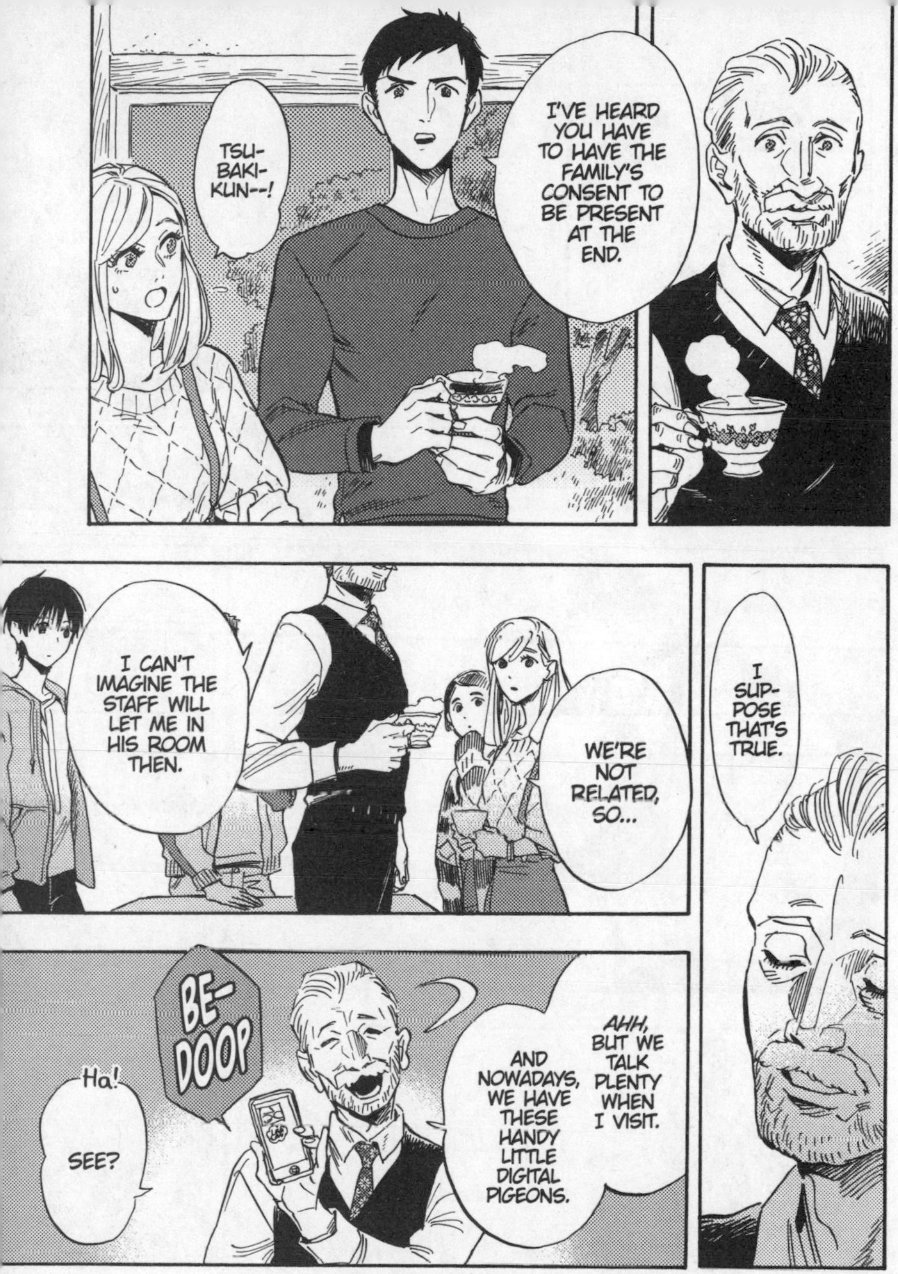
I'VE HEARD YOU HAVE TO HAVE THE FAMILY'S CONSENT TO BE PRESENT AT THE END.
TSU-BAKI-KUN--!
WE'RE NOT RELATED, SO...
I CAN'T IMAGINE THE STAFF WILL LET ME IN HIS ROOM THEN.
I SUP-POSE THAT'S TRUE.
AHH, BUT WE TALK PLENTY WHEN I VISIT.
AND NOWADAYS, WE HAVE THESE HANDY LITTLE DIGITAL PIGEONS.
BE-DOOP
Ha!
SEE?

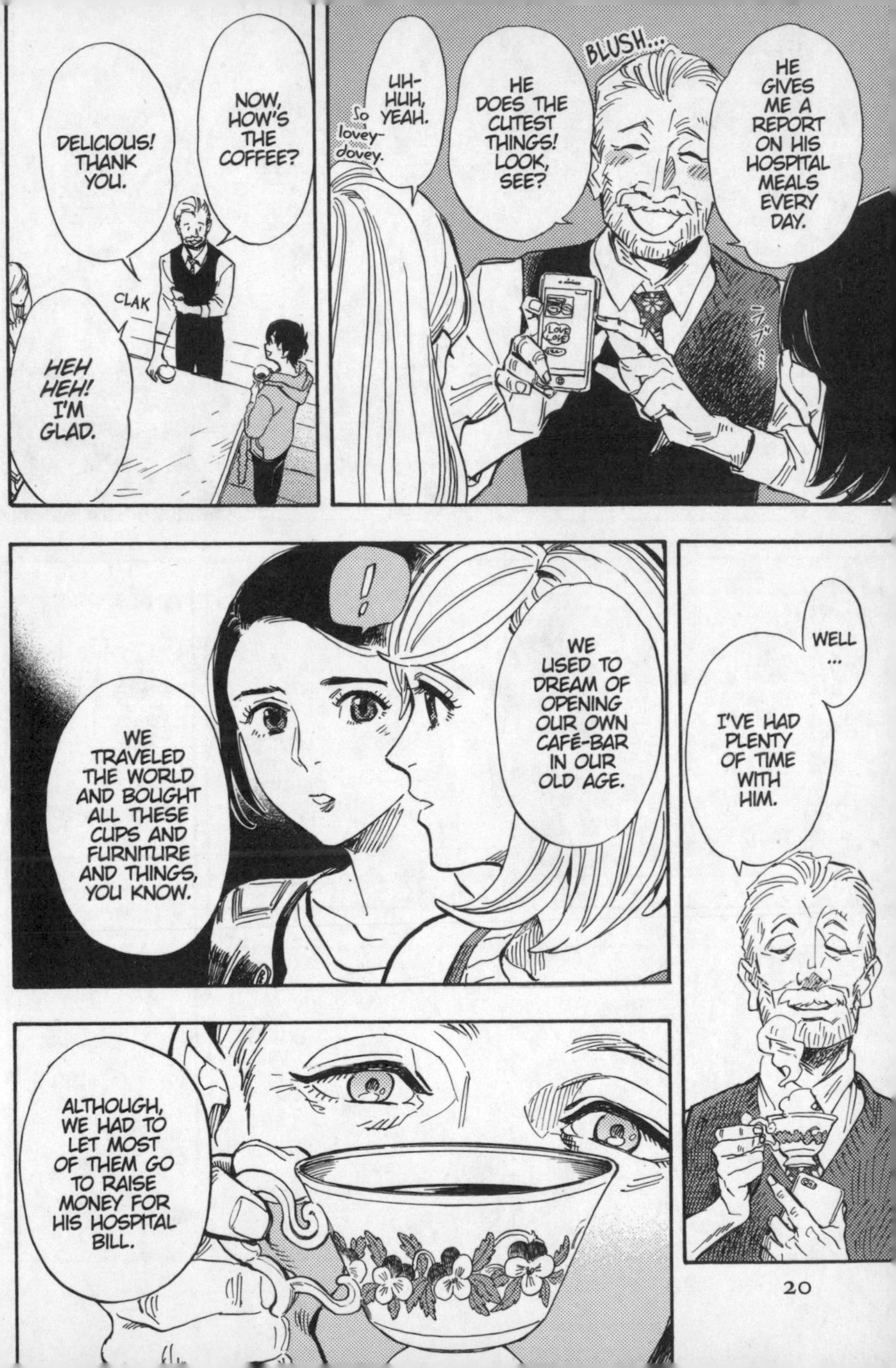
BLUSH...
HE GIVES ME A REPORT ON HIS HOSPITAL MEALS EVERY DAY.
HE DOES THE CUTEST THINGS! LOOK, SEE?
UH-HUH, YEAH.
So lovey-dovey.
NOW, HOW'S THE COFFEE?
DELICIOUS! THANK YOU.
CLAK
HEH HEH! I'M GLAD.
WELL ...
I'VE HAD PLENTY OF TIME WITH HIM.
!
WE USED TO DREAM OF OPENING OUR OWN CAFÉ-BAR IN OUR OLD AGE.
WE TRAVELED THE WORLD AND BOUGHT ALL THESE CUPS AND FURNITURE AND THINGS, YOU KNOW.
ALTHOUGH, WE HAD TO LET MOST OF THEM GO TO RAISE MONEY FOR HIS HOSPITAL BILL.

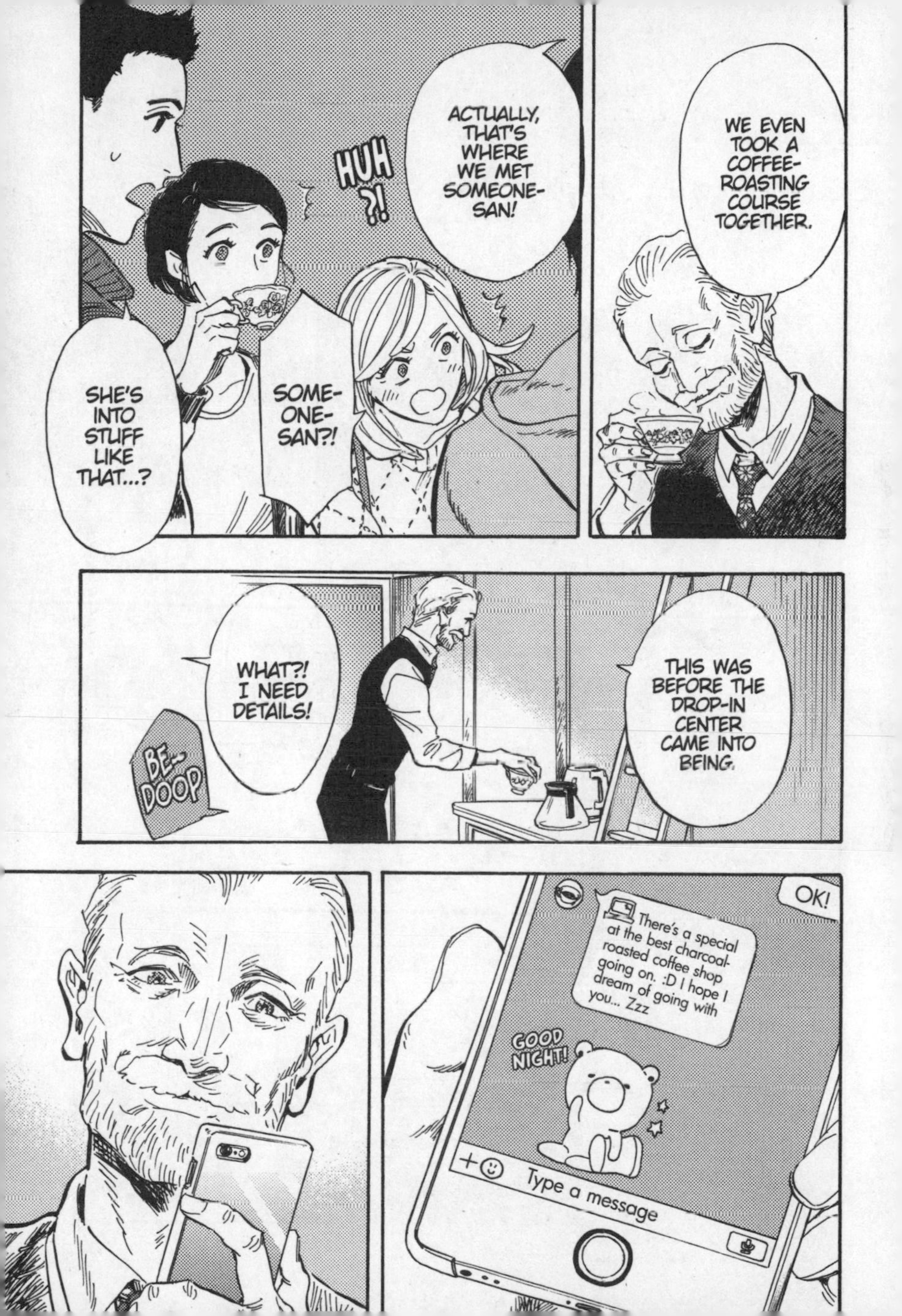
WE EVEN TOOK A COFFEE-ROASTING COURSE TOGETHER.
ACTUALLY, THAT'S WHERE WE MET SOMEONE-SAN!
HUH ?!
SOME-ONE-SAN?!
SHE'S INTO STUFF LIKE THAT...?
THIS WAS BEFORE THE DROP-IN CENTER CAME INTO BEING.
WHAT?! I NEED DETAILS!
BE-DOOP
OK!
There's a special at the best charcoal-roasted coffee shop going on. :D I hope I dream of going with you... Zzz
GOOD NIGHT!
Type a message

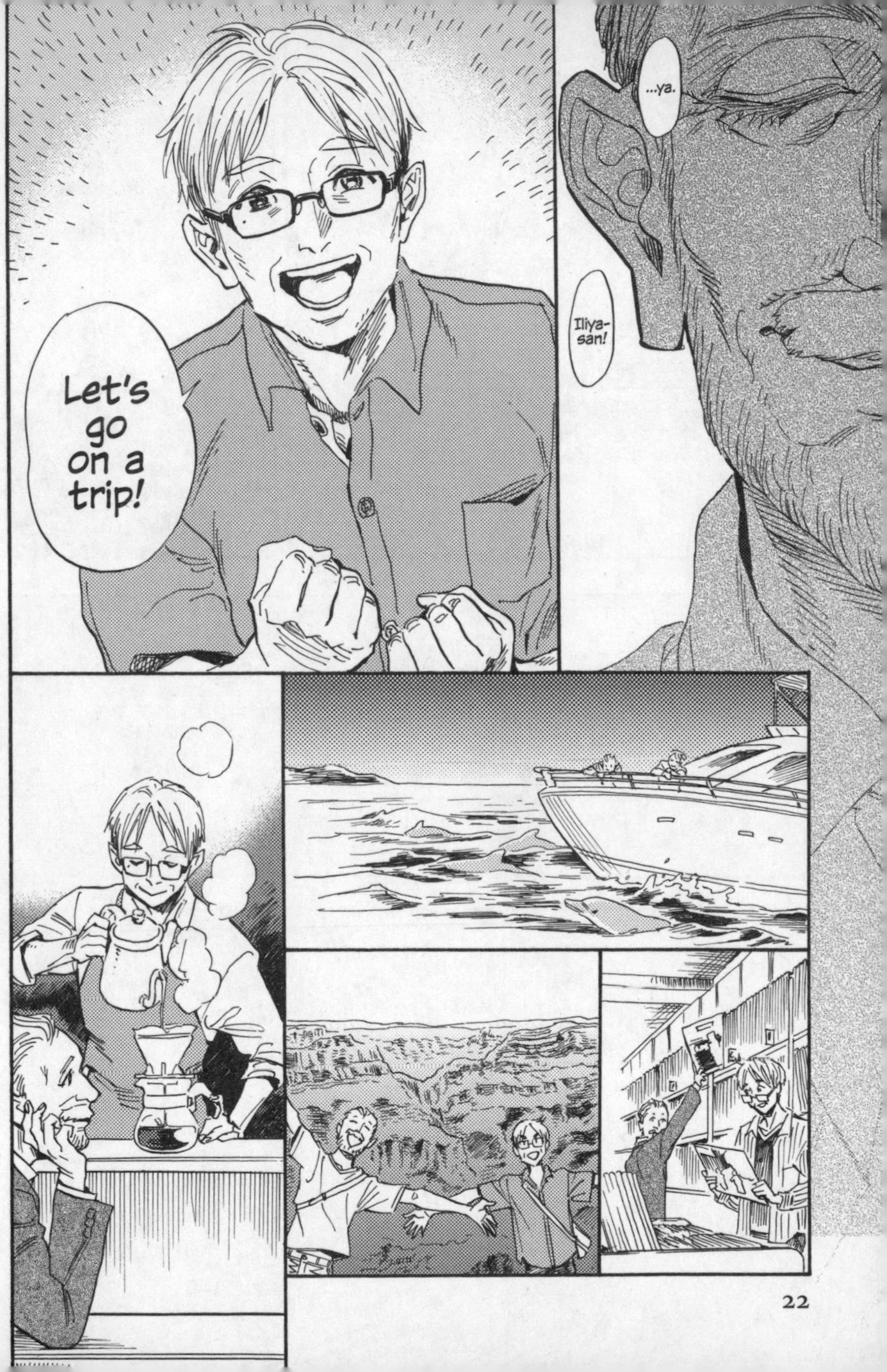
...ya.
Iliya-san!
Let's go on a trip!

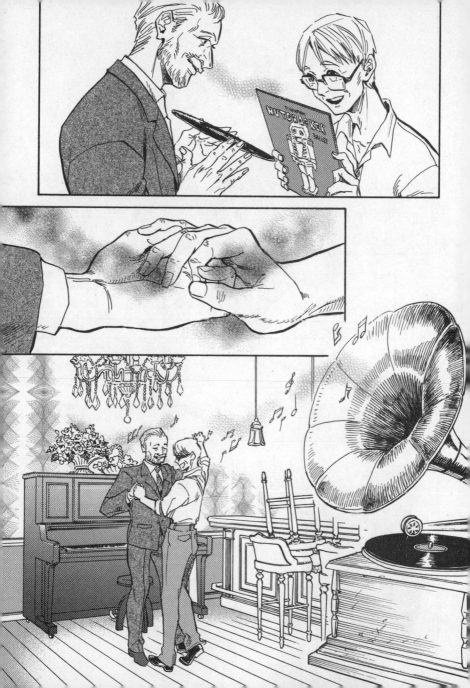

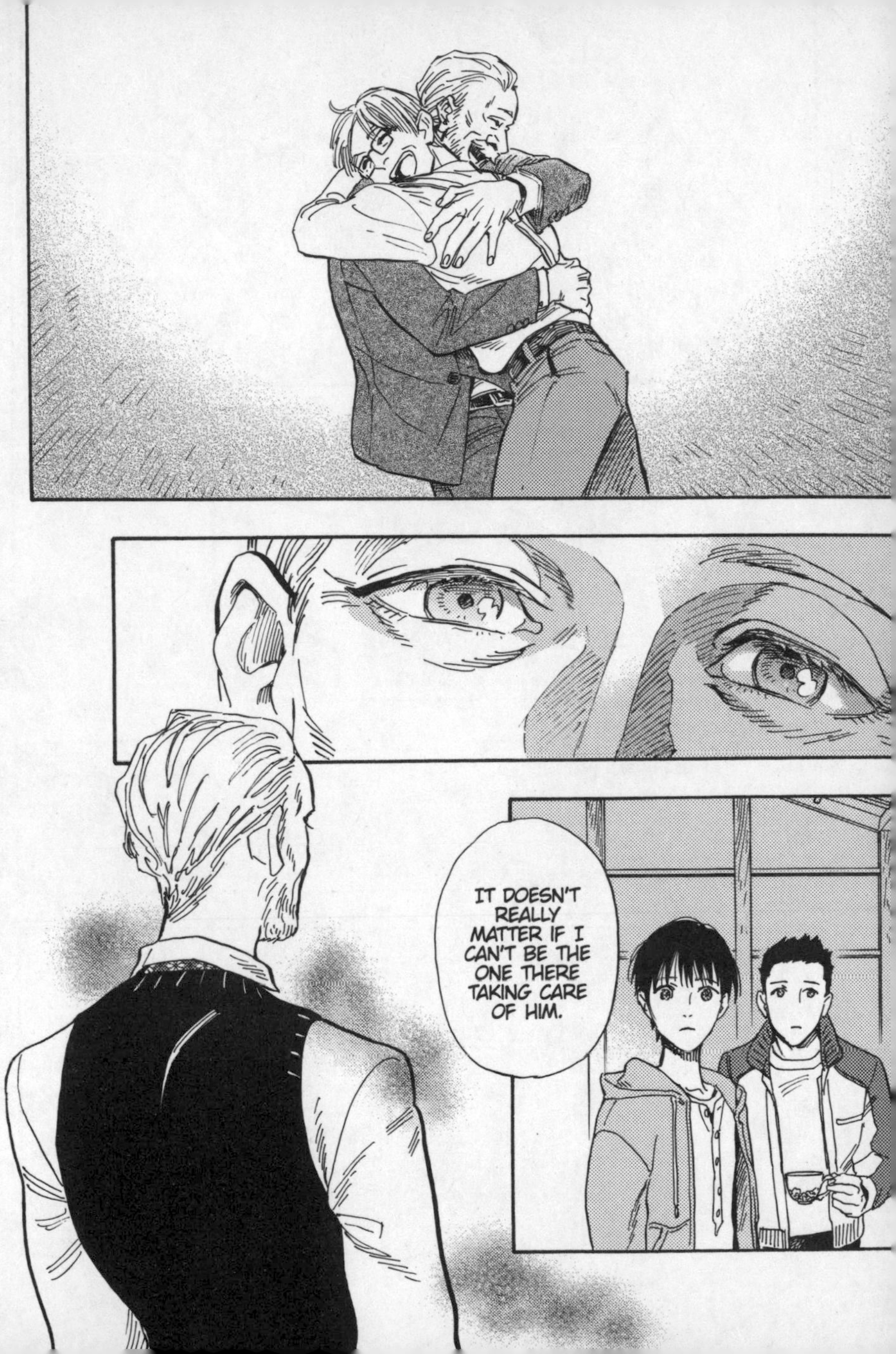
IT DOESN'T REALLY MATTER IF I CAN'T BE THE ONE THERE TAKING CARE OF HIM.

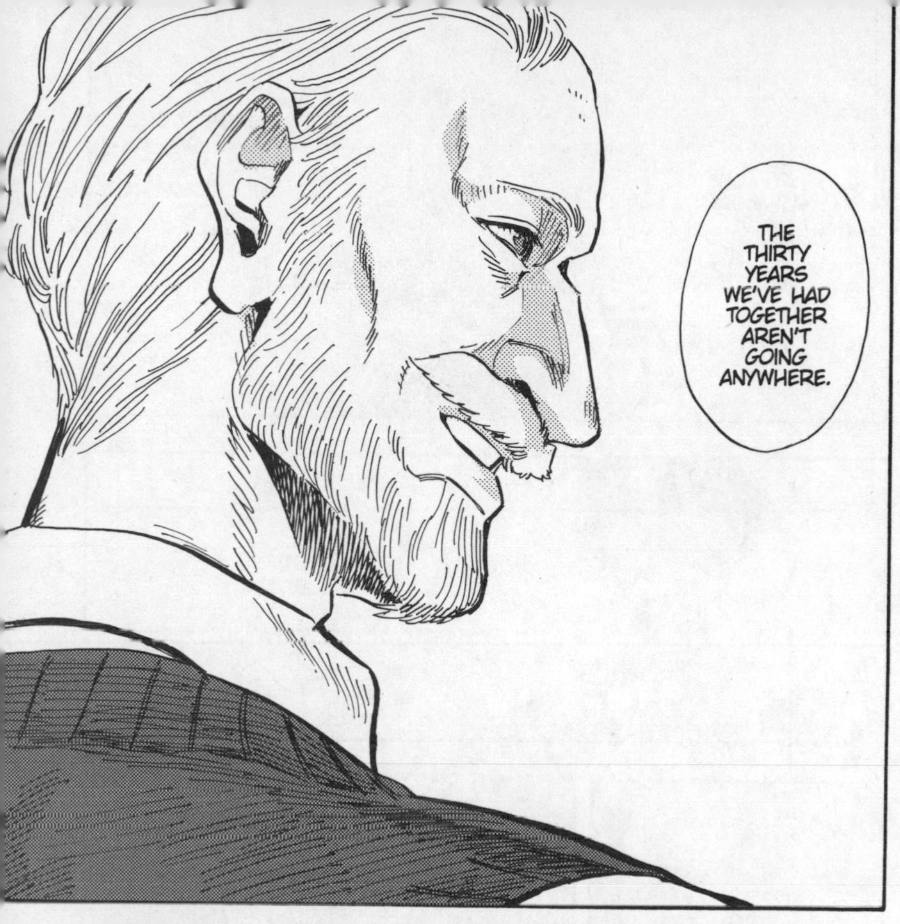
THE THIRTY YEARS WE'VE HAD TOGETHER AREN'T GOING ANYWHERE.

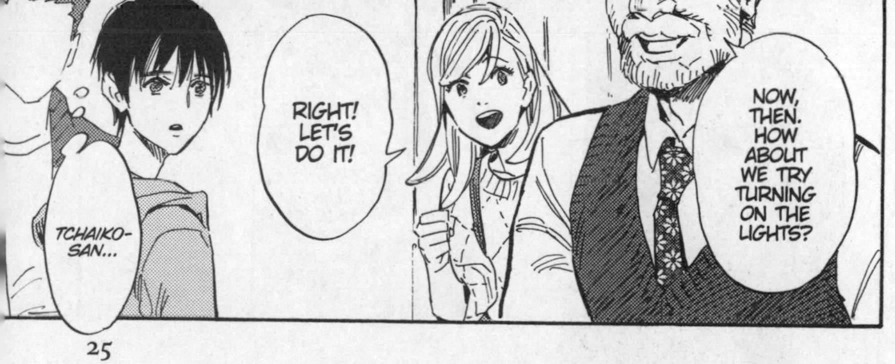
NOW, THEN. HOW ABOUT WE TRY TURNING ON THE LIGHTS?
RIGHT! LET'S DO IT!
TCHAIKO-SAN...

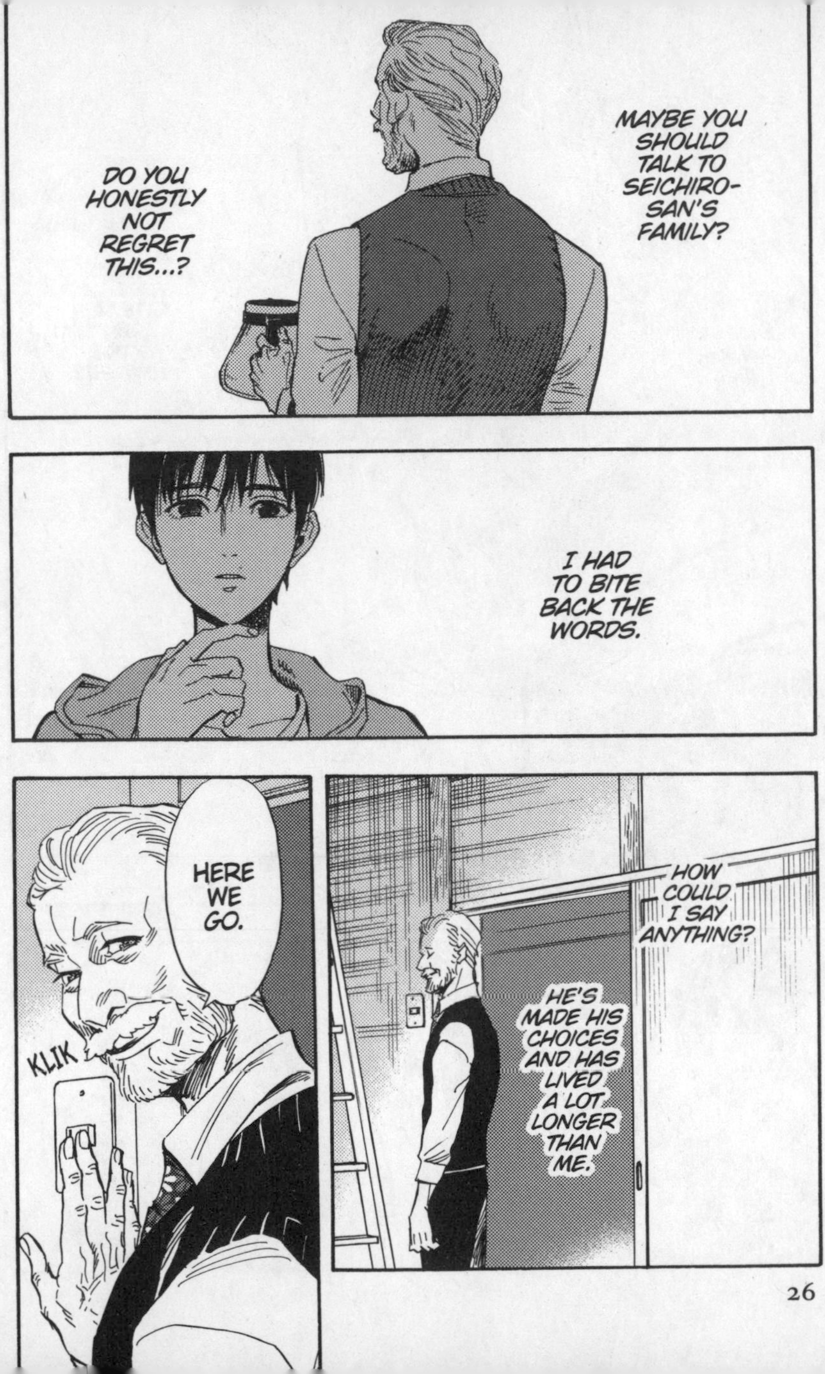
MAYBE YOU SHOULD TALK TO SEICHIRO-SAN'S FAMILY?
DO YOU HONESTLY NOT REGRET THIS...?
I HAD TO BITE BACK THE WORDS.
HOW COULD I SAY ANYTHING?
HE'S MADE HIS CHOICES AND HAS LIVED A LOT LONGER THAN ME.
HERE WE GO.
KLIK

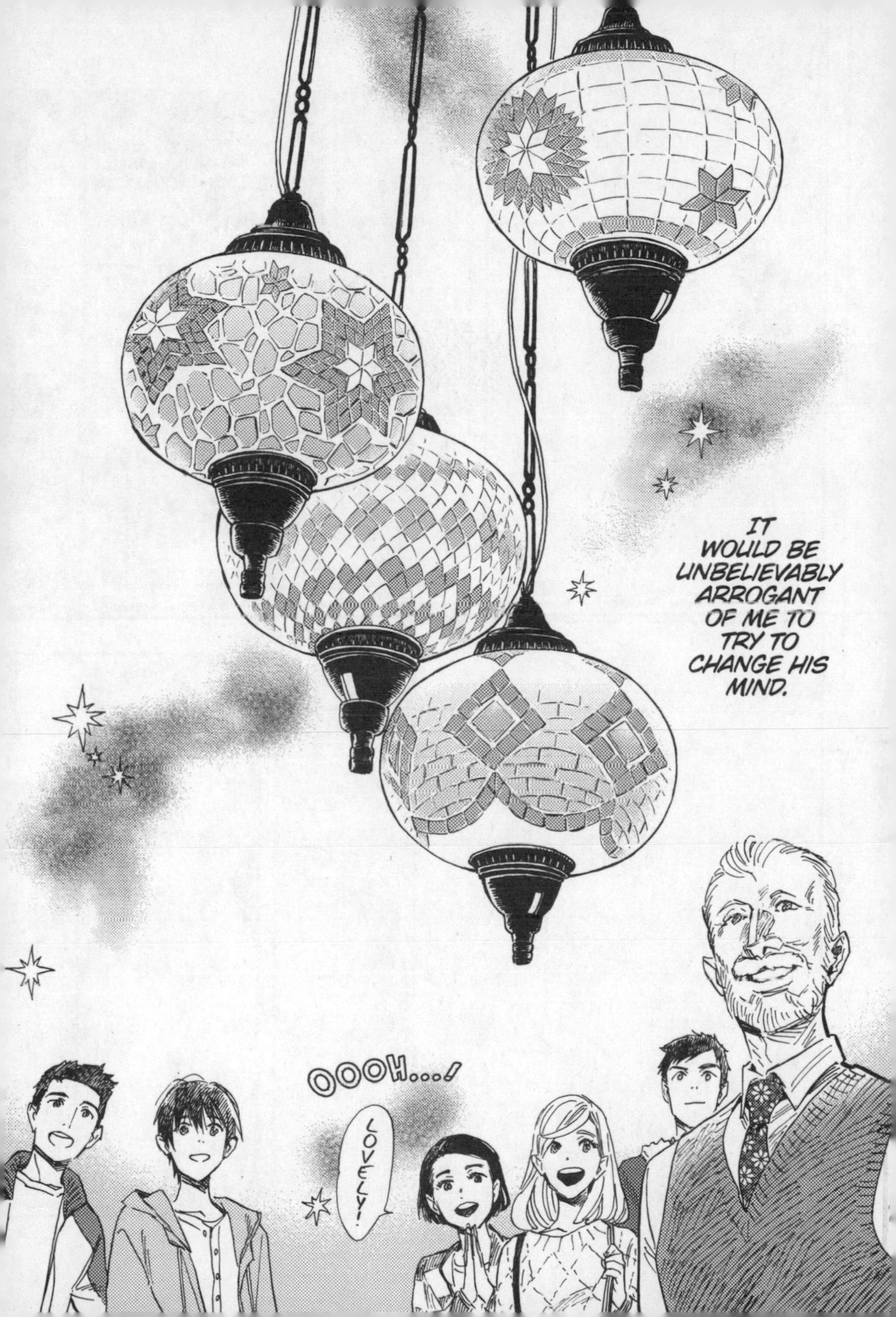
IT WOULD BE UNBELIEVABLY ARROGANT OF ME TO TRY TO CHANGE HIS MIND.
OOOH...!
LOVELY!

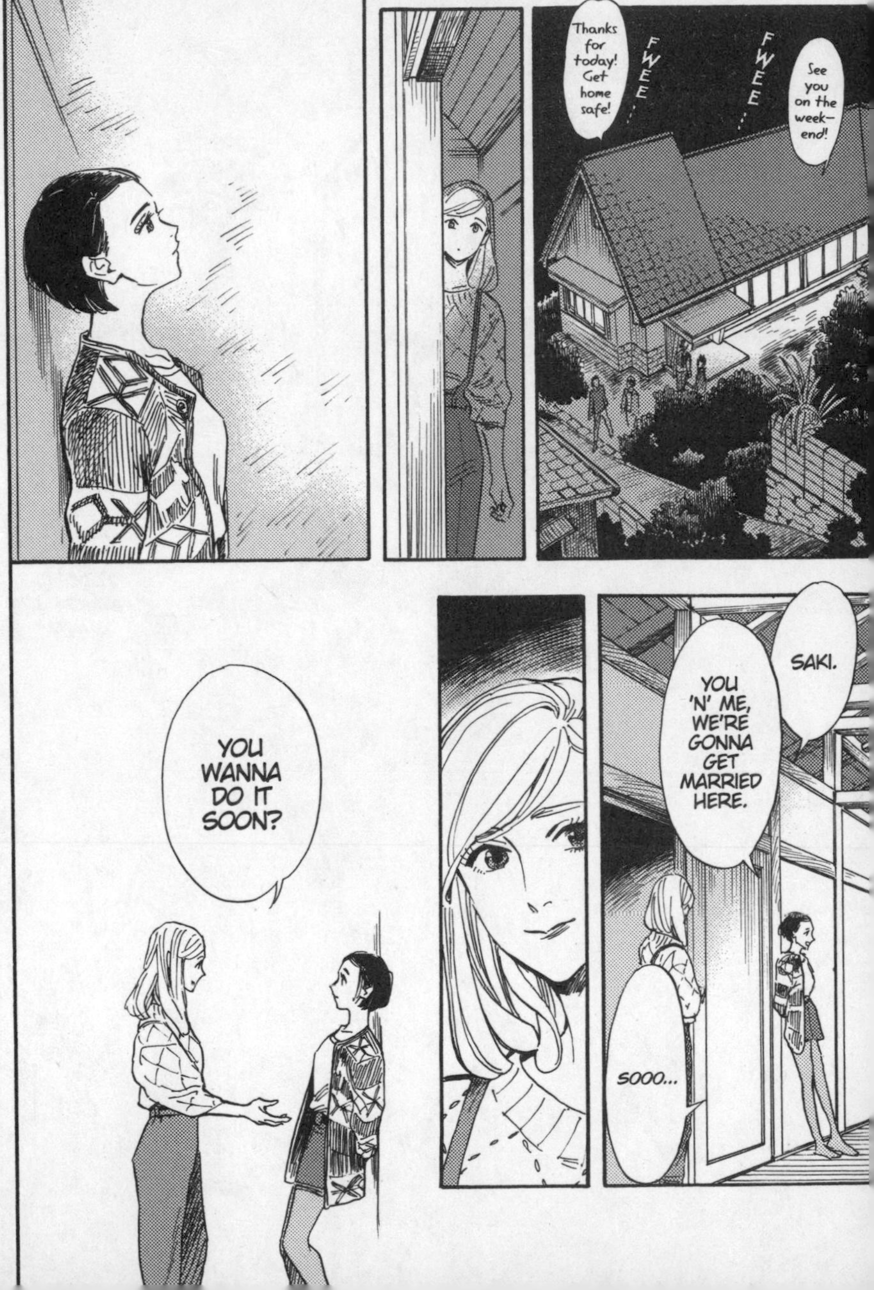
See you on the week-end!
FWEE...
Thanks for today! Get home safe!
FWEE...
SAKI.
YOU 'N' ME, WE'RE GONNA GET MARRIED HERE.
SOOO...
YOU WANNA DO IT SOON?

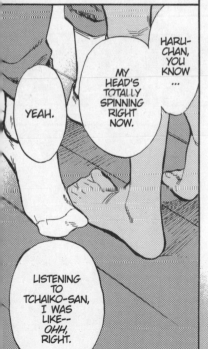

HARU-CHAN, YOU KNOW...

MY HEAD'S TOTALLY SPINNING RIGHT NOW.

YEAH.

LISTENING TO TCHAIKO-SAN, I WAS LIKE-- OHH, RIGHT.

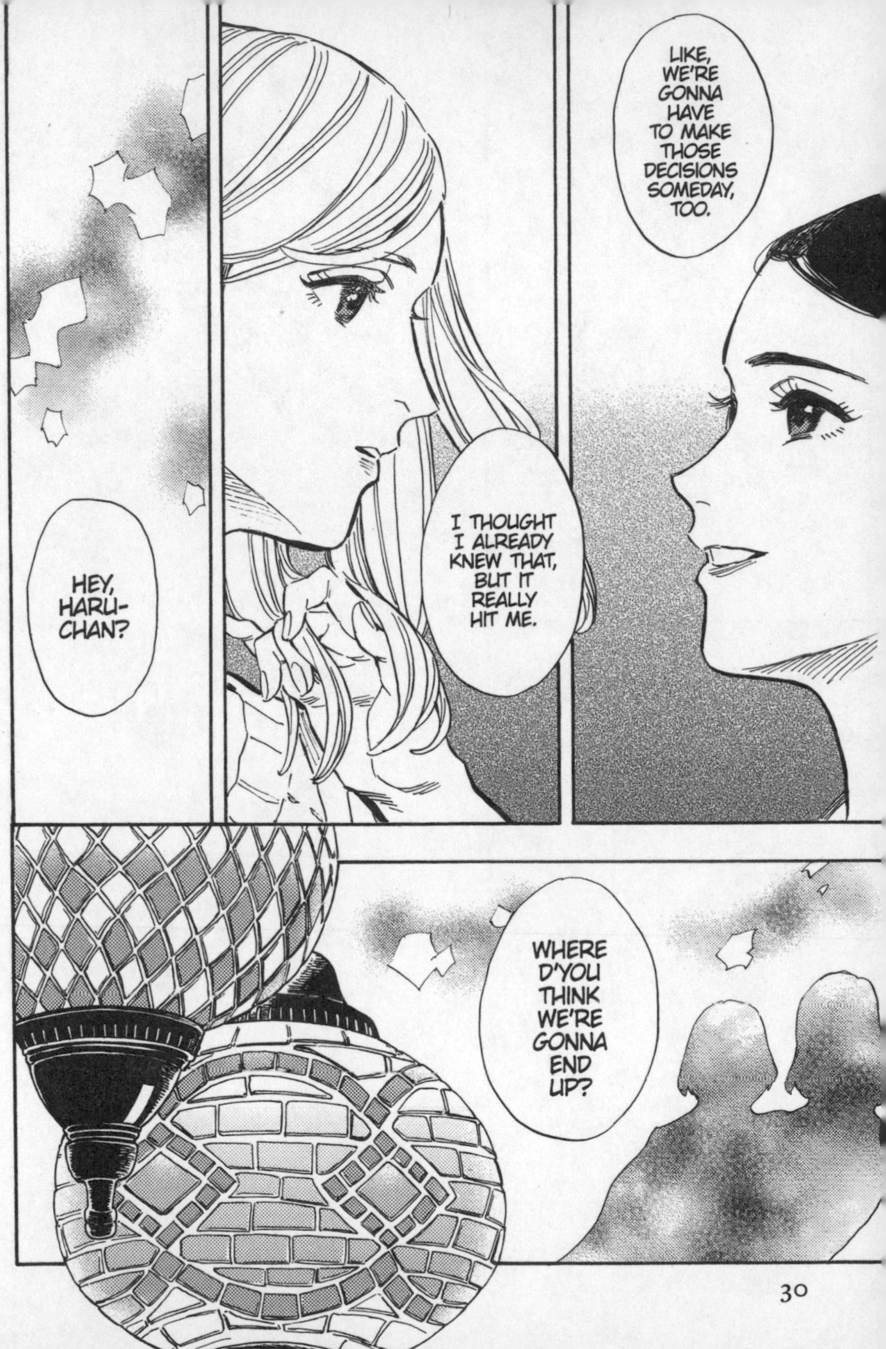
LIKE, WE'RE GONNA HAVE TO MAKE THOSE DECISIONS SOMEDAY, TOO.
I THOUGHT I ALREADY KNEW THAT, BUT IT REALLY HIT ME.
HEY, HARU-CHAN?
WHERE D'YOU THINK WE'RE GONNA END UP?

Our Dreams at Dusk
SHIMANAMI TASOGARE

Onomichi
Betcha
Festival

(Every
November
1-3.)

Chapter 17

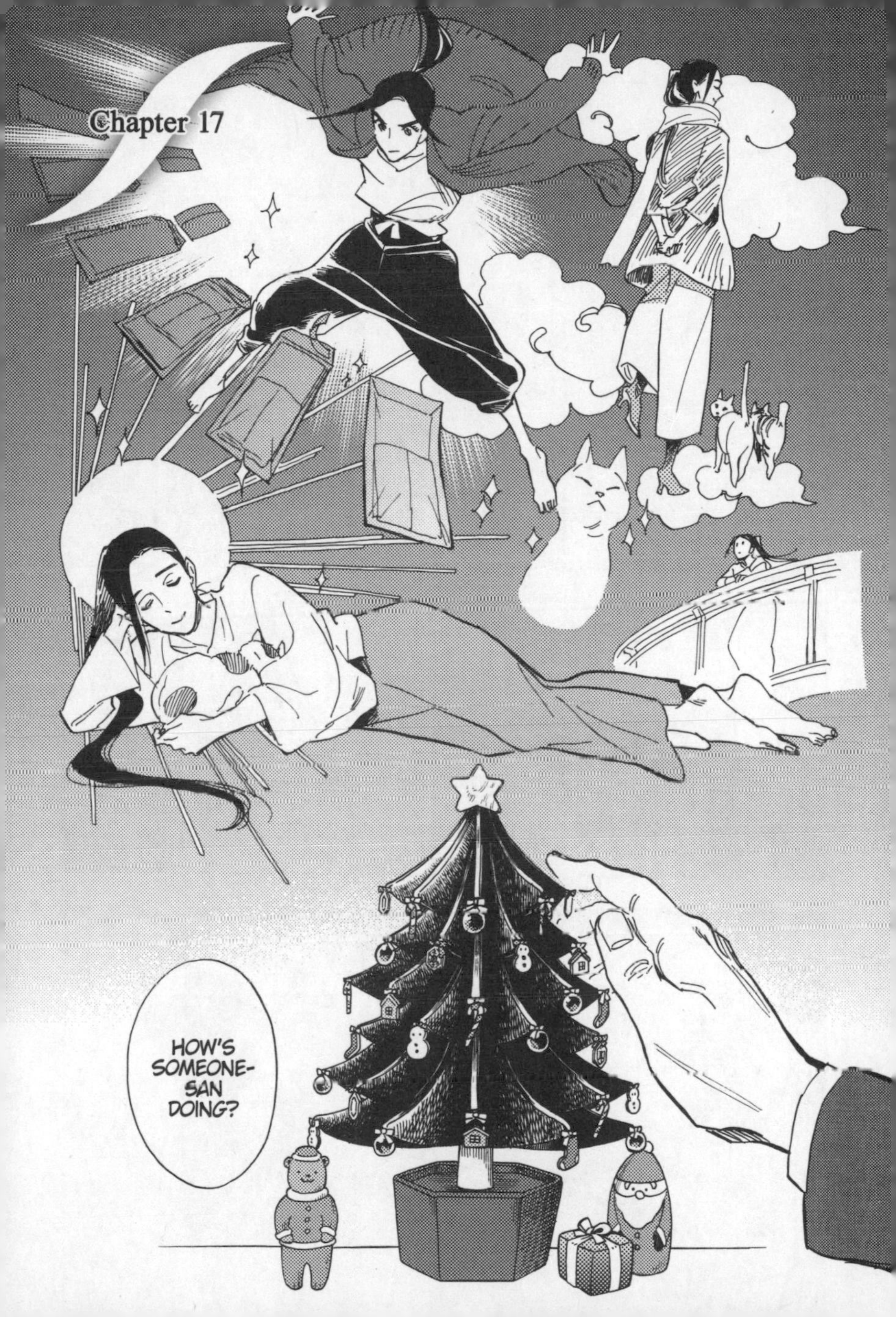
HOW'S SOMEONE-SAN DOING?

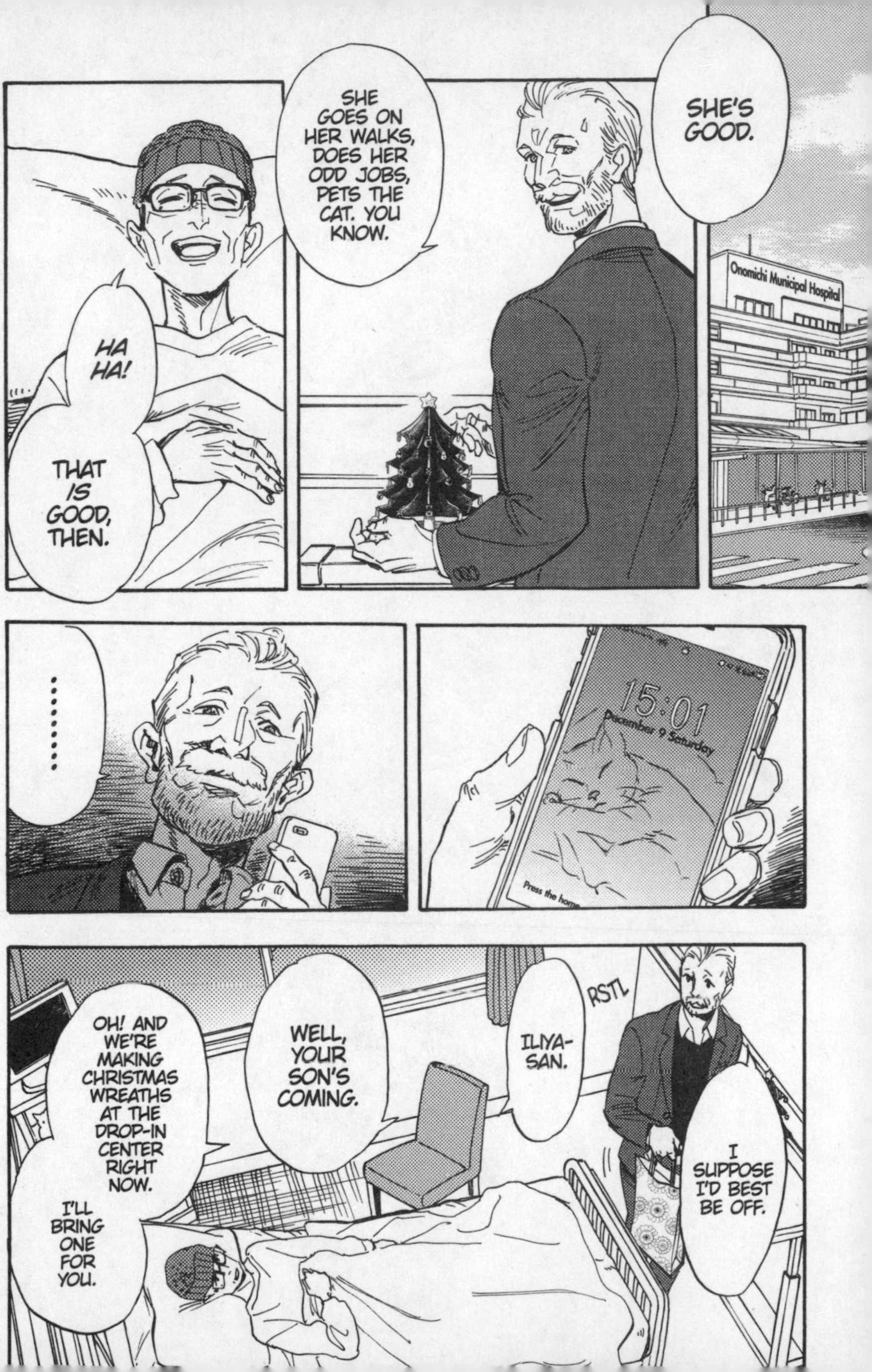
SHE'S GOOD.
Onomichi Municipal Hospital
SHE GOES ON HER WALKS, DOES HER ODD JOBS, PETS THE CAT. YOU KNOW.
HA HA!
THAT IS GOOD, THEN.
15:01
December 9 Saturday
Press the home
......
RSTL
ILIYA-SAN.
I SUPPOSE I'D BEST BE OFF.
WELL, YOUR SON'S COMING.
OH! AND WE'RE MAKING CHRISTMAS WREATHS AT THE DROP-IN CENTER RIGHT NOW.
I'LL BRING ONE FOR YOU.

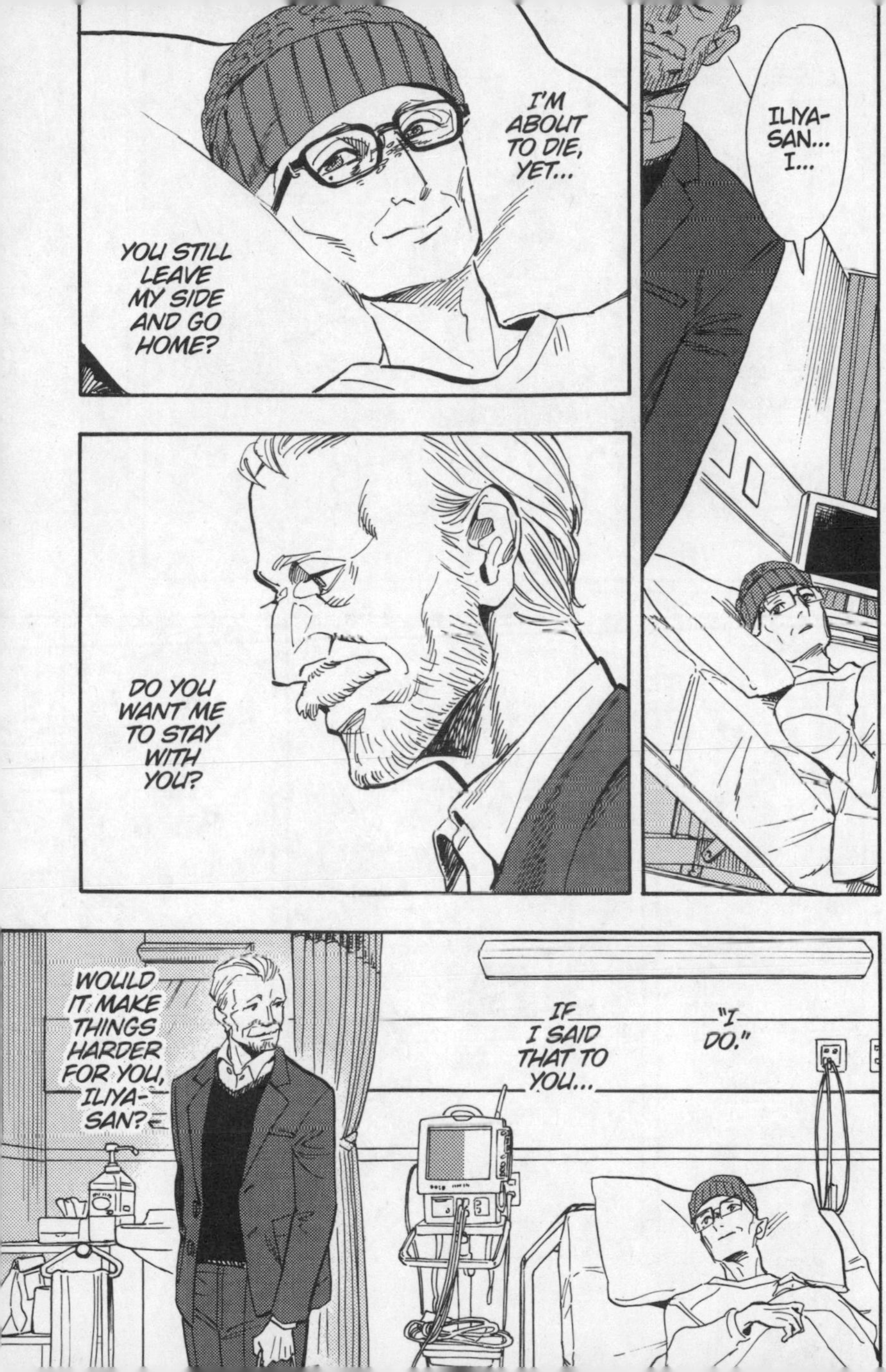
ILIYA-SAN... I...
I'M ABOUT TO DIE, YET...
YOU STILL LEAVE MY SIDE AND GO HOME?
DO YOU WANT ME TO STAY WITH YOU?
"I DO."
IF I SAID THAT TO YOU...
WOULD IT MAKE THINGS HARDER FOR YOU, ILIYA-SAN?

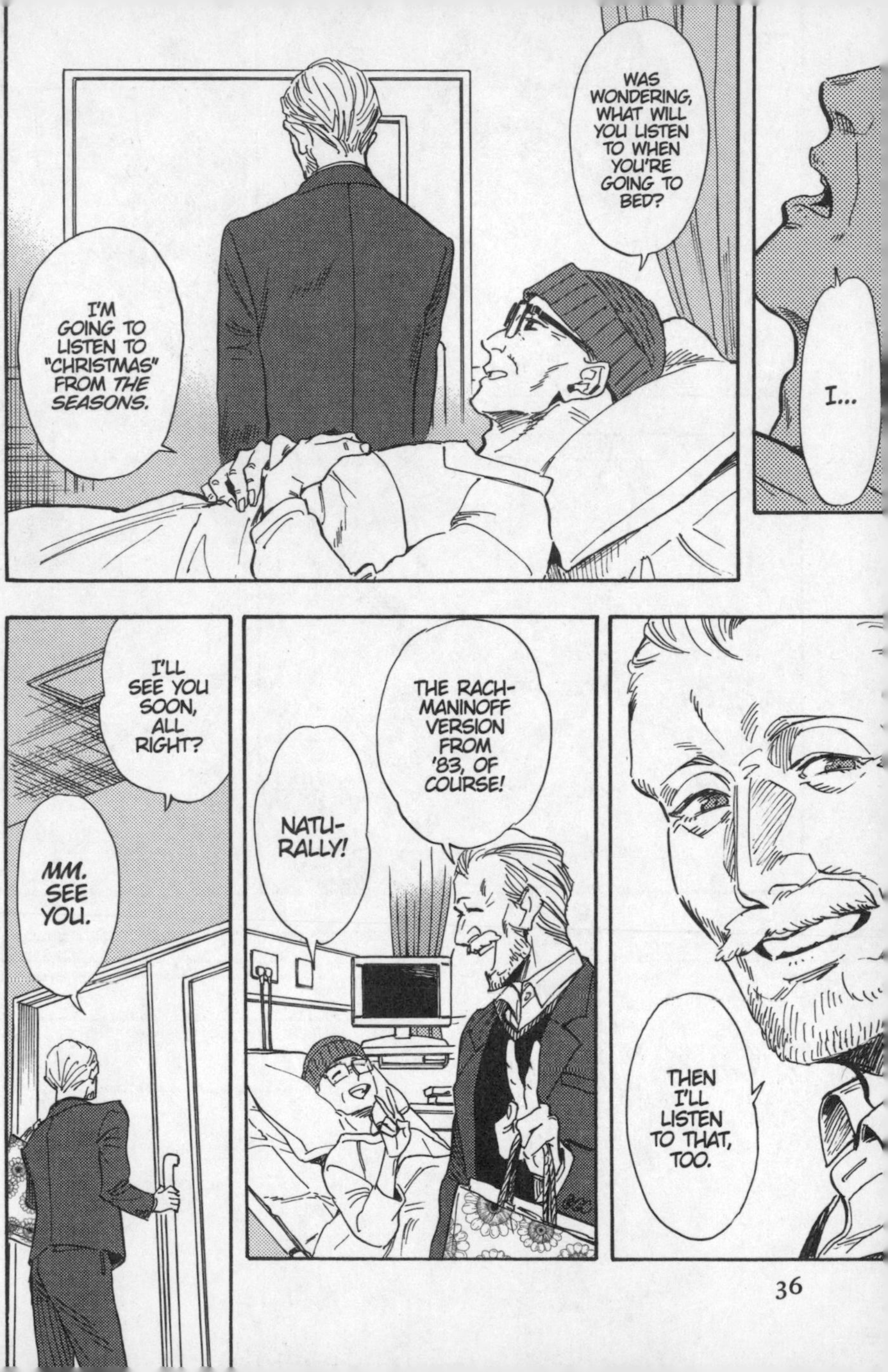
I...
WAS WONDERING, WHAT WILL YOU LISTEN TO WHEN YOU'RE GOING TO BED?
I'M GOING TO LISTEN TO "CHRISTMAS" FROM *THE SEASONS.*
THEN I'LL LISTEN TO THAT, TOO.
THE RACH-MANINOFF VERSION FROM '83, OF COURSE!
NATU-RALLY!
I'LL SEE YOU SOON, ALL RIGHT?
MM. SEE YOU.

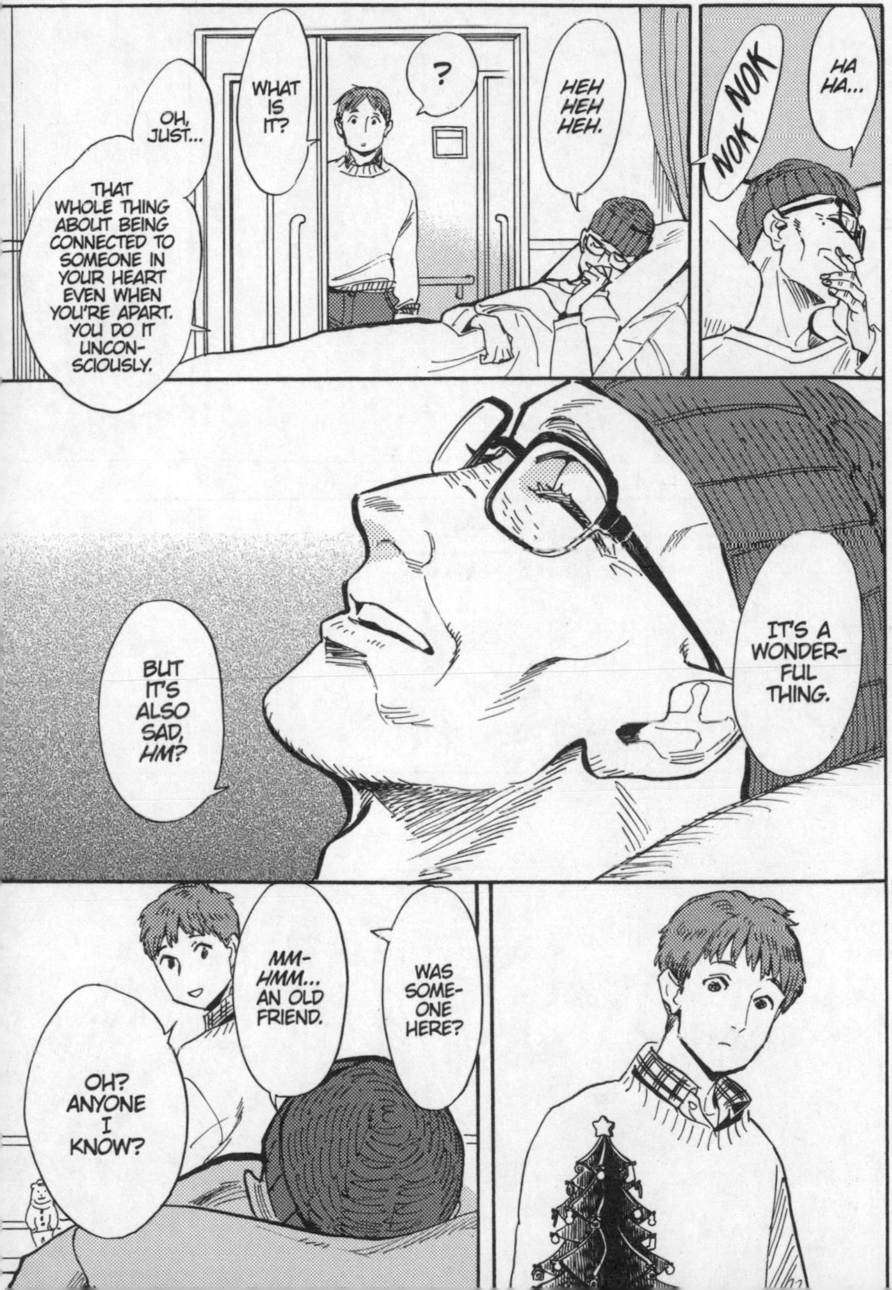
HA HA...
NOK NOK
HEH HEH HEH.
?
WHAT IS IT?
OH, JUST...
THAT WHOLE THING ABOUT BEING CONNECTED TO SOMEONE IN YOUR HEART EVEN WHEN YOU'RE APART. YOU DO IT UNCON-SCIOUSLY.
IT'S A WONDER-FUL THING.
BUT IT'S ALSO SAD, HM?
WAS SOME-ONE HERE?
MM-HMM... AN OLD FRIEND.
OH? ANYONE I KNOW?

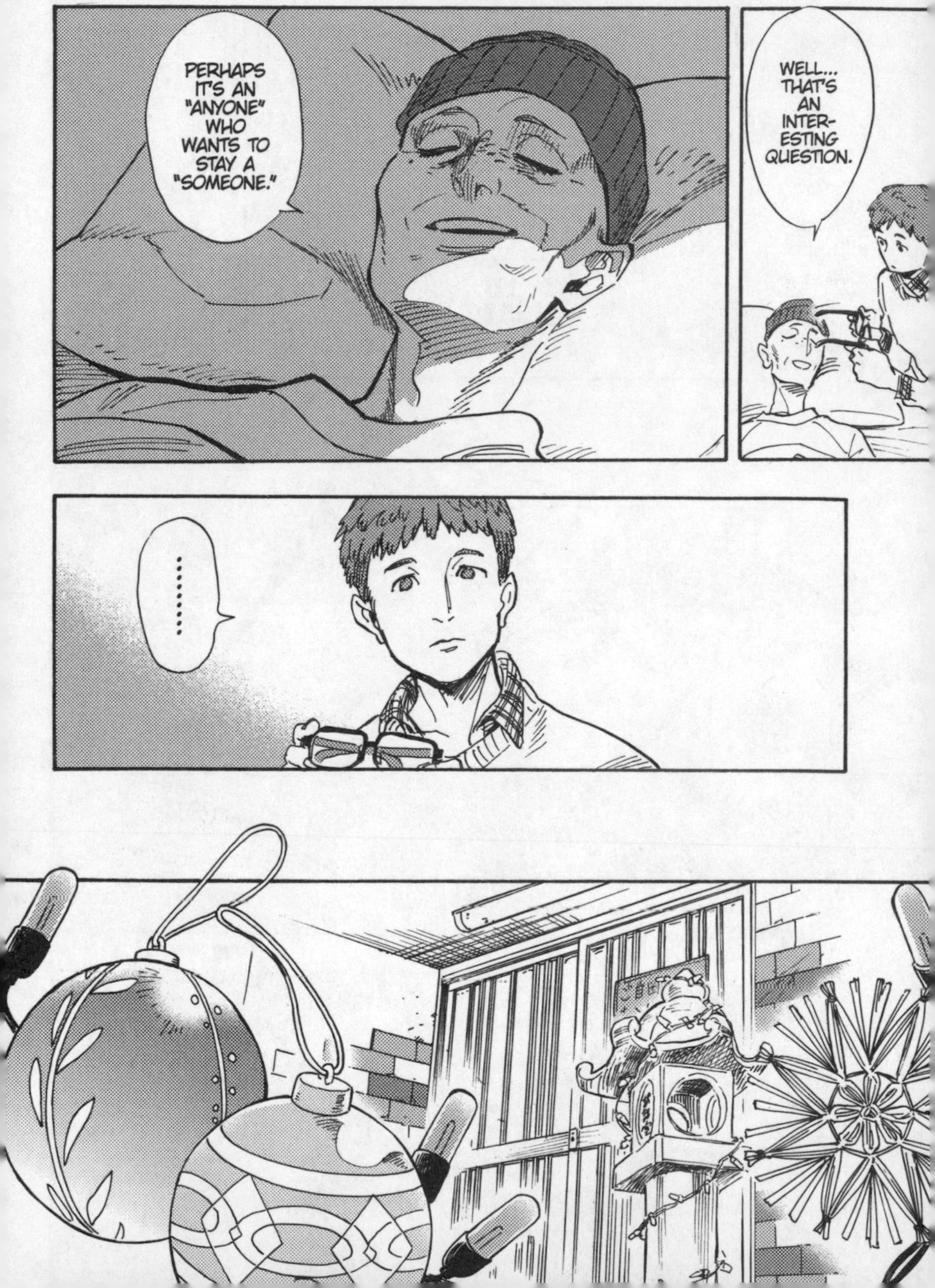
WELL... THAT'S AN INTER-ESTING QUESTION.
PERHAPS IT'S AN "ANYONE" WHO WANTS TO STAY A "SOMEONE."
......

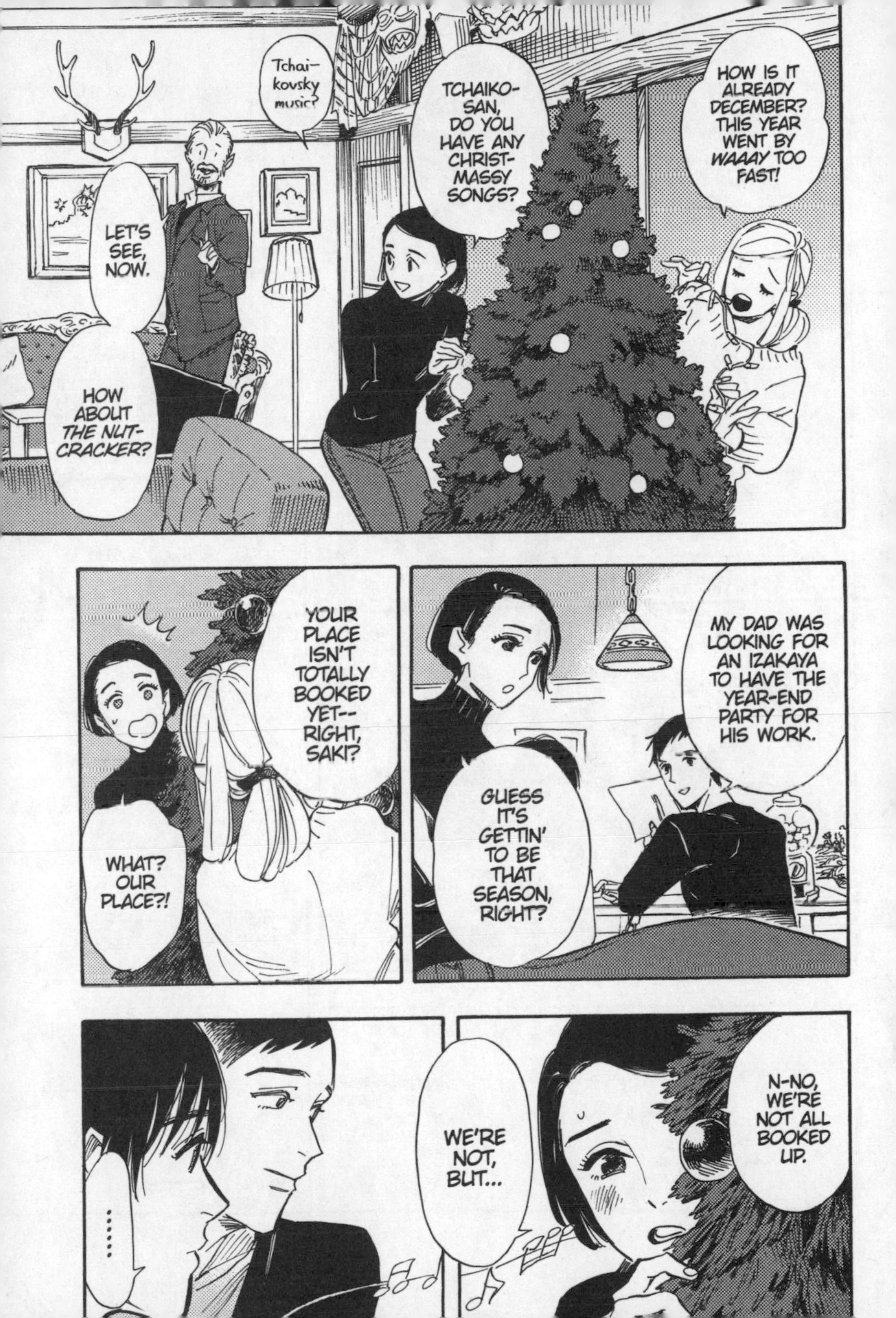
HOW IS IT ALREADY DECEMBER? THIS YEAR WENT BY WAAAY TOO FAST!
TCHAIKO-SAN, DO YOU HAVE ANY CHRISTMASSY SONGS?
Tchaikovsky music?
LET'S SEE, NOW.
HOW ABOUT THE NUTCRACKER?
MY DAD WAS LOOKING FOR AN IZAKAYA TO HAVE THE YEAR-END PARTY FOR HIS WORK.
GUESS IT'S GETTIN' TO BE THAT SEASON, RIGHT?
YOUR PLACE ISN'T TOTALLY BOOKED YET--RIGHT, SAKI?
WHAT? OUR PLACE?!
N-NO, WE'RE NOT ALL BOOKED UP.
WE'RE NOT, BUT...
......

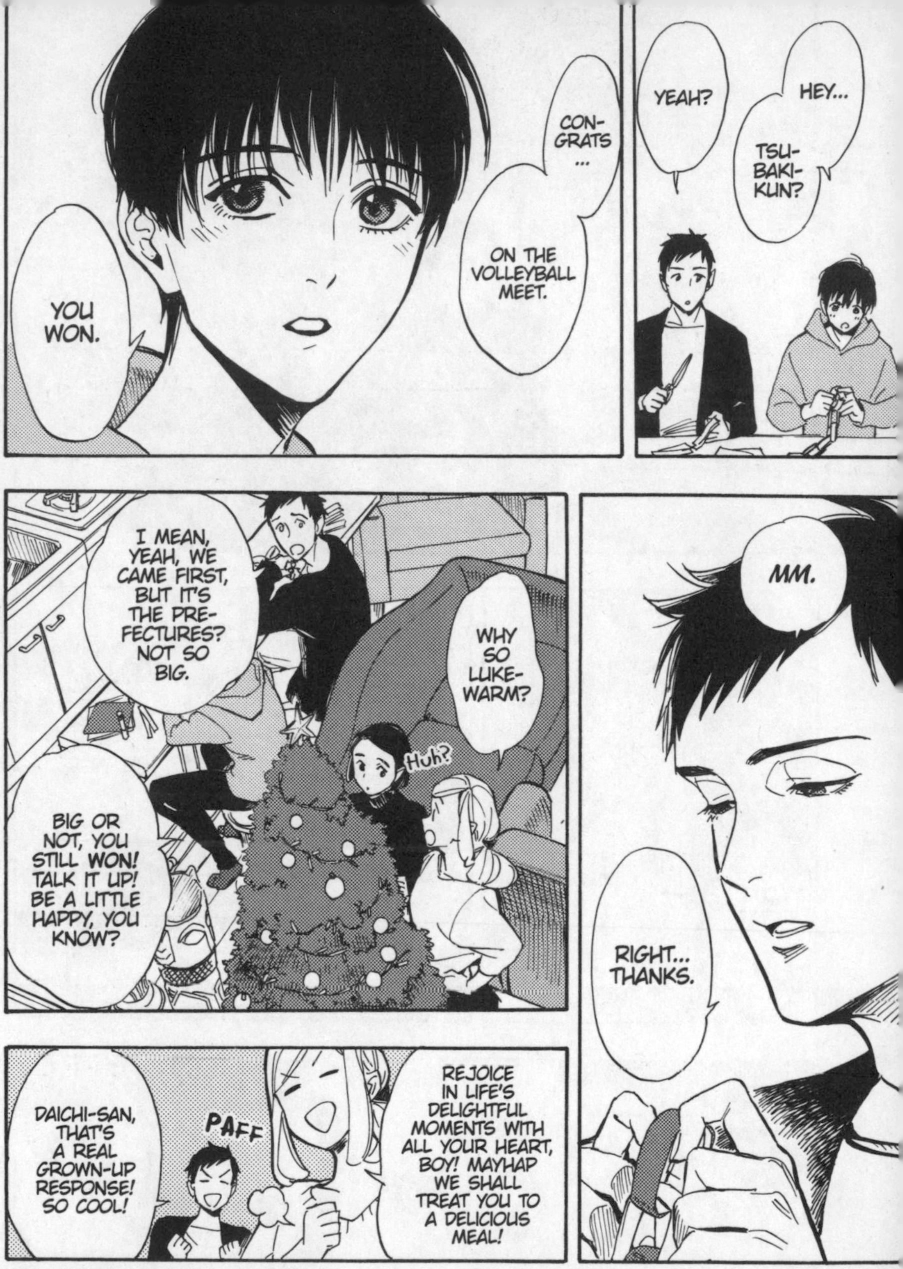
HEY... TSUBAKI-KUN?
YEAH?
CONGRATS...
ON THE VOLLEYBALL MEET.
YOU WON.
MM.
RIGHT... THANKS.
WHY SO LUKEWARM?
Huh?
I MEAN, YEAH, WE CAME FIRST, BUT IT'S THE PREFECTURES? NOT SO BIG.
BIG OR NOT, YOU STILL WON! TALK IT UP! BE A LITTLE HAPPY, YOU KNOW?
REJOICE IN LIFE'S DELIGHTFUL MOMENTS WITH ALL YOUR HEART, BOY! MAYHAP WE SHALL TREAT YOU TO A DELICIOUS MEAL!
PAFF
DAICHI-SAN, THAT'S A REAL GROWN-UP RESPONSE! SO COOL!

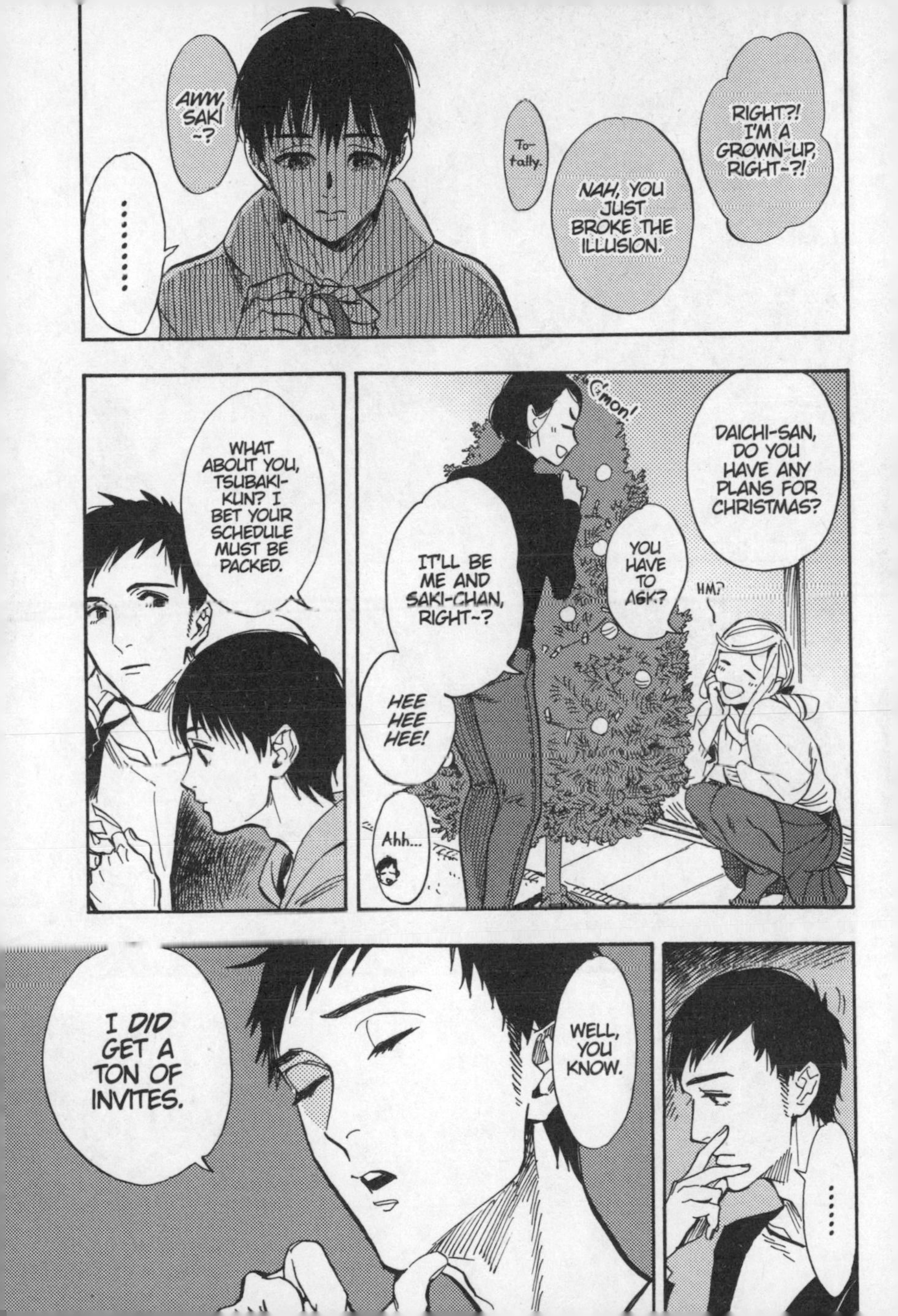
RIGHT?! I'M A GROWN-UP, RIGHT~?!
NAH, YOU JUST BROKE THE ILLUSION.
To-tally.
AWW, SAKI ~?
......
C'mon!
DAICHI-SAN, DO YOU HAVE ANY PLANS FOR CHRISTMAS?
HM?
YOU HAVE TO ASK?
IT'LL BE ME AND SAKI-CHAN, RIGHT~?
HEE HEE HEE!
Ahh...
WHAT ABOUT YOU, TSUBAKI-KUN? I BET YOUR SCHEDULE MUST BE PACKED.
......
WELL, YOU KNOW.
I *DID* GET A TON OF INVITES.

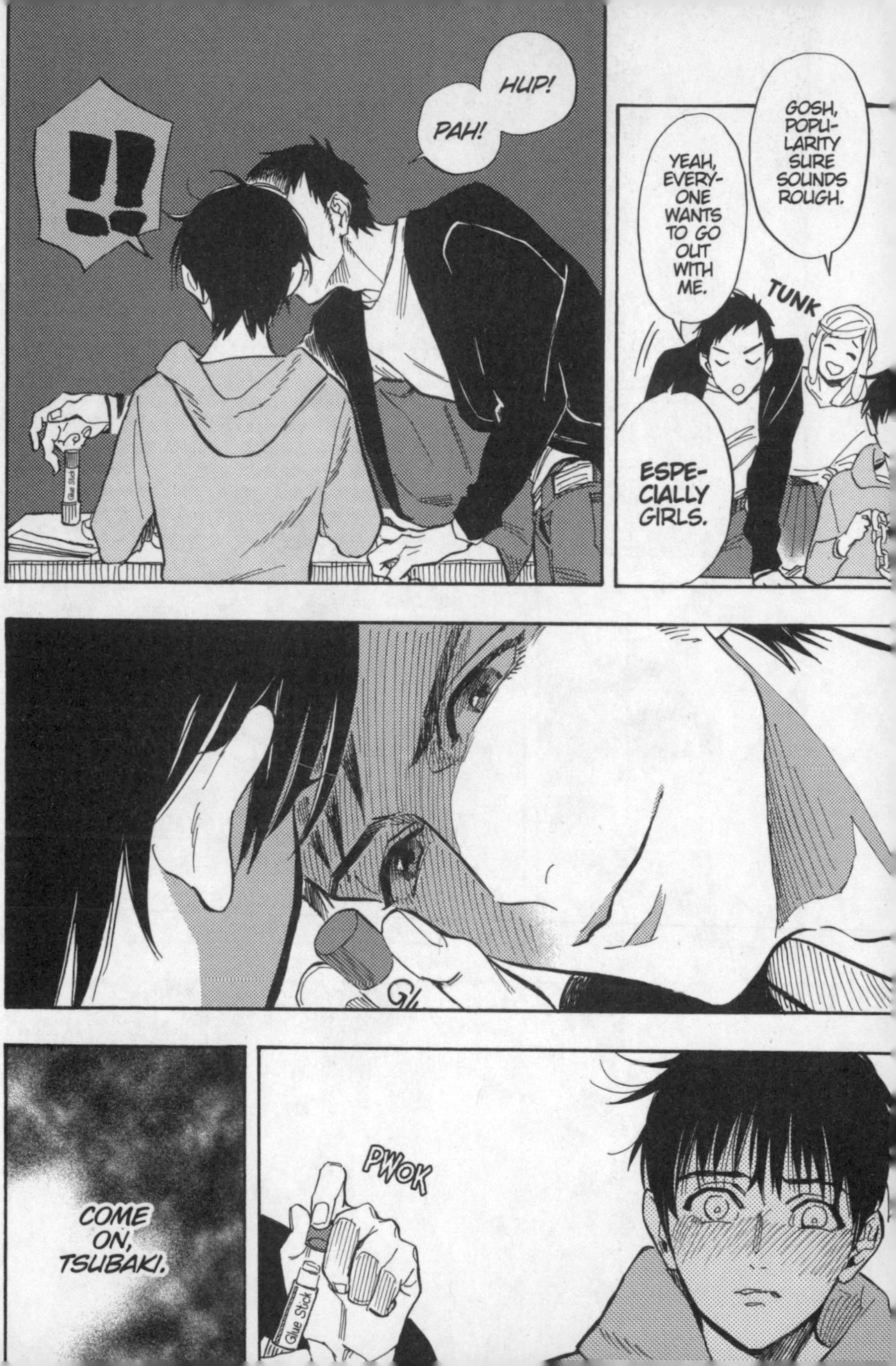
GOSH, POPULARITY SURE SOUNDS ROUGH.
YEAH, EVERYONE WANTS TO GO OUT WITH ME.
TUNK
ESPECIALLY GIRLS.
HUP!
PAH!
!!
PWOK
COME ON, TSUBAKI.

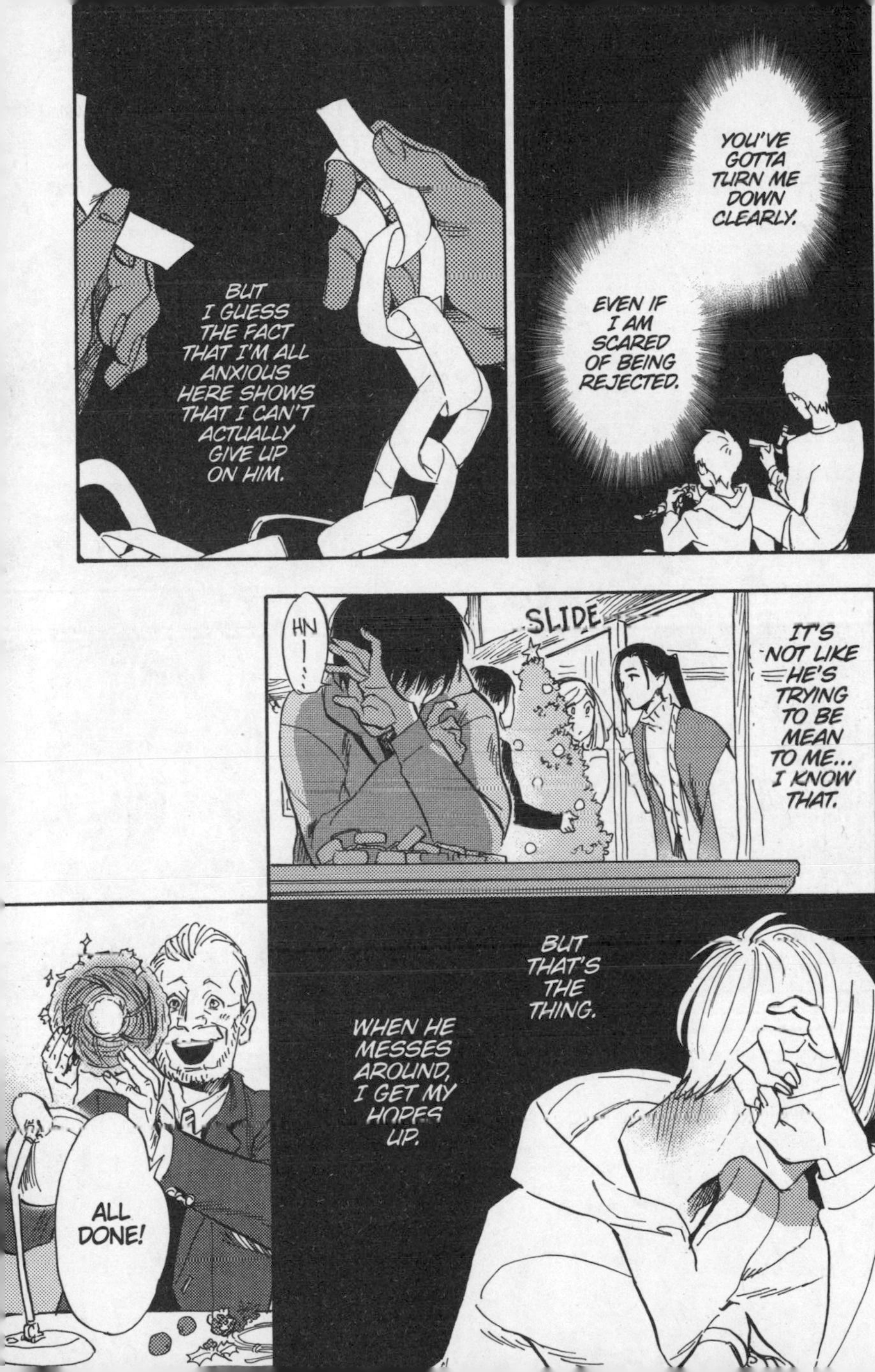
YOU'VE GOTTA TURN ME DOWN CLEARLY.
EVEN IF I AM SCARED OF BEING REJECTED.
BUT I GUESS THE FACT THAT I'M ALL ANXIOUS HERE SHOWS THAT I CAN'T ACTUALLY GIVE UP ON HIM.
IT'S NOT LIKE HE'S TRYING TO BE MEAN TO ME... I KNOW THAT.
SLIDE
HN!..
BUT THAT'S THE THING.
WHEN HE MESSES AROUND, I GET MY HOPES UP.
ALL DONE!

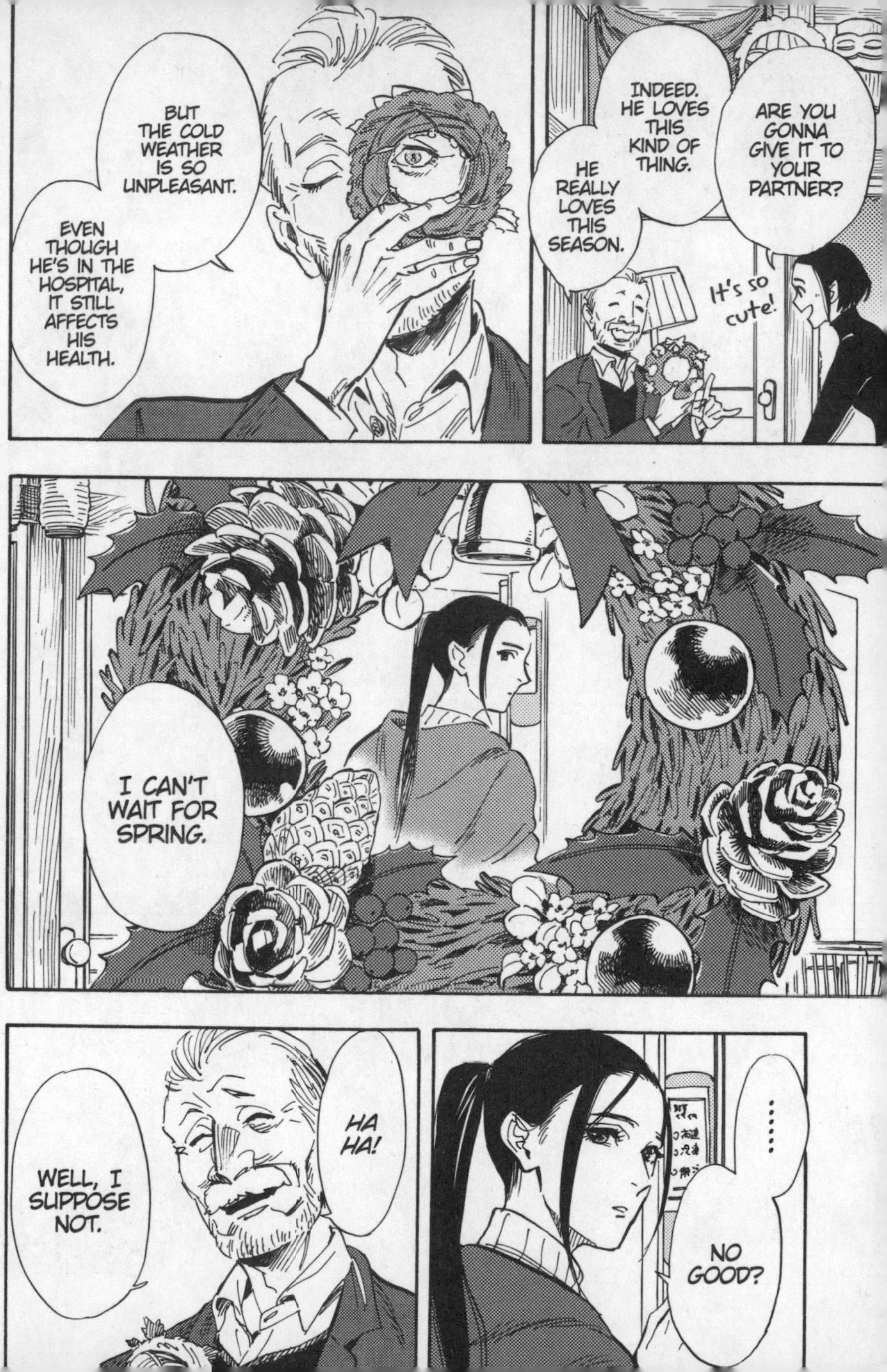
ARE YOU GONNA GIVE IT TO YOUR PARTNER?
It's so cute!
INDEED. HE LOVES THIS KIND OF THING.
HE REALLY LOVES THIS SEASON.
BUT THE COLD WEATHER IS SO UNPLEASANT.
EVEN THOUGH HE'S IN THE HOSPITAL, IT STILL AFFECTS HIS HEALTH.
I CAN'T WAIT FOR SPRING.
......
NO GOOD?
HA HA!
WELL, I SUPPOSE NOT.

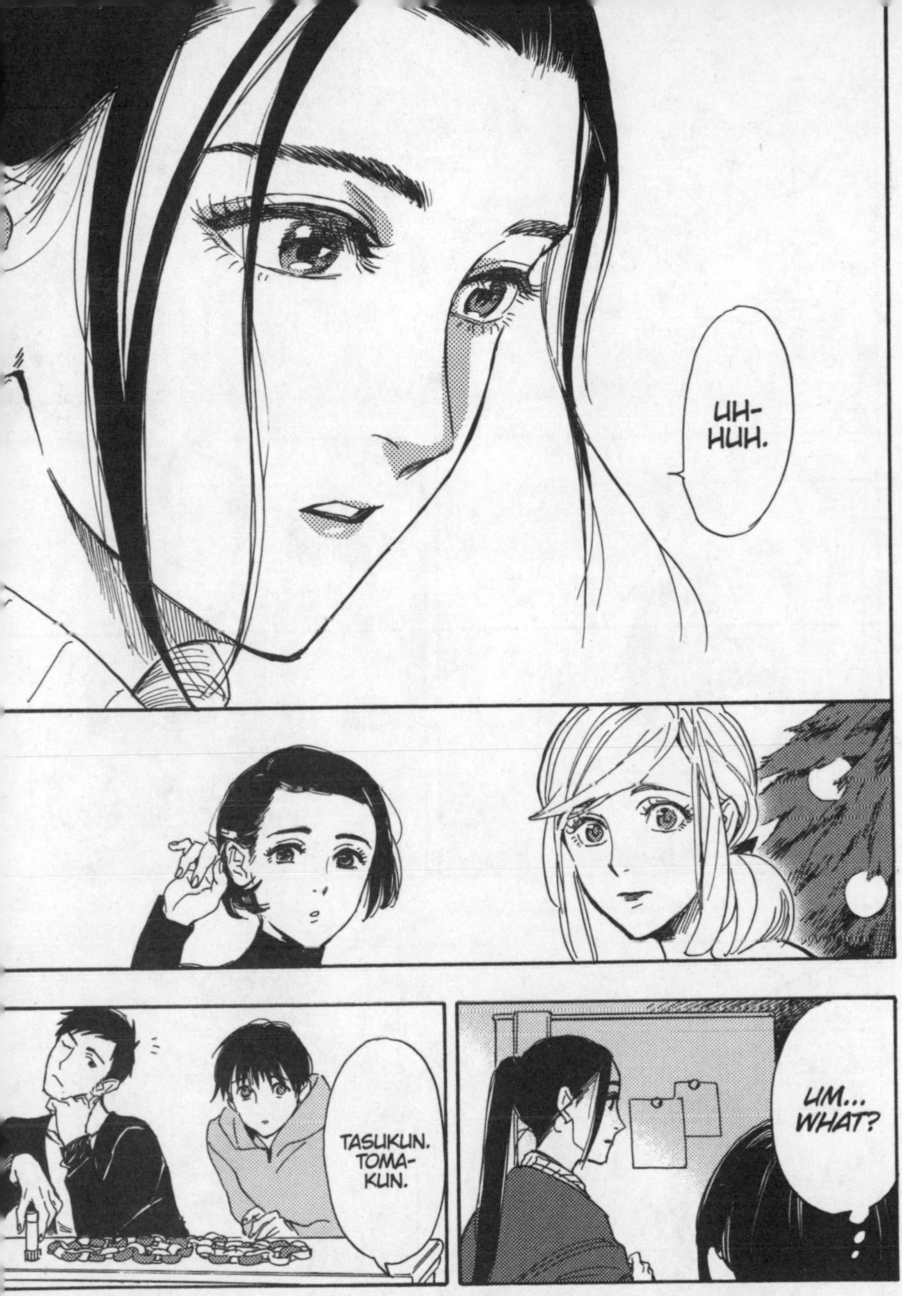
UH-HUH.
UM... WHAT?
TASUKUN. TOMA-KUN.

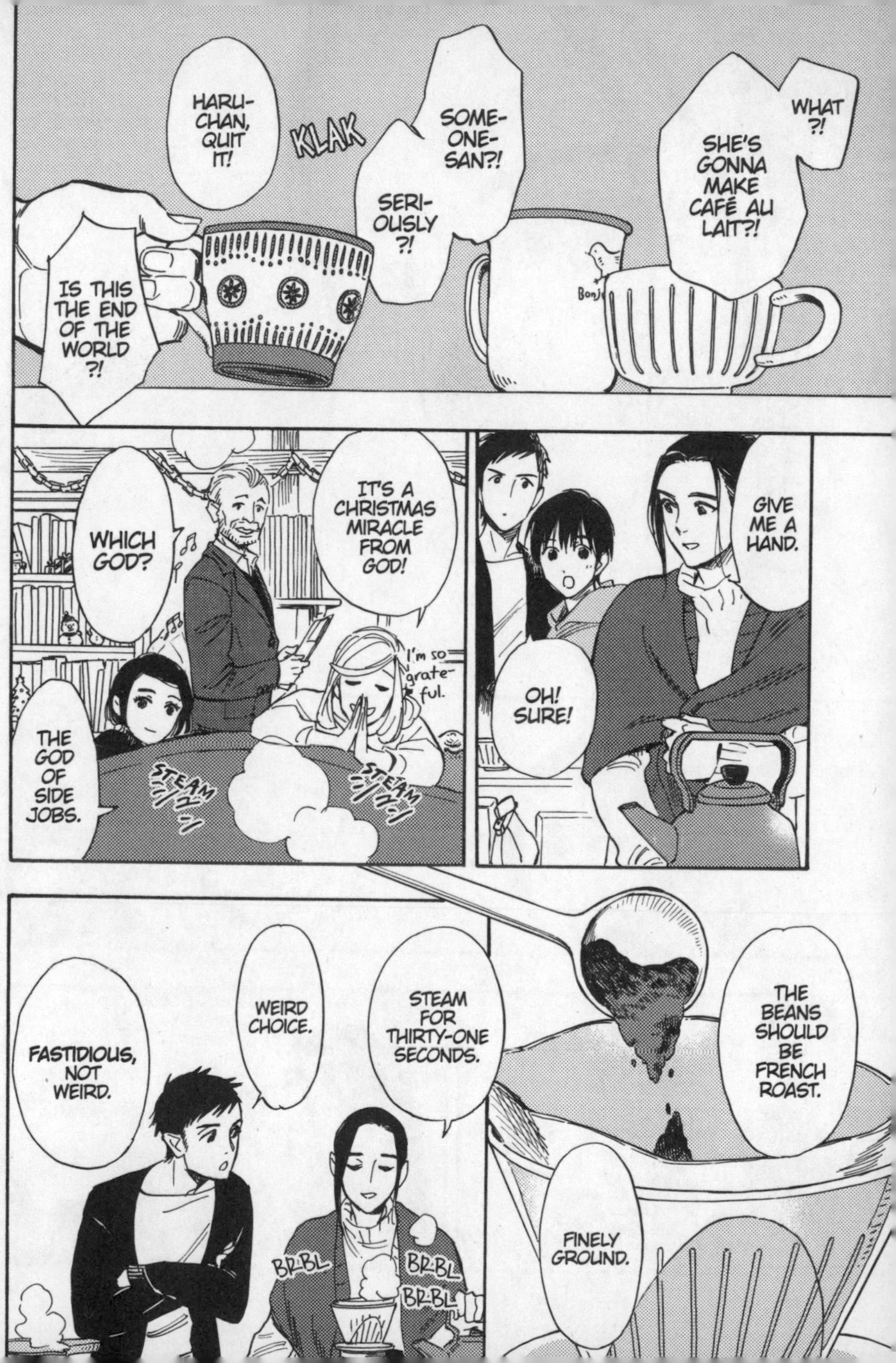
WHAT ?!
SHE'S GONNA MAKE CAFÉ AU LAIT?!
SOME-ONE-SAN?!
SERI-OUSLY ?!
KLAK
HARU-CHAN, QUIT IT!
IS THIS THE END OF THE WORLD ?!
GIVE ME A HAND.
OH! SURE!
IT'S A CHRISTMAS MIRACLE FROM GOD!
I'm so grateful.
WHICH GOD?
THE GOD OF SIDE JOBS.
STEAM
STEAM
THE BEANS SHOULD BE FRENCH ROAST.
FINELY GROUND.
STEAM FOR THIRTY-ONE SECONDS.
WEIRD CHOICE.
FASTIDIOUS, NOT WEIRD.
BR-BL
BR-BL
BR-BL

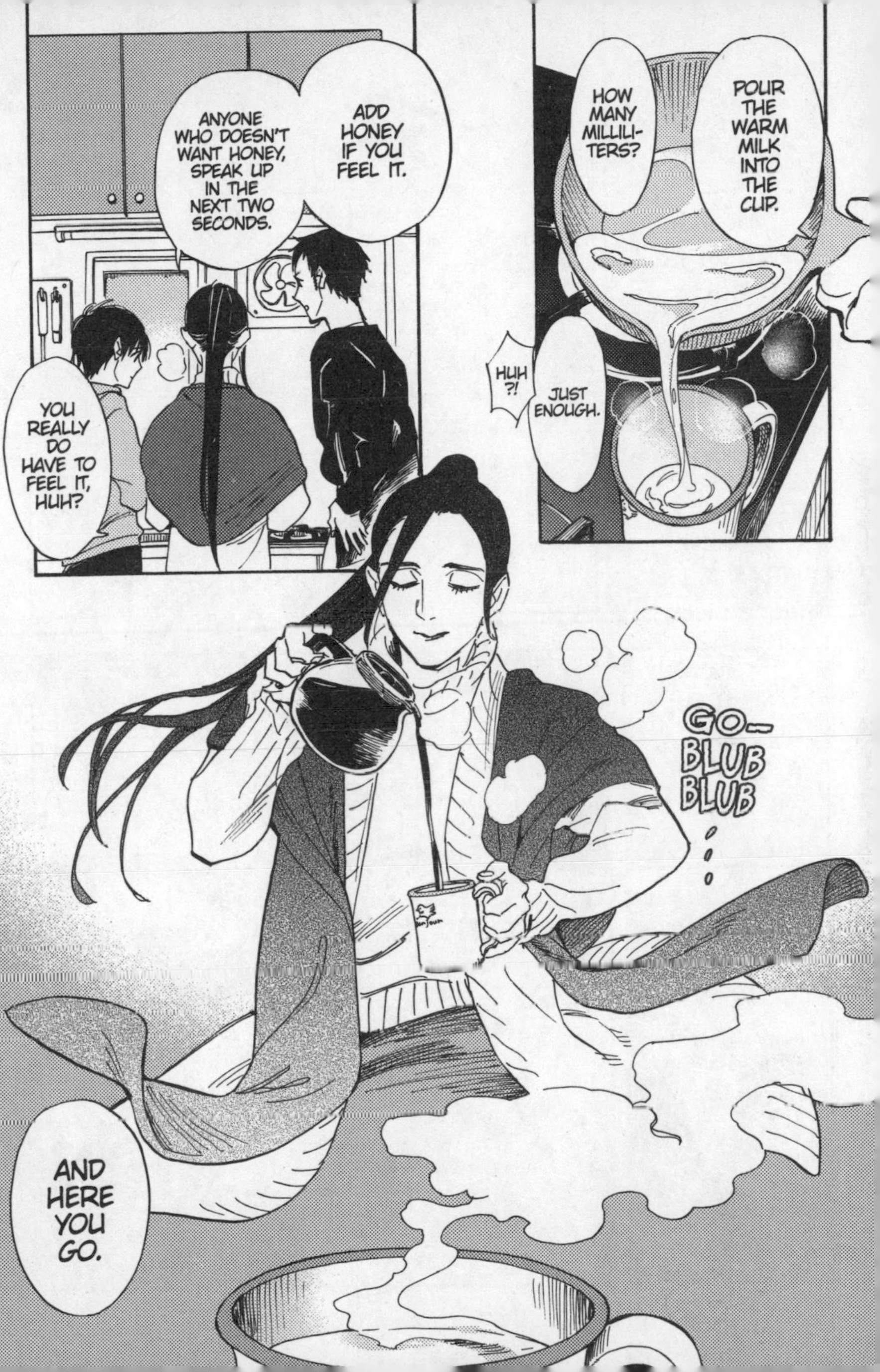
POUR THE WARM MILK INTO THE CUP.
HOW MANY MILLILI-TERS?
JUST ENOUGH.
HUH?!
ADD HONEY IF YOU FEEL IT.
ANYONE WHO DOESN'T WANT HONEY, SPEAK UP IN THE NEXT TWO SECONDS.
YOU REALLY DO HAVE TO FEEL IT, HUH?
GO-BLUB BLUB...
AND HERE YOU GO.

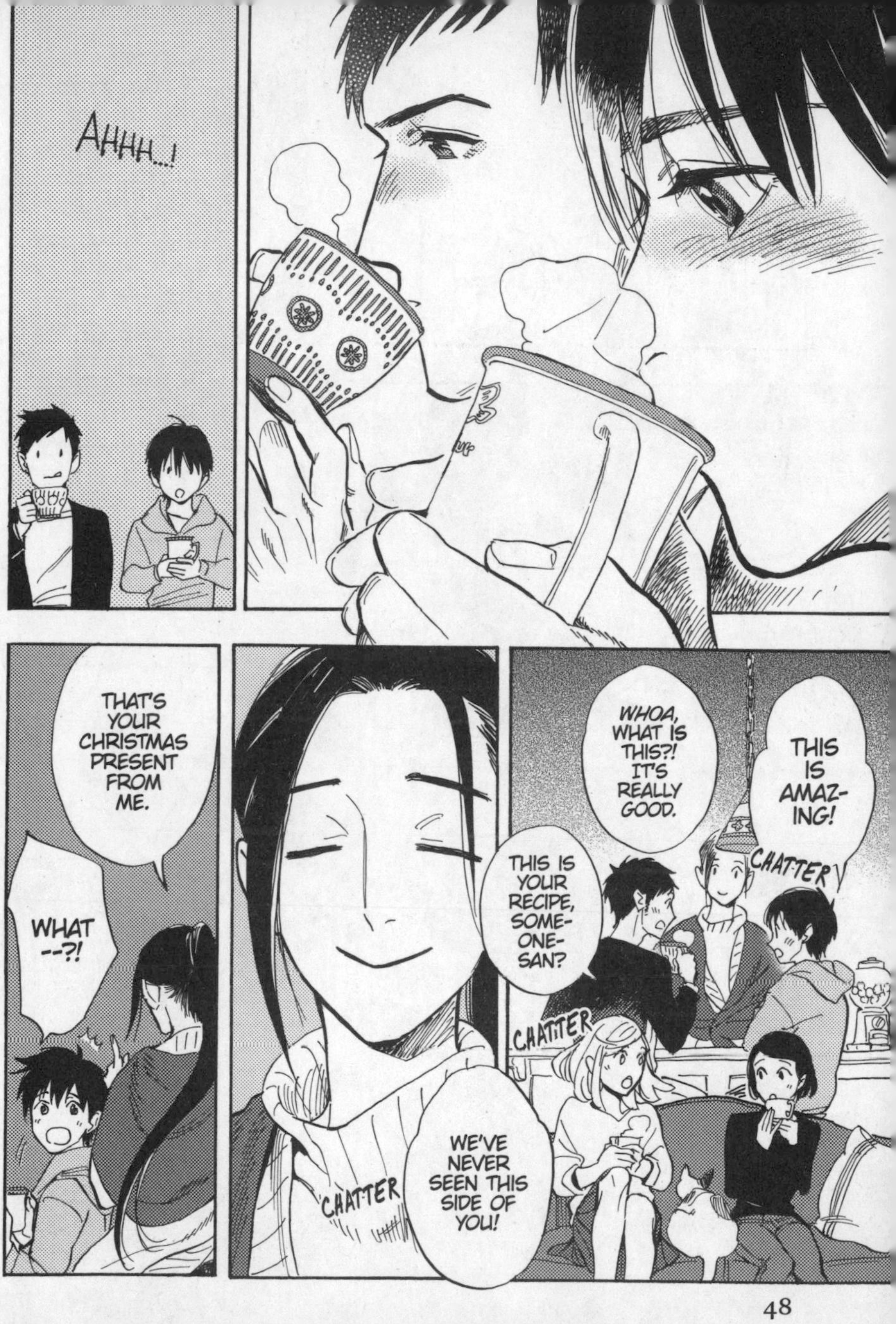
AHHH...!
THIS IS AMAZ-ING!
WHOA, WHAT IS THIS?! IT'S REALLY GOOD.
CHATTER
THIS IS YOUR RECIPE, SOME-ONE-SAN?
CHATTER
WE'VE NEVER SEEN THIS SIDE OF YOU!
CHATTER
THAT'S YOUR CHRISTMAS PRESENT FROM ME.
WHAT --?!

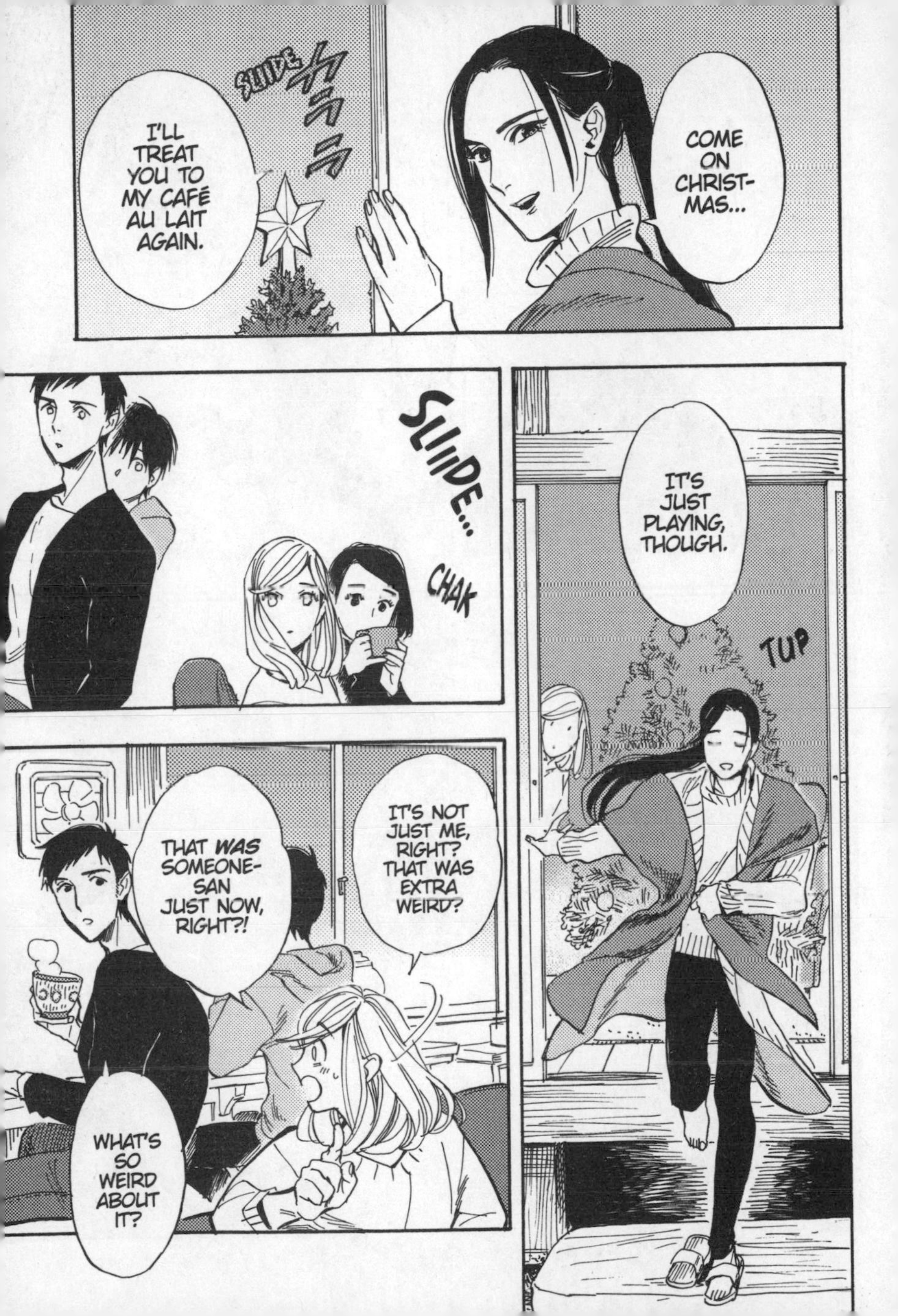
COME ON CHRIST-MAS...
SLIIDE
I'LL TREAT YOU TO MY CAFÉ AU LAIT AGAIN.
IT'S JUST PLAYING, THOUGH.
TUP
SLIIDE...
CHAK
IT'S NOT JUST ME, RIGHT? THAT WAS EXTRA WEIRD?
THAT *WAS* SOMEONE-SAN JUST NOW, RIGHT?!
WHAT'S SO WEIRD ABOUT IT?

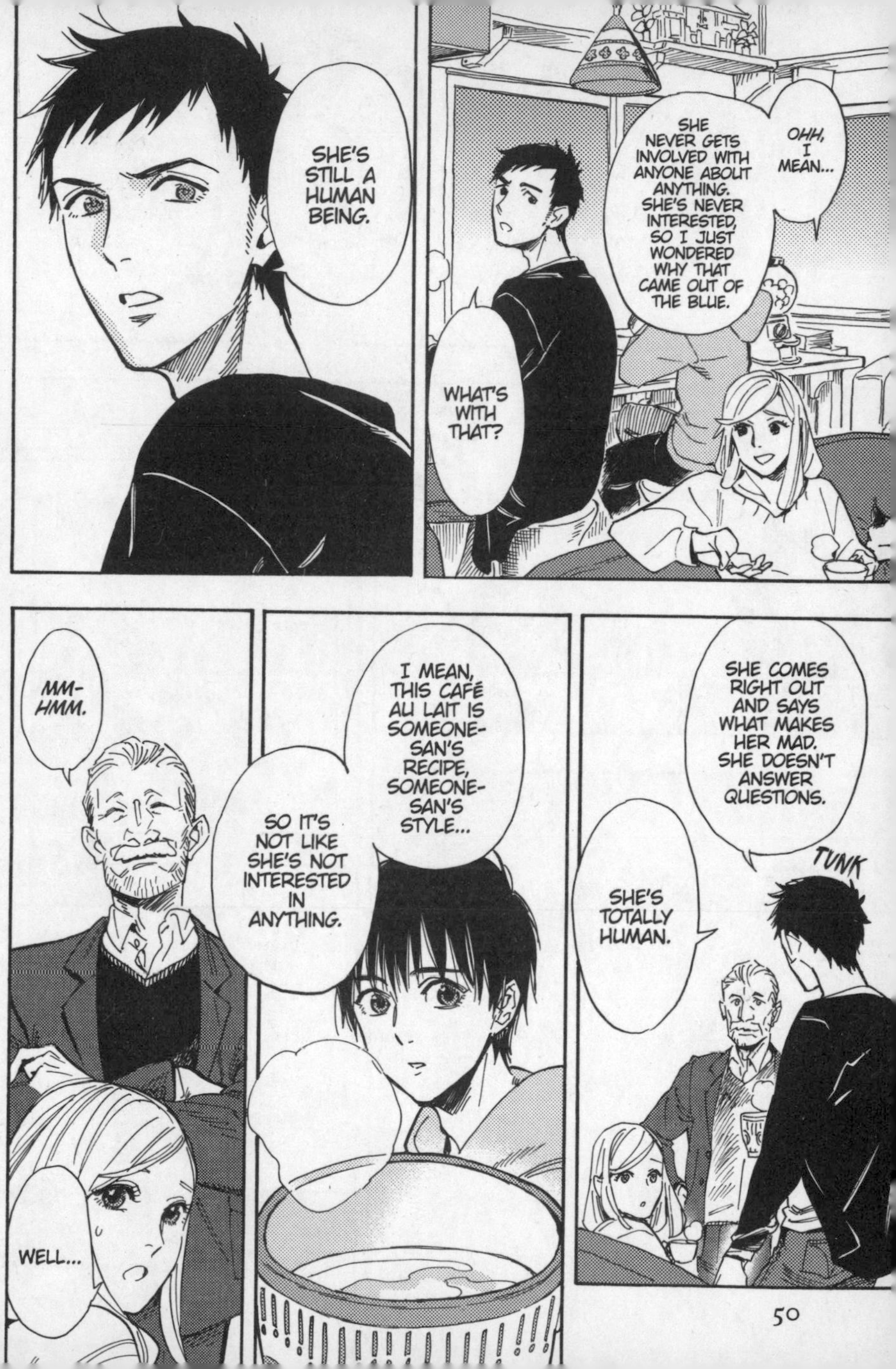
OHH, I MEAN...
SHE NEVER GETS INVOLVED WITH ANYONE ABOUT ANYTHING. SHE'S NEVER INTERESTED, SO I JUST WONDERED WHY THAT CAME OUT OF THE BLUE.
WHAT'S WITH THAT?
SHE'S STILL A HUMAN BEING.
SHE COMES RIGHT OUT AND SAYS WHAT MAKES HER MAD. SHE DOESN'T ANSWER QUESTIONS.
TUNK
SHE'S TOTALLY HUMAN.
I MEAN, THIS CAFÉ AU LAIT IS SOMEONE-SAN'S RECIPE, SOMEONE-SAN'S STYLE...
SO IT'S NOT LIKE SHE'S NOT INTERESTED IN ANYTHING.
MM-HMM.
WELL...

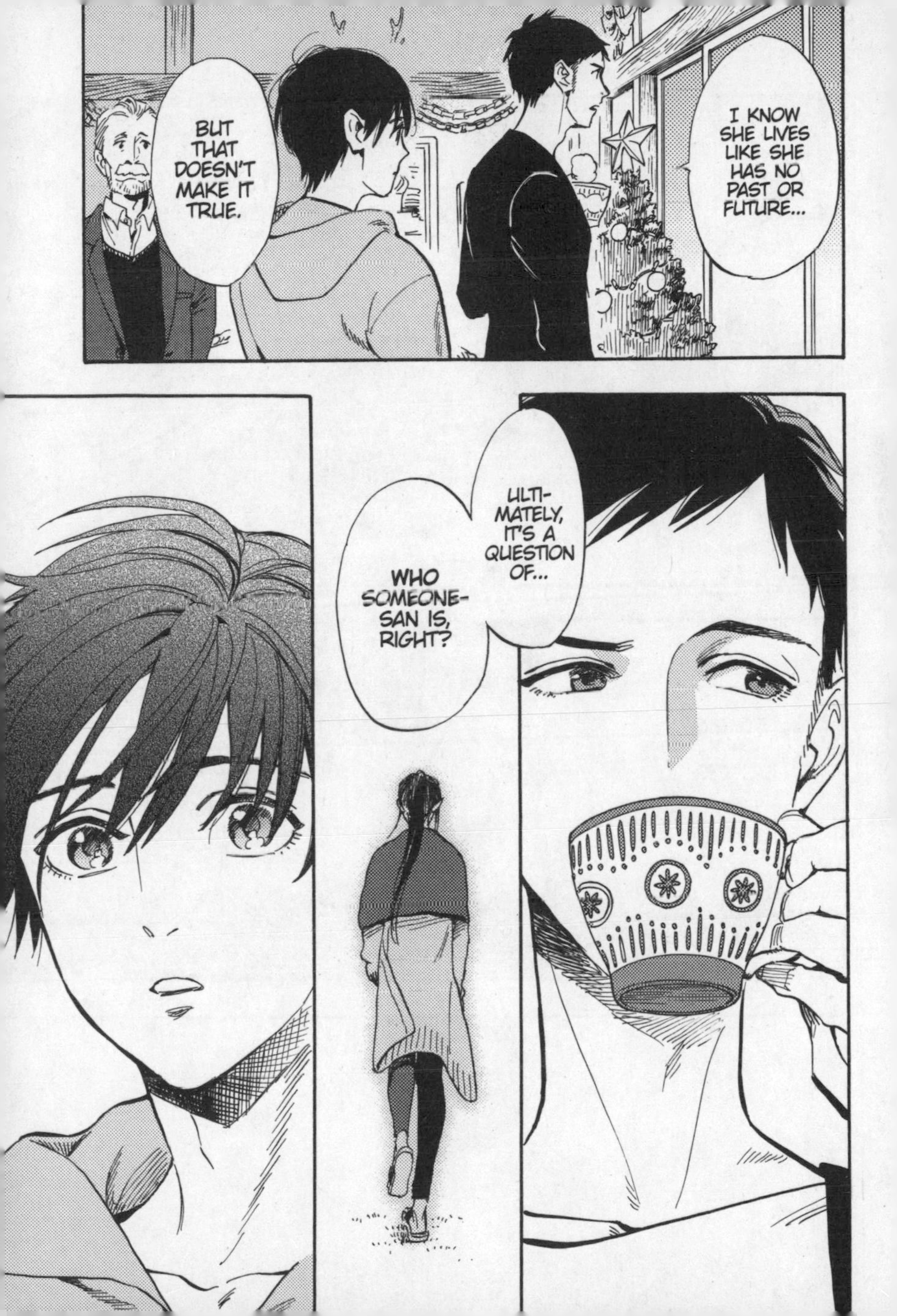
I KNOW SHE LIVES LIKE SHE HAS NO PAST OR FUTURE...
BUT THAT DOESN'T MAKE IT TRUE.
ULTI-MATELY, IT'S A QUESTION OF...
WHO SOMEONE-SAN IS, RIGHT?

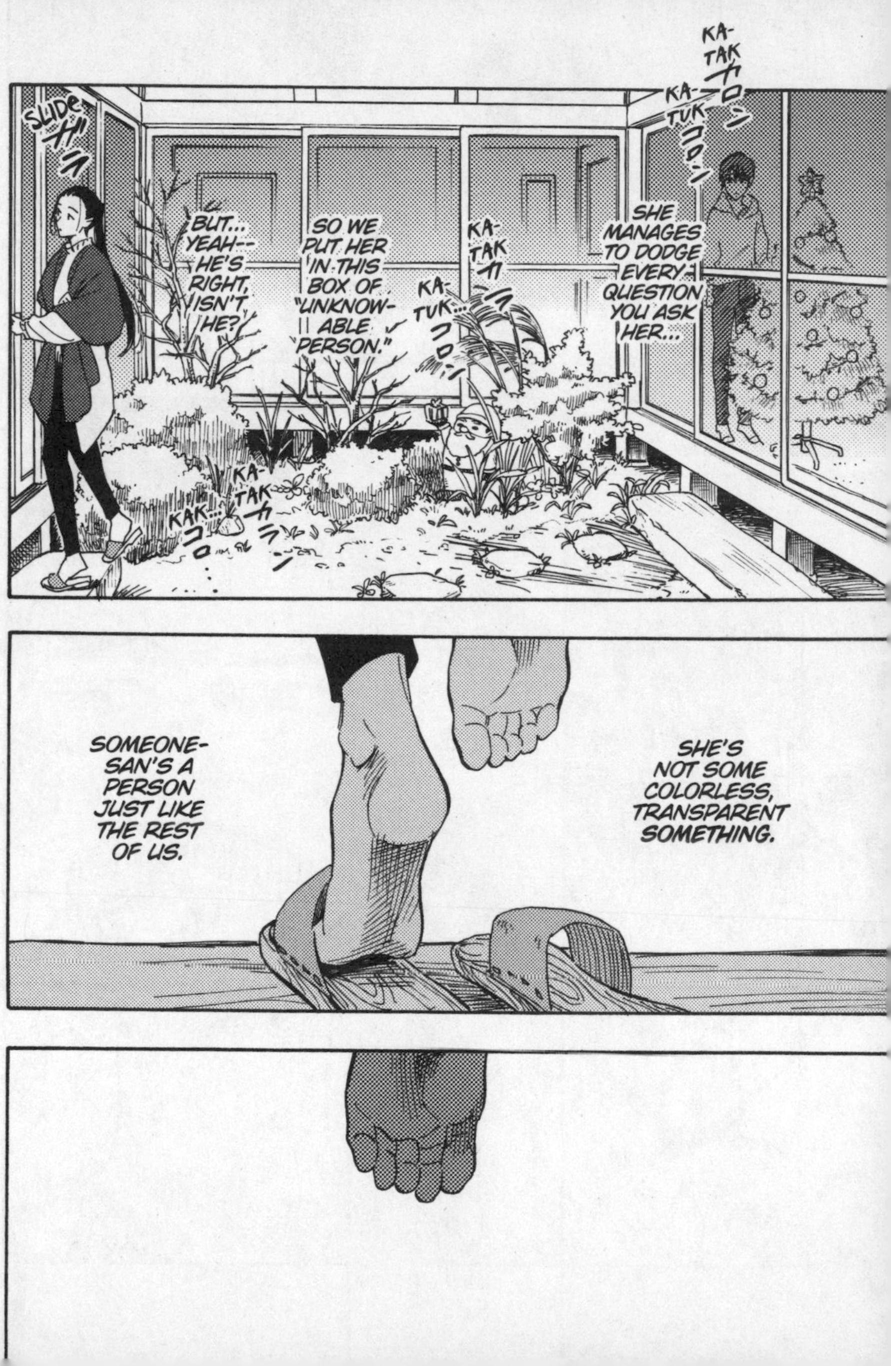
KA-TAK
KA-TUK
SHE MANAGES TO DODGE EVERY QUESTION YOU ASK HER...
KA-TAK
KA-TUK...
SO WE PUT HER IN THIS BOX OF "UNKNOWABLE PERSON."
BUT... YEAH-- HE'S RIGHT, ISN'T HE?
KA-TAK
KAK...
SLIDE
SHE'S NOT SOME COLORLESS, TRANSPARENT SOMETHING.
SOMEONE-SAN'S A PERSON JUST LIKE THE REST OF US.

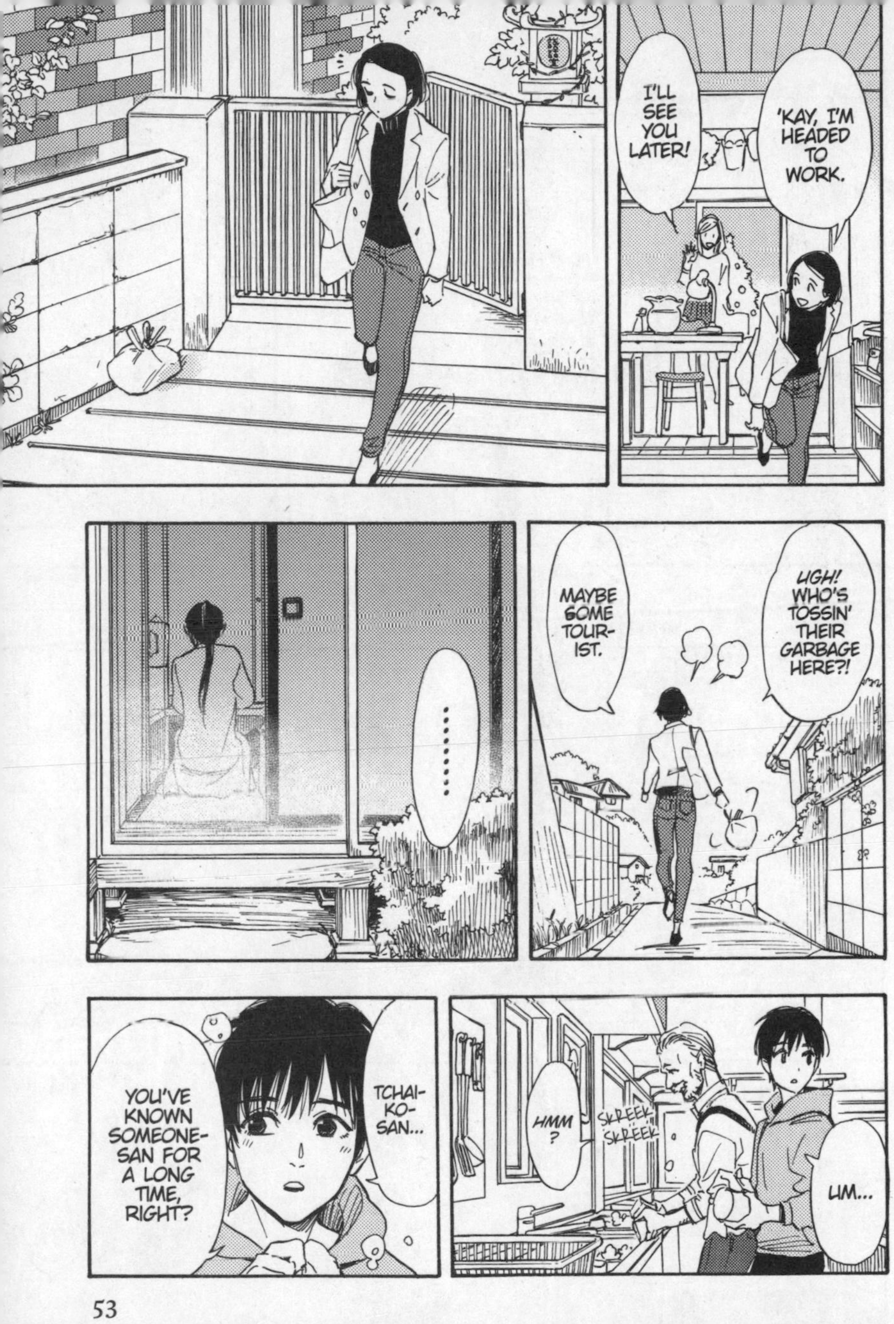
'KAY, I'M HEADED TO WORK.
I'LL SEE YOU LATER!
UGH! WHO'S TOSSIN' THEIR GARBAGE HERE?!
MAYBE SOME TOURIST.
....
UM...
SKREEK SKREEK
HMM?
TCHAIKO-SAN...
YOU'VE KNOWN SOMEONE-SAN FOR A LONG TIME, RIGHT?

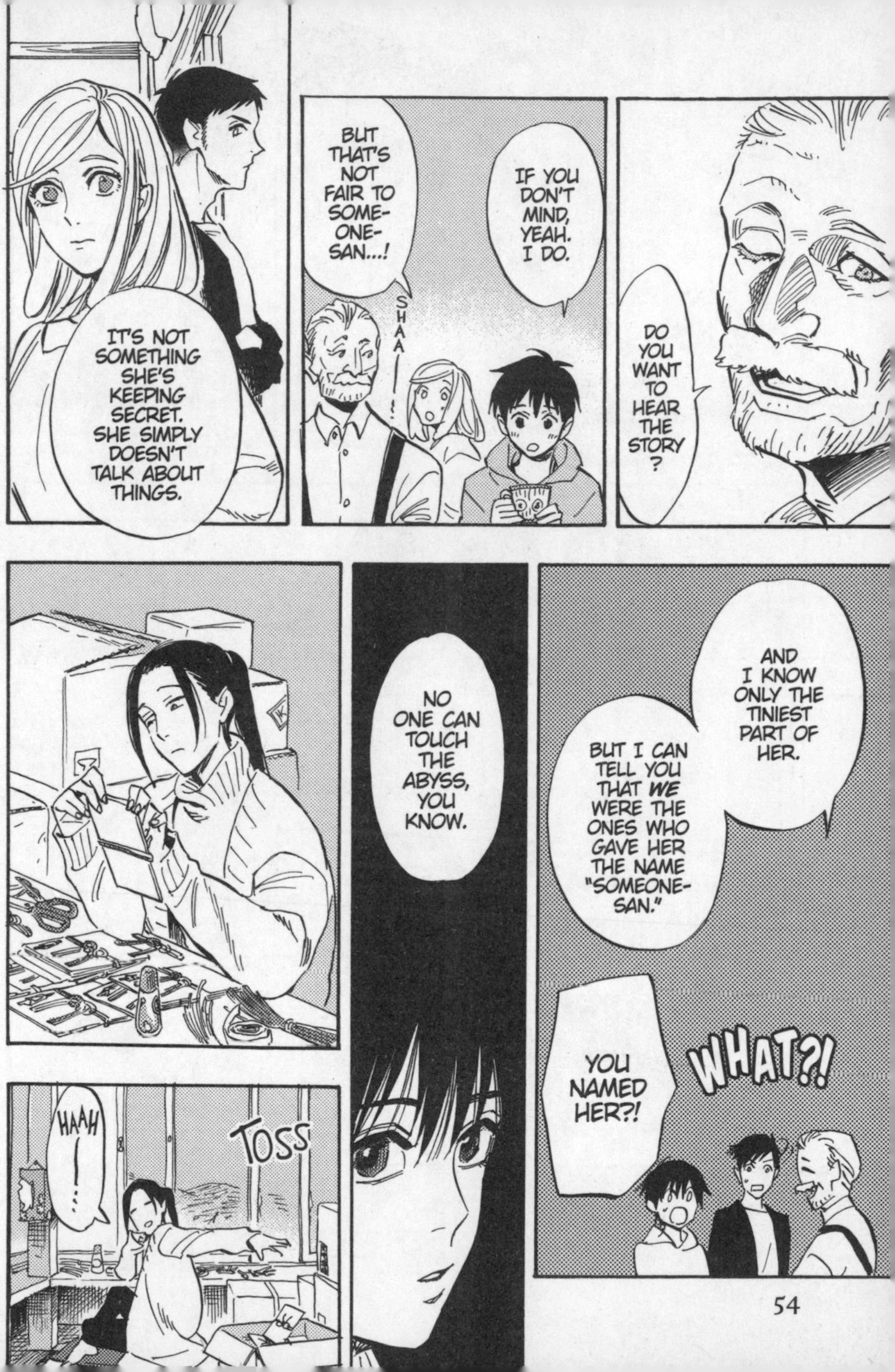
DO YOU WANT TO HEAR THE STORY?
IF YOU DON'T MIND, YEAH. I DO.
BUT THAT'S NOT FAIR TO SOMEONE-SAN...!
SHAA
IT'S NOT SOMETHING SHE'S KEEPING SECRET. SHE SIMPLY DOESN'T TALK ABOUT THINGS.
AND I KNOW ONLY THE TINIEST PART OF HER.
BUT I CAN TELL YOU THAT *WE* WERE THE ONES WHO GAVE HER THE NAME "SOMEONE-SAN."
WHAT?!
YOU NAMED HER?!
NO ONE CAN TOUCH THE ABYSS, YOU KNOW.
TOSS
HAAH...!

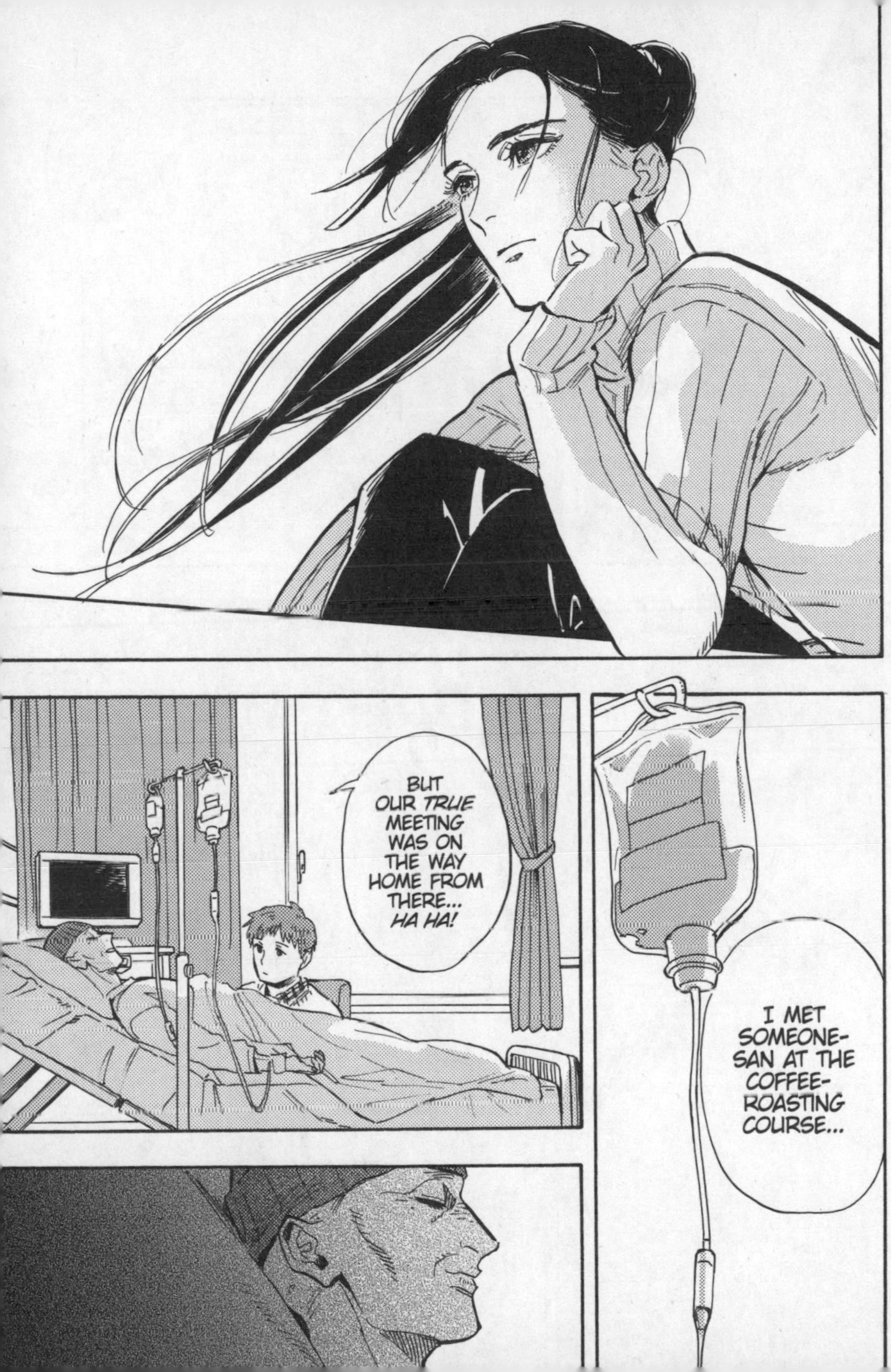
I MET SOMEONE-SAN AT THE COFFEE-ROASTING COURSE...
BUT OUR *TRUE* MEETING WAS ON THE WAY HOME FROM THERE... *HA HA!*

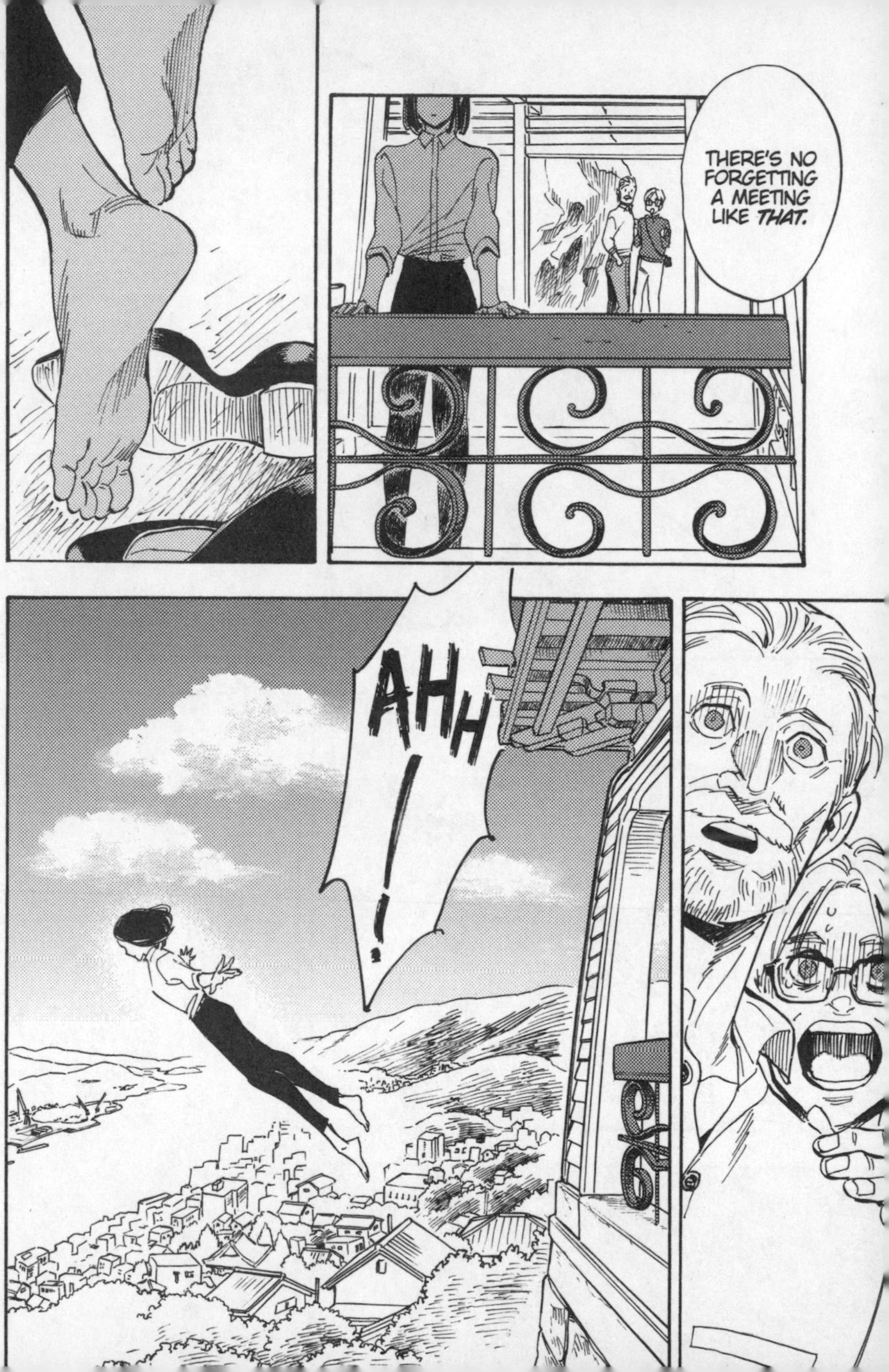
THERE'S NO FORGETTING A MEETING LIKE *THAT.*
AHH!

Our Dreams at Dusk
SHIMANAMI **TASOGARE**

Innoshima
Suigun
Festival

Murakami
Suigun

Kobaya
wooden
ship race.

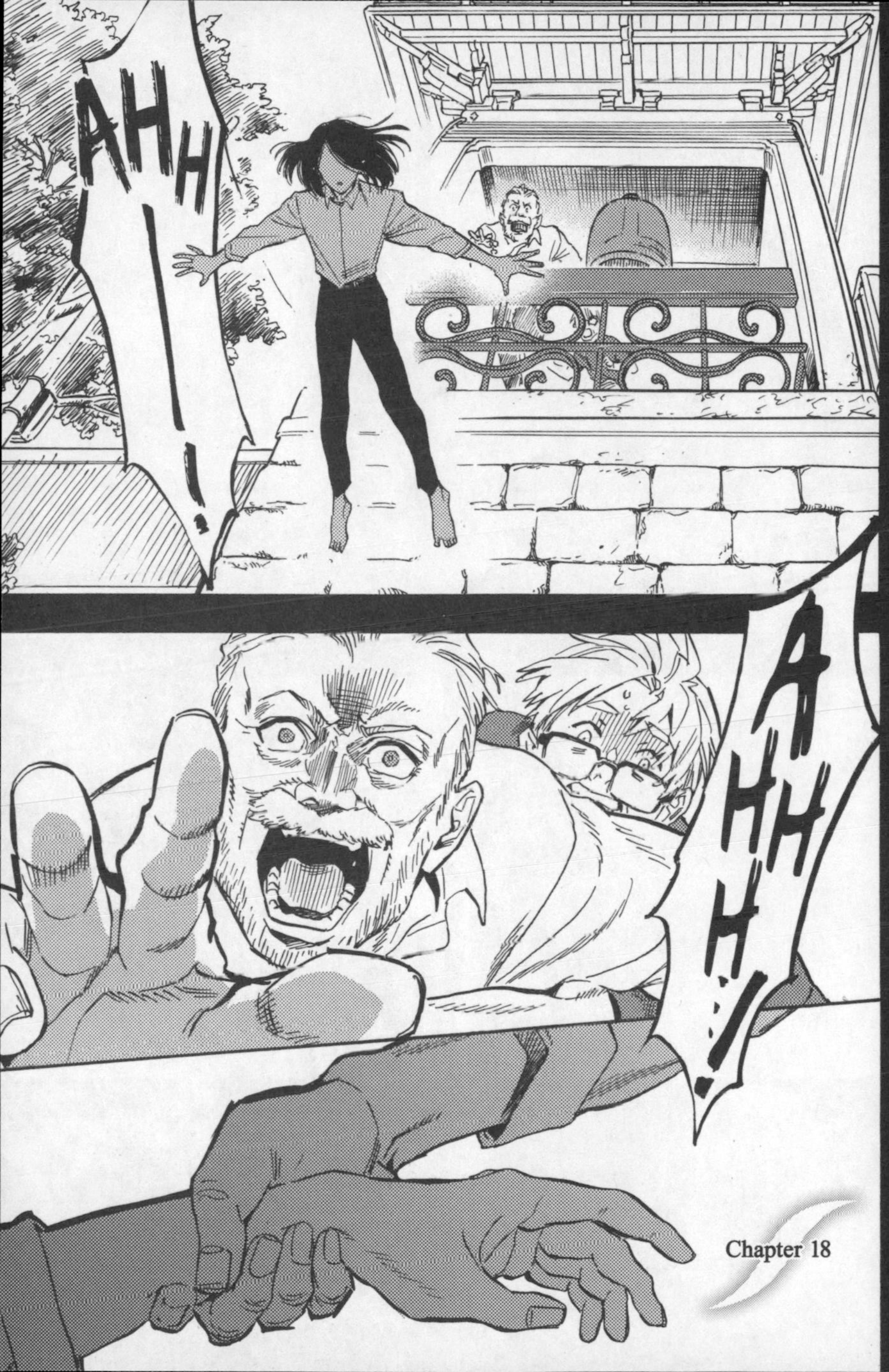
AHH!!
AHHHH...!
Chapter 18

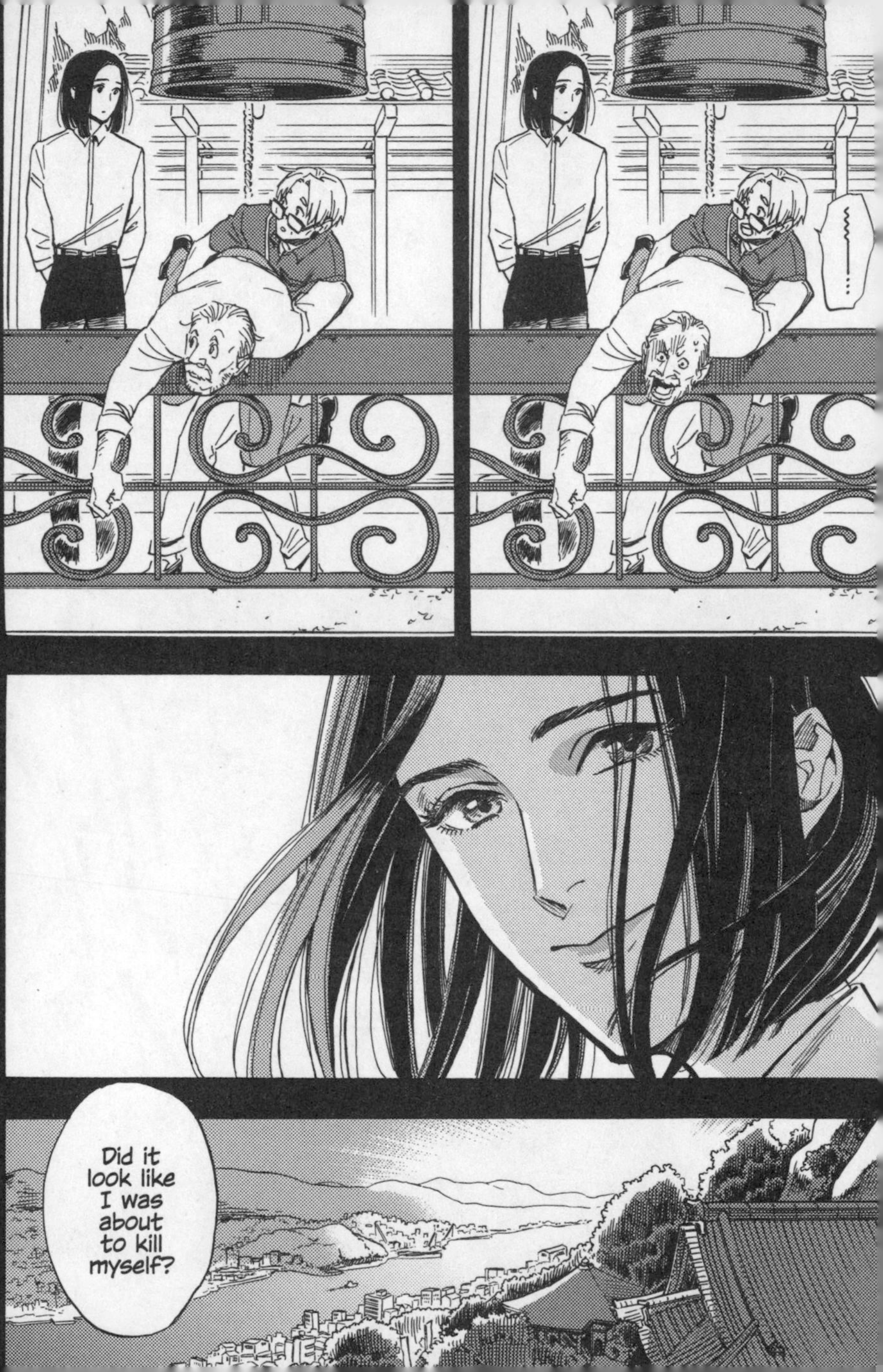
Did it look like I was about to kill myself?

Chapter 18

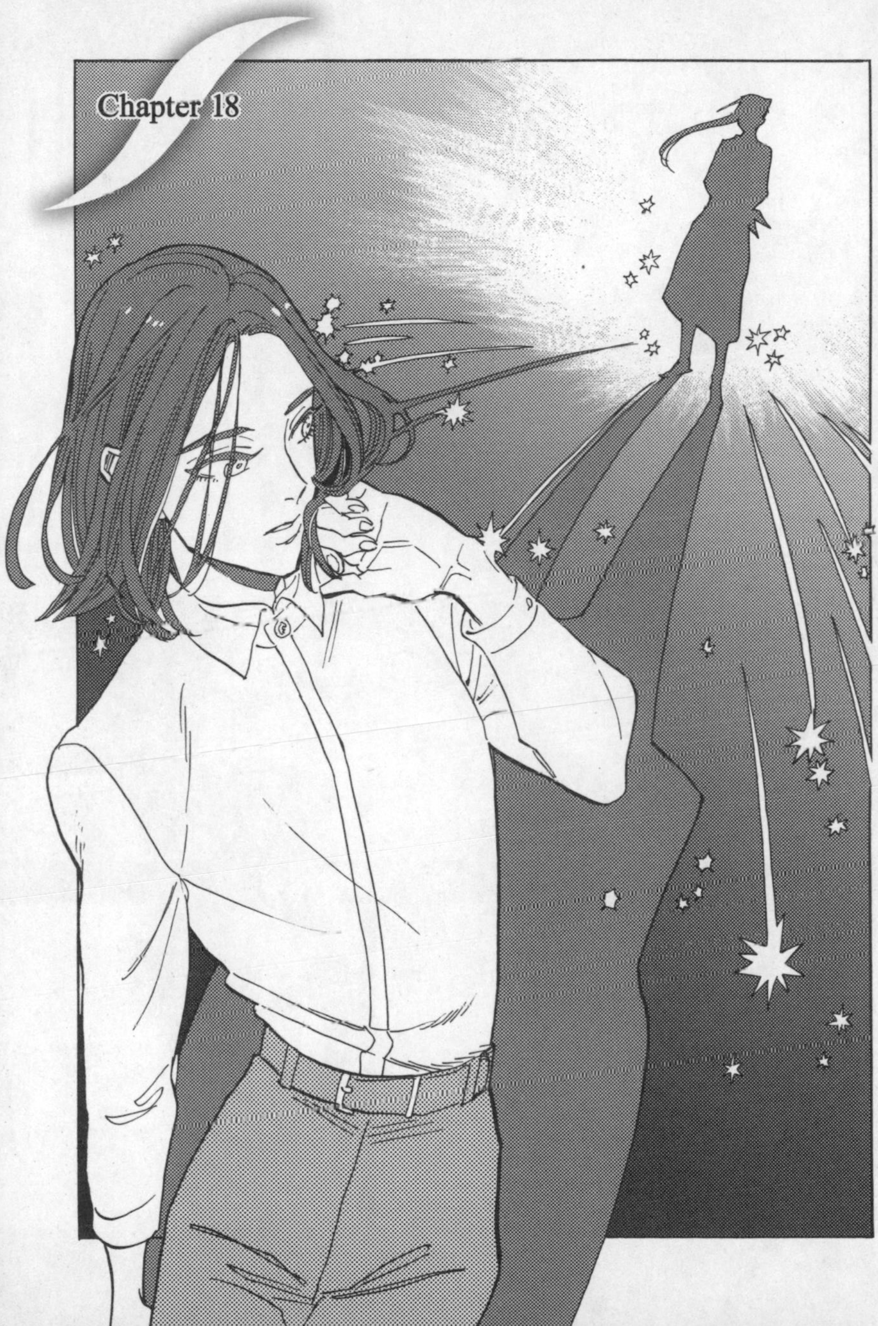

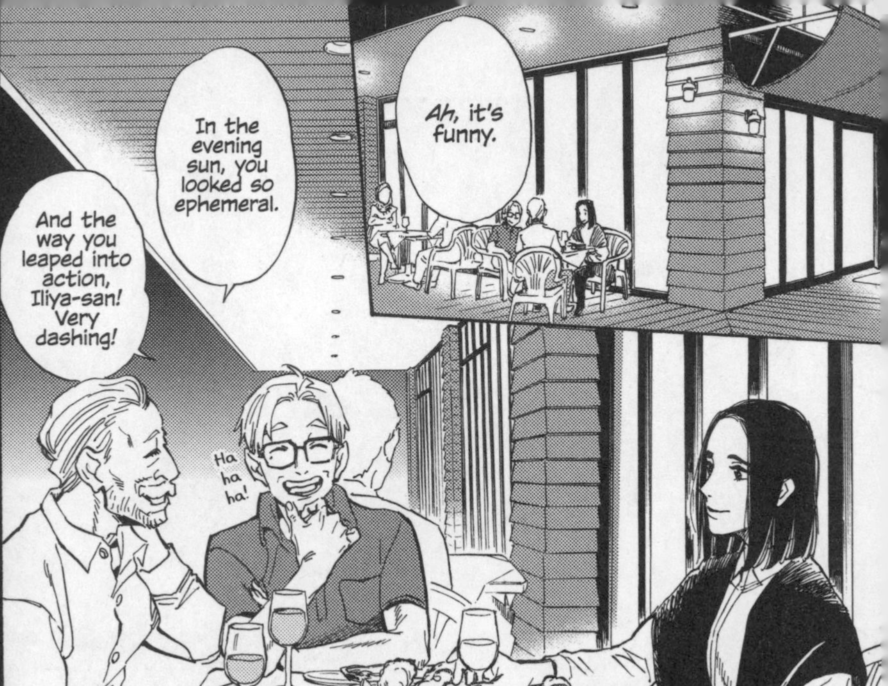
Ah, it's funny.
In the evening sun, you looked so ephemeral.
And the way you leaped into action, Iliya-san! Very dashing!
Ha ha ha!
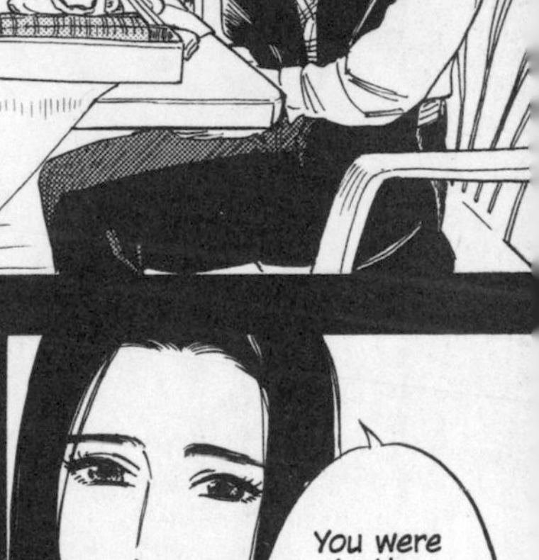
You were in the coffee class this afternoon, weren't you?
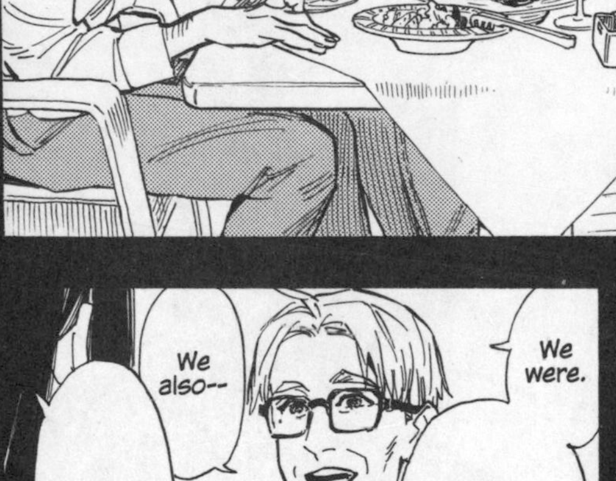
We were.
We also--
Do you like coffee?
Not especially, no.

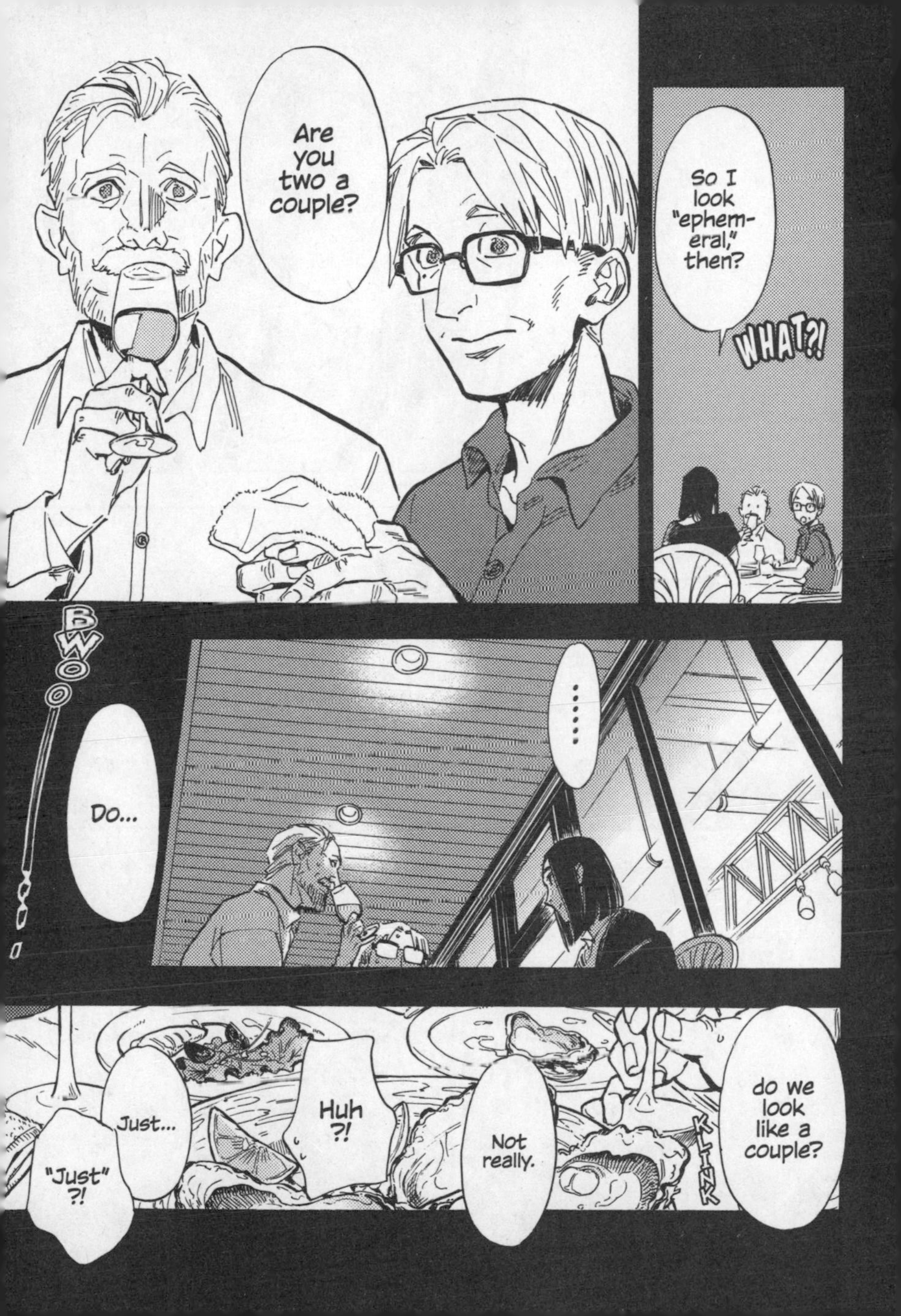
So I look "ephemeral," then?
WHAT?!
Are you two a couple?
......
BWOO
Do...
do we look like a couple?
KLINK
Not really.
Huh?!
Just...
"Just"?!

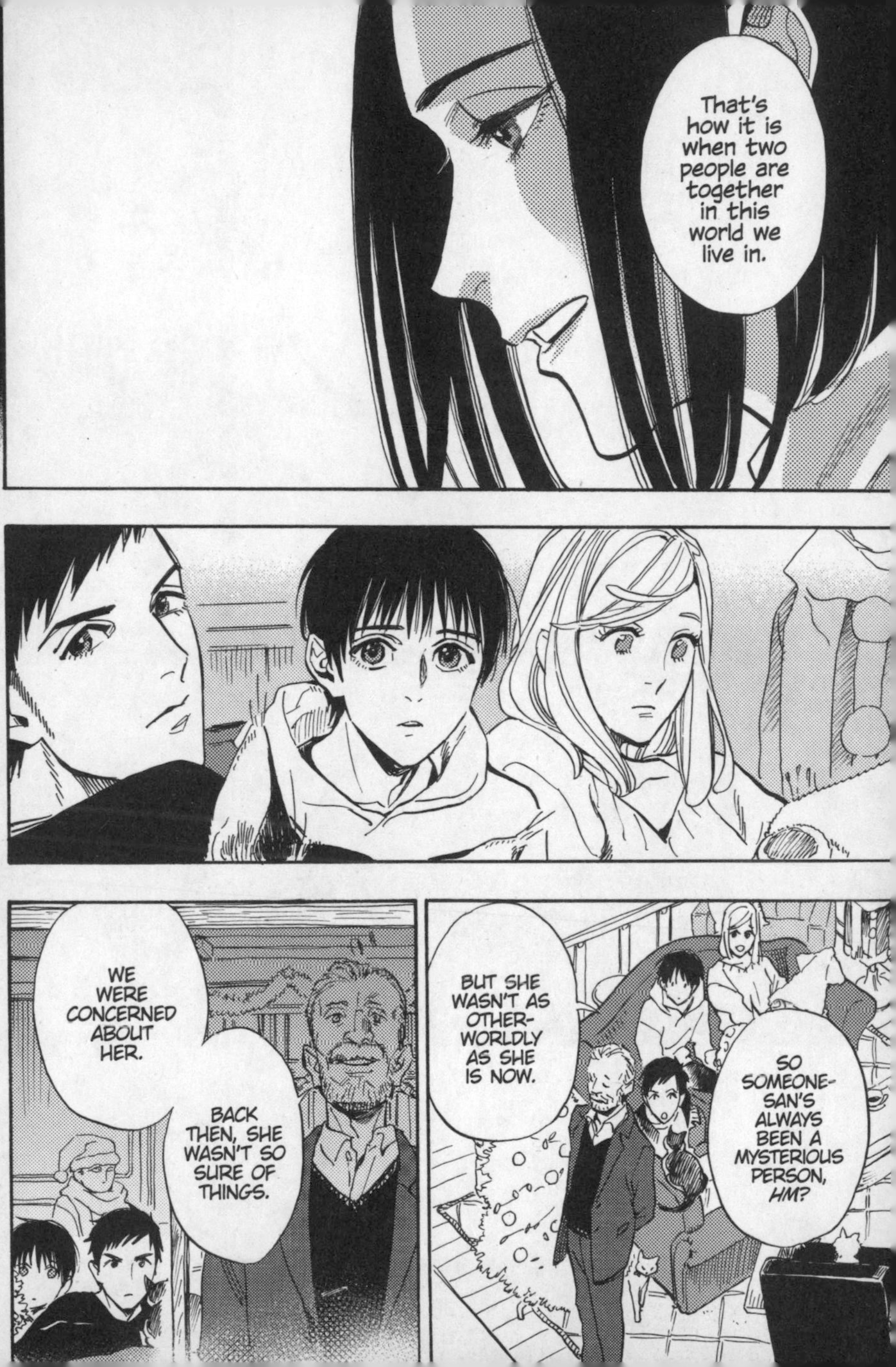
That's how it is when two people are together in this world we live in.
SO SOMEONE-SAN'S ALWAYS BEEN A MYSTERIOUS PERSON, HM?
BUT SHE WASN'T AS OTHER-WORLDLY AS SHE IS NOW.
BACK THEN, SHE WASN'T SO SURE OF THINGS.
WE WERE CONCERNED ABOUT HER.

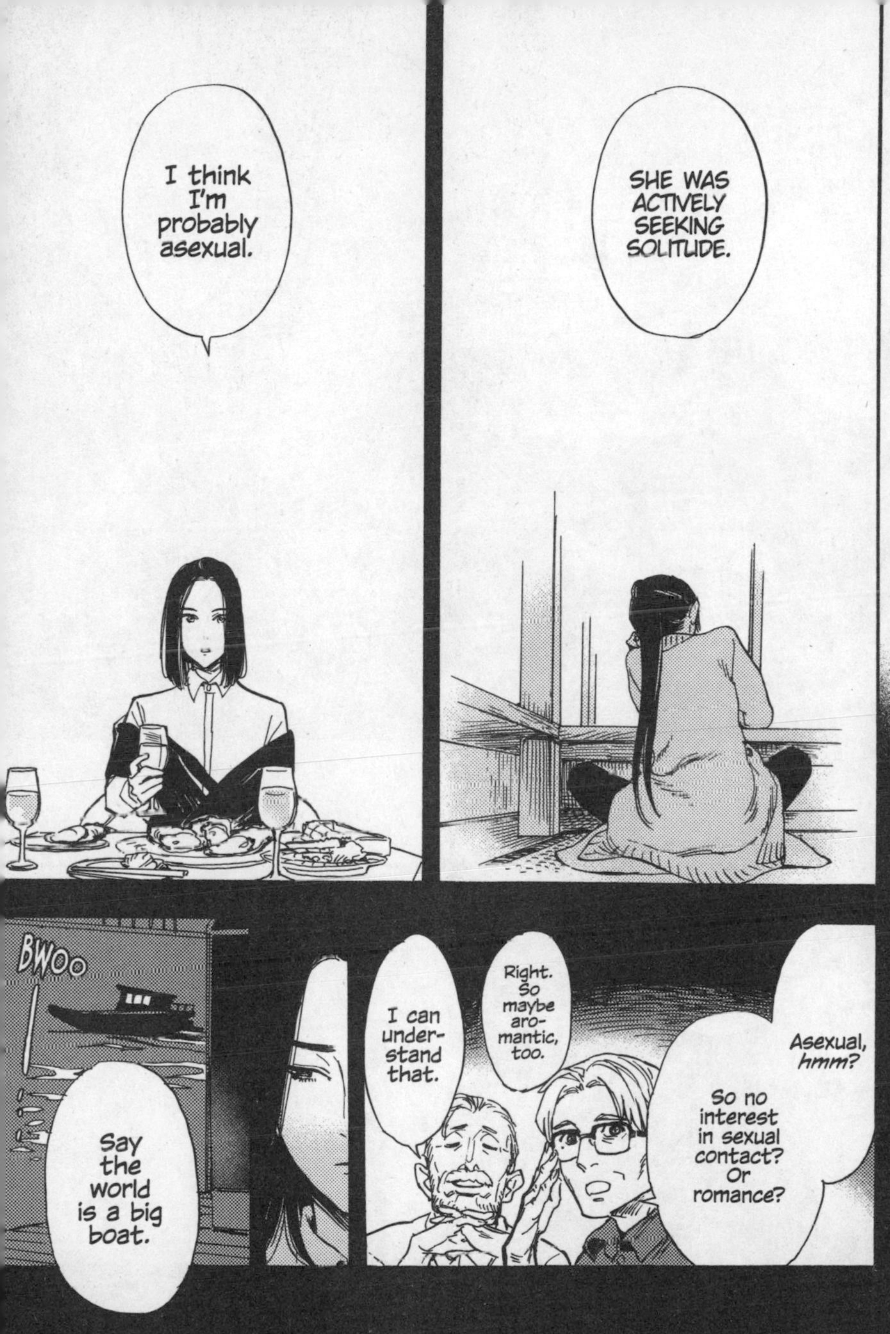
SHE WAS ACTIVELY SEEKING SOLITUDE.
I think I'm probably asexual.
Asexual, *hmm?*
So no interest in sexual contact? Or romance?
Right. So maybe aro-mantic, too.
I can under-stand that.
BWOo
Say the world is a big boat.

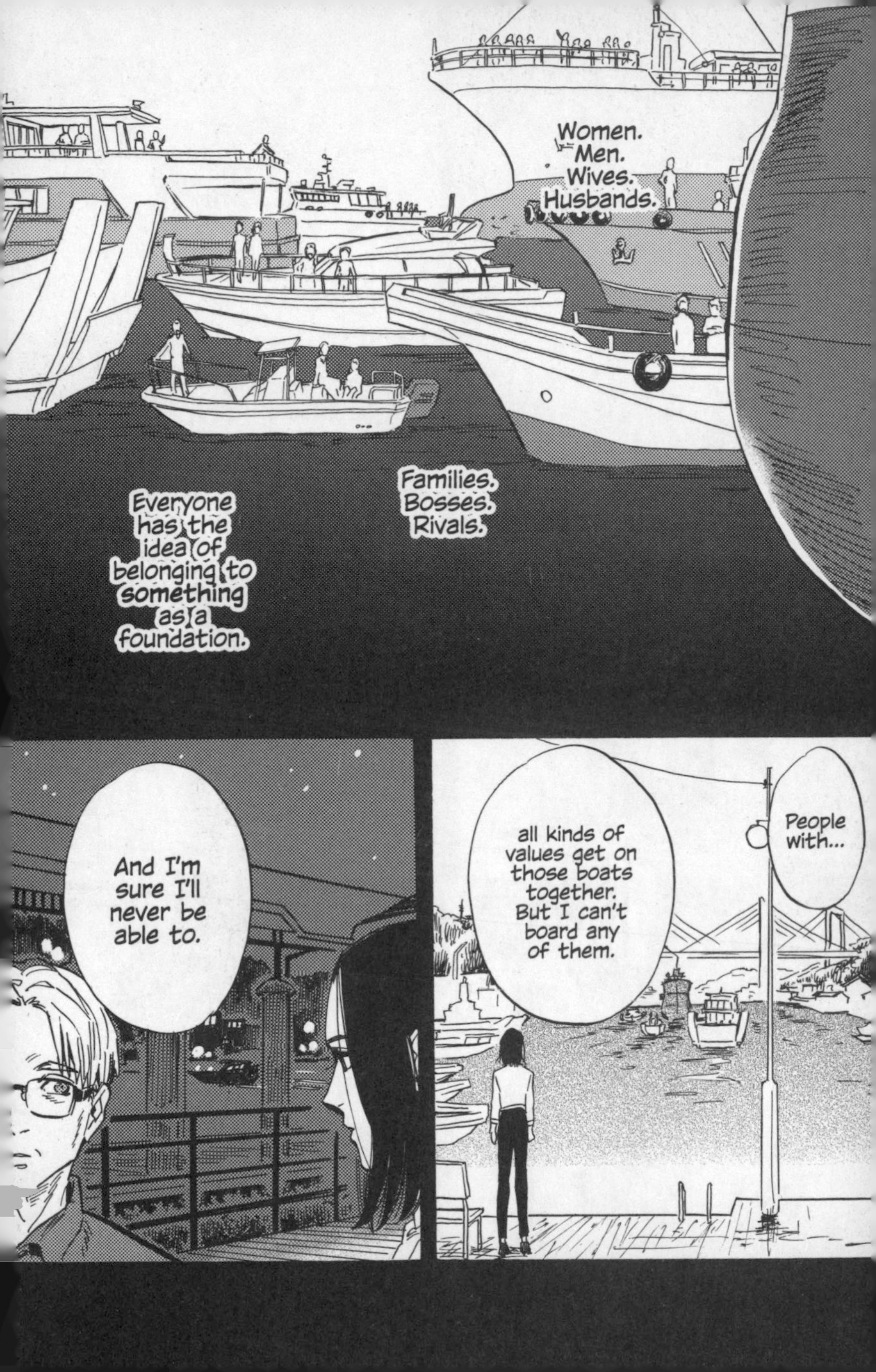
Women. Men. Wives. Husbands.
Families. Bosses. Rivals.
Everyone has the idea of belonging to something as a foundation.
People with...
all kinds of values get on those boats together. But I can't board any of them.
And I'm sure I'll never be able to.

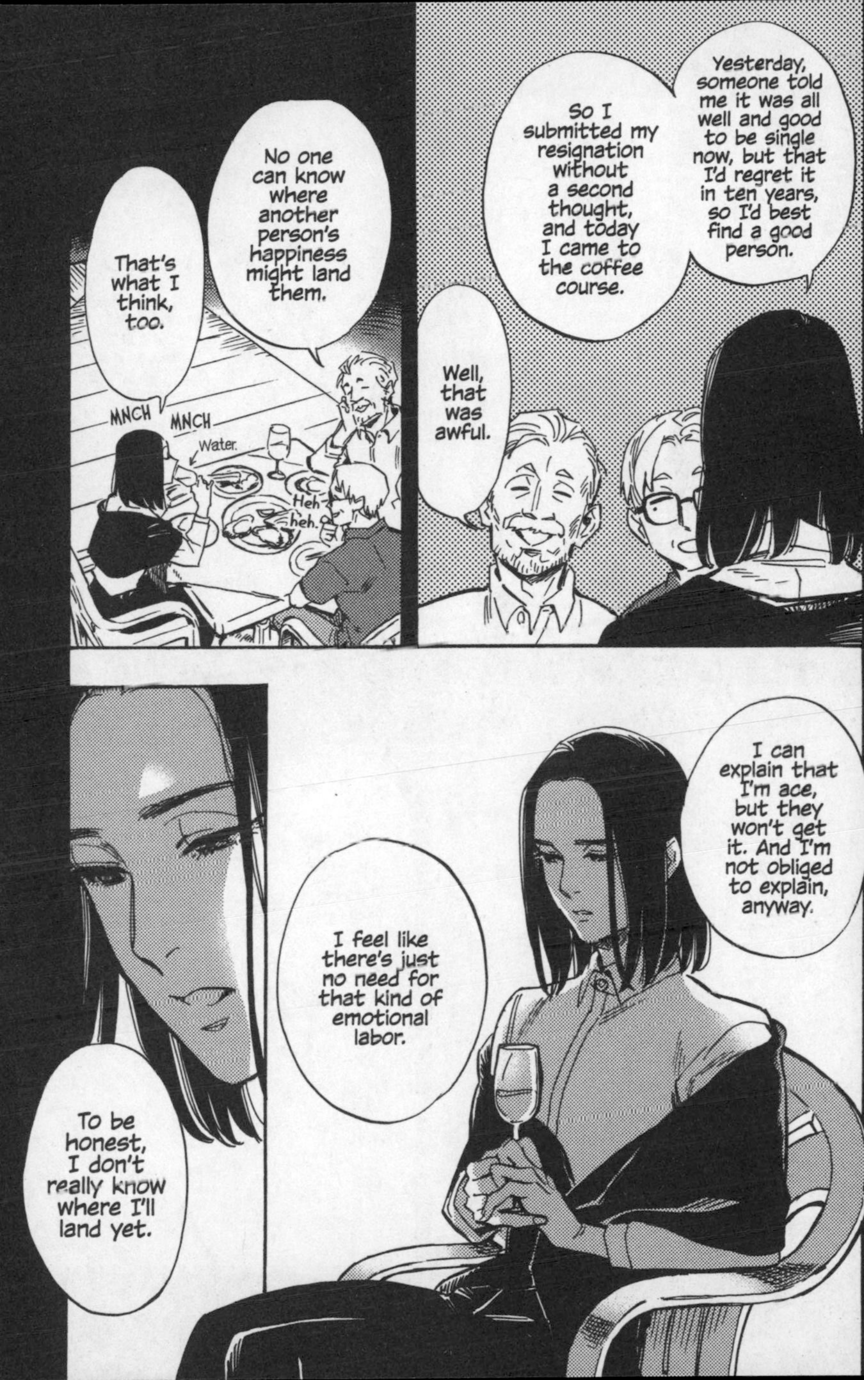
Yesterday, someone told me it was all well and good to be single now, but that I'd regret it in ten years, so I'd best find a good person.
So I submitted my resignation without a second thought, and today I came to the coffee course.
Well, that was awful.
No one can know where another person's happiness might land them.
That's what I think, too.
MNCH MNCH
Water.
Heh heh.
I can explain that I'm ace, but they won't get it. And I'm not obliged to explain, anyway.
I feel like there's just no need for that kind of emotional labor.
To be honest, I don't really know where I'll land yet.

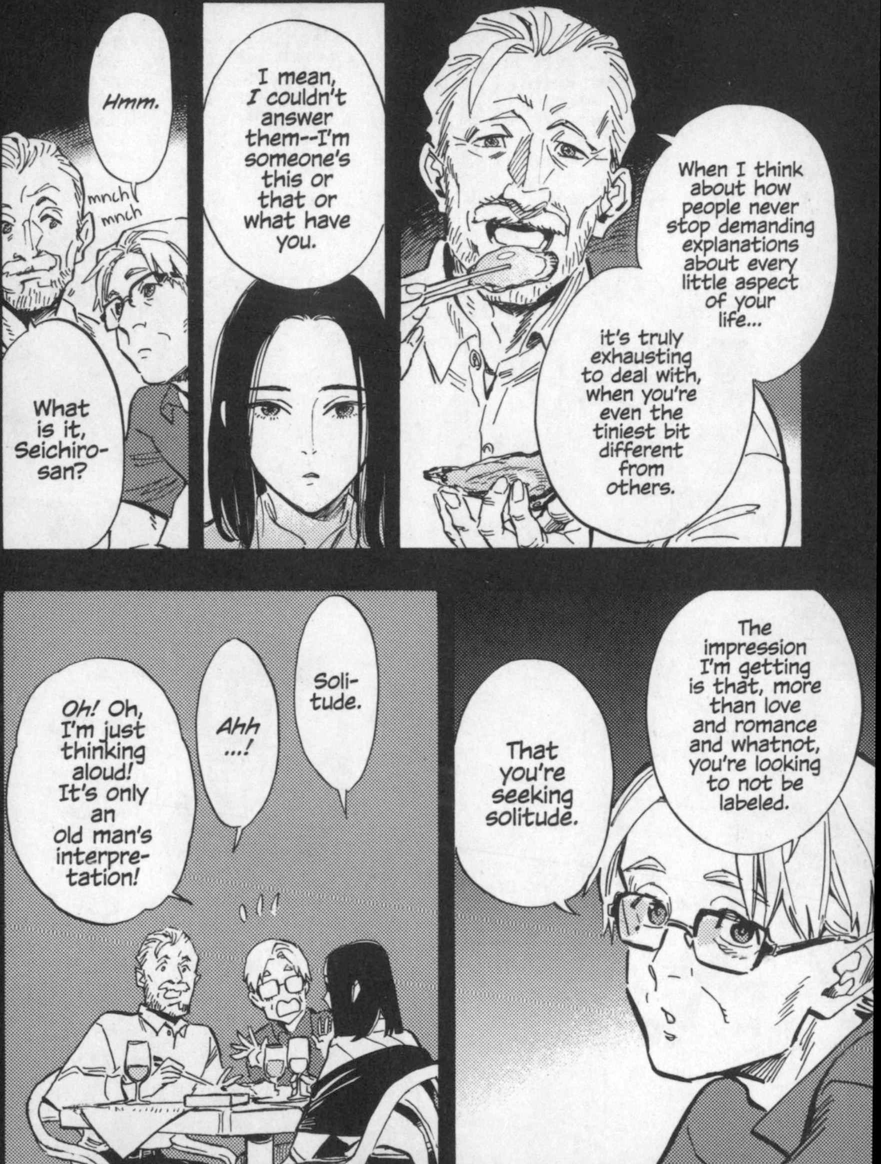
When I think about how people never stop demanding explanations about every little aspect of your life...
it's truly exhausting to deal with, when you're even the tiniest bit different from others.
I mean, *I* couldn't answer them--I'm someone's this or that or what have you.
Hmm.
mnch mnch
What is it, Seichiro-san?
The impression I'm getting is that, more than love and romance and whatnot, you're looking to not be labeled.
That you're seeking solitude.
Soli-tude.
Ahh ...!
Oh! Oh, I'm just thinking aloud! It's only an old man's interpretation!

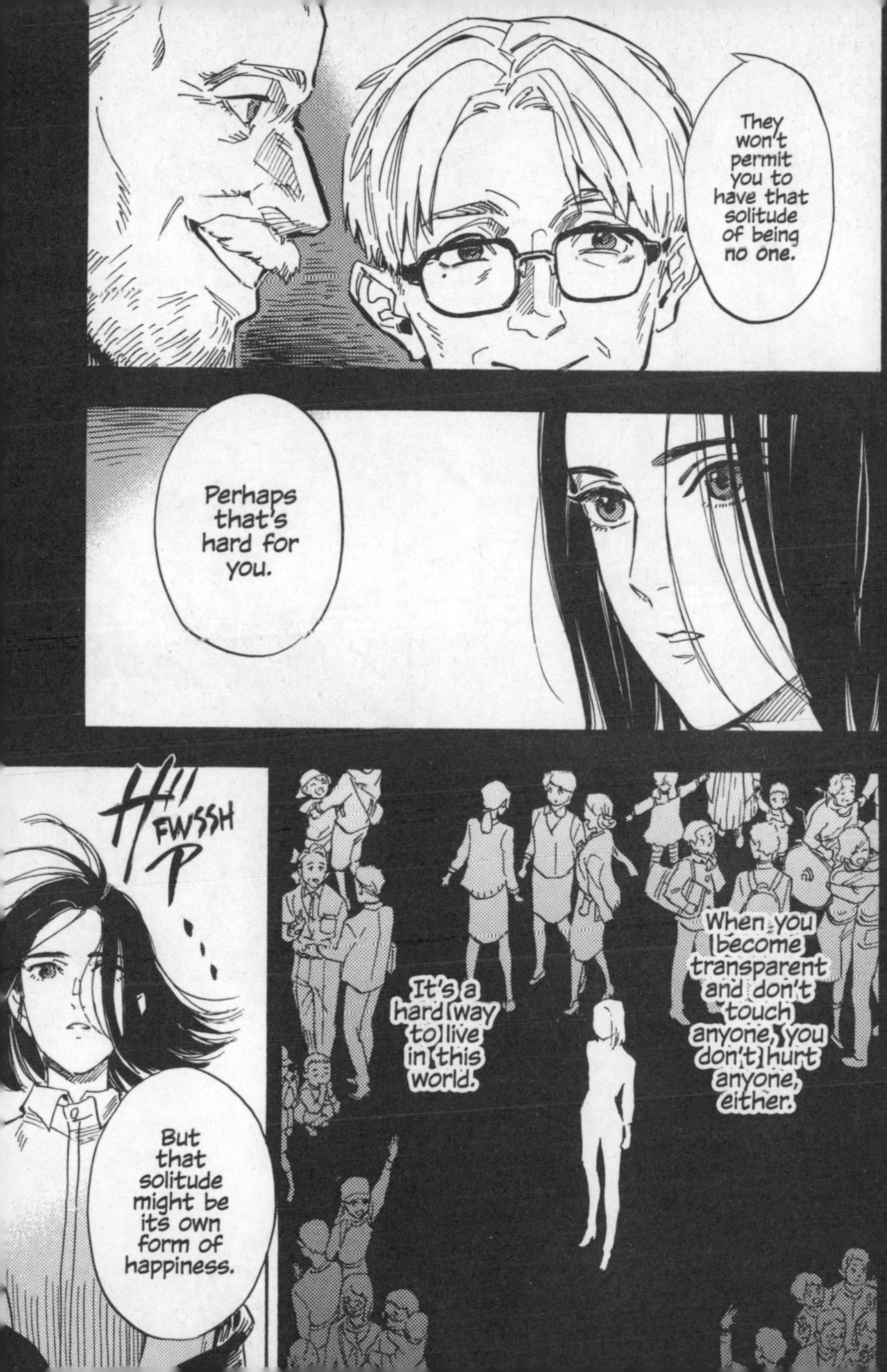
They won't permit you to have that solitude of being no one.
Perhaps that's hard for you.
When you become transparent and don't touch anyone, you don't hurt anyone, either.
It's a hard way to live in this world.
FWSSH
But that solitude might be its own form of happiness.

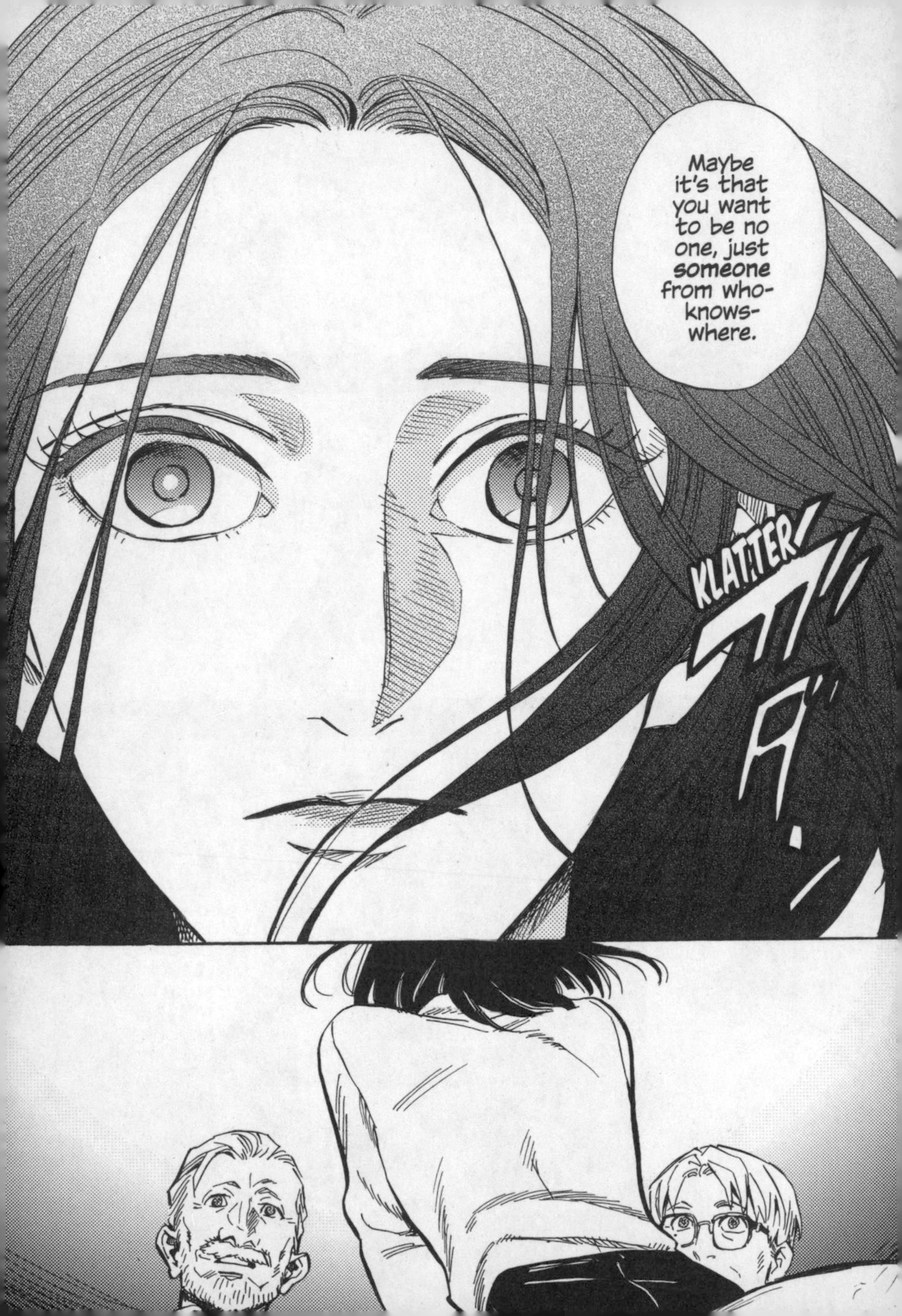
Maybe it's that you want to be no one, just someone from who-knows-where.
KLATTER!

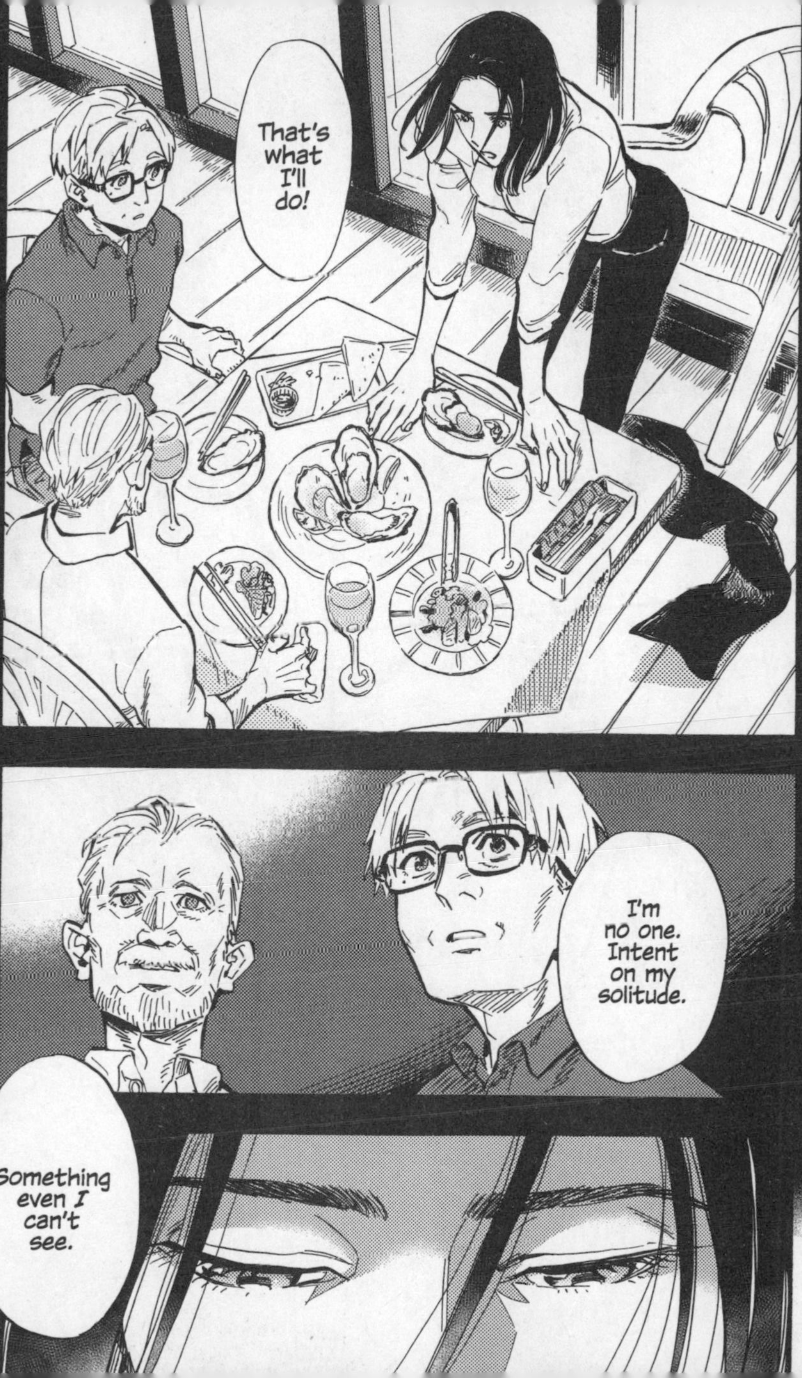
That's what I'll do!
I'm no one. Intent on my solitude.
Something even *I* can't see.

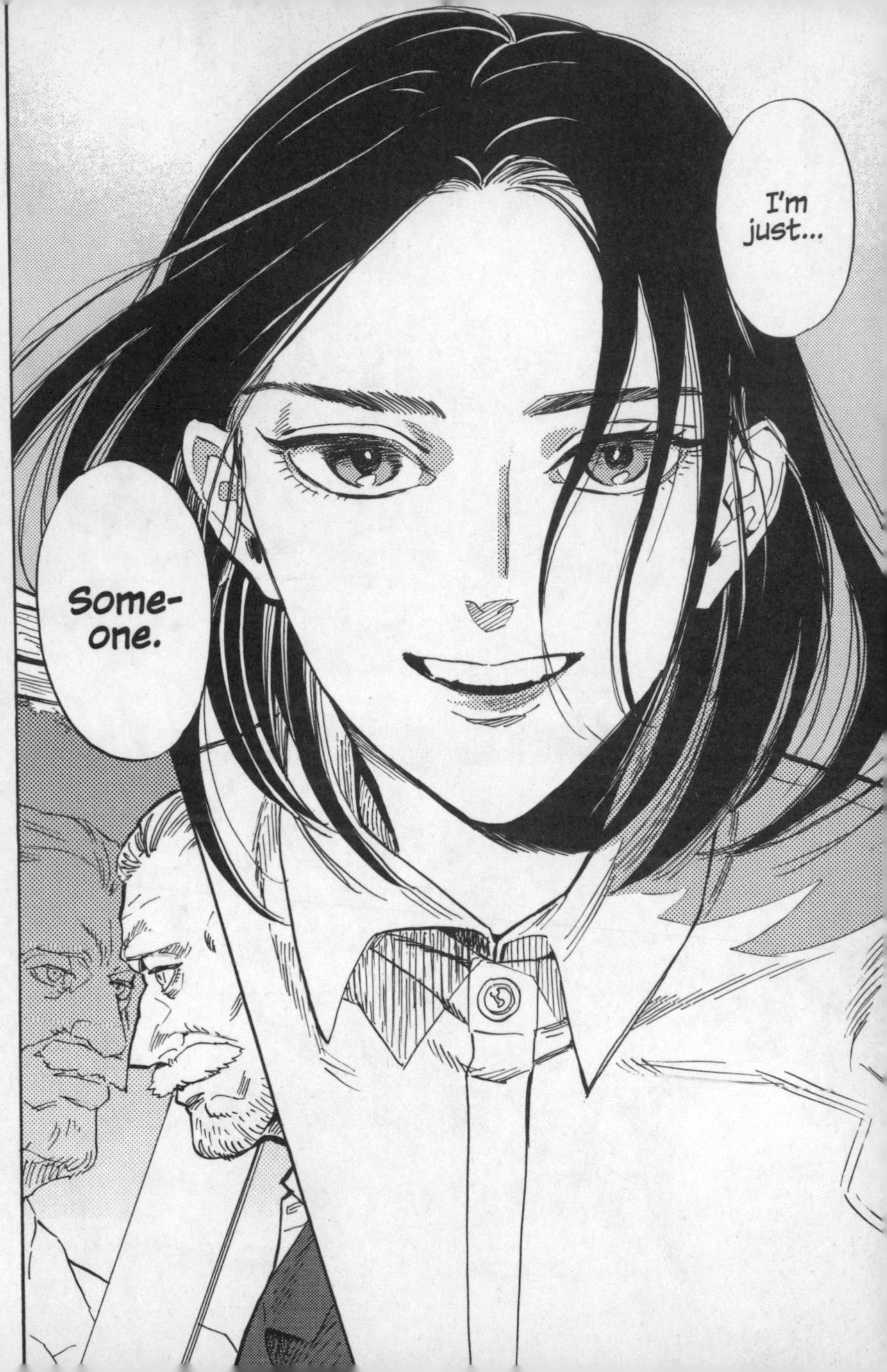
I'm just...
Some-one.

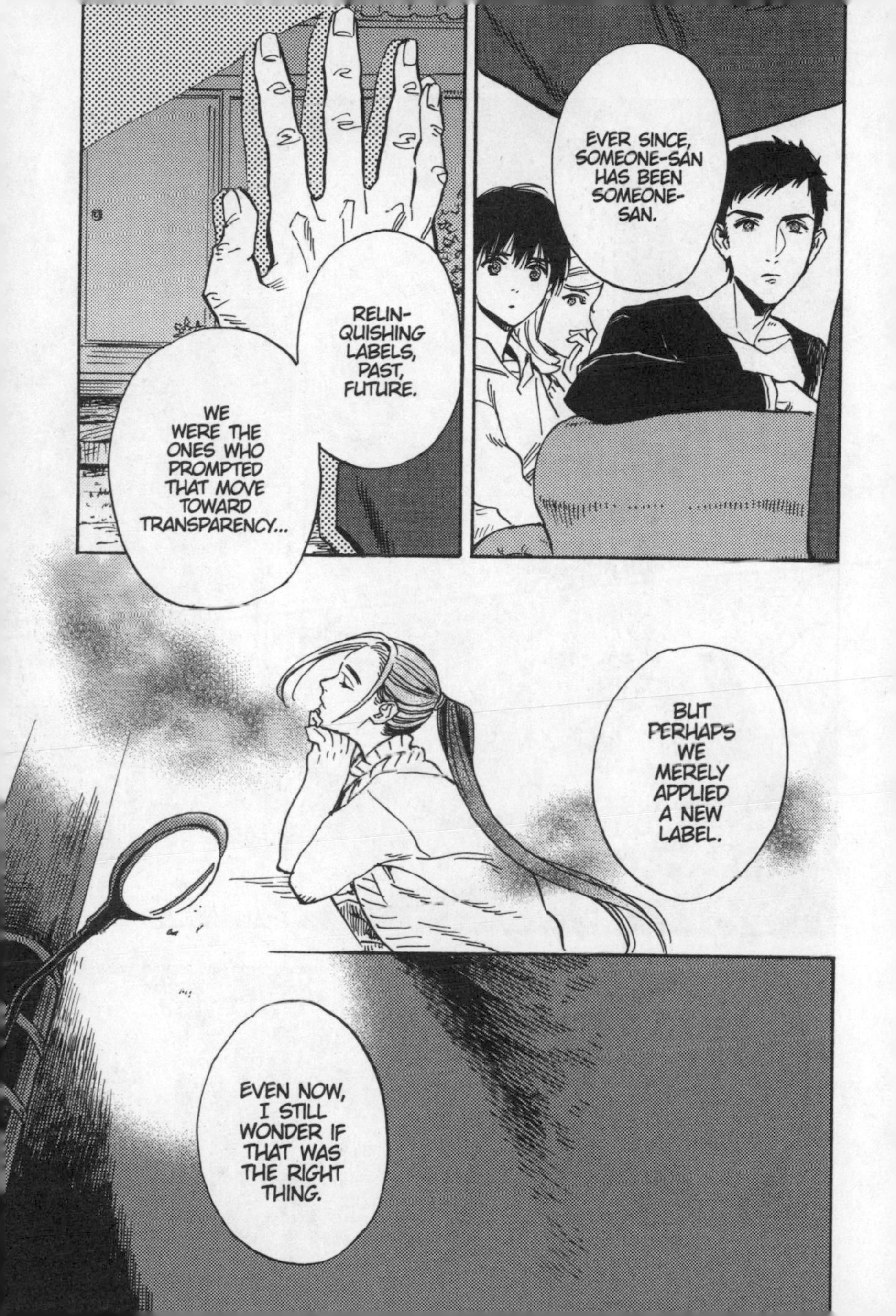
EVER SINCE, SOMEONE-SAN HAS BEEN SOMEONE-SAN.
RELIN-QUISHING LABELS, PAST, FUTURE.
WE WERE THE ONES WHO PROMPTED THAT MOVE TOWARD TRANSPARENCY...
BUT PERHAPS WE MERELY APPLIED A NEW LABEL.
EVEN NOW, I STILL WONDER IF THAT WAS THE RIGHT THING.

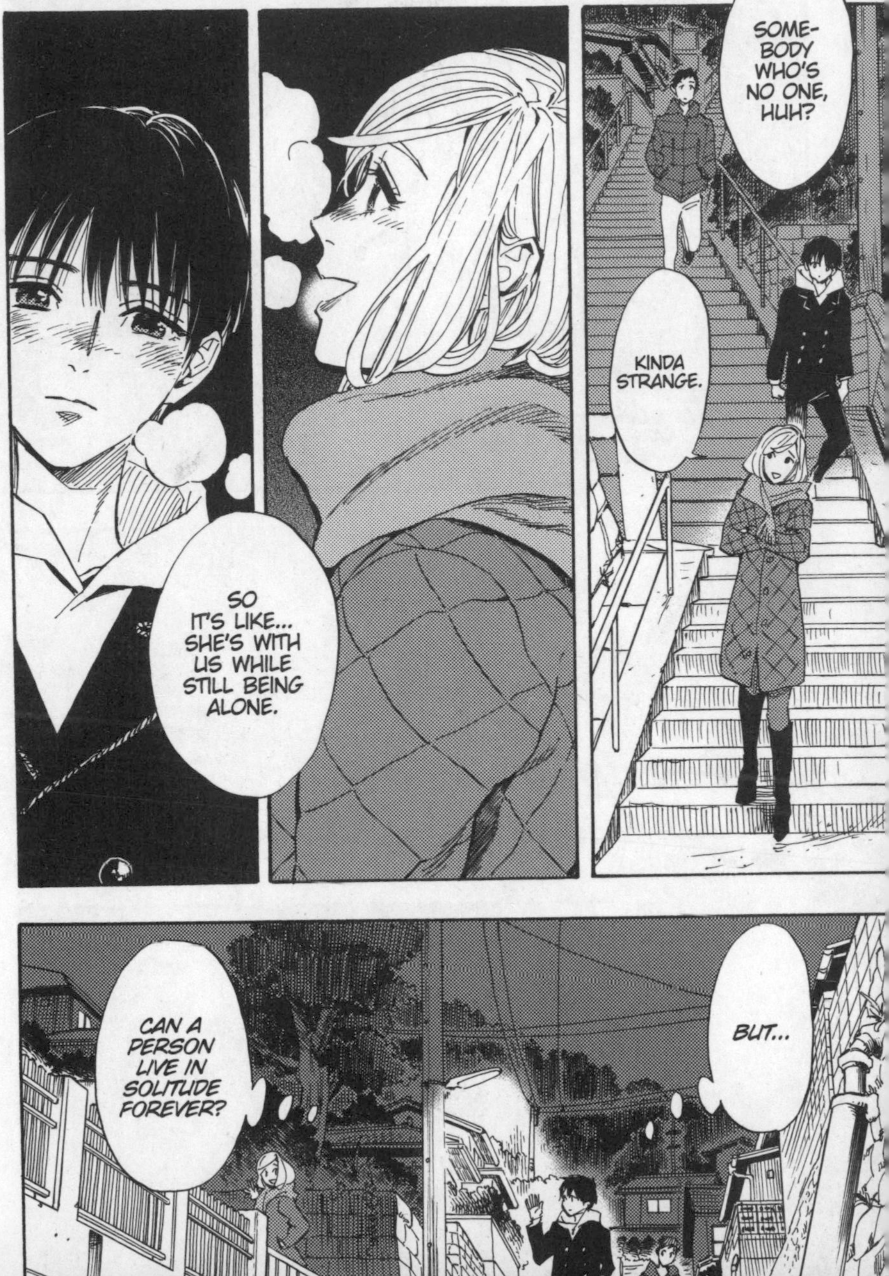
SOME-BODY WHO'S NO ONE, HUH?
KINDA STRANGE.
SO IT'S LIKE... SHE'S WITH US WHILE STILL BEING ALONE.
BUT...
CAN A PERSON LIVE IN SOLITUDE FOREVER?

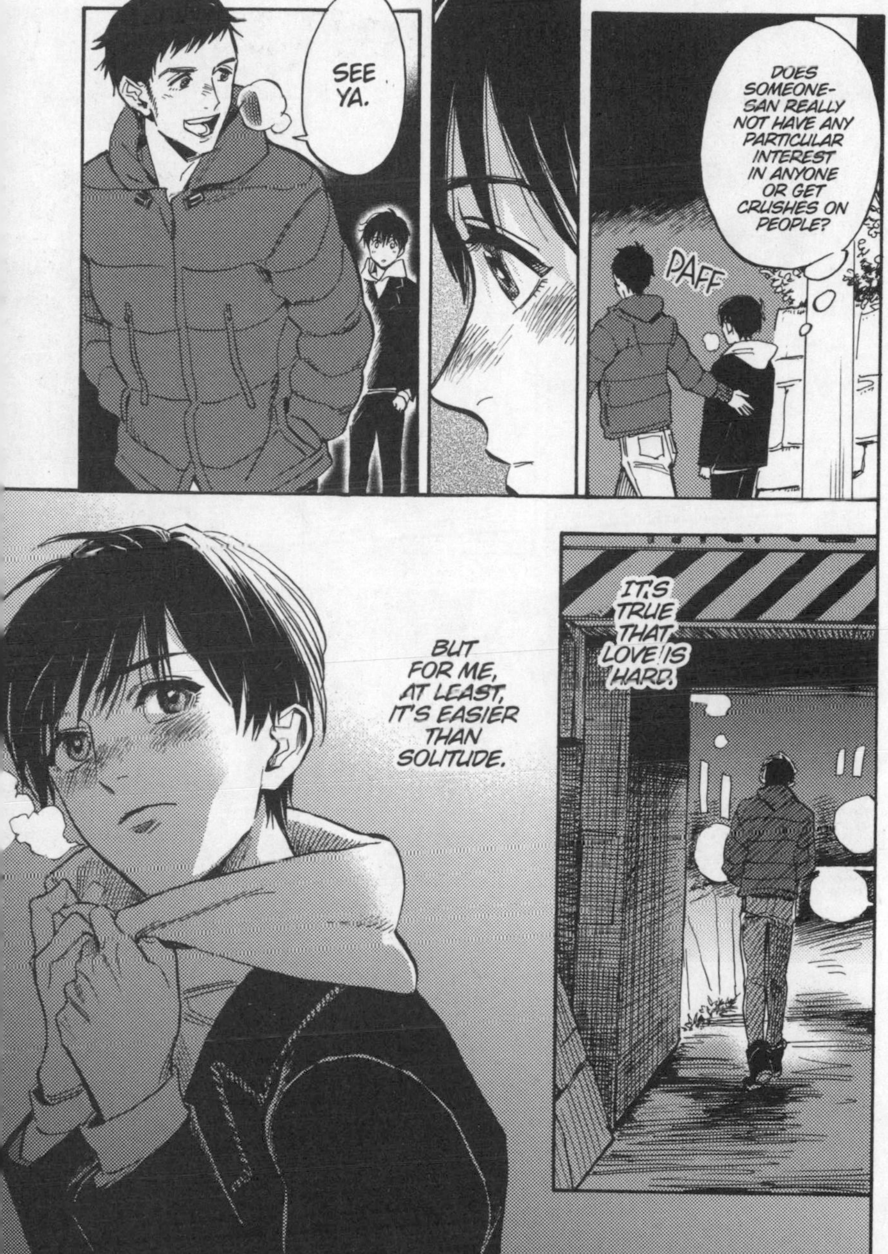
DOES SOMEONE-SAN REALLY NOT HAVE ANY PARTICULAR INTEREST IN ANYONE OR GET CRUSHES ON PEOPLE?
PAFF
SEE YA.
IT'S TRUE THAT LOVE IS HARD.
BUT FOR ME, AT LEAST, IT'S EASIER THAN SOLITUDE.

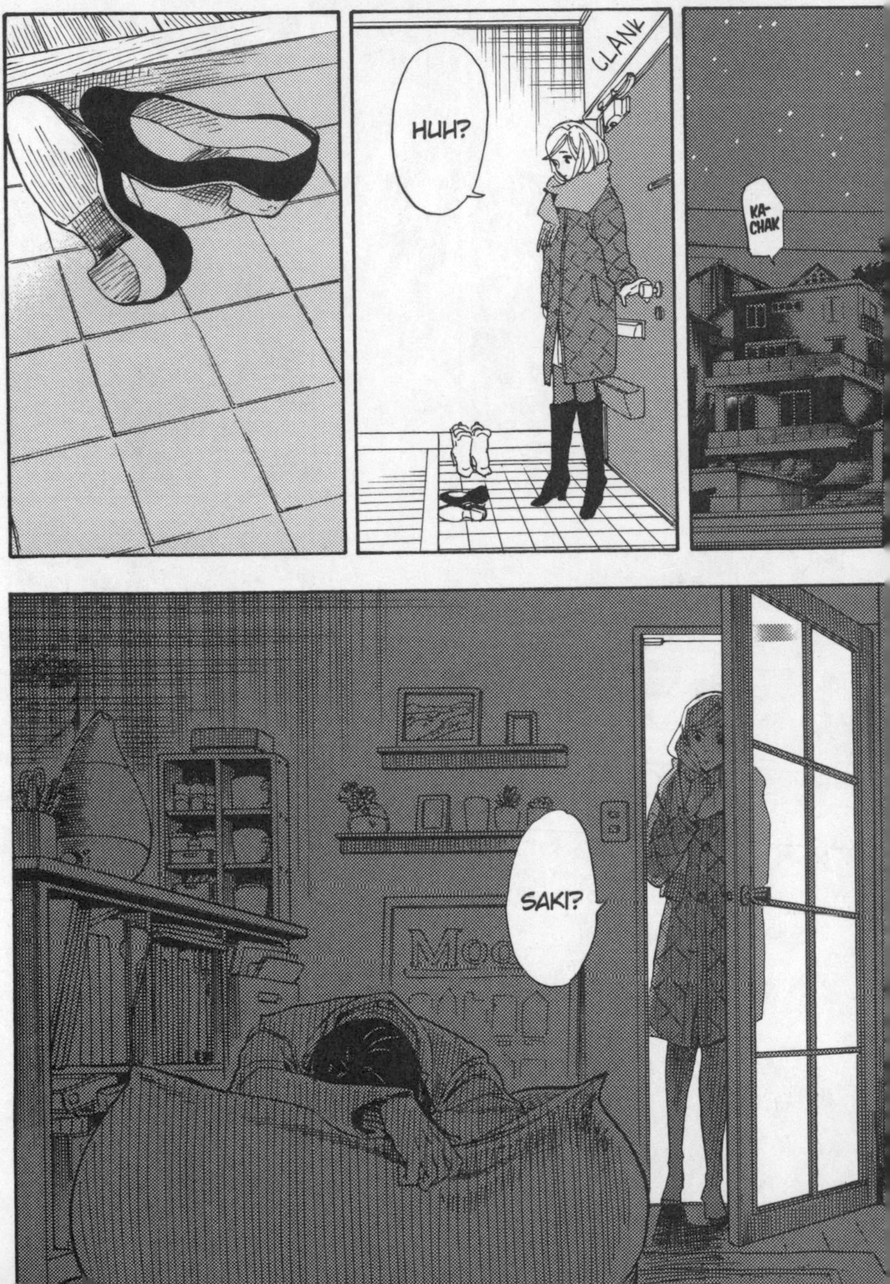
KA-CHAK
CLANK
HUH?
SAKI?

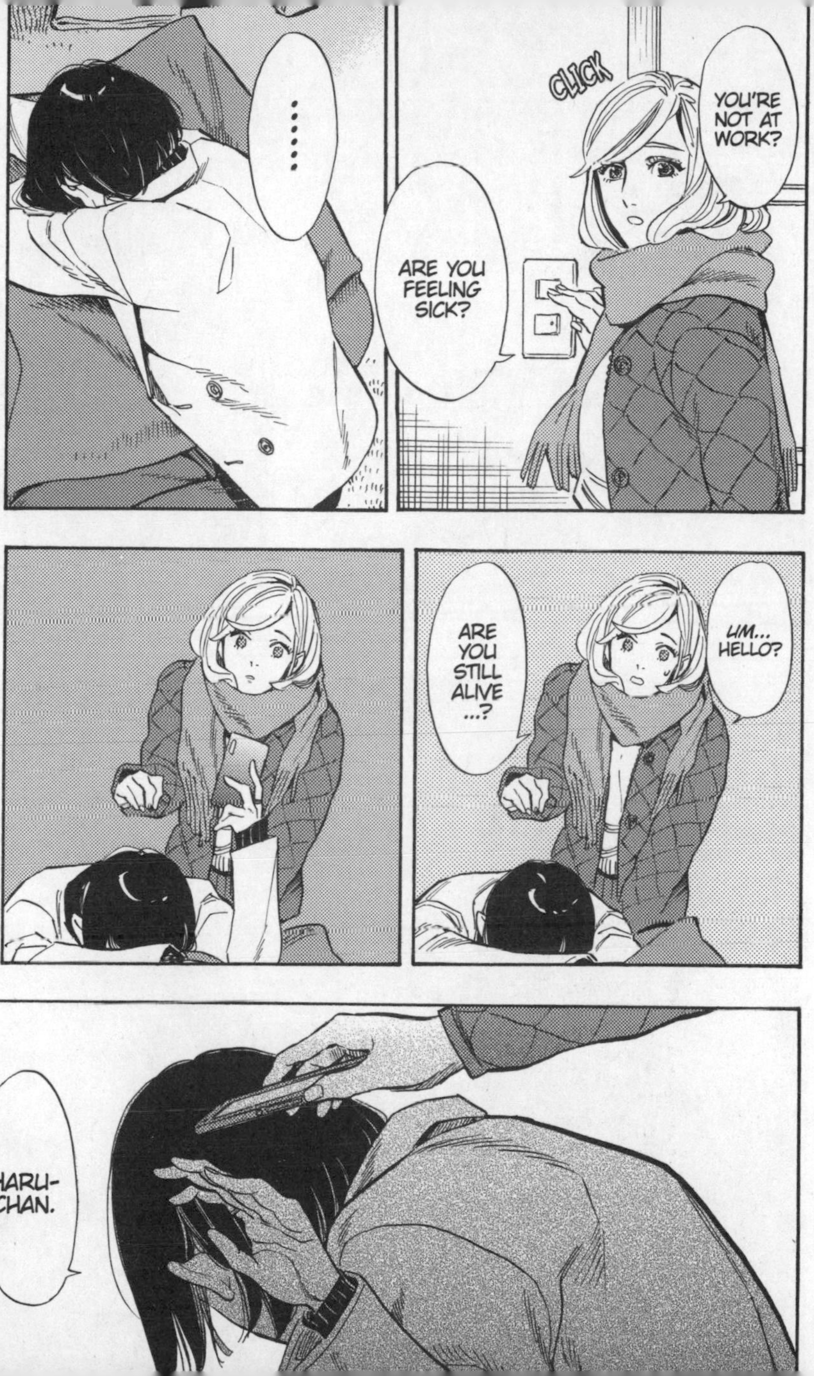
CLICK
YOU'RE NOT AT WORK?
ARE YOU FEELING SICK?
......
UM... HELLO?
ARE YOU STILL ALIVE ...?
HARU-CHAN.

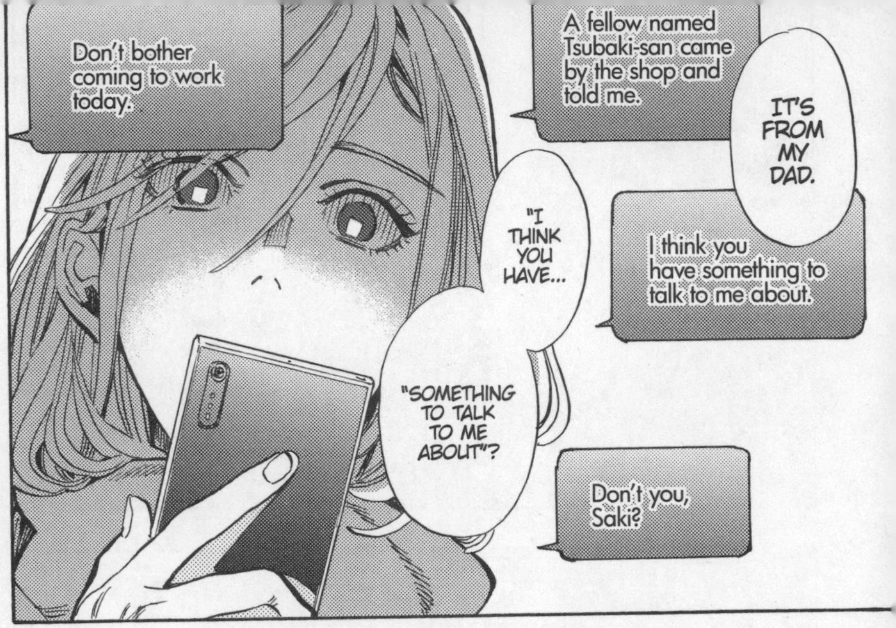
IT'S FROM MY DAD.
Don't bother coming to work today.
A fellow named Tsubaki-san came by the shop and told me.
I think you have something to talk to me about.
"I THINK YOU HAVE...
"SOMETHING TO TALK TO ME ABOUT"?
Don't you, Saki?

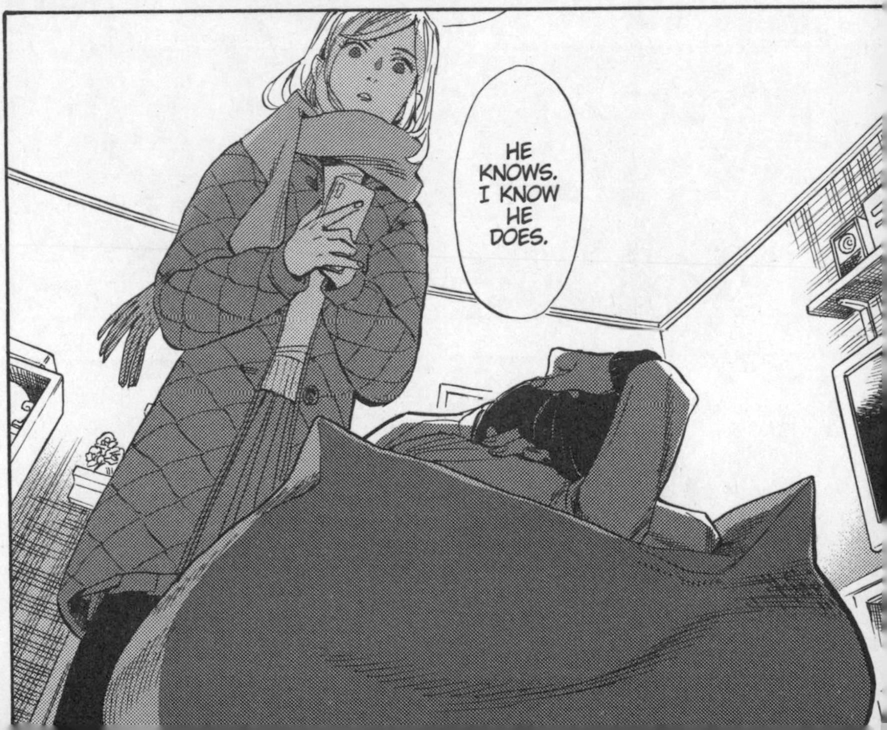
HE KNOWS. I KNOW HE DOES.

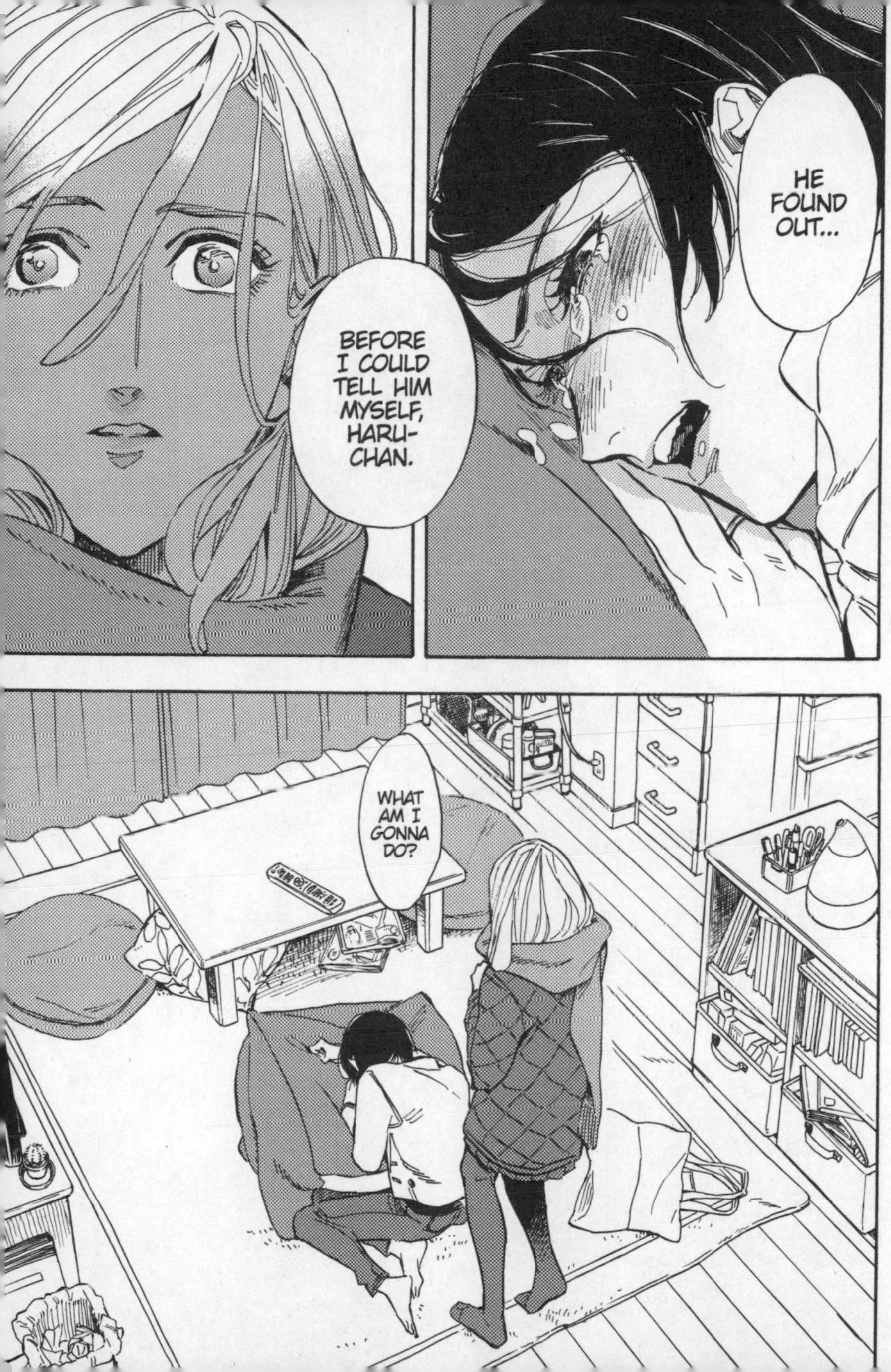
HE FOUND OUT...
BEFORE I COULD TELL HIM MYSELF, HARU-CHAN.
WHAT AM I GONNA DO?

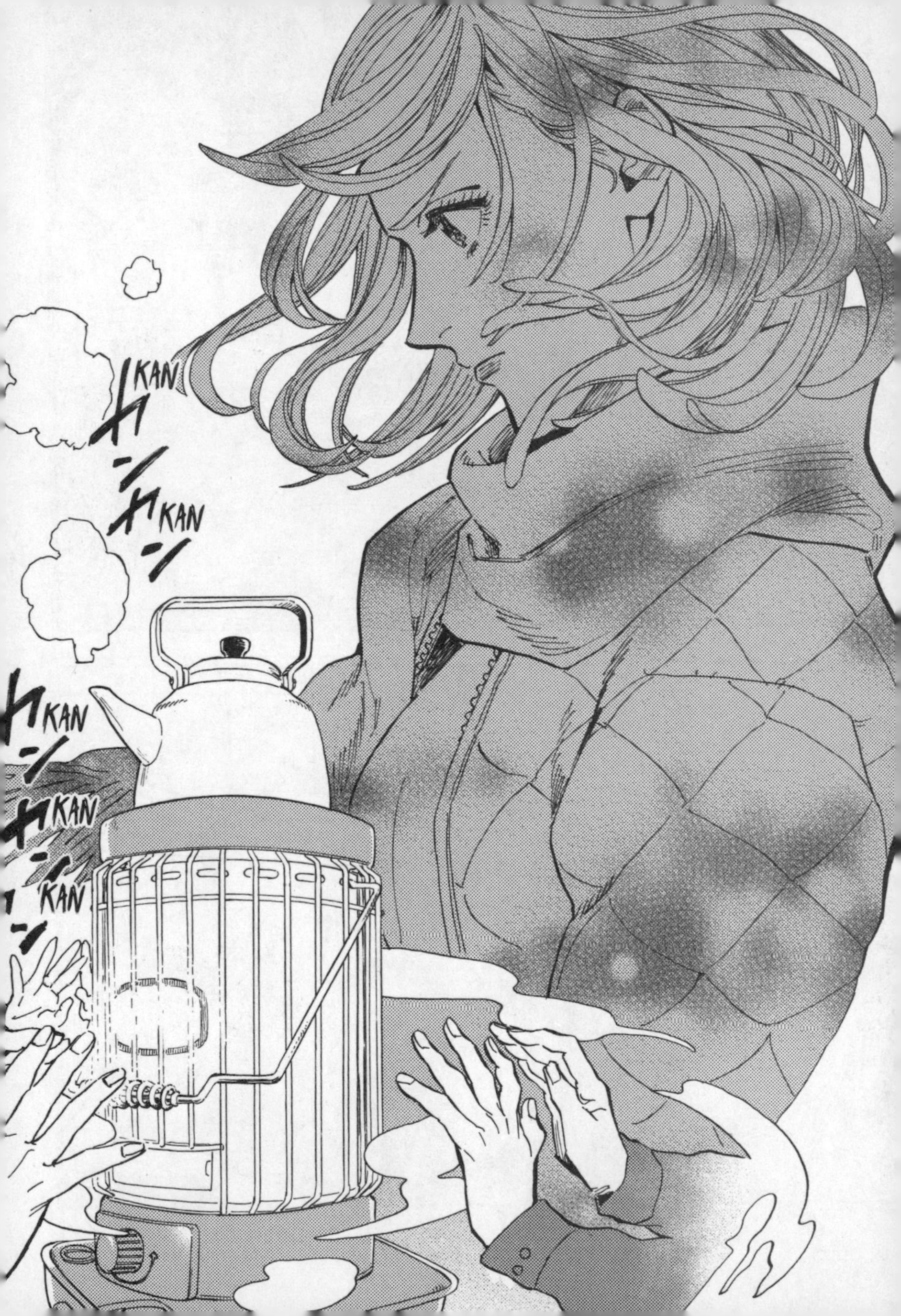
KAN
KAN
KAN
KAN
KAN

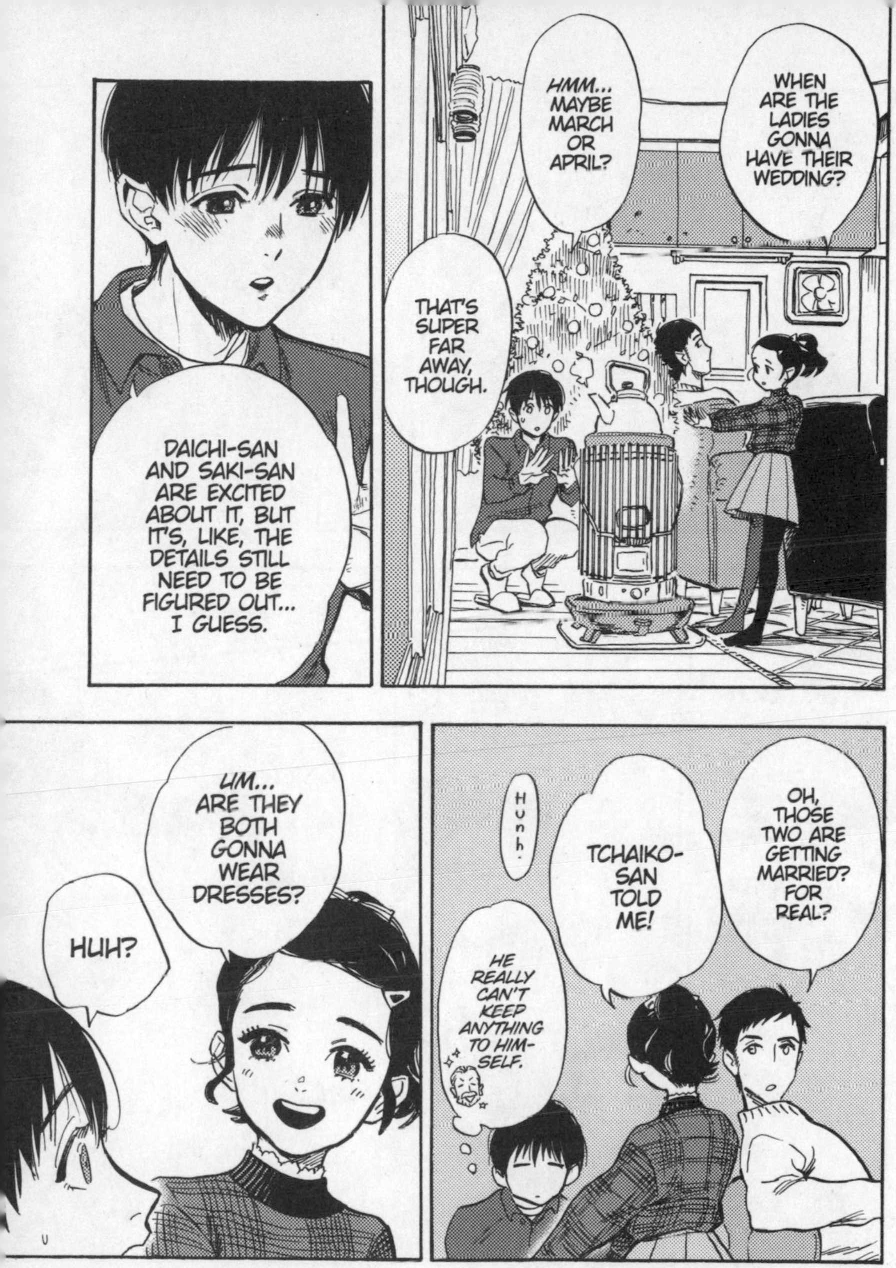
WHEN ARE THE LADIES GONNA HAVE THEIR WEDDING?
HMM... MAYBE MARCH OR APRIL?
THAT'S SUPER FAR AWAY, THOUGH.
DAICHI-SAN AND SAKI-SAN ARE EXCITED ABOUT IT, BUT IT'S, LIKE, THE DETAILS STILL NEED TO BE FIGURED OUT... I GUESS.
OH, THOSE TWO ARE GETTING MARRIED? FOR REAL?
TCHAIKO-SAN TOLD ME!
Hunh.
HE REALLY CAN'T KEEP ANYTHING TO HIMSELF.
UM... ARE THEY BOTH GONNA WEAR DRESSES?
HUH?

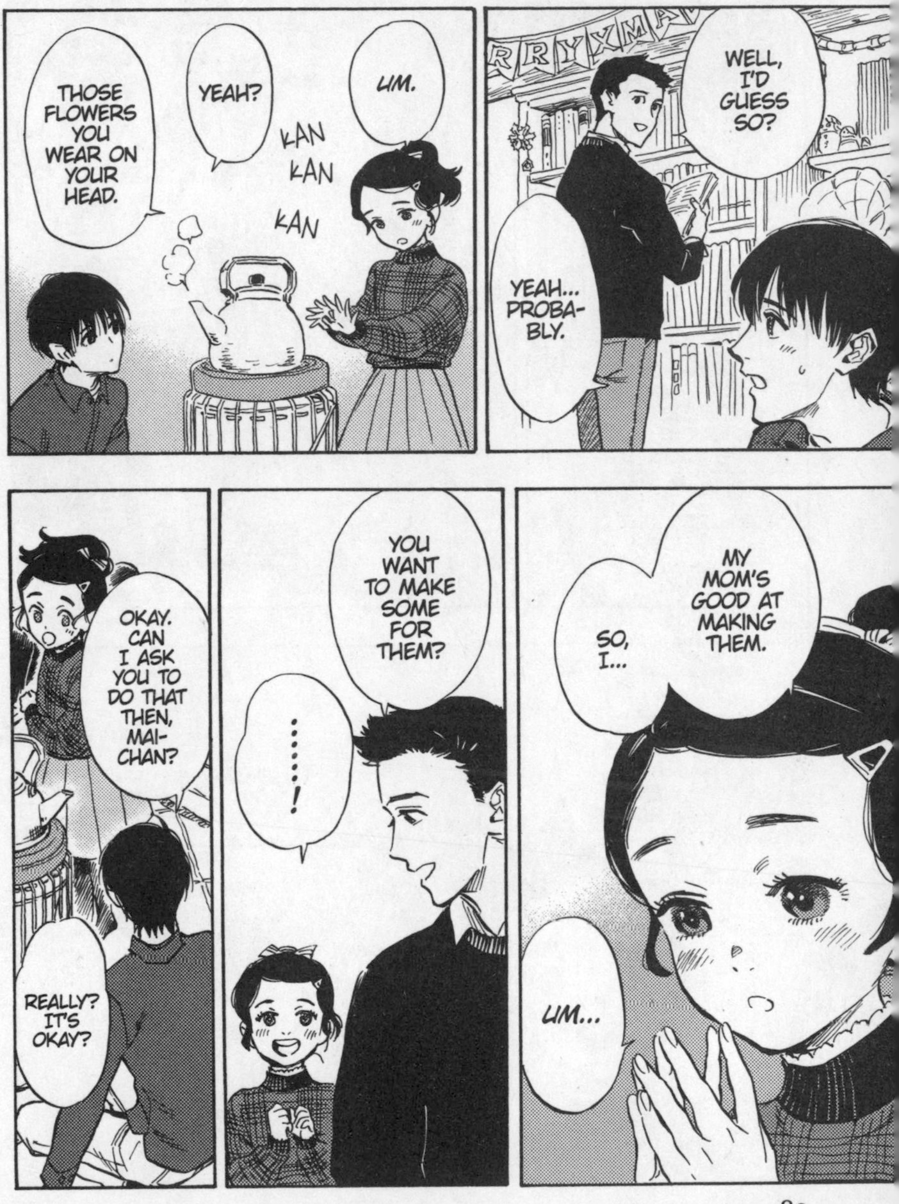
WELL, I'D GUESS SO?
YEAH... PROBABLY.
UM.
KAN
KAN
KAN
YEAH?
THOSE FLOWERS YOU WEAR ON YOUR HEAD.
MY MOM'S GOOD AT MAKING THEM.
SO, I...
UM...
YOU WANT TO MAKE SOME FOR THEM?
......!
OKAY. CAN I ASK YOU TO DO THAT THEN, MAI-CHAN?
REALLY? IT'S OKAY?

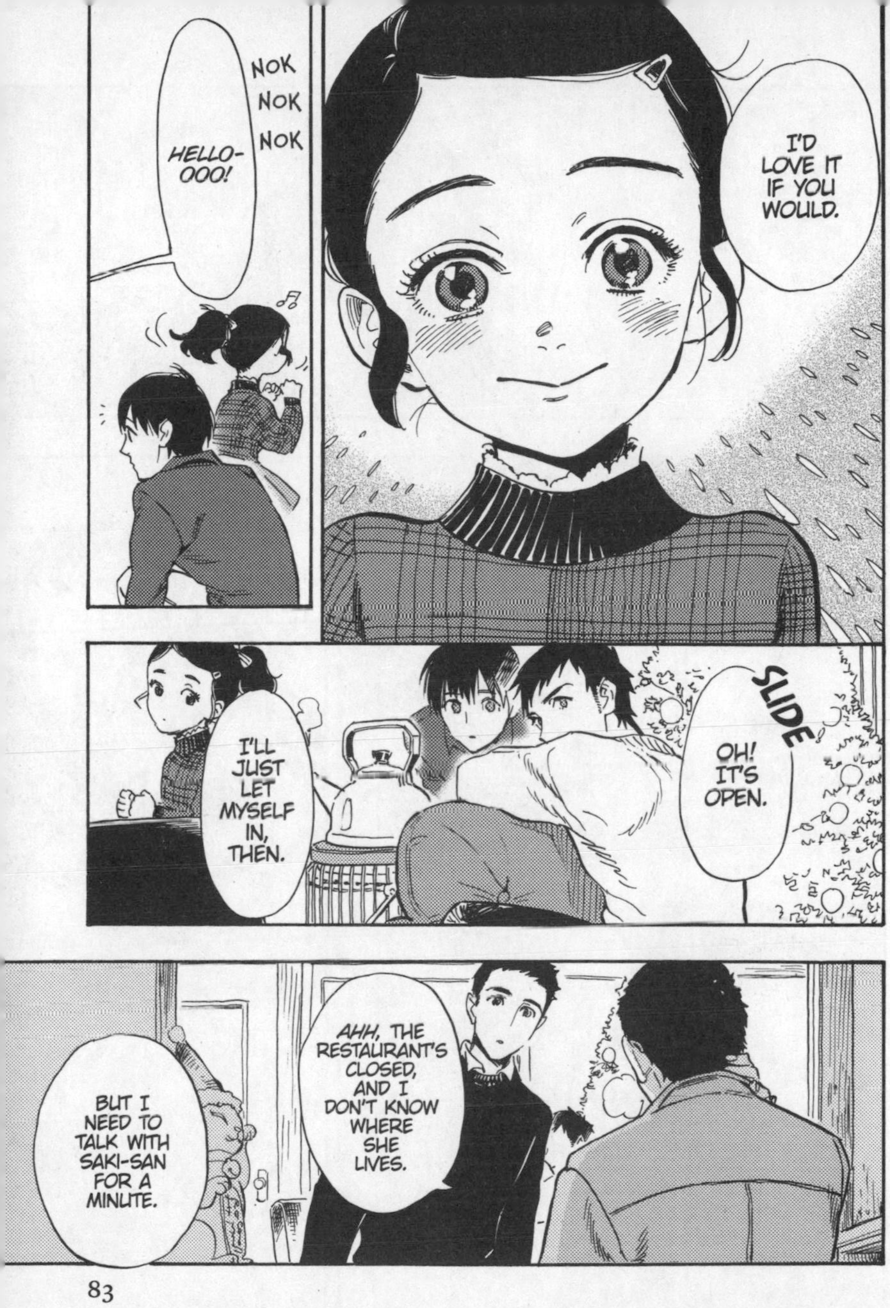
I'D LOVE IT IF YOU WOULD.
NOK NOK NOK
HELLO-OOO!
SLIDE
OH! IT'S OPEN.
I'LL JUST LET MYSELF IN, THEN.
AHH, THE RESTAURANT'S CLOSED, AND I DON'T KNOW WHERE SHE LIVES.
BUT I NEED TO TALK WITH SAKI-SAN FOR A MINUTE.

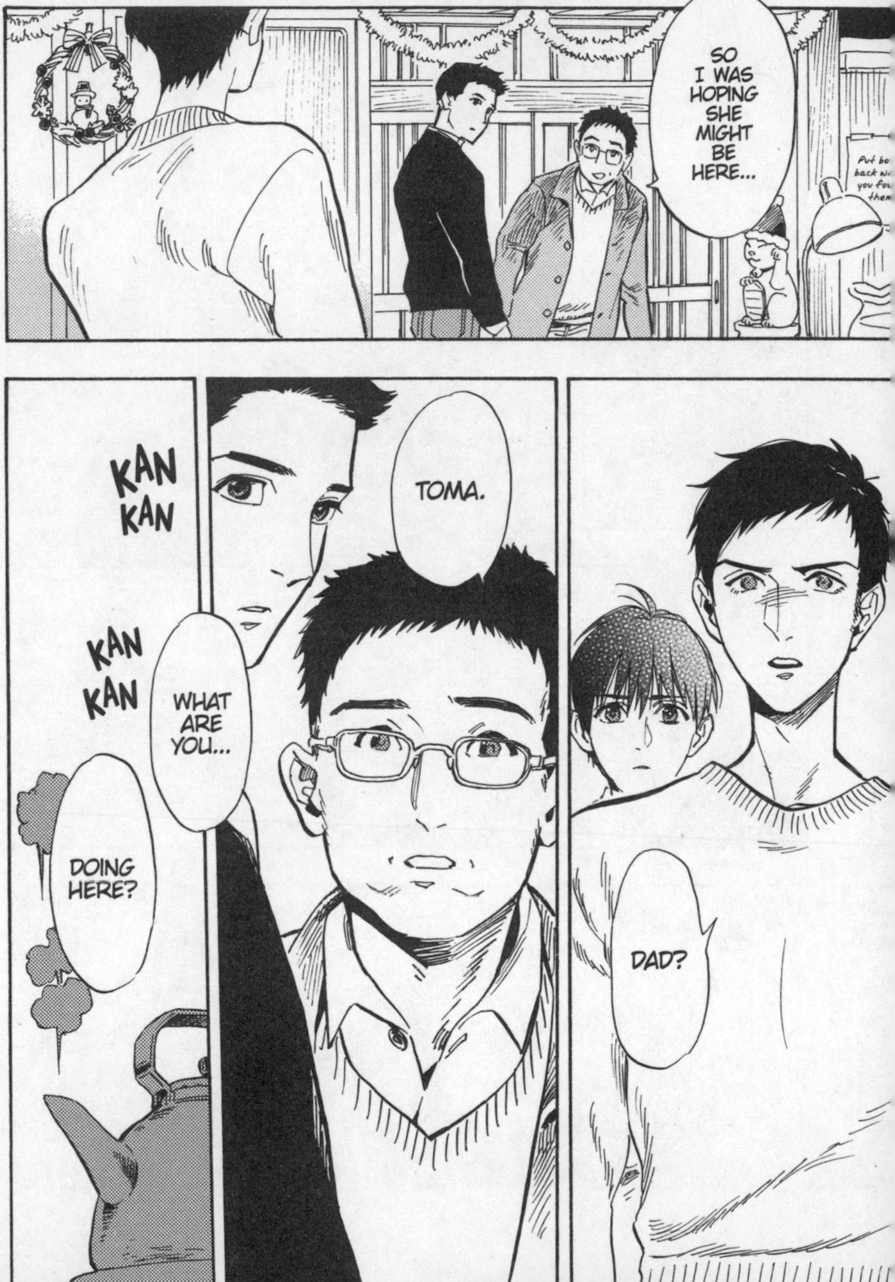
SO I WAS HOPING SHE MIGHT BE HERE...
DAD?
TOMA.
WHAT ARE YOU...
DOING HERE?
KAN KAN
KAN KAN

Our Dreams at Dusk

SHIMANAMI TASOGARE

Hassaku Daifuku

Hassaku is a citrus fruit that
originated in Onomichi's Innoshima.
They're a delicious combination
of sourness, bitterness,
and sweetness.

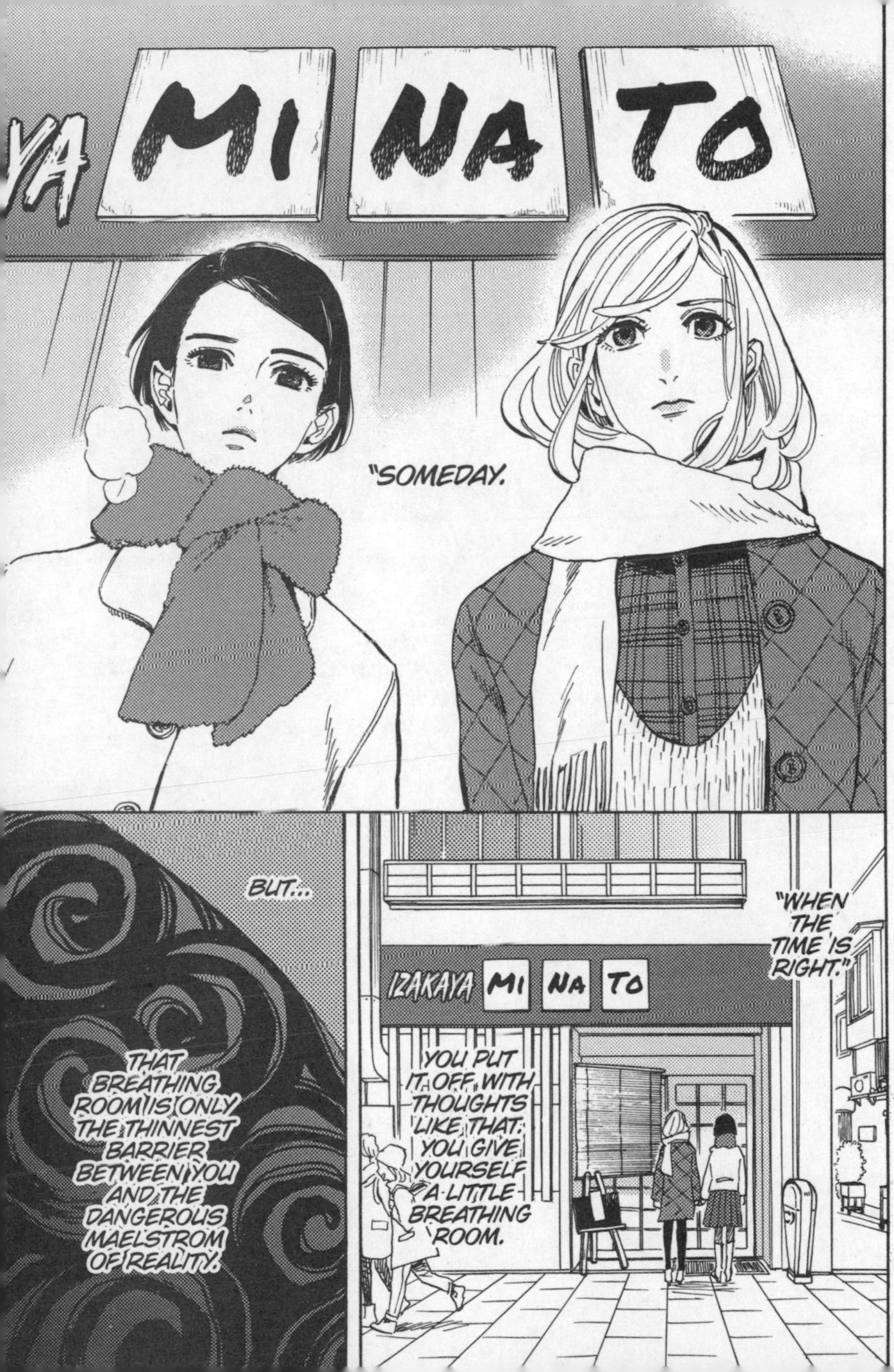
YA MI NA TO
"SOMEDAY.
IZAKAYA MI NA TO
"WHEN THE TIME IS RIGHT."
YOU PUT IT OFF WITH THOUGHTS LIKE THAT. YOU GIVE YOURSELF A LITTLE BREATHING ROOM.
BUT...
THAT BREATHING ROOM IS ONLY THE THINNEST BARRIER BETWEEN YOU AND THE DANGEROUS MAELSTROM OF REALITY.

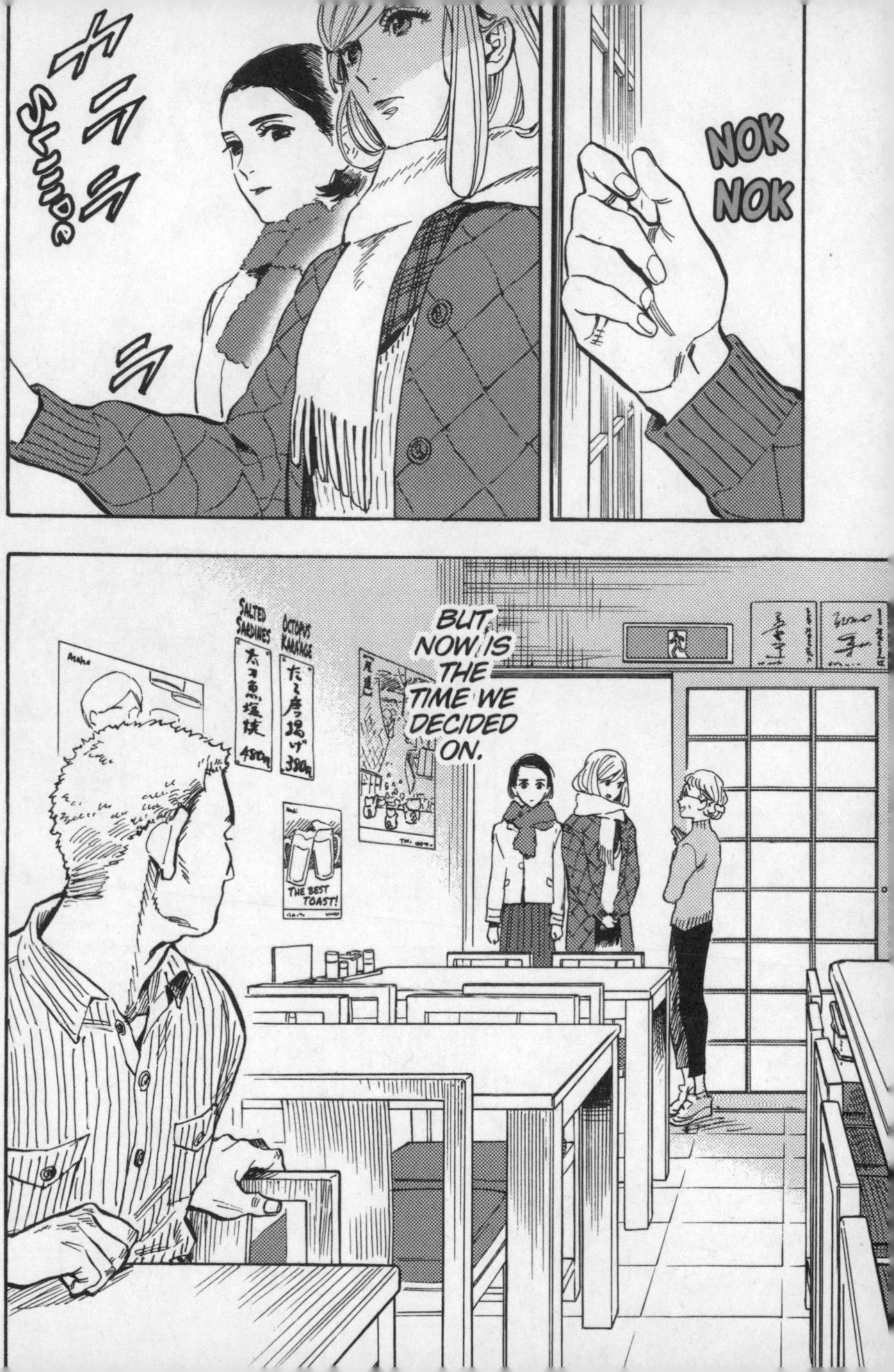
NOK
NOK
SLIDE
SALTED SARDINES
OCTOPUS KARAAGE
THE BEST TOAST!
BUT NOW IS THE TIME WE DECIDED ON.

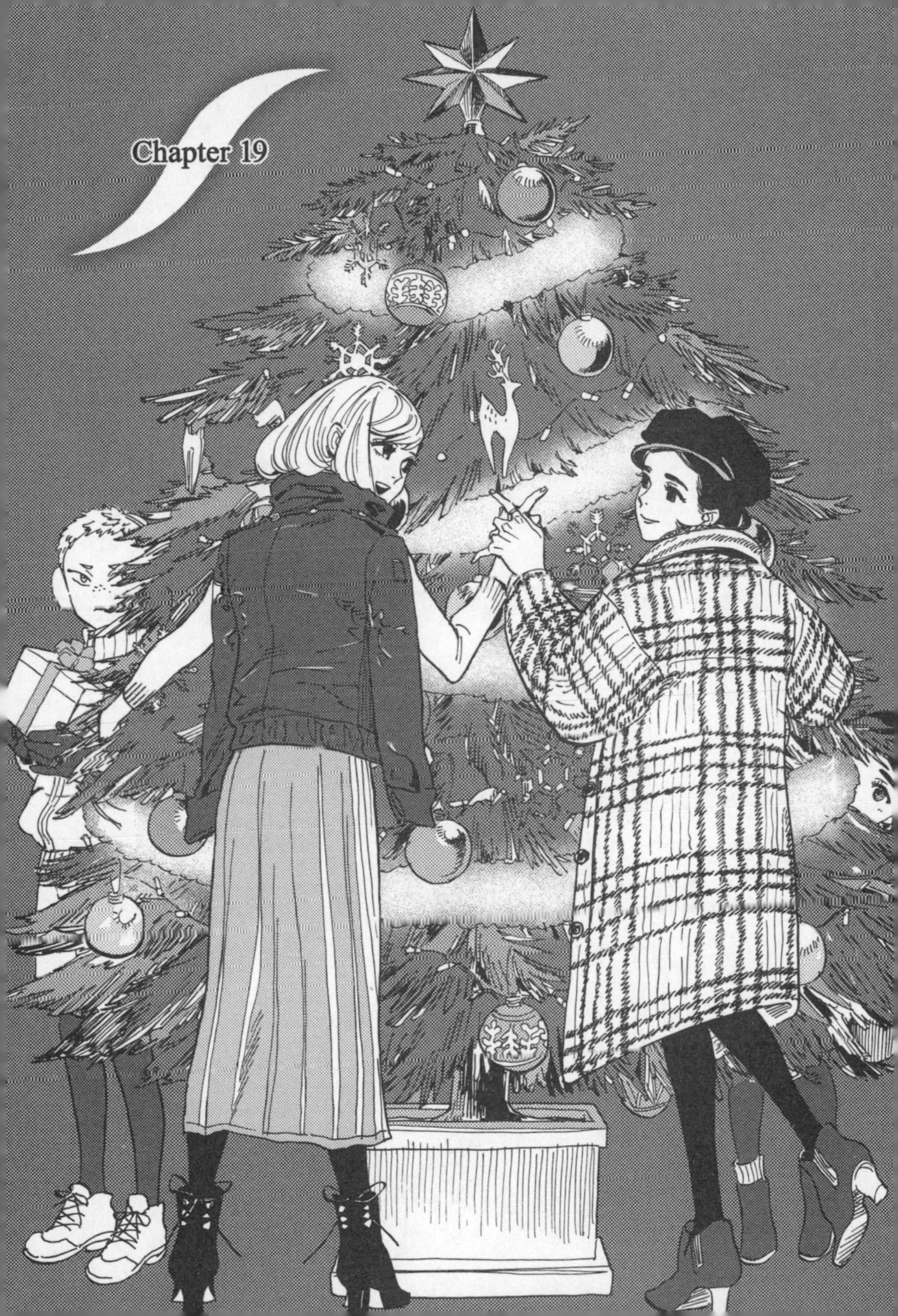
Chapter 19

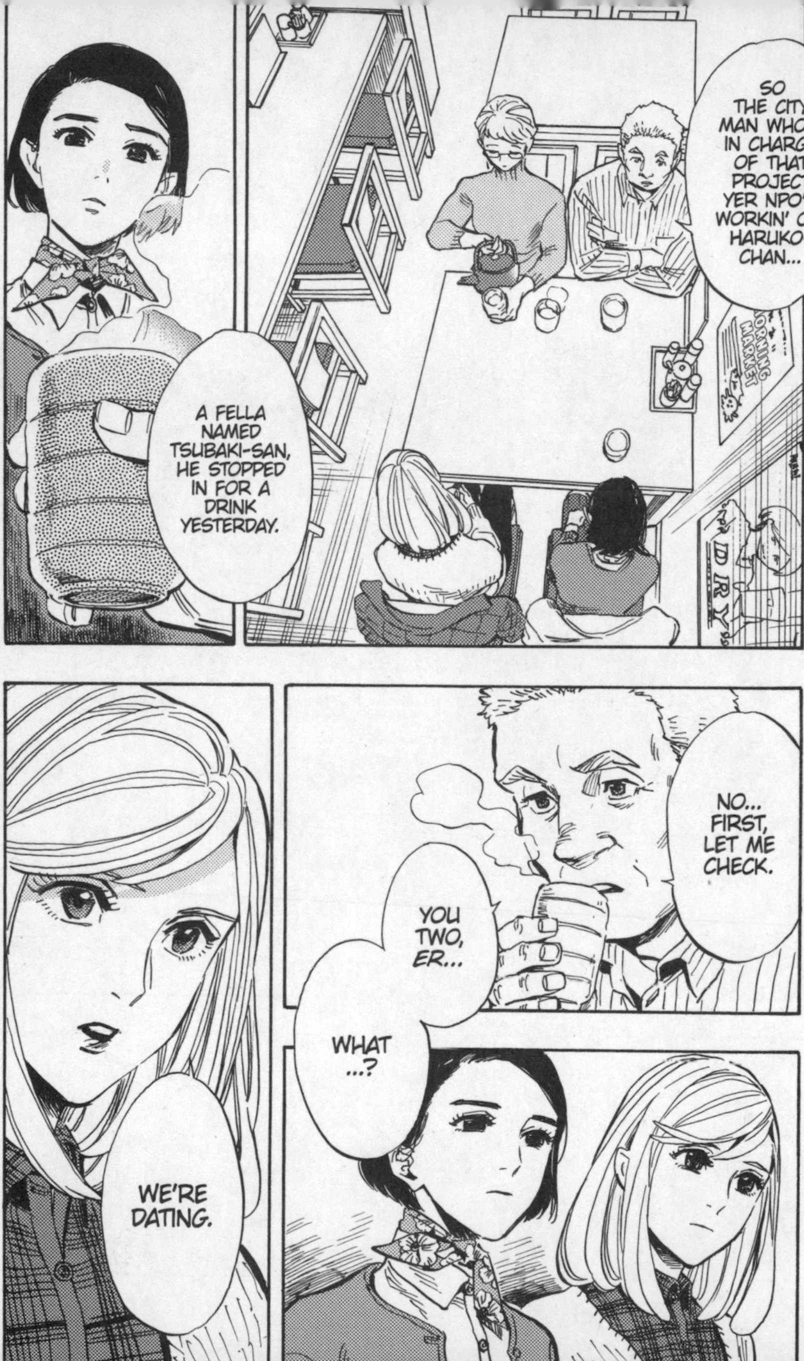
SO THE CITY MAN WHO'S IN CHARGE OF THAT PROJECT YER NPO'S WORKIN' ON, HARUKO-CHAN...
A FELLA NAMED TSUBAKI-SAN, HE STOPPED IN FOR A DRINK YESTERDAY.
NO... FIRST, LET ME CHECK.
YOU TWO, ER...
WHAT ...?
WE'RE DATING.

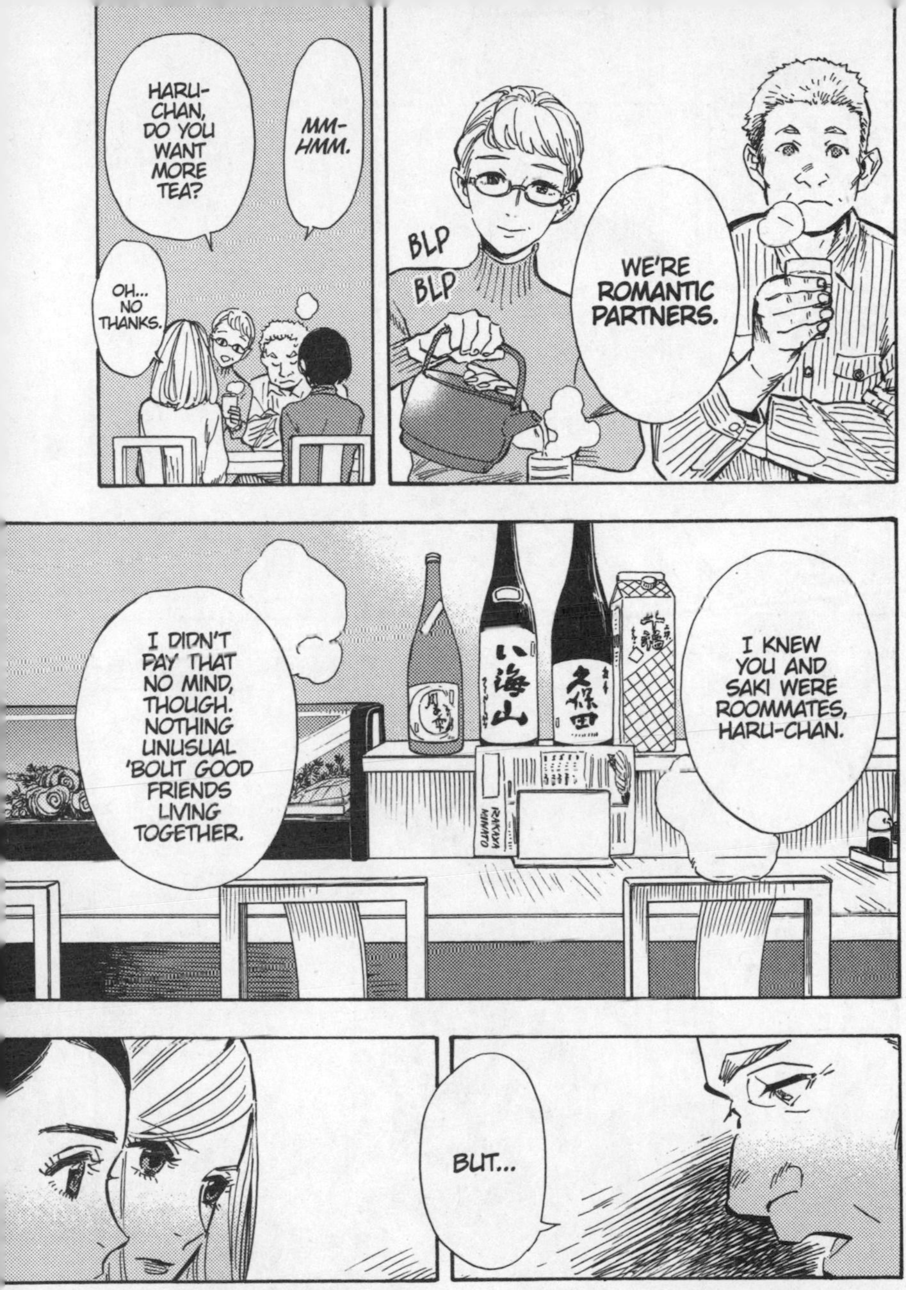
BLP
BLP
WE'RE ROMANTIC PARTNERS.
MM-HMM.
HARU-CHAN, DO YOU WANT MORE TEA?
OH... NO THANKS.
I KNEW YOU AND SAKI WERE ROOMMATES, HARU-CHAN.
I DIDN'T PAY THAT NO MIND, THOUGH. NOTHING UNUSUAL 'BOUT GOOD FRIENDS LIVING TOGETHER.
BUT...

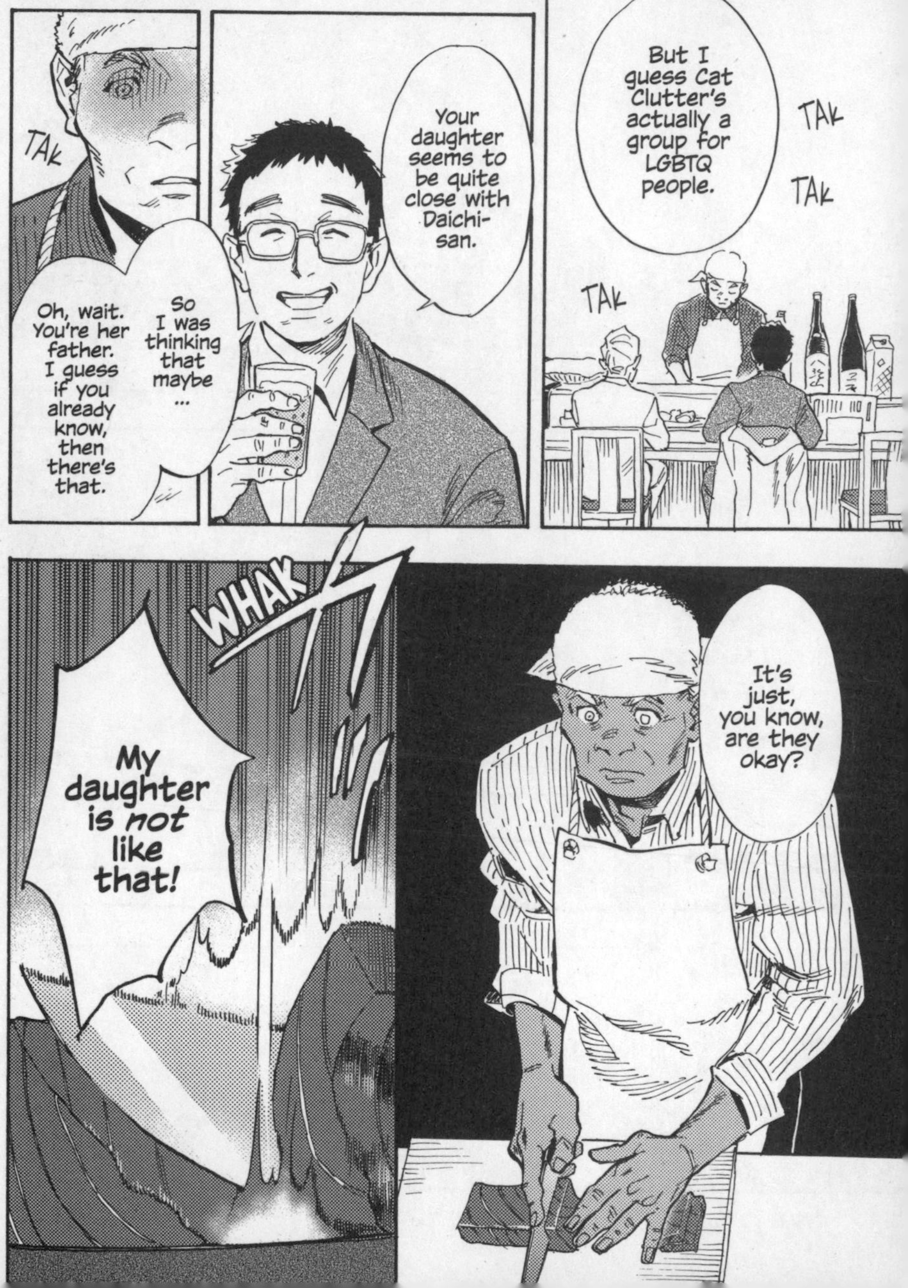
But I guess Cat Clutter's actually a group for LGBTQ people.
TAK
TAK
TAK
Your daughter seems to be quite close with Daichi-san.
So I was thinking that maybe ...
Oh, wait. You're her father. I guess if you already know, then there's that.
TAK
It's just, you know, are they okay?
WHAK
My daughter is *not* like that!

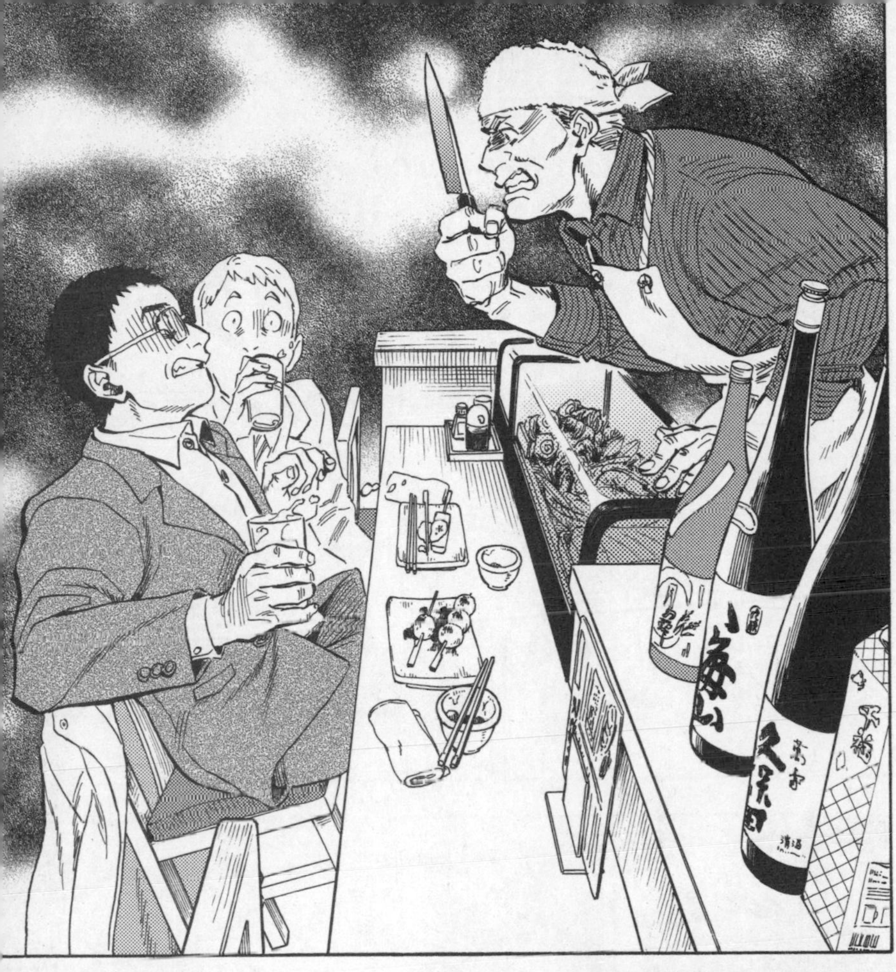

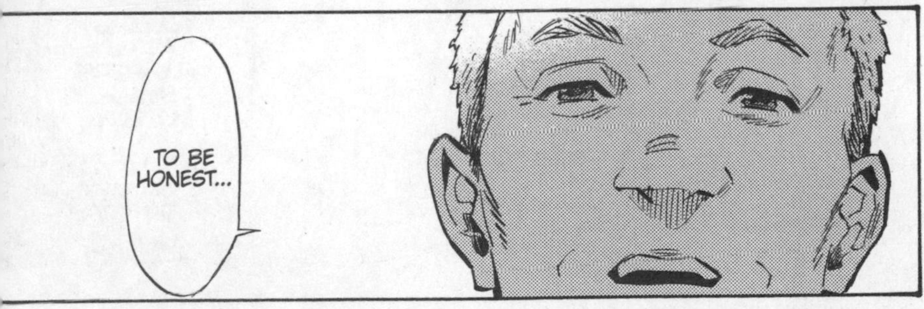
TO BE HONEST...

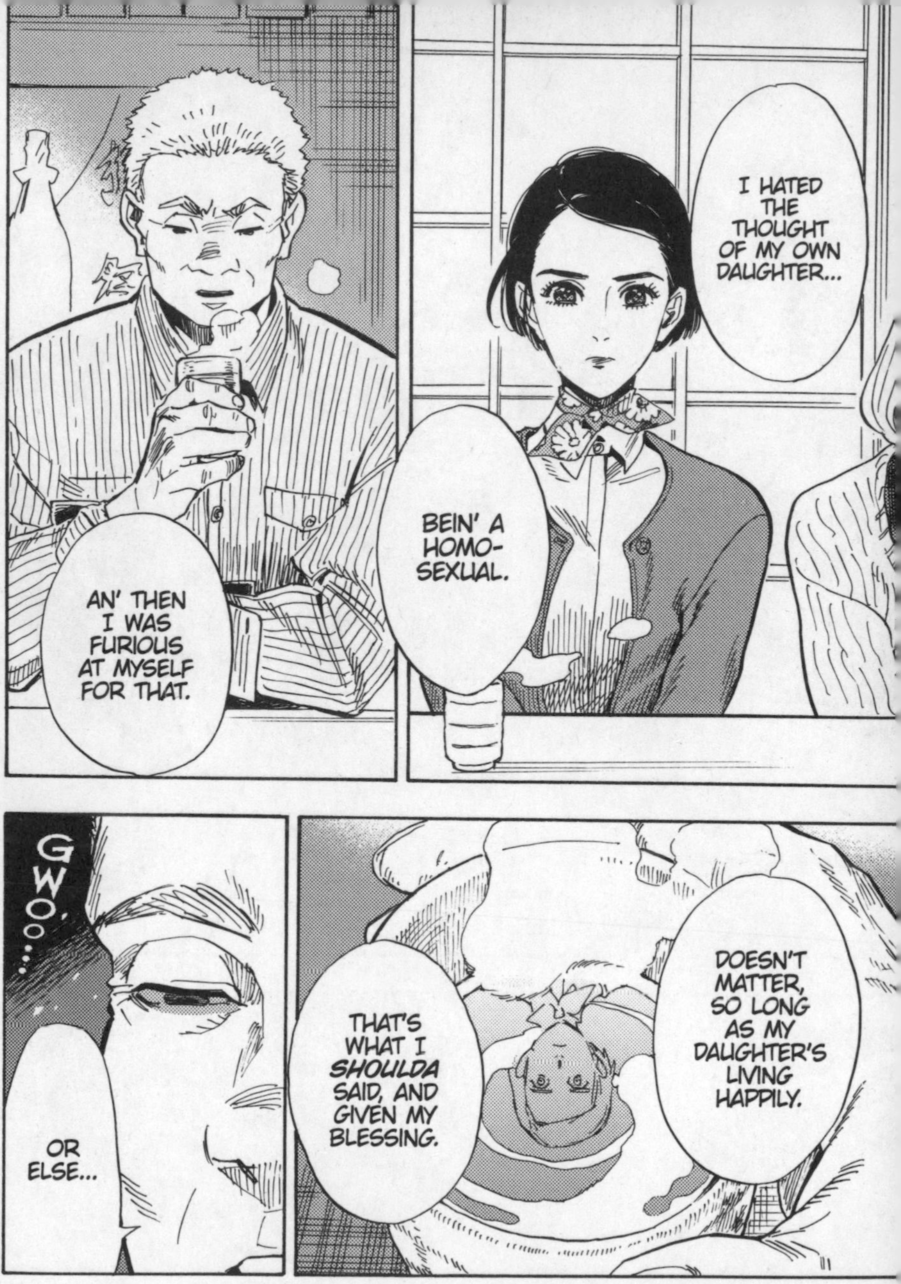
I HATED THE THOUGHT OF MY OWN DAUGHTER...
BEIN' A HOMO-SEXUAL.
AN' THEN I WAS FURIOUS AT MYSELF FOR THAT.
DOESN'T MATTER, SO LONG AS MY DAUGHTER'S LIVING HAPPILY.
THAT'S WHAT I *SHOULDA* SAID, AND GIVEN MY BLESSING.
GWOO...
OR ELSE...

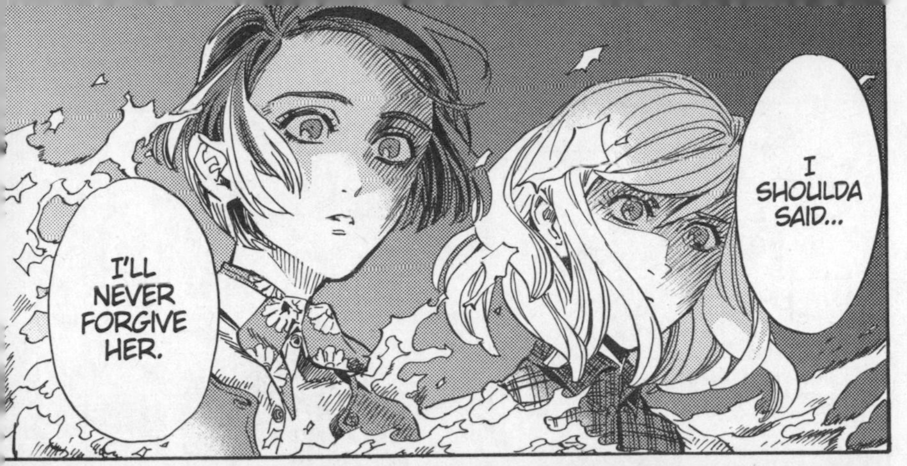
I SHOULDA SAID...
I'LL NEVER FORGIVE HER.
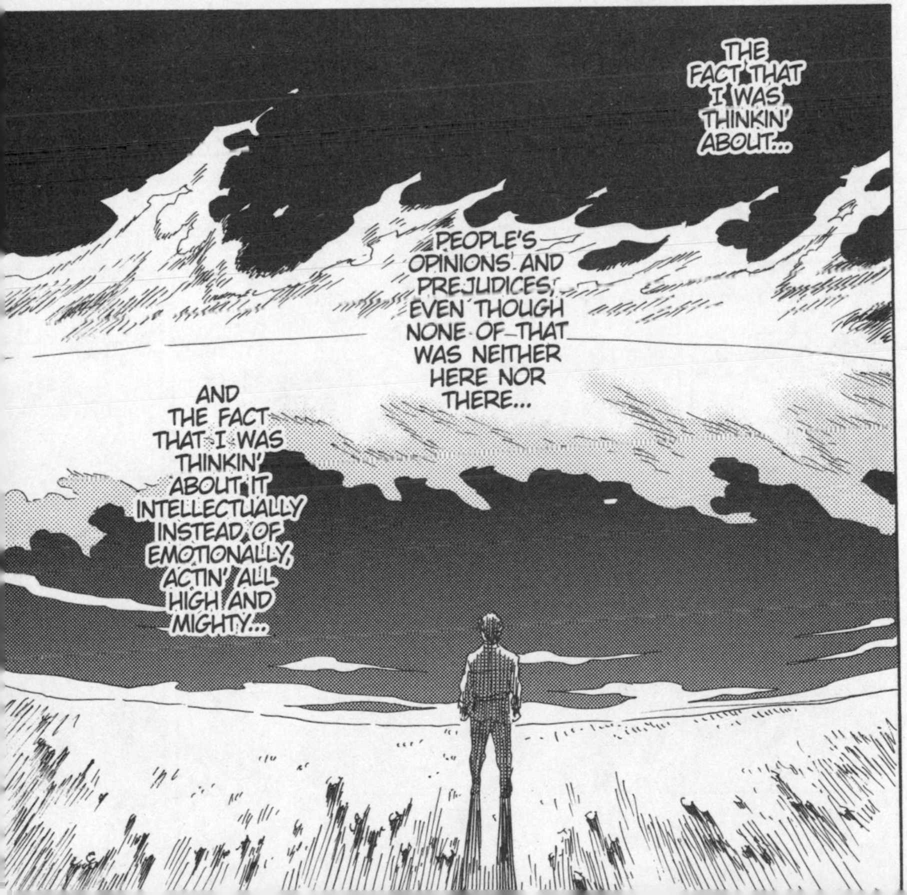
THE FACT THAT I WAS THINKIN' ABOUT...
PEOPLE'S OPINIONS AND PREJUDICES, EVEN THOUGH NONE OF THAT WAS NEITHER HERE NOR THERE...
AND THE FACT THAT I WAS THINKIN' ABOUT IT INTELLECTUALLY INSTEAD OF EMOTIONALLY, ACTIN' ALL HIGH AND MIGHTY...

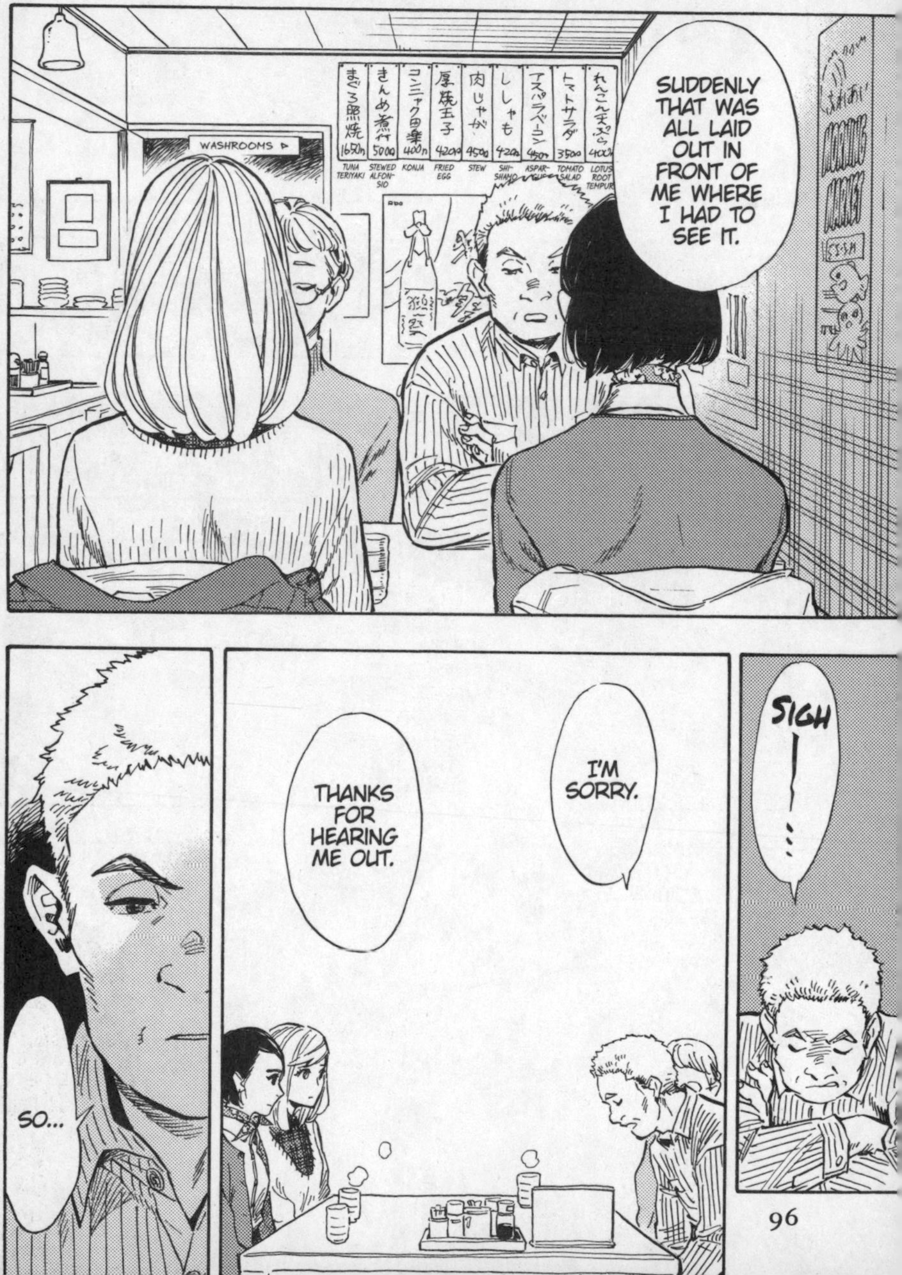

WASHROOMS
TUNA TERIYAKI
STEWED ALFONSIO
KONJA
FRIED EGG
STEW
SHISHAMO
TOMATO SALAD
SUDDENLY THAT WAS ALL LAID OUT IN FRONT OF ME WHERE I HAD TO SEE IT.
SIGH ...
I'M SORRY.
THANKS FOR HEARING ME OUT.
SO...

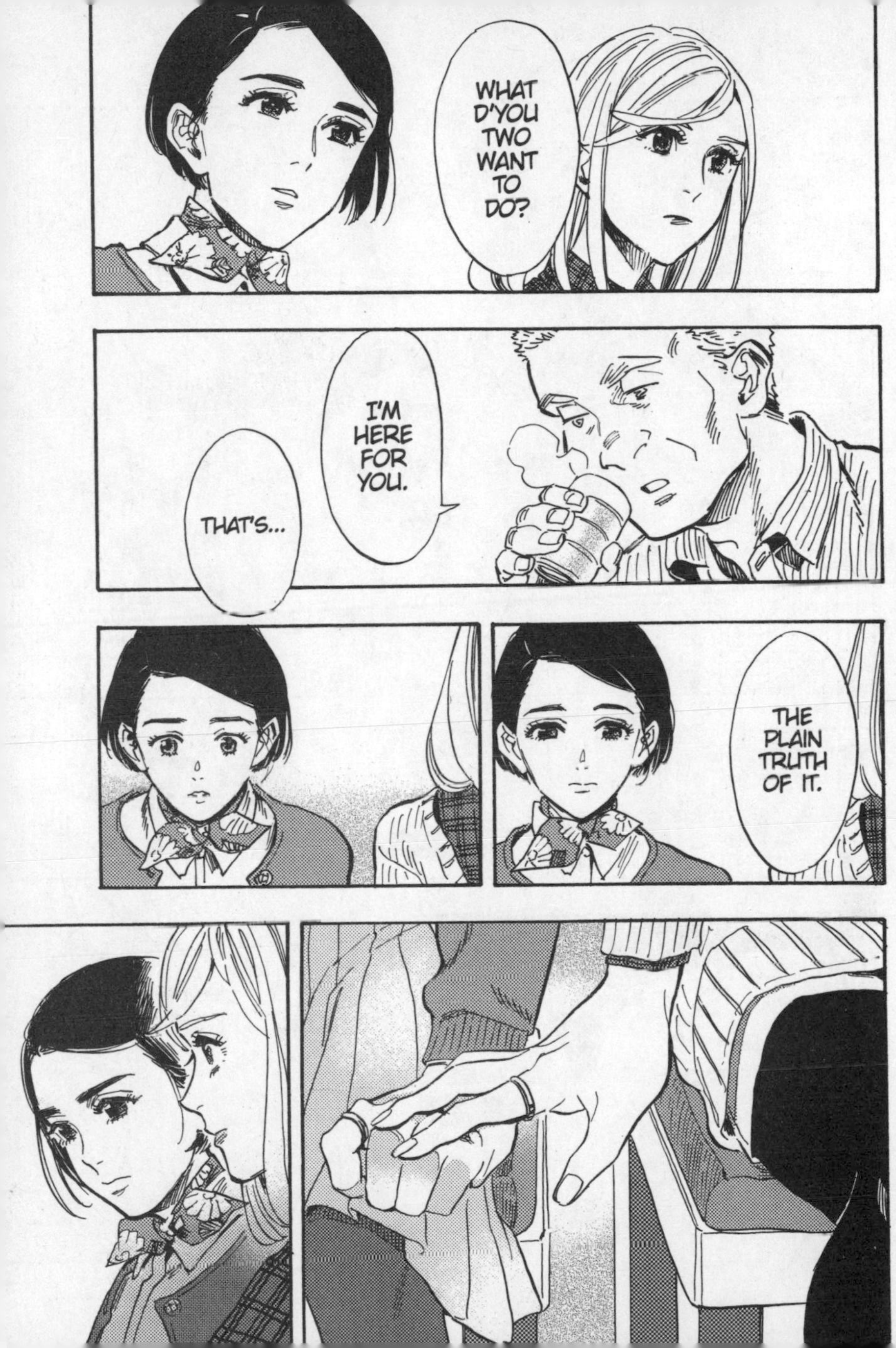
WHAT D'YOU TWO WANT TO DO?
I'M HERE FOR YOU.
THAT'S...
THE PLAIN TRUTH OF IT.

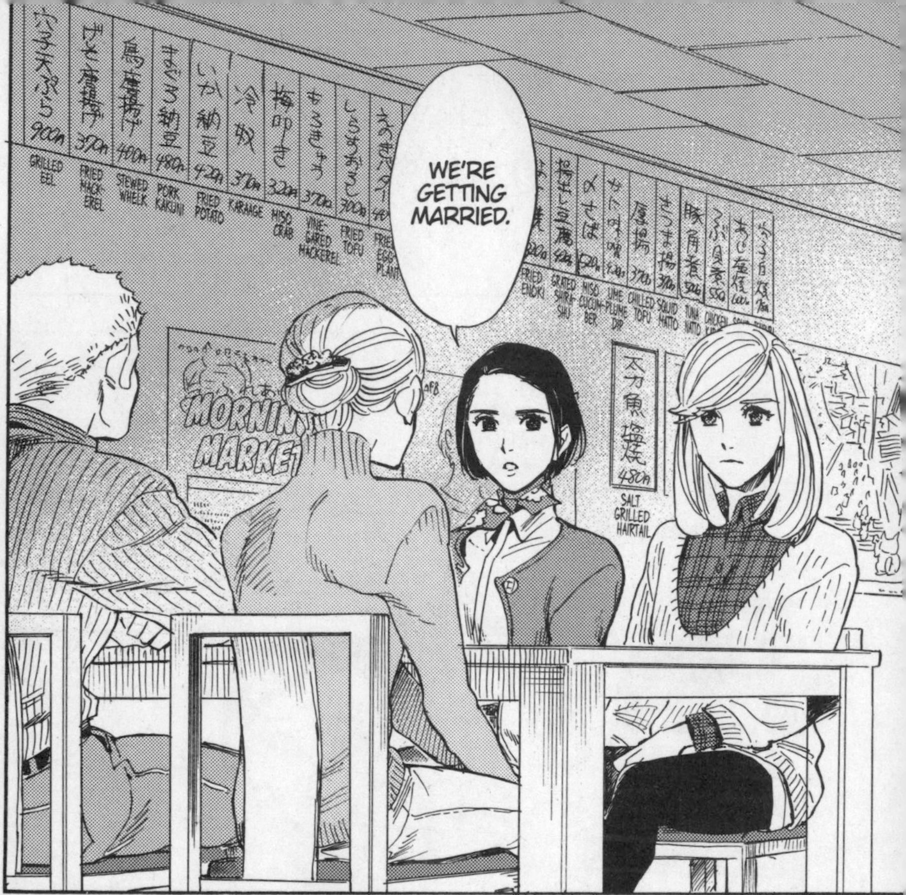
WE'RE GETTING MARRIED.
GRILLED EEL
FRIED MACKEREL
STEWED WHELK
PORK KAKUNI
FRIED POTATO
KARAAGE
MISO CRAB
VINEGARED MACKEREL
FRIED TOFU
FRIED ENOKI
GRATED SHIRASU
MISO CUCUMBER
UME PLUM DIP
CHILLED TOFU
SQUID NATTO
TUNA NATTO
SALT GRILLED HAIRTAIL

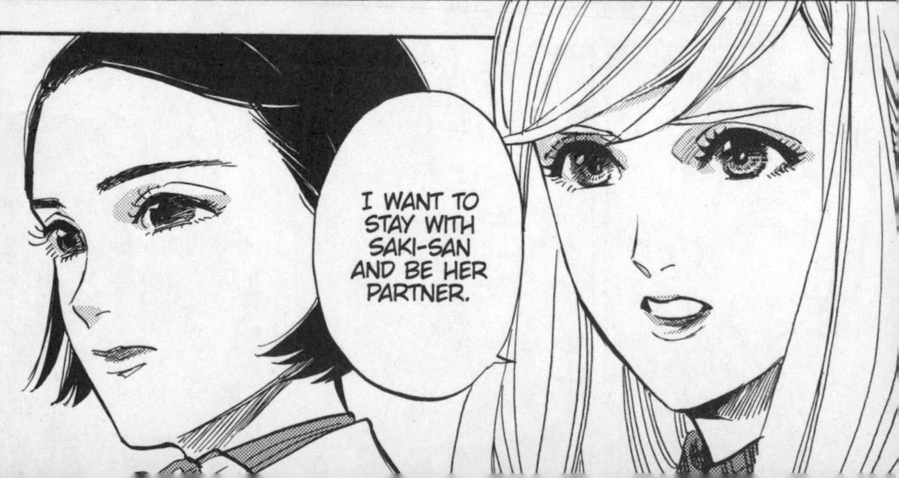
I WANT TO STAY WITH SAKI-SAN AND BE HER PARTNER.

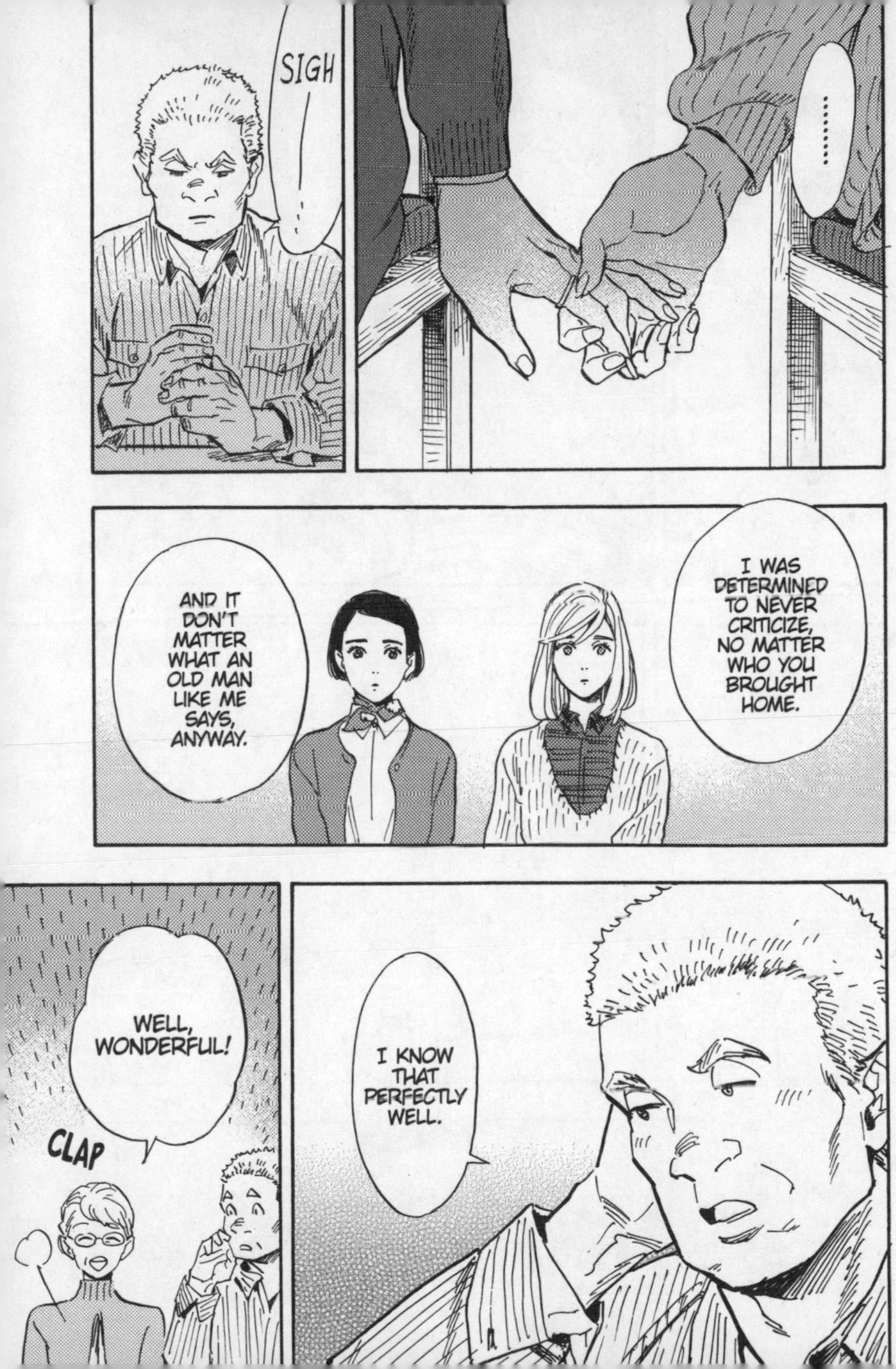
......
SIGH
I WAS DETERMINED TO NEVER CRITICIZE, NO MATTER WHO YOU BROUGHT HOME.
AND IT DON'T MATTER WHAT AN OLD MAN LIKE ME SAYS, ANYWAY.
I KNOW THAT PERFECTLY WELL.
WELL, WONDERFUL!
CLAP

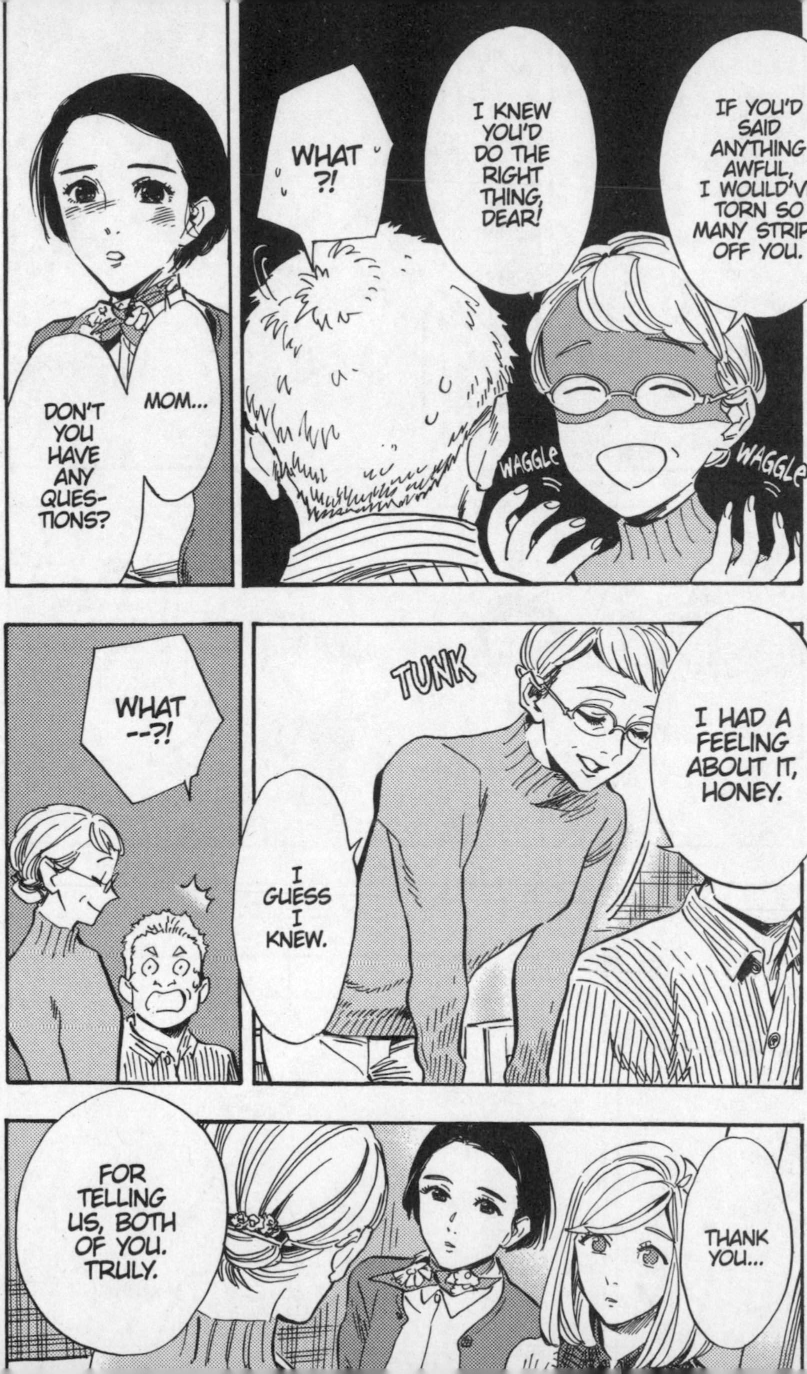
IF YOU'D SAID ANYTHING AWFUL, I WOULD'VE TORN SO MANY STRIPS OFF YOU.
I KNEW YOU'D DO THE RIGHT THING, DEAR!
WAGGLE
WAGGLE
WHAT ?!
MOM...
DON'T YOU HAVE ANY QUES-TIONS?
I HAD A FEELING ABOUT IT, HONEY.
TUNK
I GUESS I KNEW.
WHAT --?!
THANK YOU...
FOR TELLING US, BOTH OF YOU. TRULY.

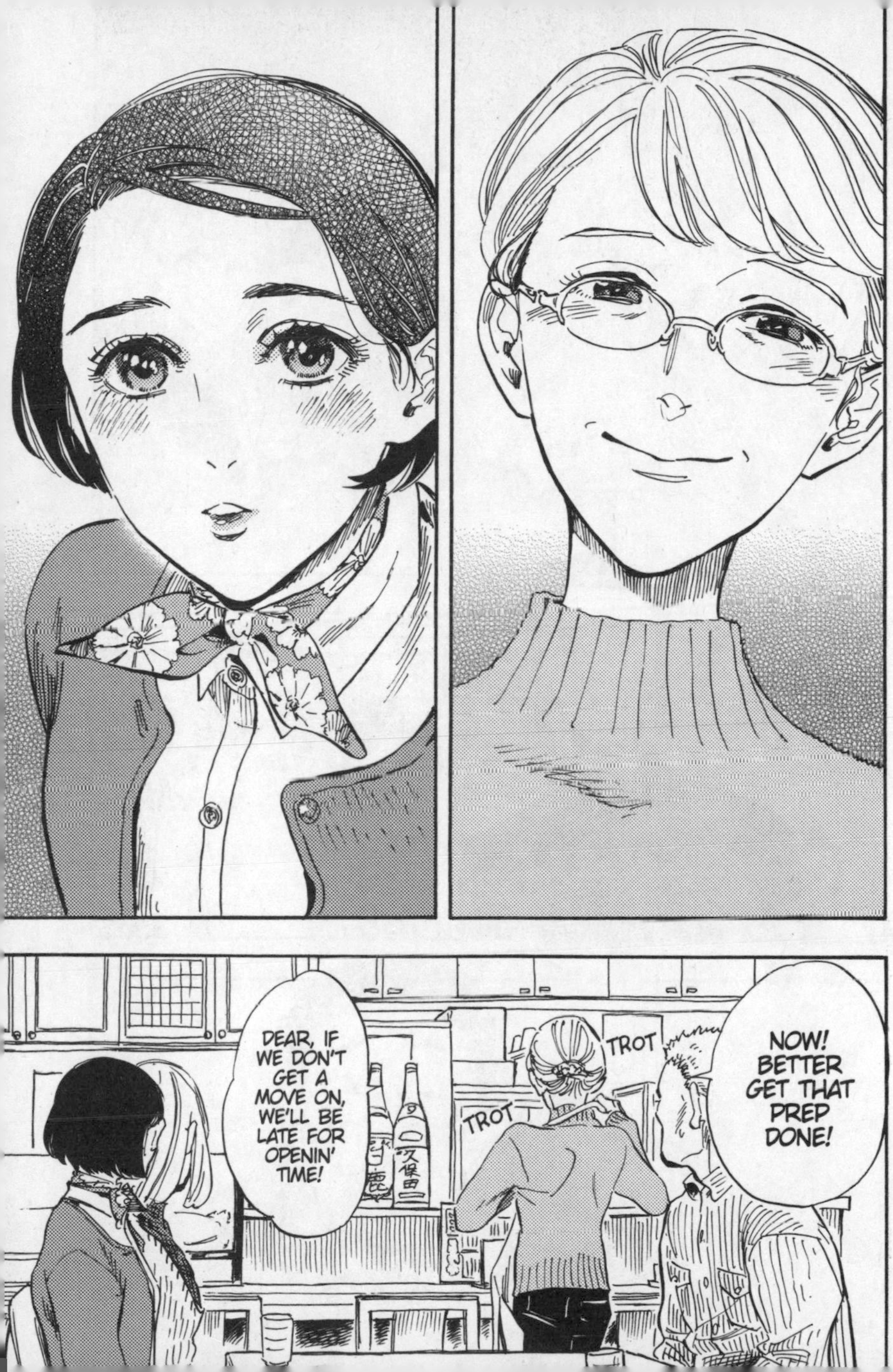
NOW! BETTER GET THAT PREP DONE!
TROT
DEAR, IF WE DON'T GET A MOVE ON, WE'LL BE LATE FOR OPENIN' TIME!
TROT

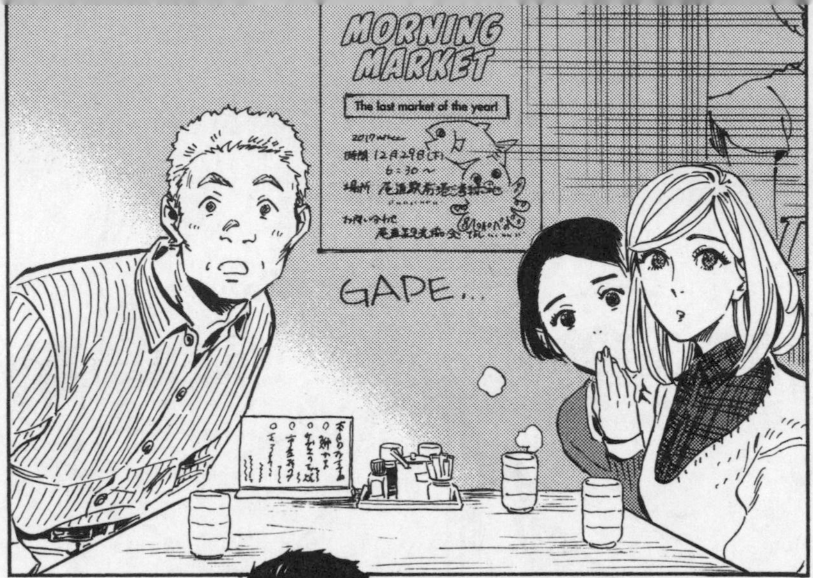
MORNING MARKET
The last market of the year!
GAPE...
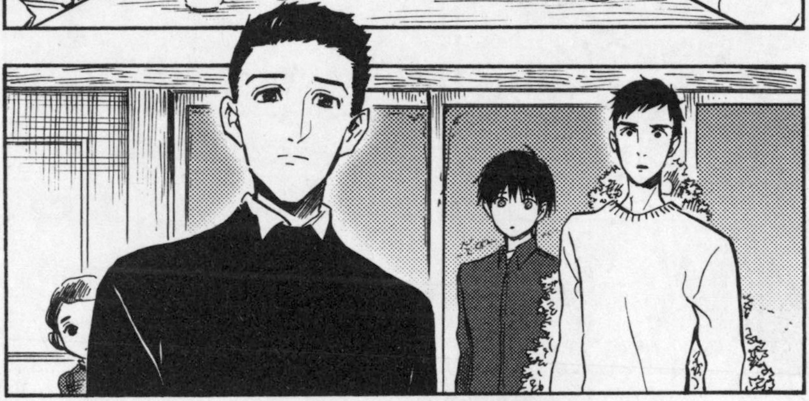
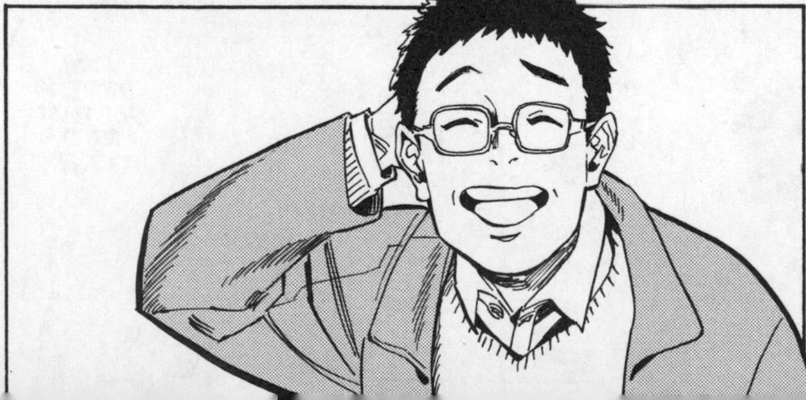

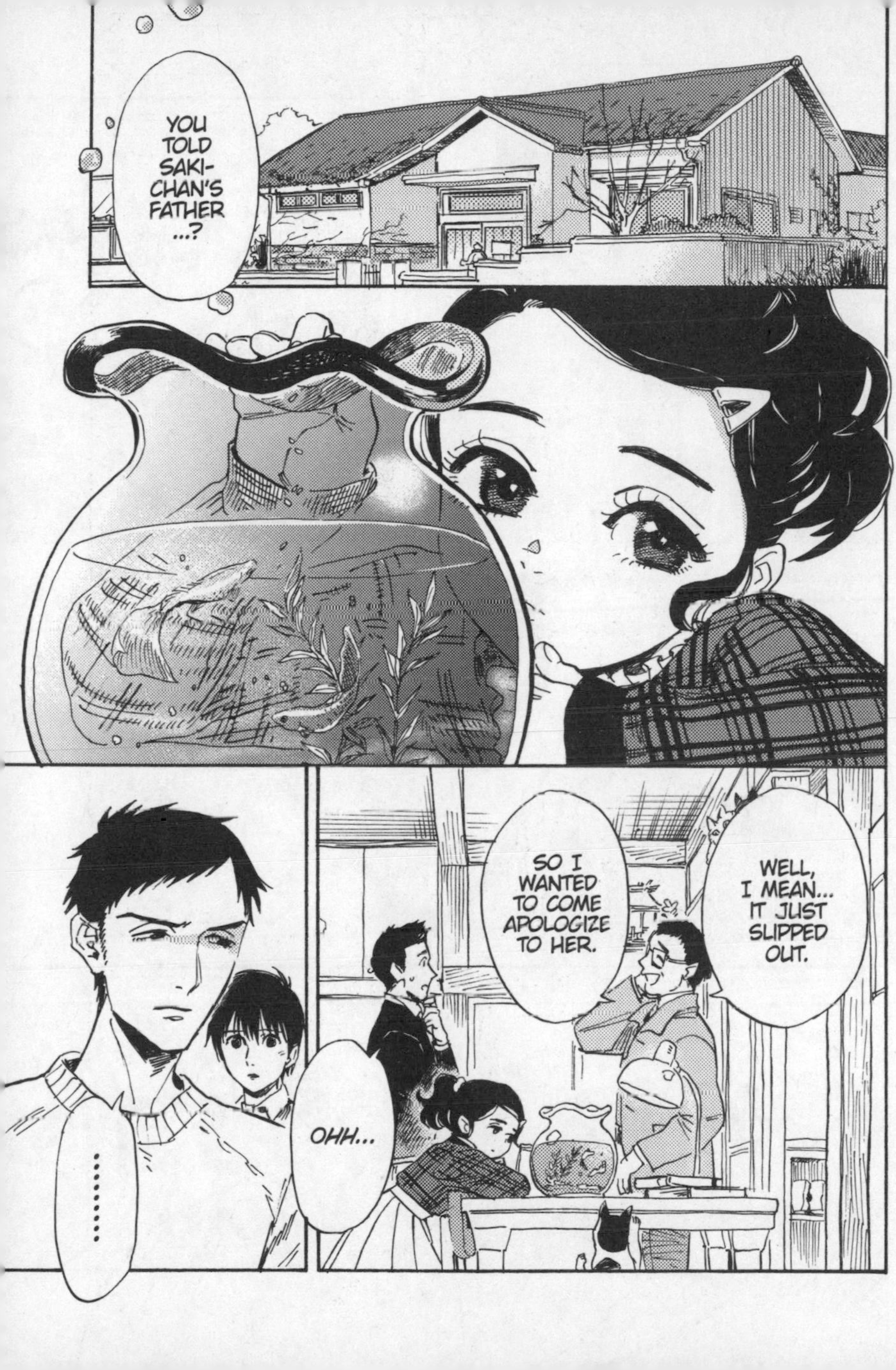
YOU TOLD SAKI-CHAN'S FATHER ...?
WELL, I MEAN... IT JUST SLIPPED OUT.
SO I WANTED TO COME APOLOGIZE TO HER.
OHH...
......

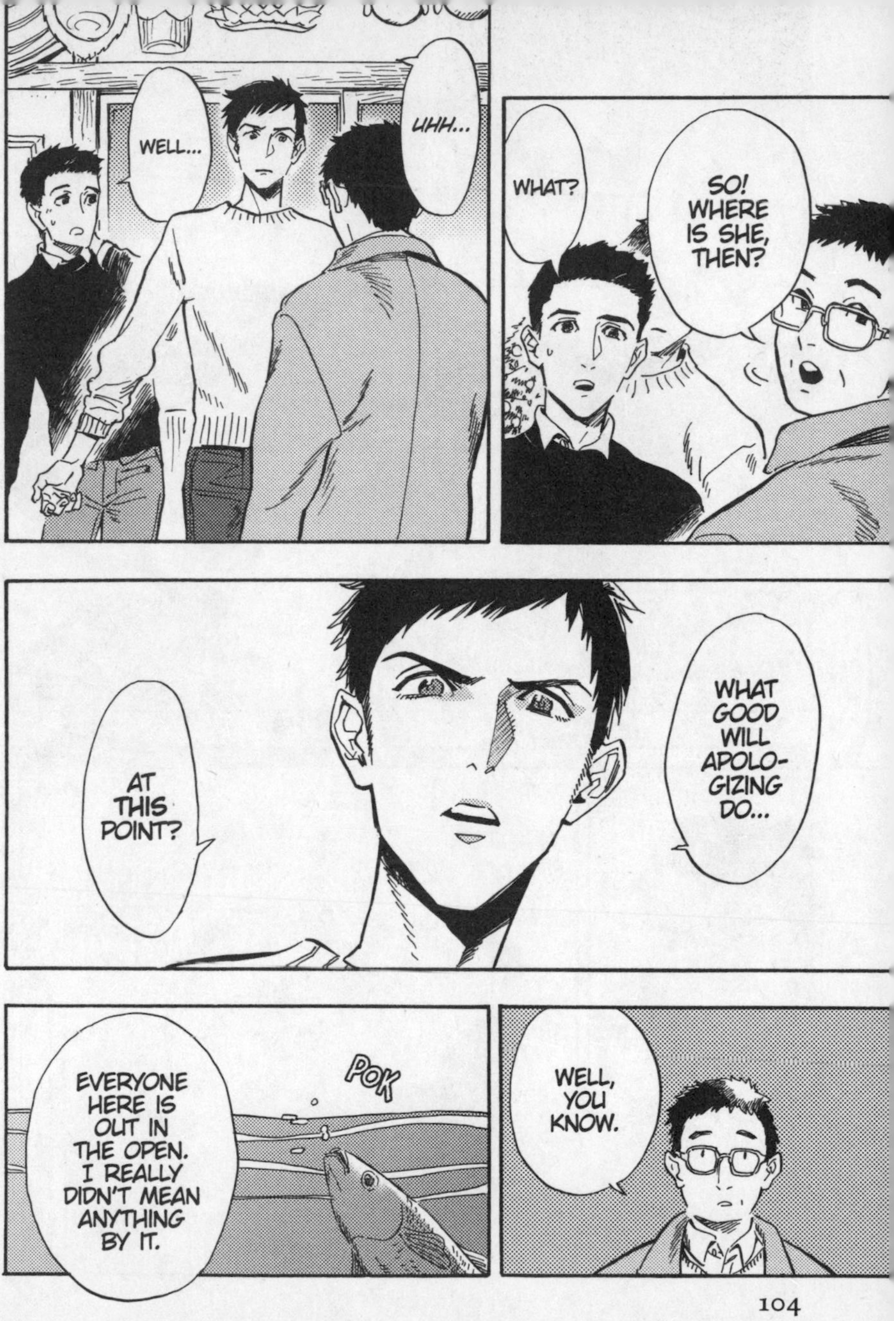
SO! WHERE IS SHE, THEN?
WHAT?
UHH...
WELL...
WHAT GOOD WILL APOLO-GIZING DO...
AT THIS POINT?
WELL, YOU KNOW.
POK
EVERYONE HERE IS OUT IN THE OPEN. I REALLY DIDN'T MEAN ANYTHING BY IT.

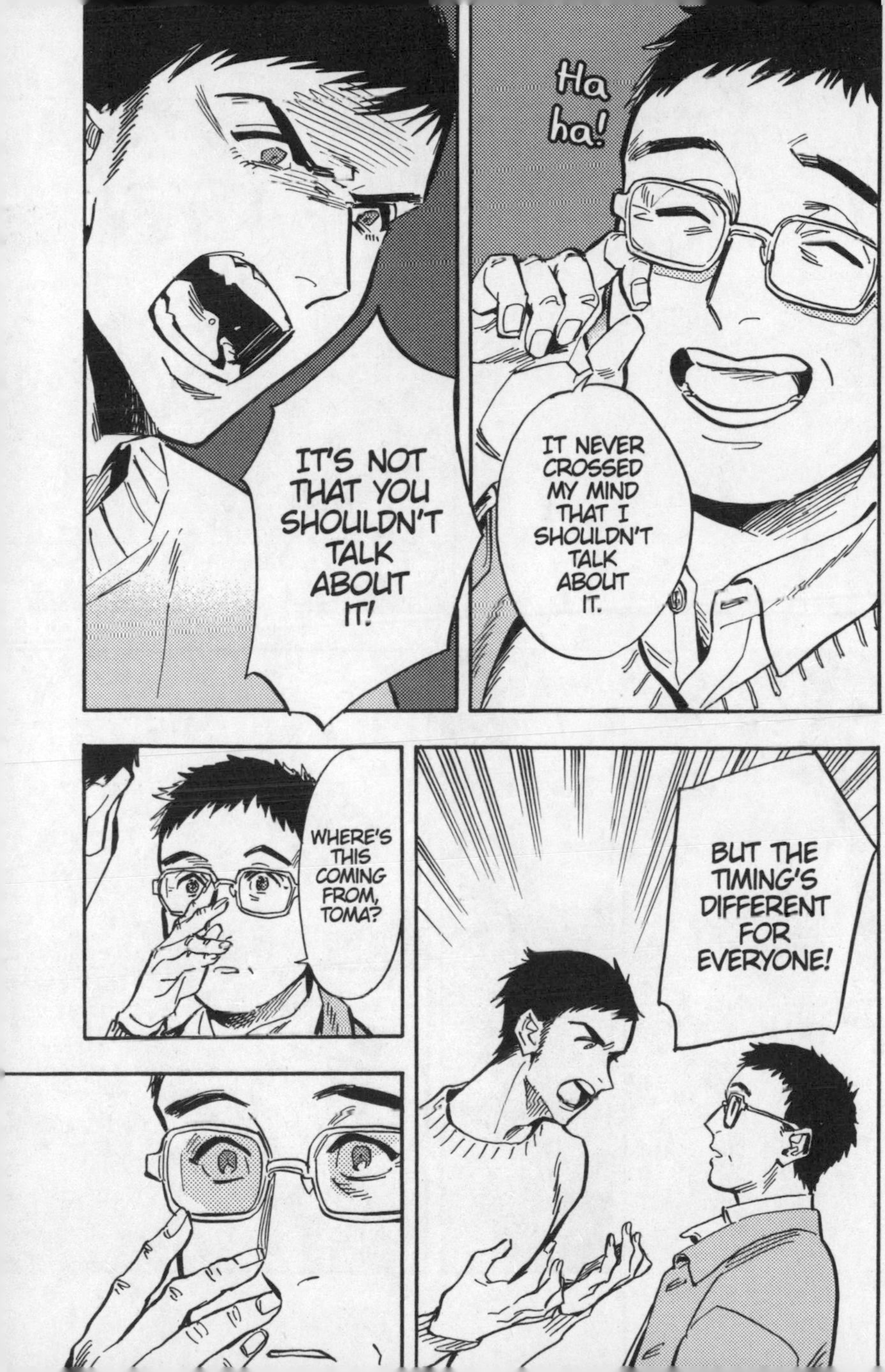
Ha ha!
IT NEVER CROSSED MY MIND THAT I SHOULDN'T TALK ABOUT IT.
IT'S NOT THAT YOU SHOULDN'T TALK ABOUT IT!
BUT THE TIMING'S DIFFERENT FOR EVERYONE!
WHERE'S THIS COMING FROM, TOMA?

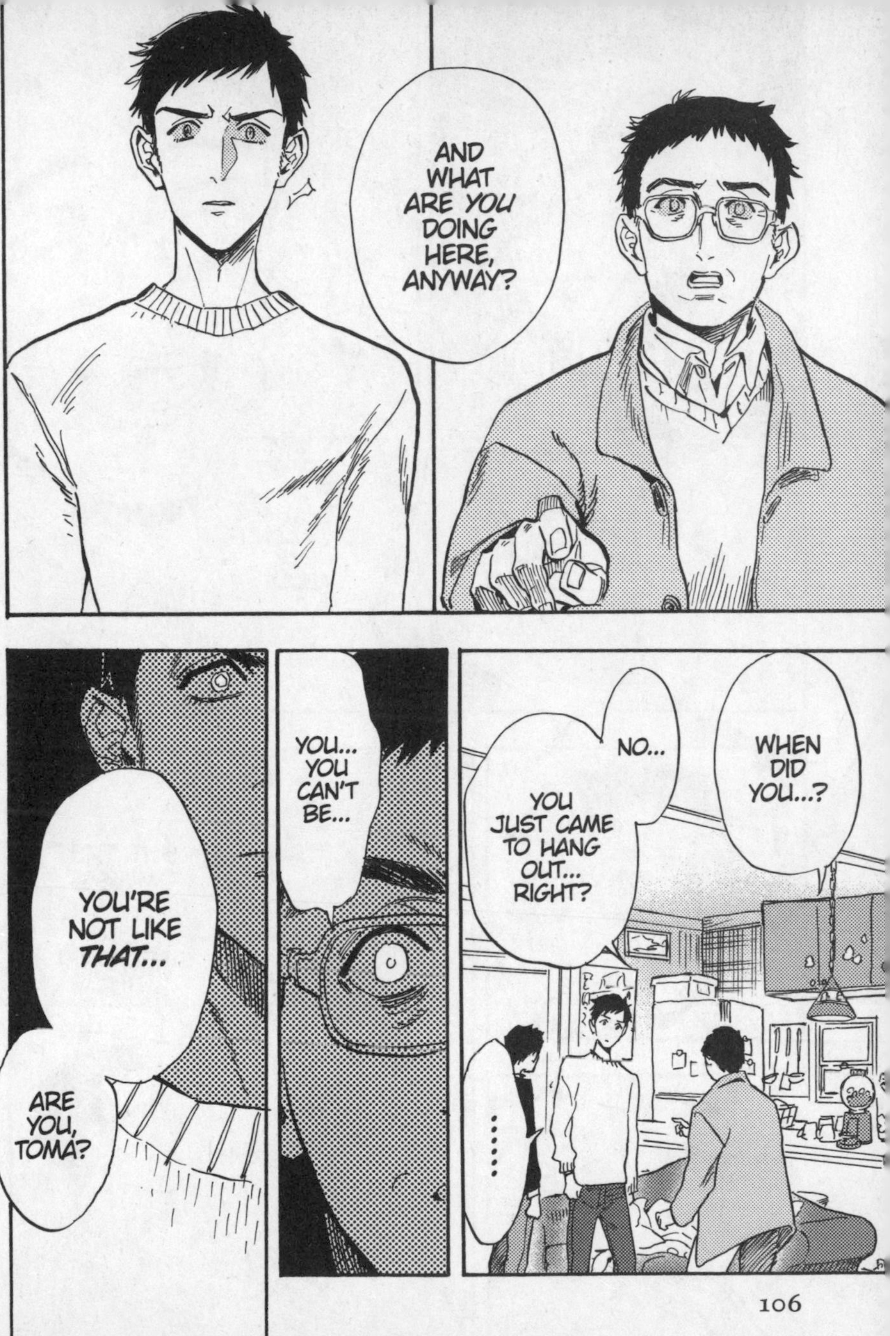
AND WHAT ARE YOU DOING HERE, ANYWAY?
WHEN DID YOU...?
NO...
YOU JUST CAME TO HANG OUT... RIGHT?
......
YOU... YOU CAN'T BE...
YOU'RE NOT LIKE *THAT...*
ARE YOU, TOMA?

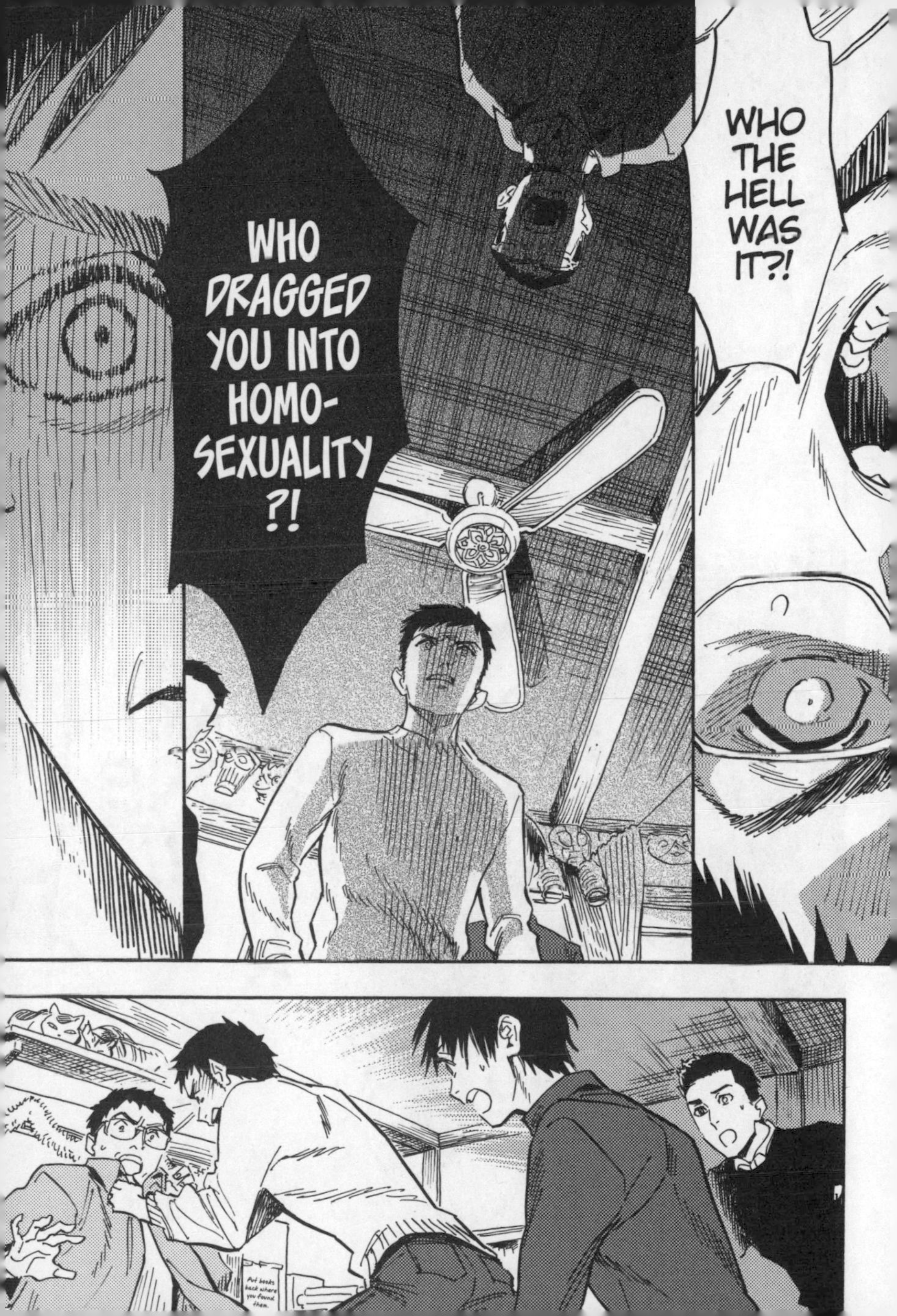
WHO THE HELL WAS IT?!
WHO DRAGGED YOU INTO HOMO-SEXUALITY ?!
Put books back where you found them.

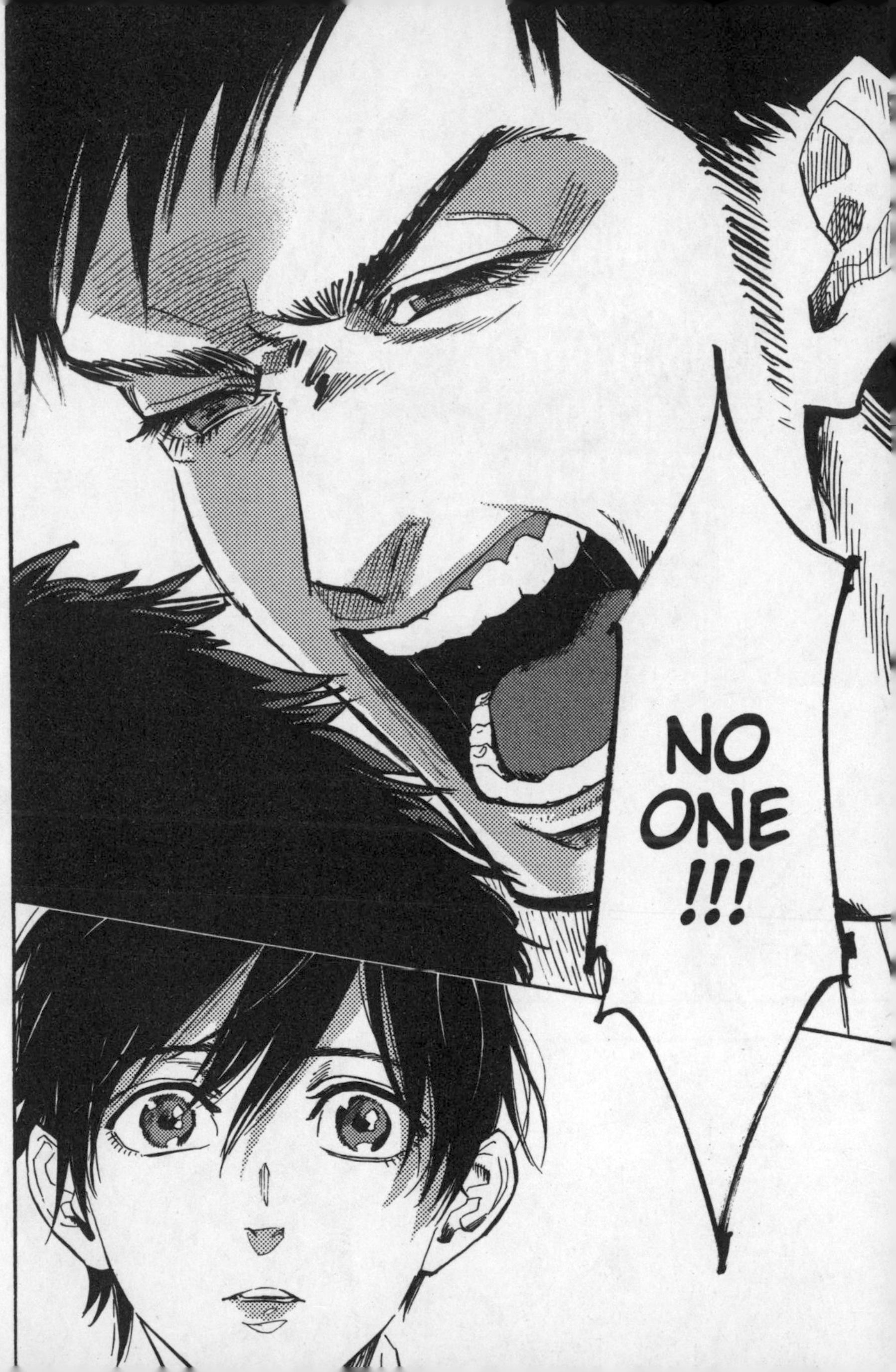
NO ONE !!!

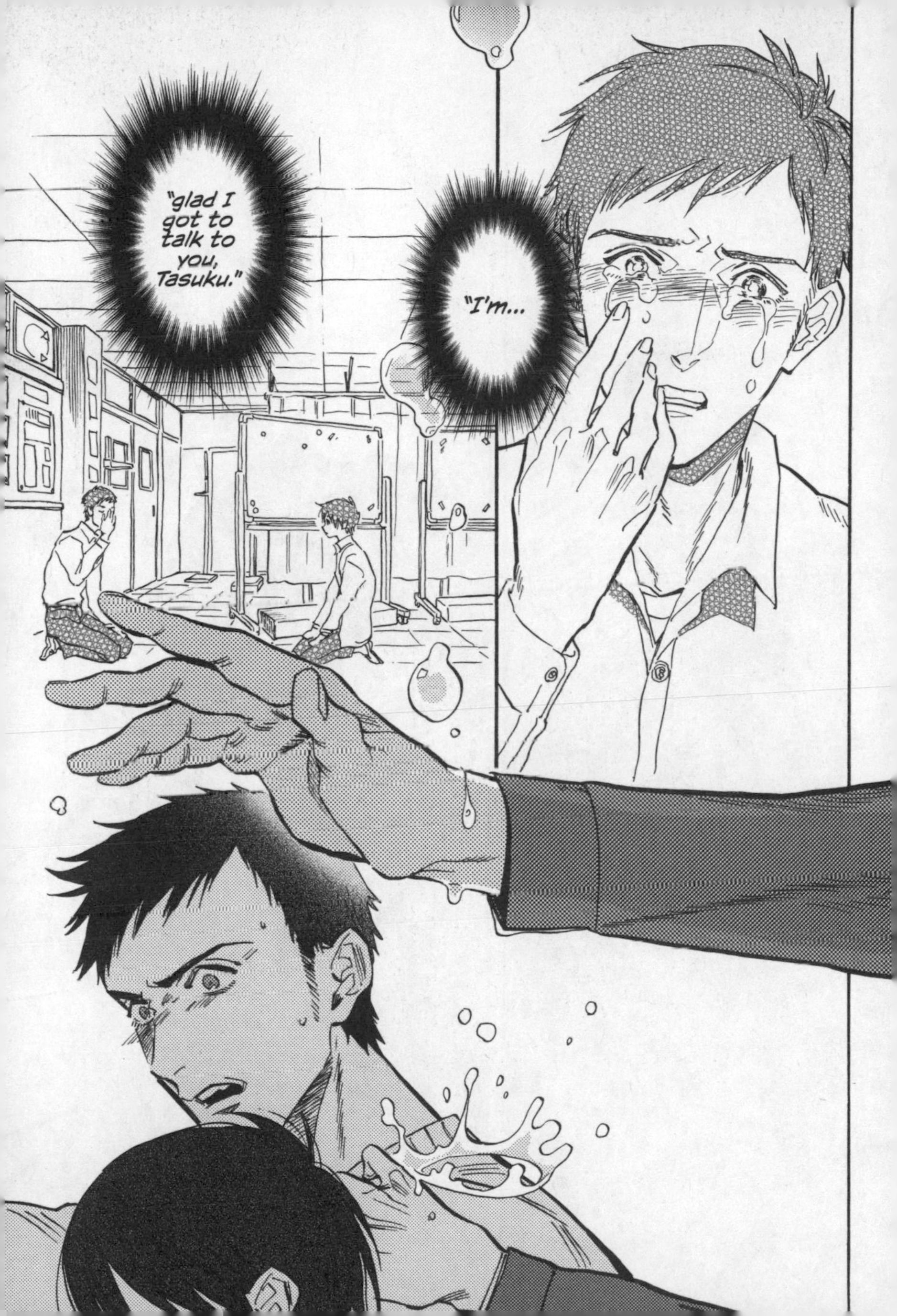
"I'm...
"glad I got to talk to you, Tasuku."

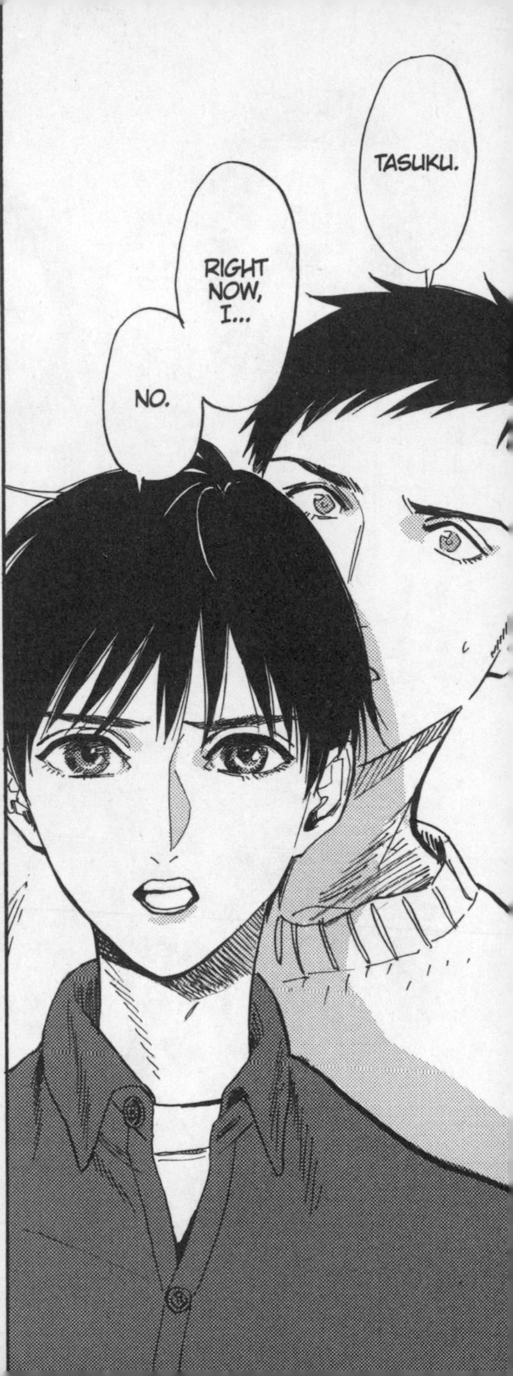
TASUKU.
RIGHT NOW, I...
NO.
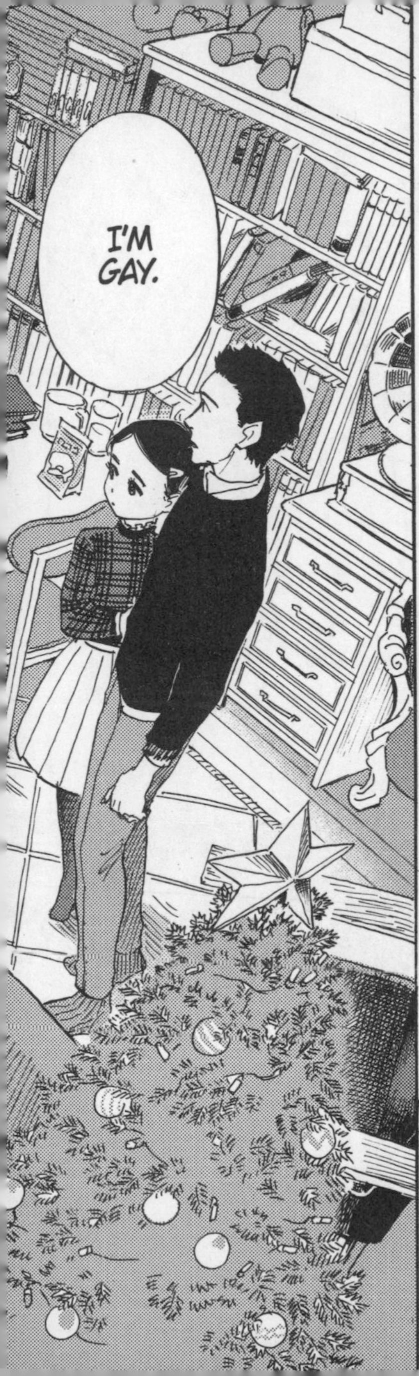
I'M GAY.

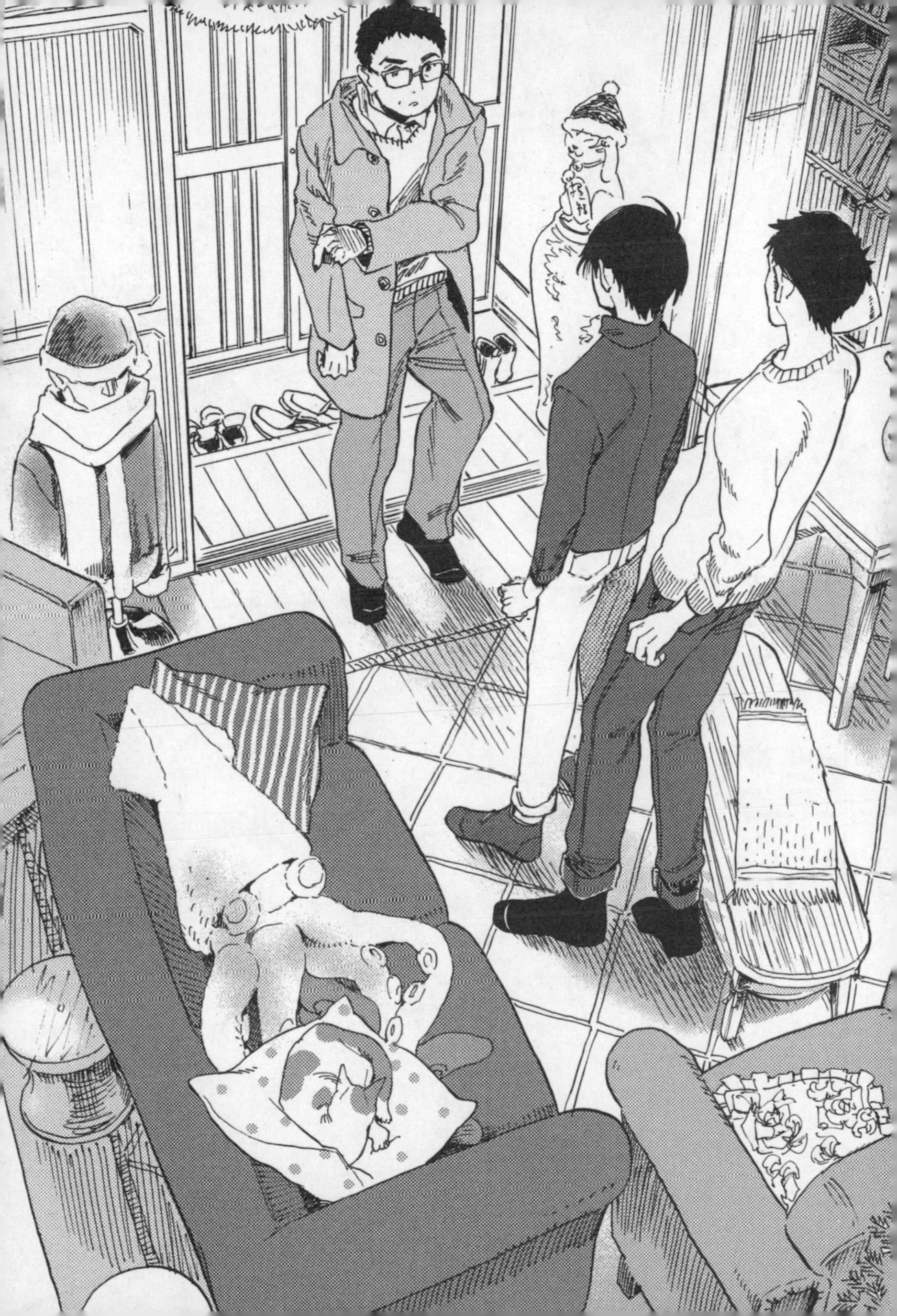

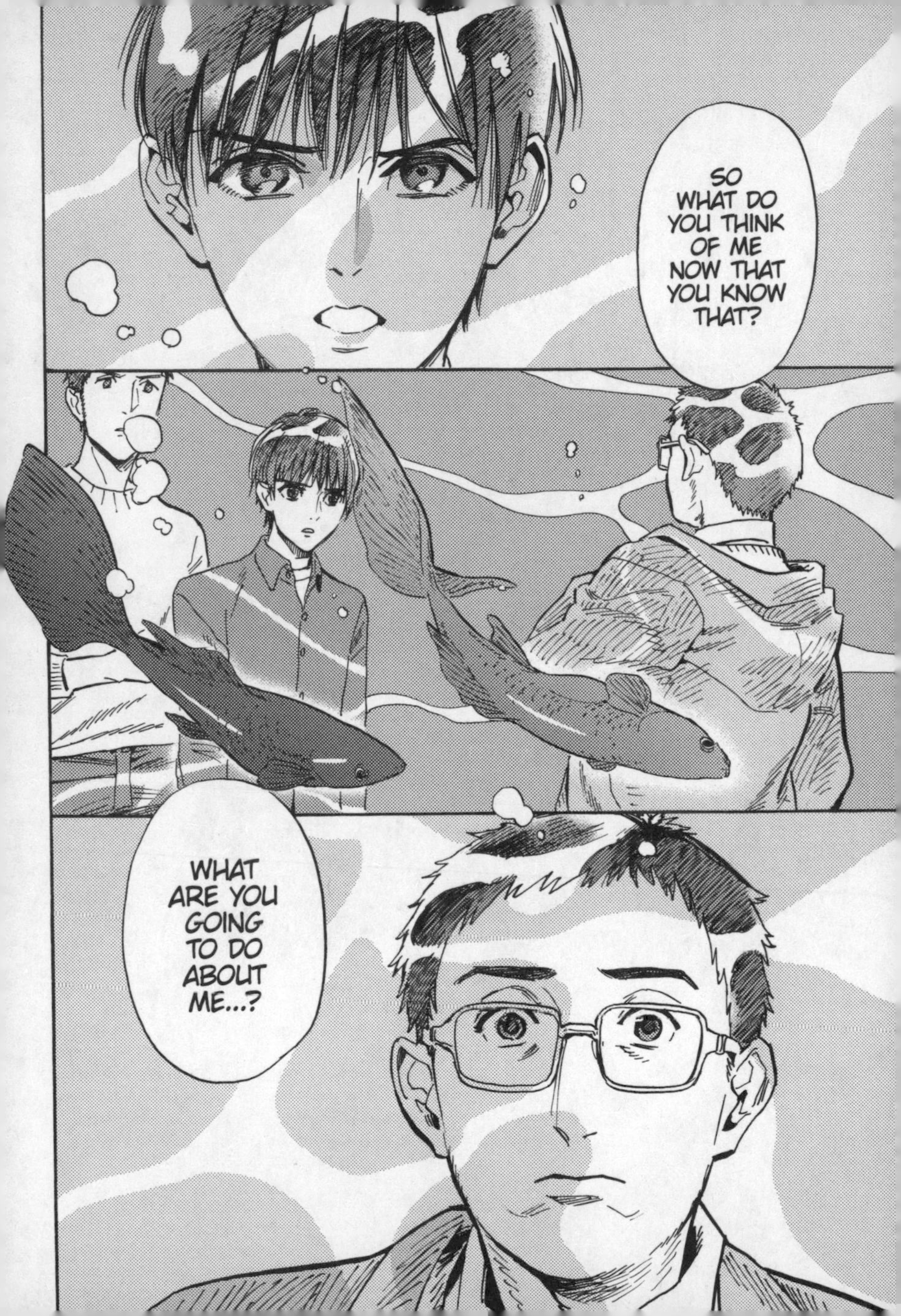
SO WHAT DO YOU THINK OF ME NOW THAT YOU KNOW THAT?
WHAT ARE YOU GOING TO DO ABOUT ME...?

Our Dreams at Dusk

SHIMANAMI TASOGARE

Onomichi Hondori Shopping Street

While the shops from way back are still there, new shops have sprung up in the empty spaces to create an arcade street that's vibrant in all kinds of ways. The total length is 1.2 kilometers.

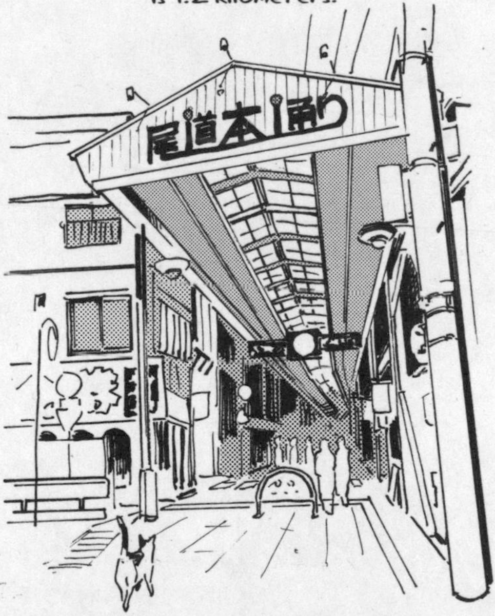
尾道本通り

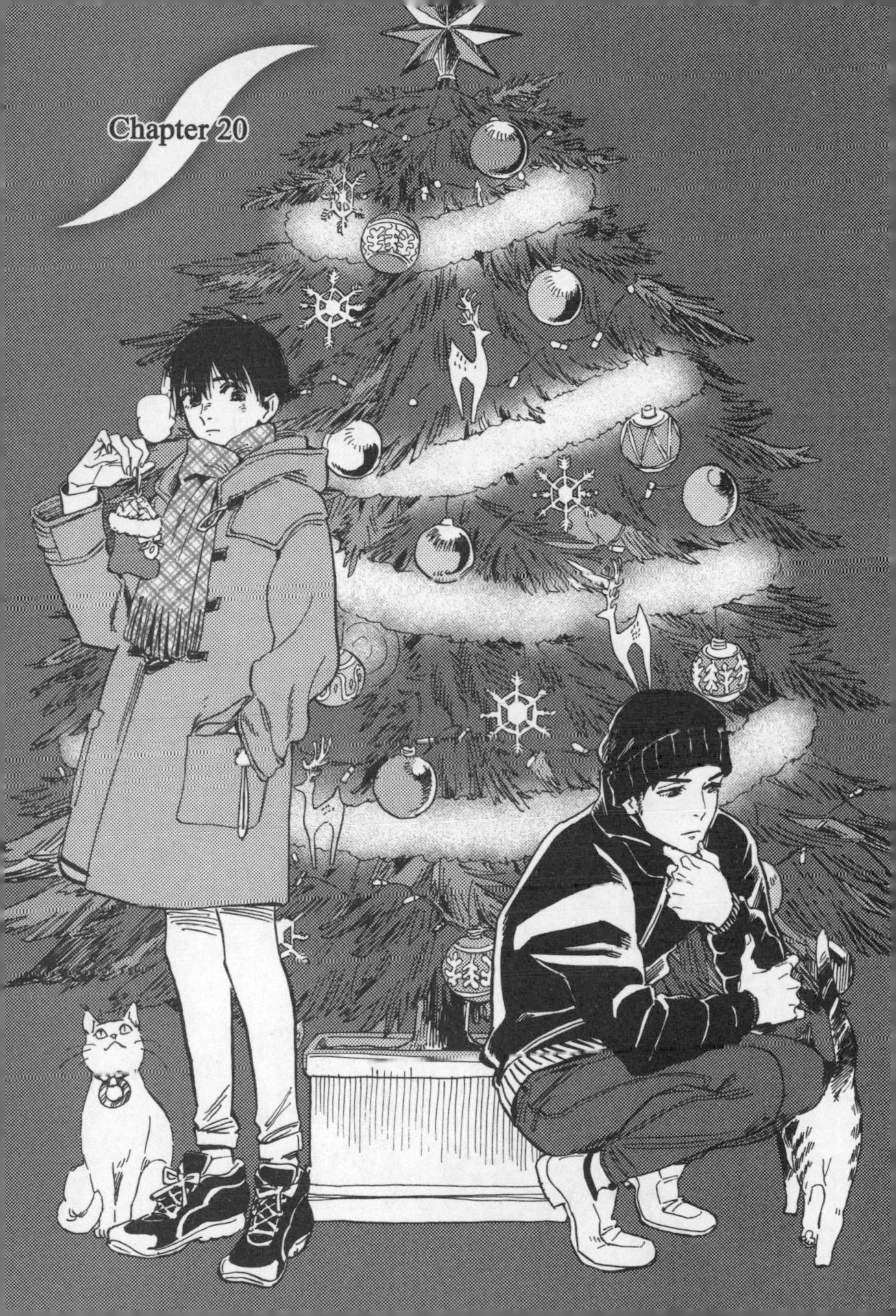
Chapter 20

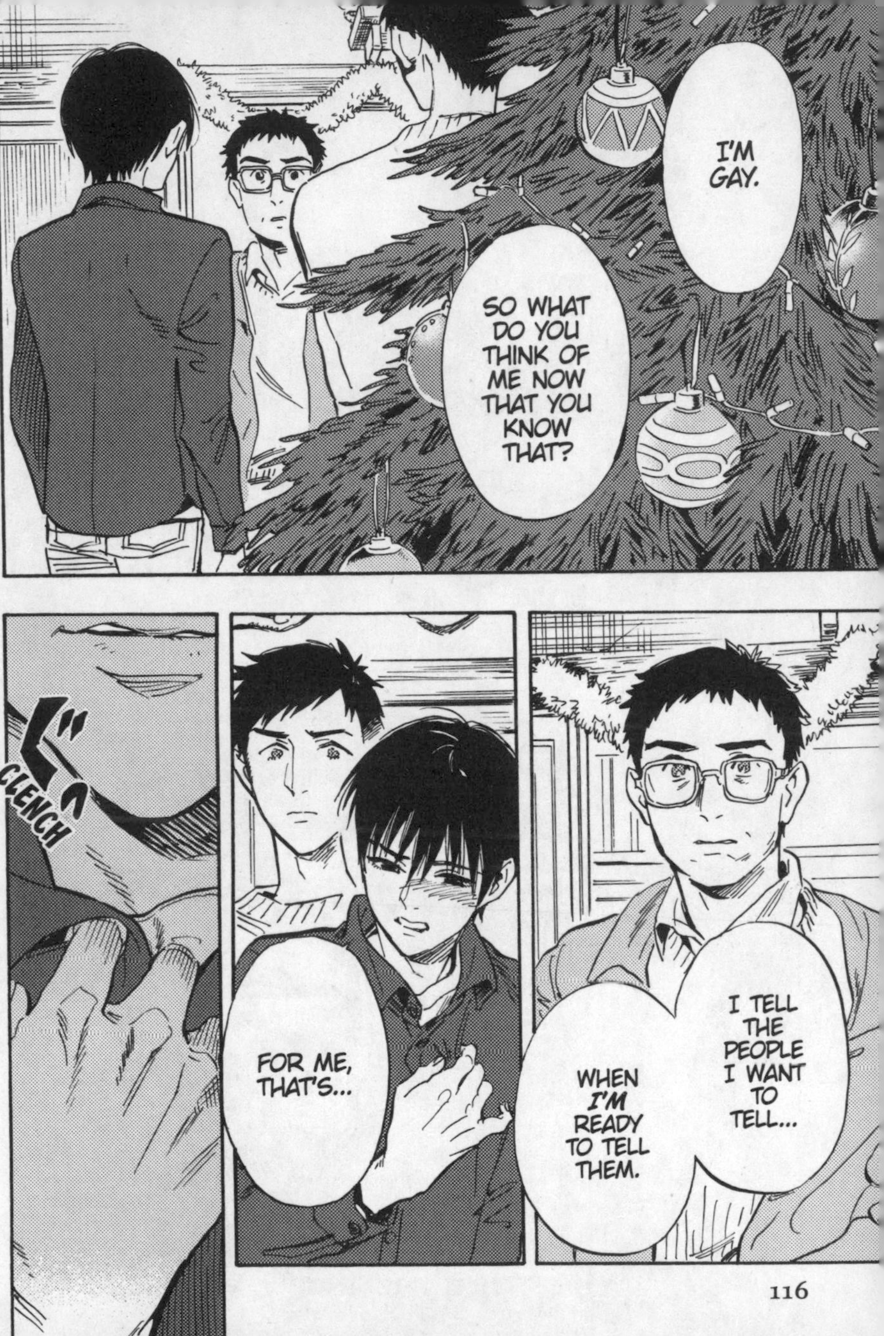
I'M GAY.
SO WHAT DO YOU THINK OF ME NOW THAT YOU KNOW THAT?
I TELL THE PEOPLE I WANT TO TELL...
WHEN *I'M* READY TO TELL THEM.
FOR ME, THAT'S...
CLENCH

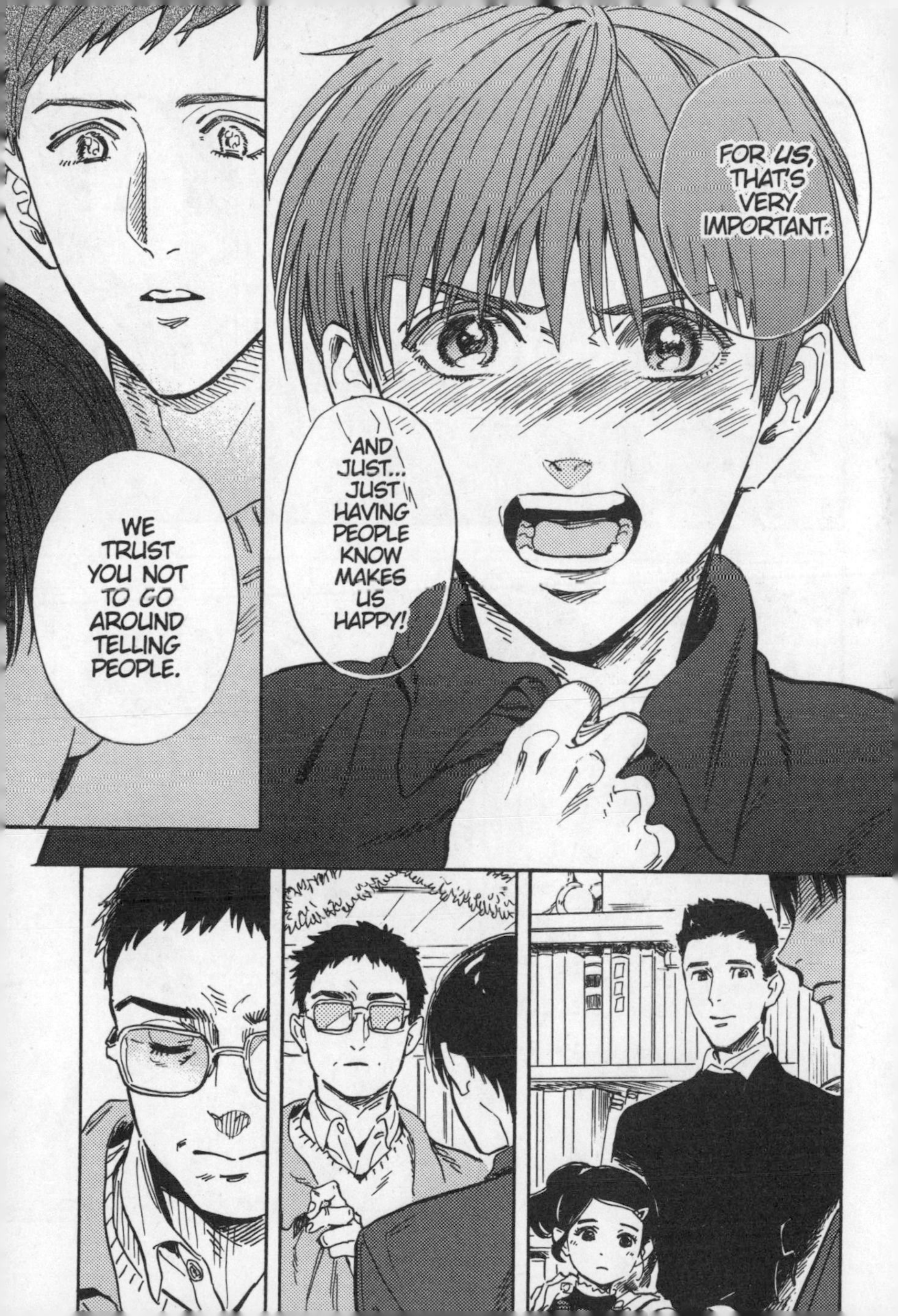
FOR US, THAT'S VERY IMPORTANT.
AND JUST... JUST HAVING PEOPLE KNOW MAKES US HAPPY!
WE TRUST YOU NOT TO GO AROUND TELLING PEOPLE.

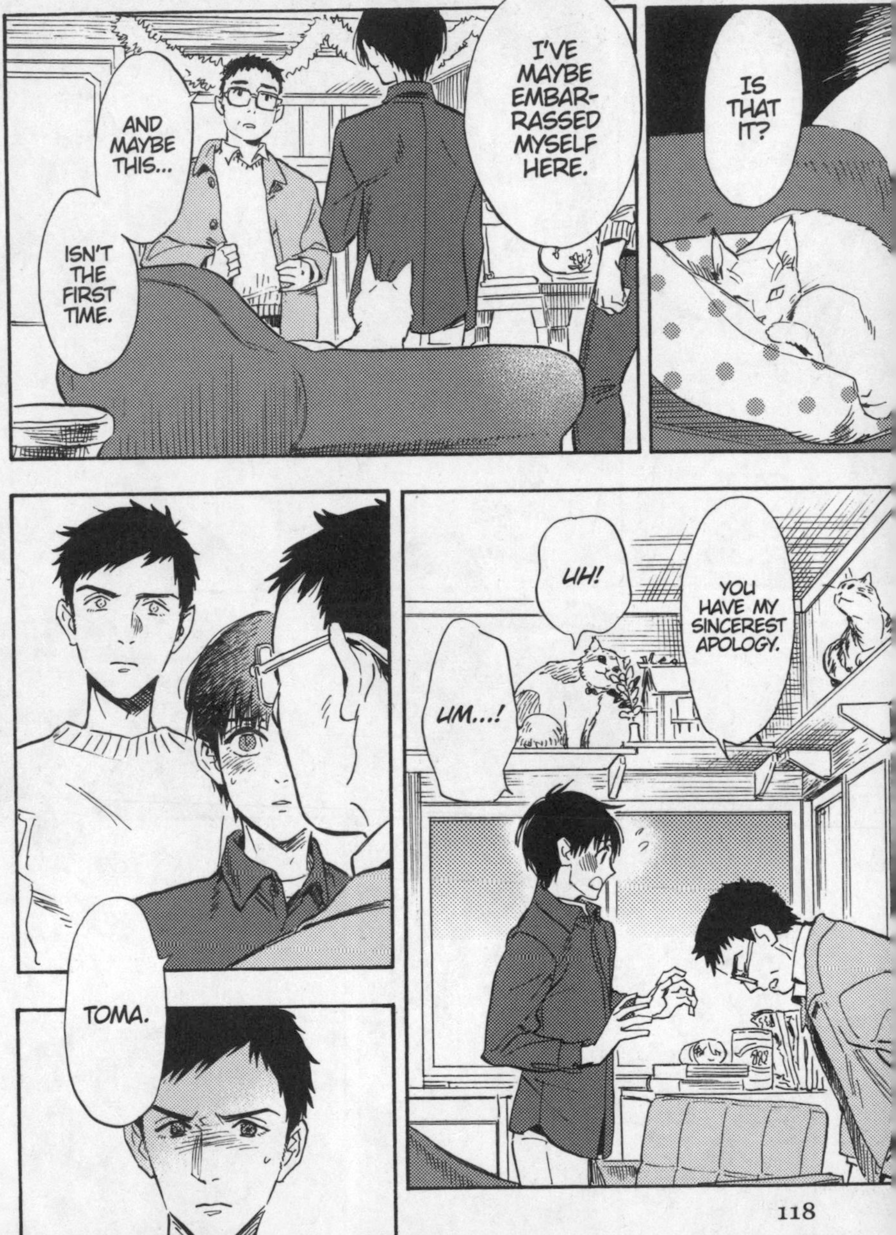
IS THAT IT?
I'VE MAYBE EMBAR-RASSED MYSELF HERE.
AND MAYBE THIS...
ISN'T THE FIRST TIME.
YOU HAVE MY SINCEREST APOLOGY.
UH!
UM...!
TOMA.

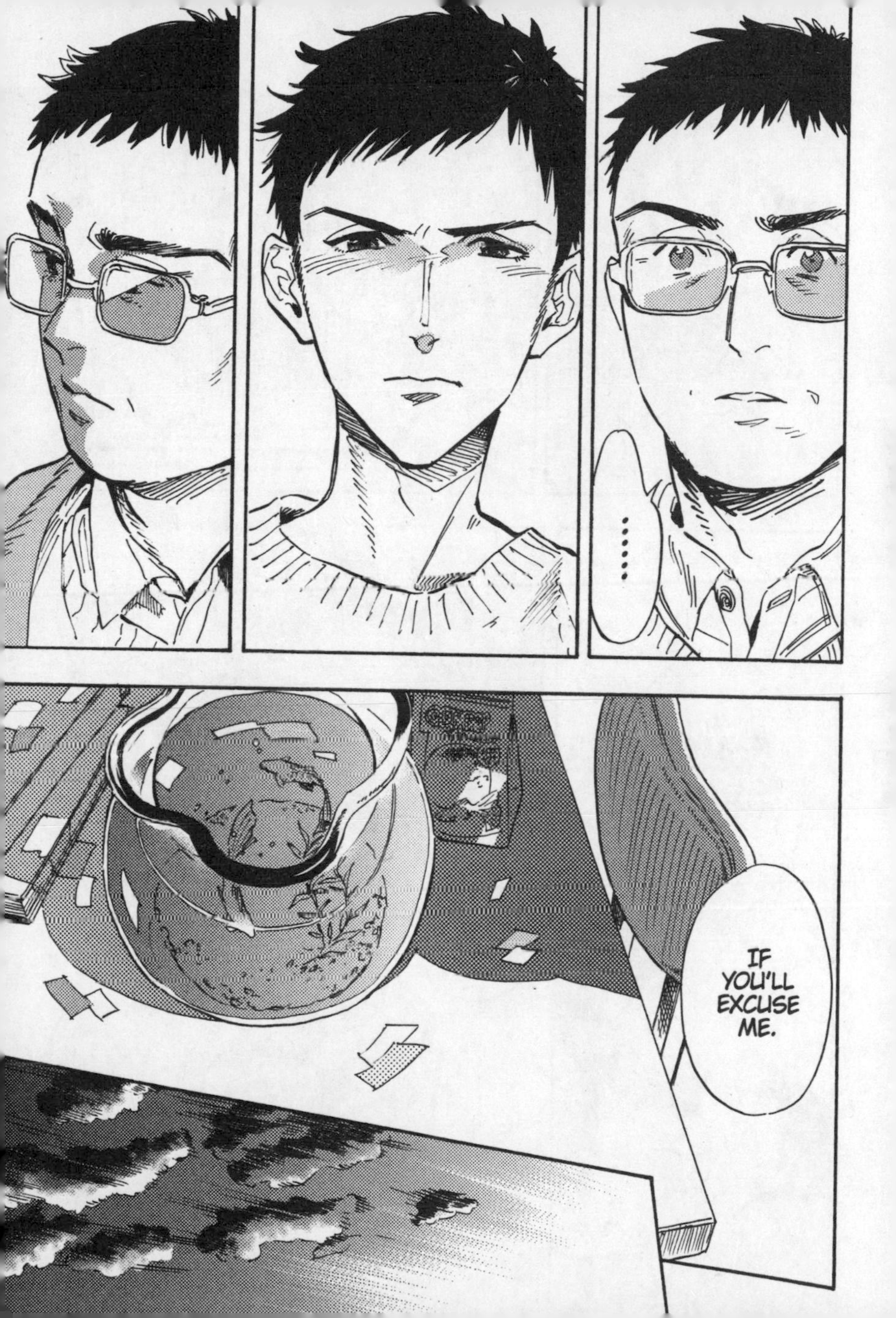
......
IF YOU'LL EXCUSE ME.

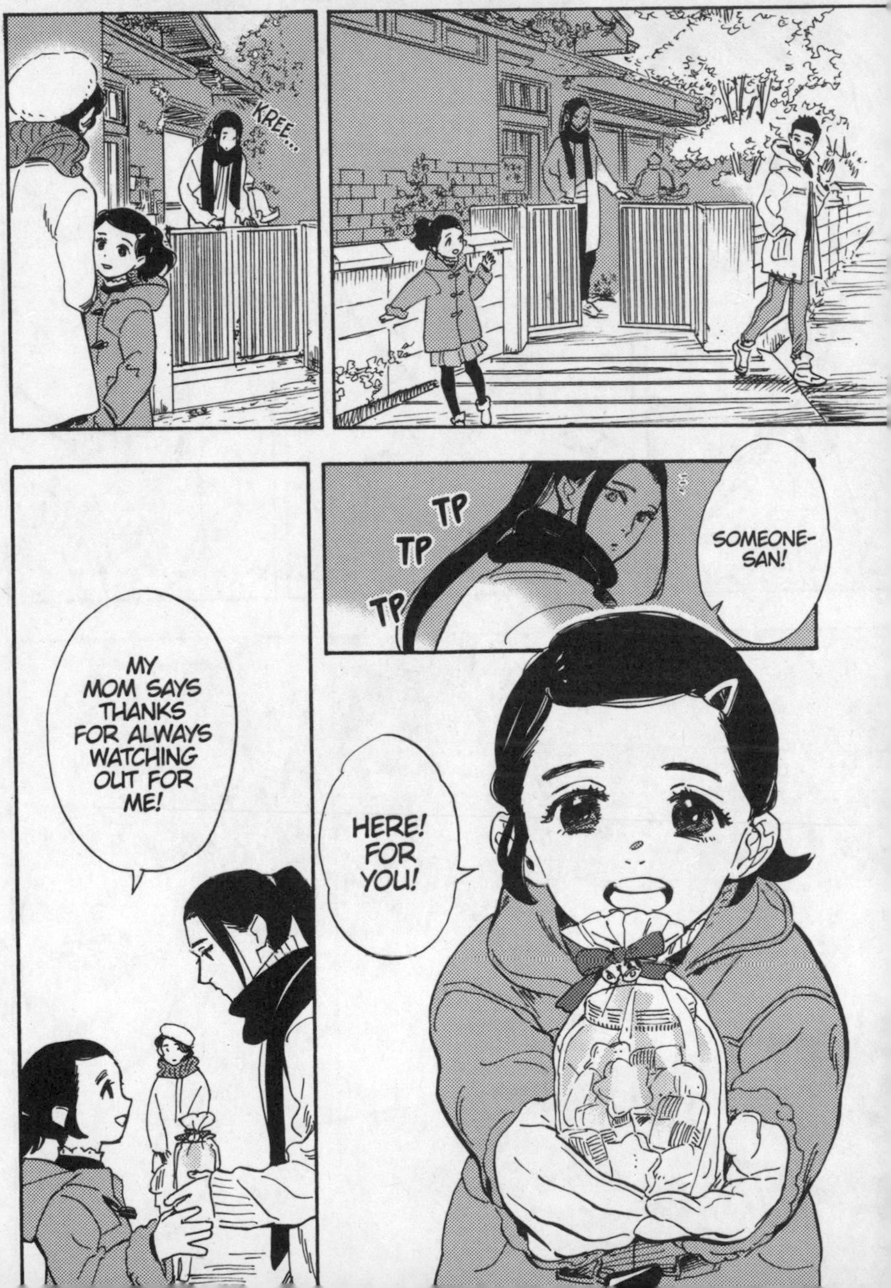
KREE...
SOMEONE-SAN!
TP
TP
TP
HERE! FOR YOU!
MY MOM SAYS THANKS FOR ALWAYS WATCHING OUT FOR ME!

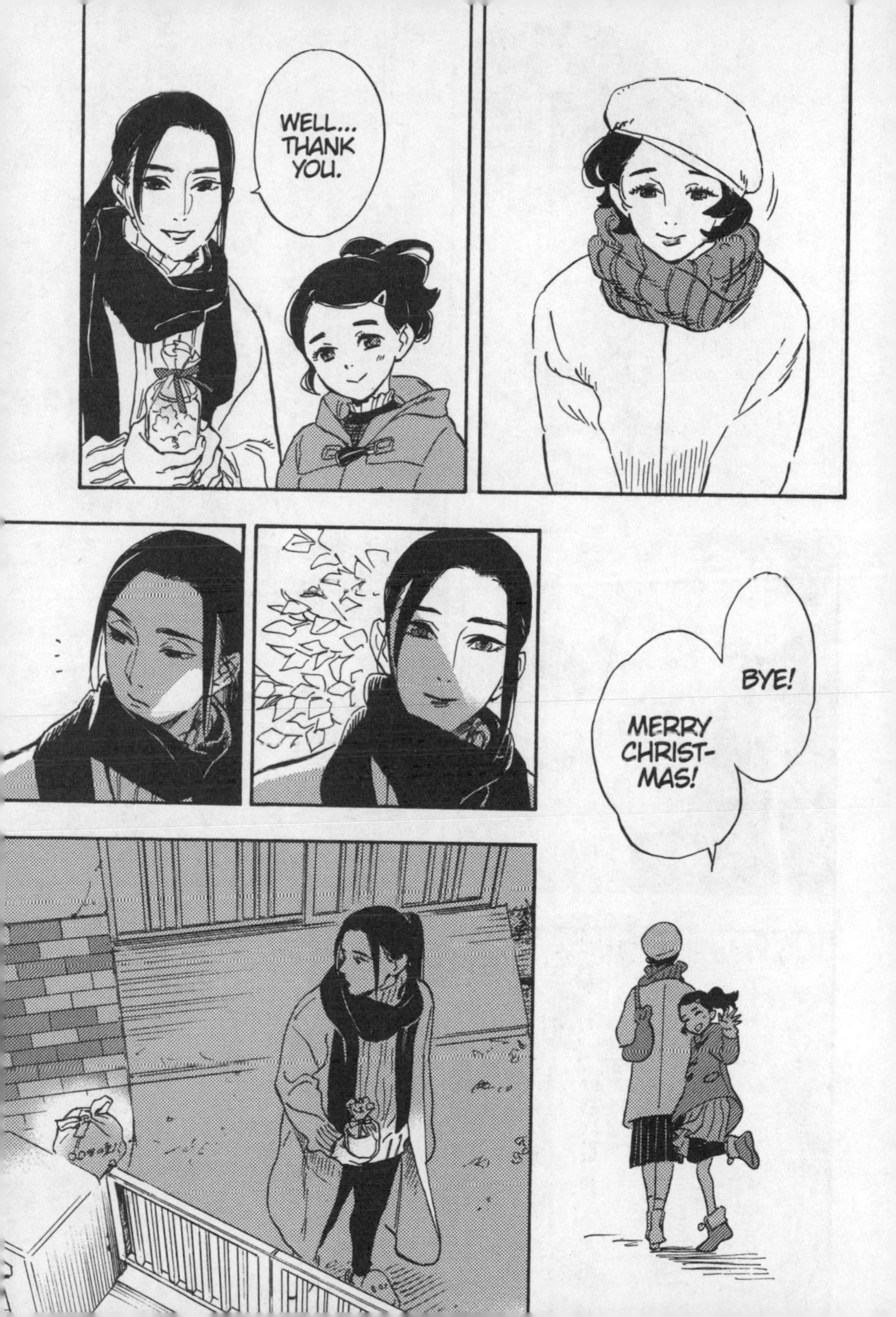
WELL... THANK YOU.
MERRY CHRISTMAS! BYE!

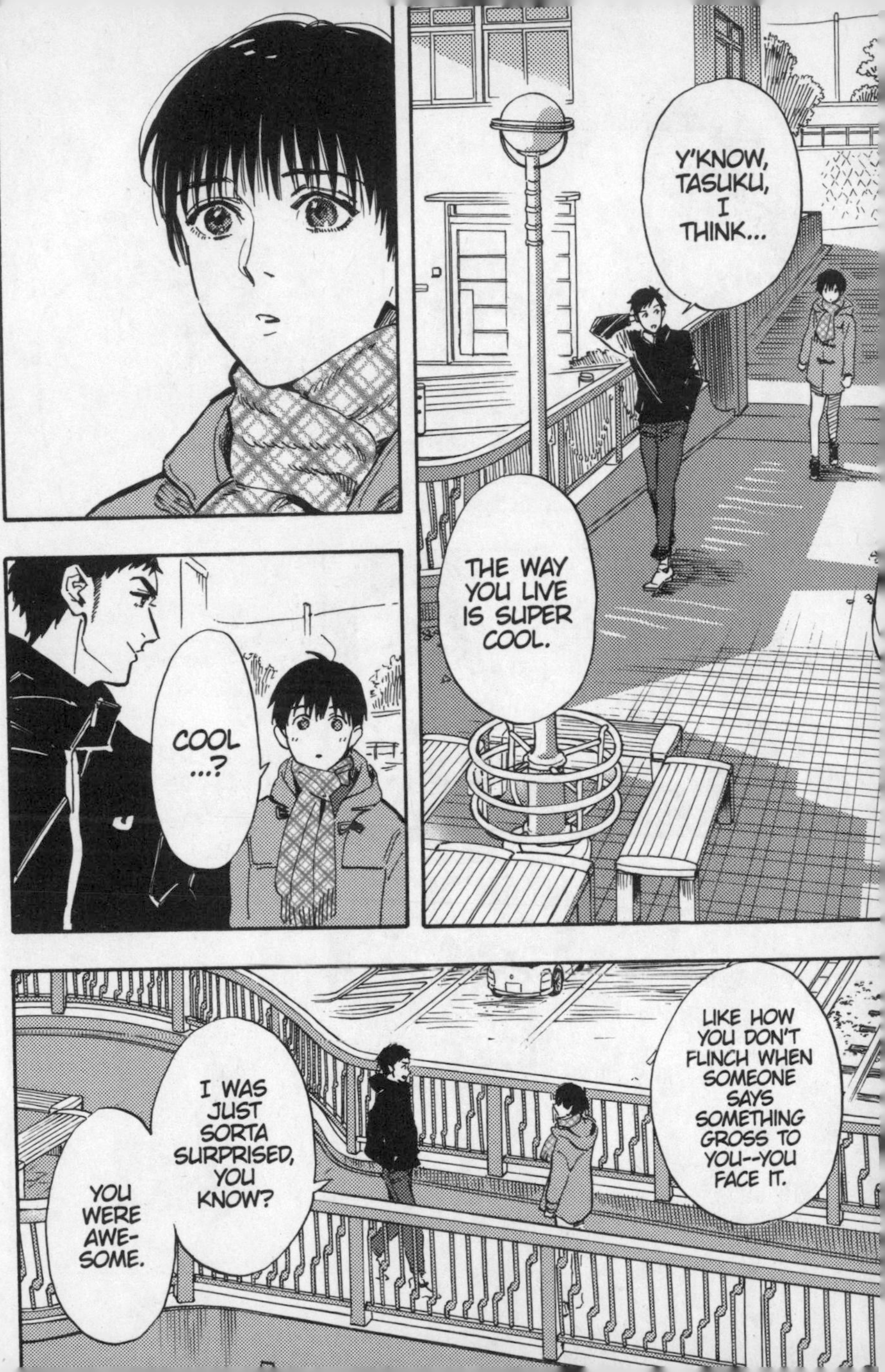
Y'KNOW, TASUKU, I THINK...
THE WAY YOU LIVE IS SUPER COOL.
COOL ...?
LIKE HOW YOU DON'T FLINCH WHEN SOMEONE SAYS SOMETHING GROSS TO YOU--YOU FACE IT.
I WAS JUST SORTA SURPRISED, YOU KNOW?
YOU WERE AWE-SOME.

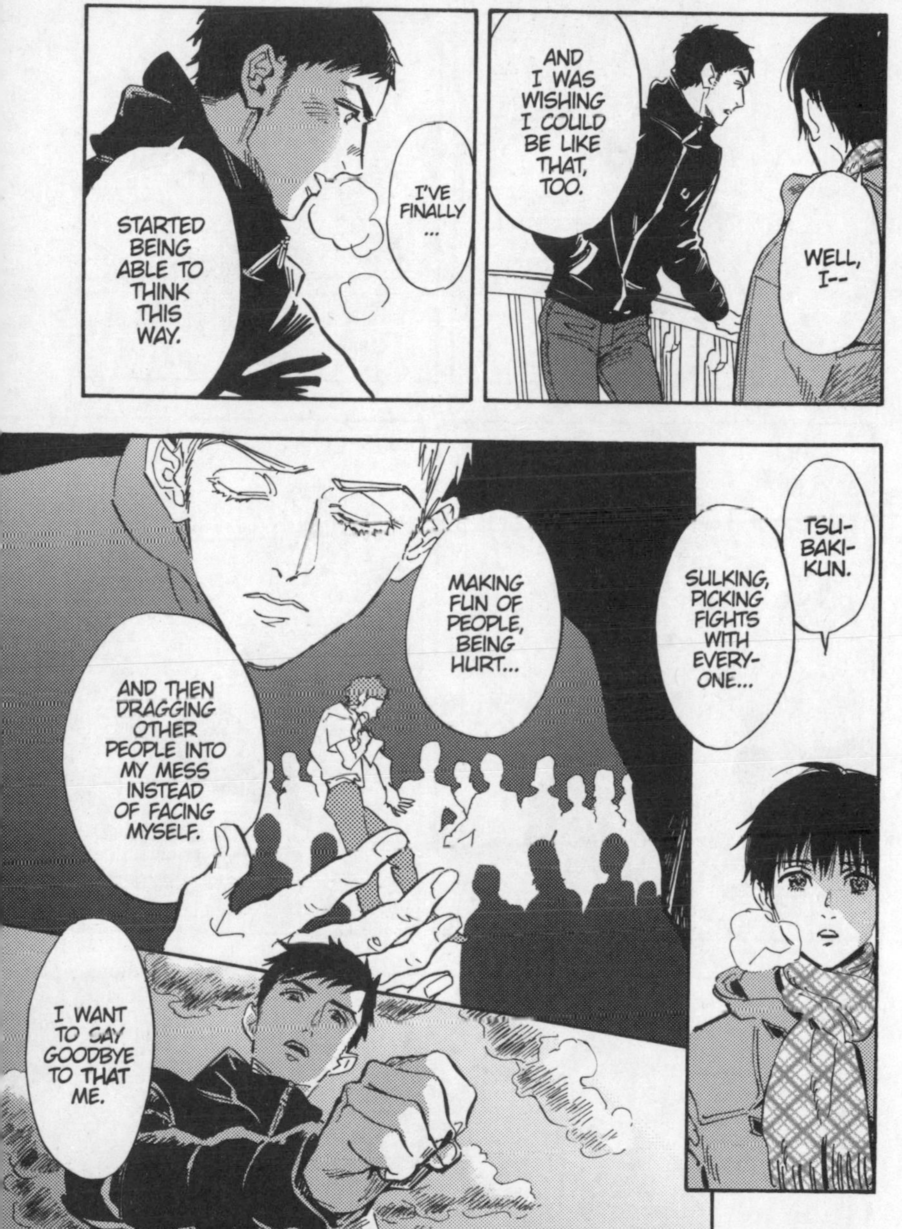
WELL, I--
AND I WAS WISHING I COULD BE LIKE THAT, TOO.
I'VE FINALLY ...
STARTED BEING ABLE TO THINK THIS WAY.
TSU-BAKI-KUN.
SULKING, PICKING FIGHTS WITH EVERY-ONE...
MAKING FUN OF PEOPLE, BEING HURT...
AND THEN DRAGGING OTHER PEOPLE INTO MY MESS INSTEAD OF FACING MYSELF.
I WANT TO SAY GOODBYE TO THAT ME.

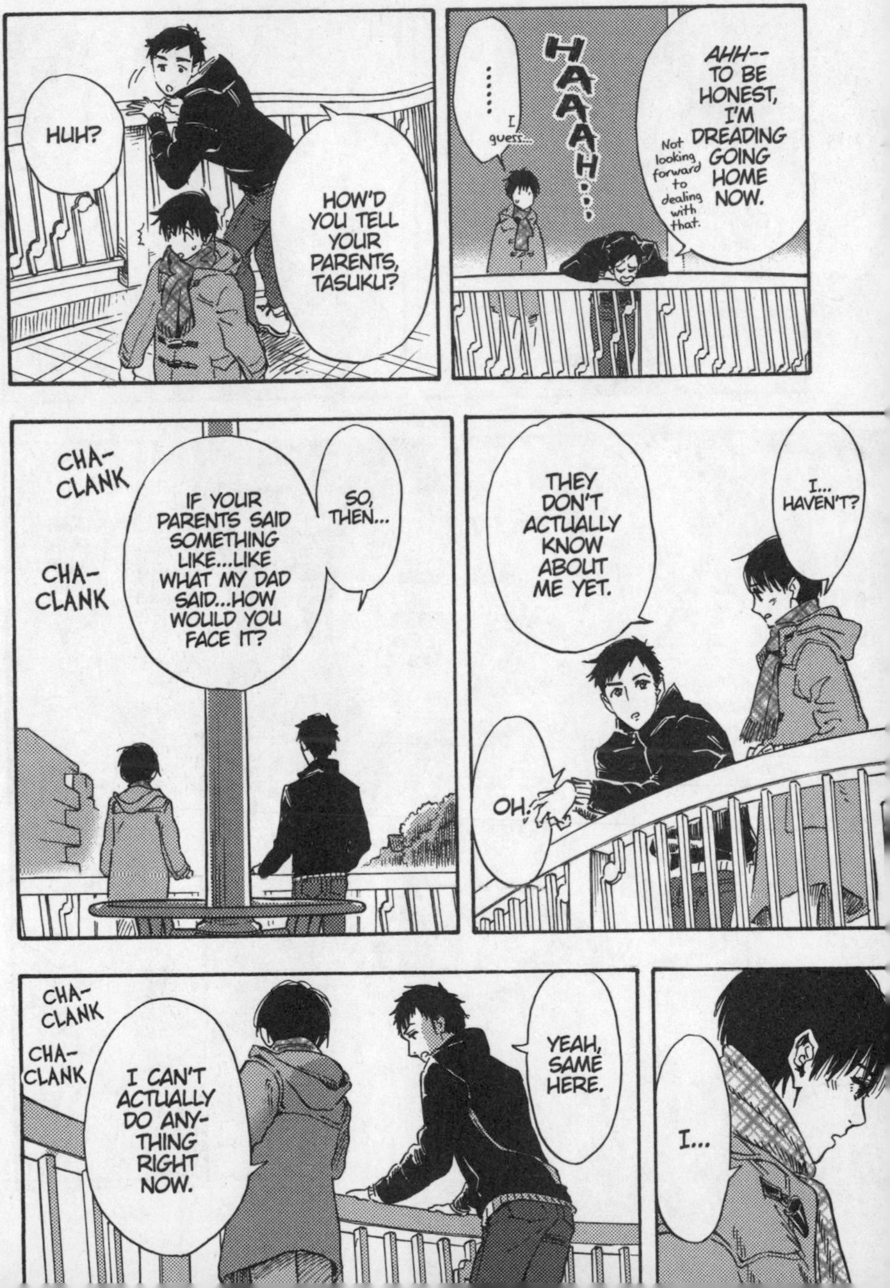
AHH-- TO BE HONEST, I'M DREADING GOING HOME NOW.
Not looking forward to dealing with that.
HAAAAH...
I guess...
......
HOW'D YOU TELL YOUR PARENTS, TASUKU?
HUH?
I... HAVEN'T?
THEY DON'T ACTUALLY KNOW ABOUT ME YET.
OH.
SO, THEN...
IF YOUR PARENTS SAID SOMETHING LIKE...LIKE WHAT MY DAD SAID...HOW WOULD YOU FACE IT?
CHA-CLANK
CHA-CLANK
I...
YEAH, SAME HERE.
I CAN'T ACTUALLY DO ANY-THING RIGHT NOW.
CHA-CLANK
CHA-CLANK

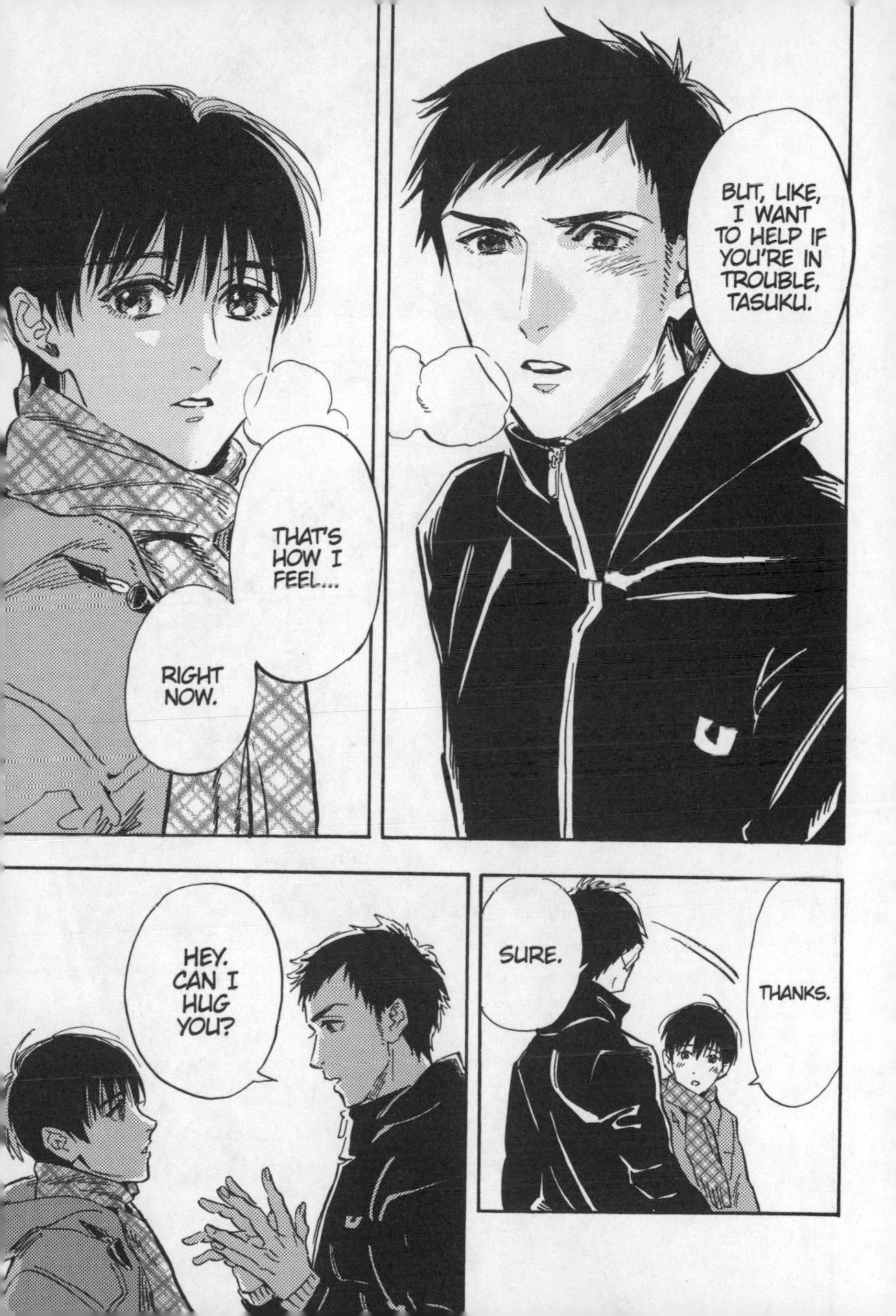
THAT'S HOW I FEEL...
RIGHT NOW.
BUT, LIKE, I WANT TO HELP IF YOU'RE IN TROUBLE, TASUKU.
HEY. CAN I HUG YOU?
SURE.
THANKS.

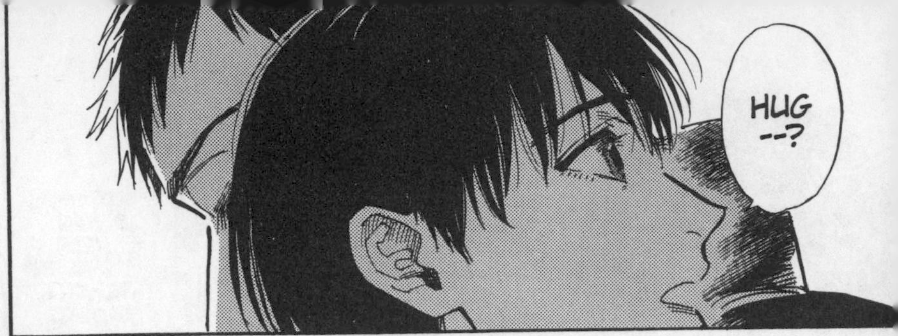
HUG --?
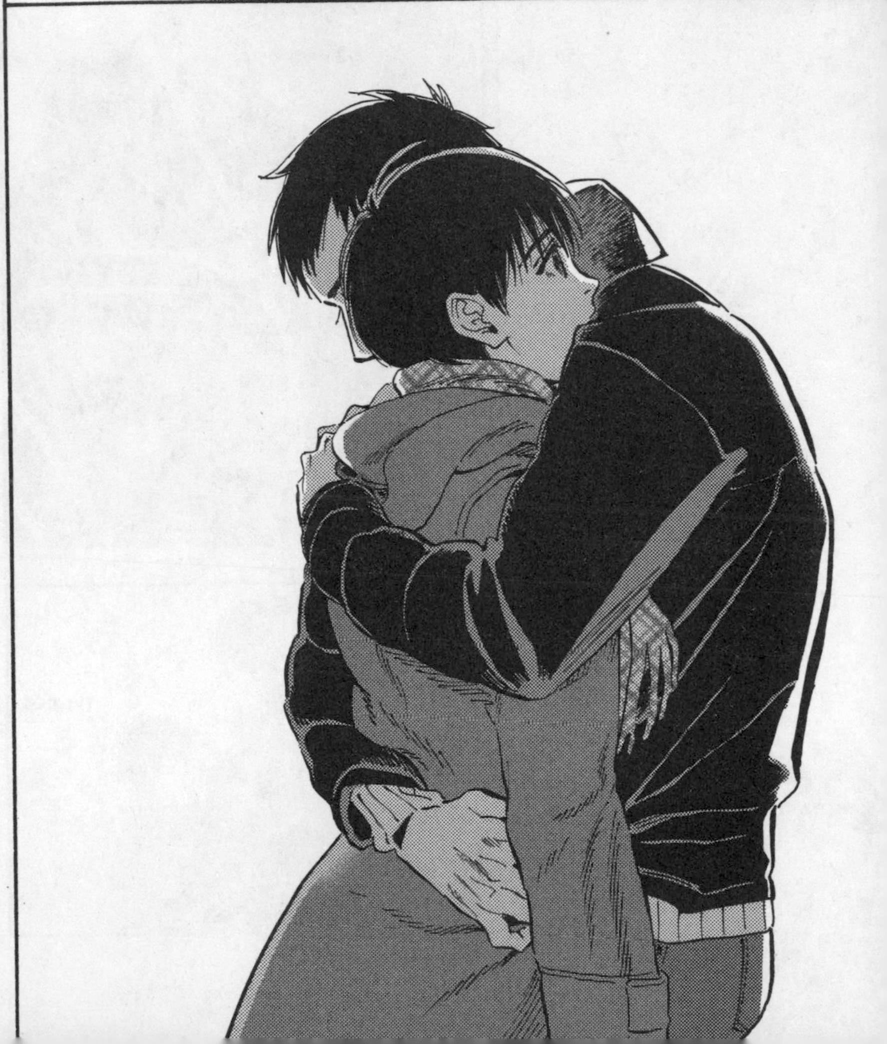

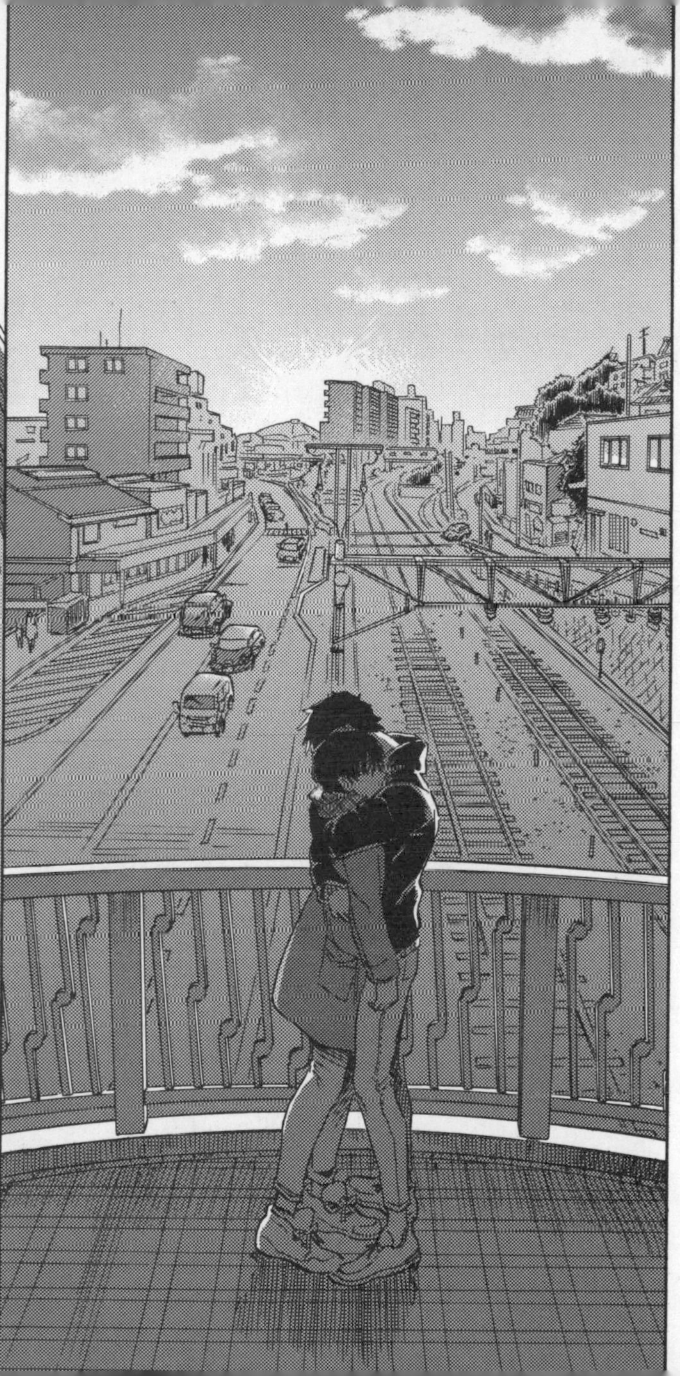

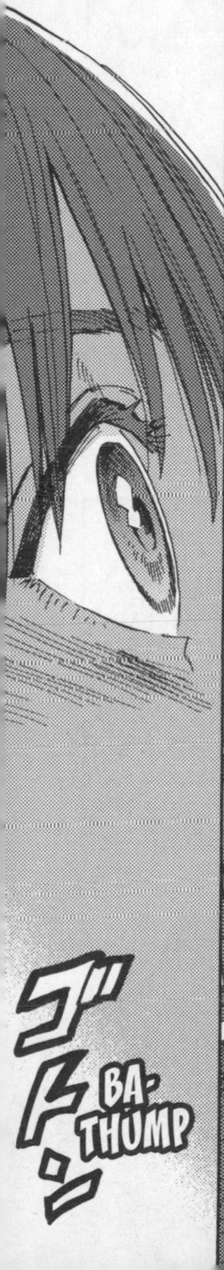
ドキン
BA-THUMP

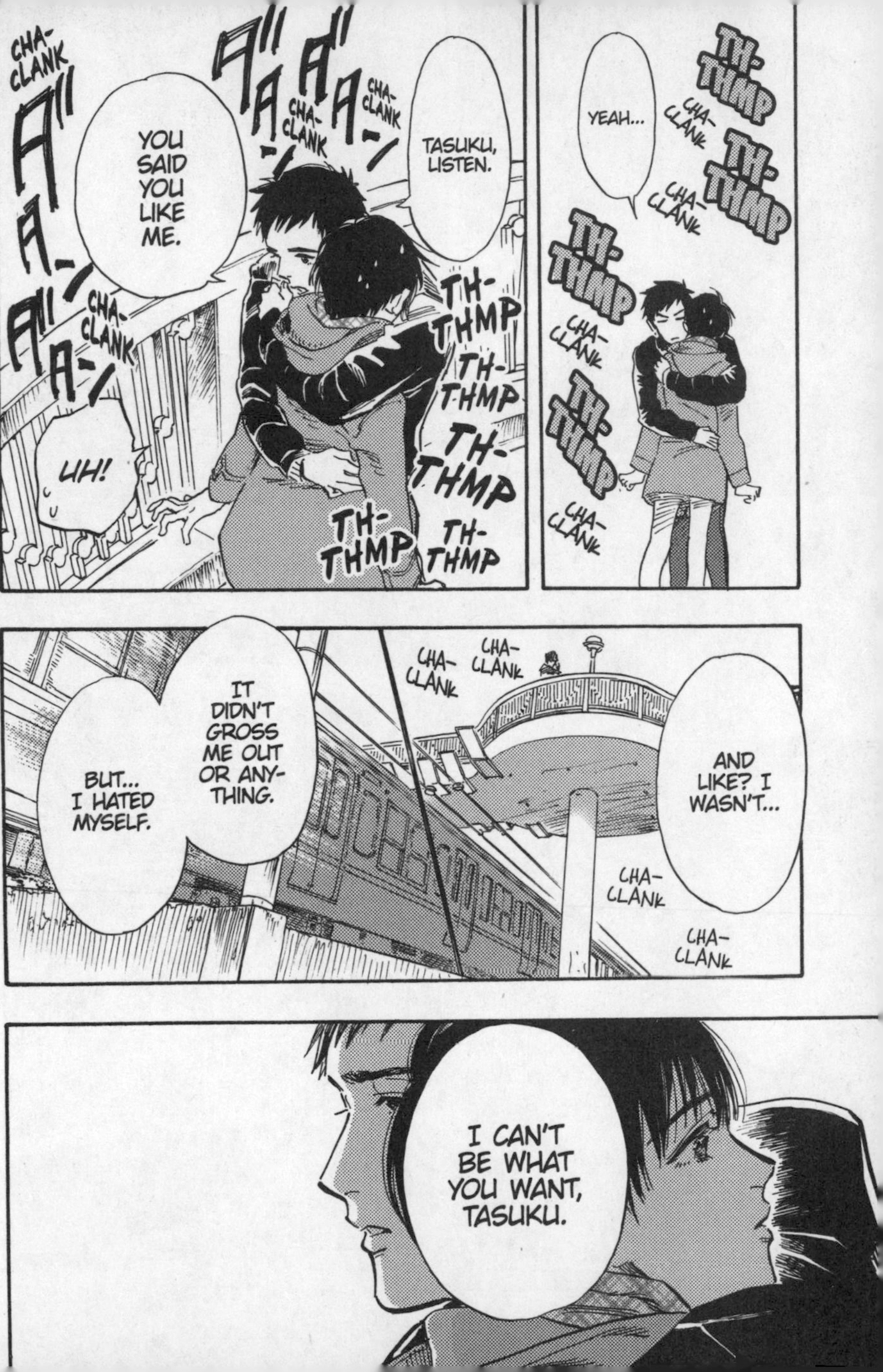
TH-THMP
CHA-CLANK
TH-THMP
CHA-CLANK
YEAH...
TH-THMP
CHA-CLANK
TH-THMP
CHA-CLANK
TASUKU, LISTEN.
CHA-CLANK
CHA-CLANK
YOU SAID YOU LIKE ME.
CHA-CLANK
CHA-CLANK
TH-THMP
TH-THMP
TH-THMP
TH-THMP
TH-THMP
UH!
CHA-CLANK
CHA-CLANK
AND LIKE? I WASN'T...
CHA-CLANK
CHA-CLANK
IT DIDN'T GROSS ME OUT OR ANY-THING.
BUT... I HATED MYSELF.
I CAN'T BE WHAT YOU WANT, TASUKU.

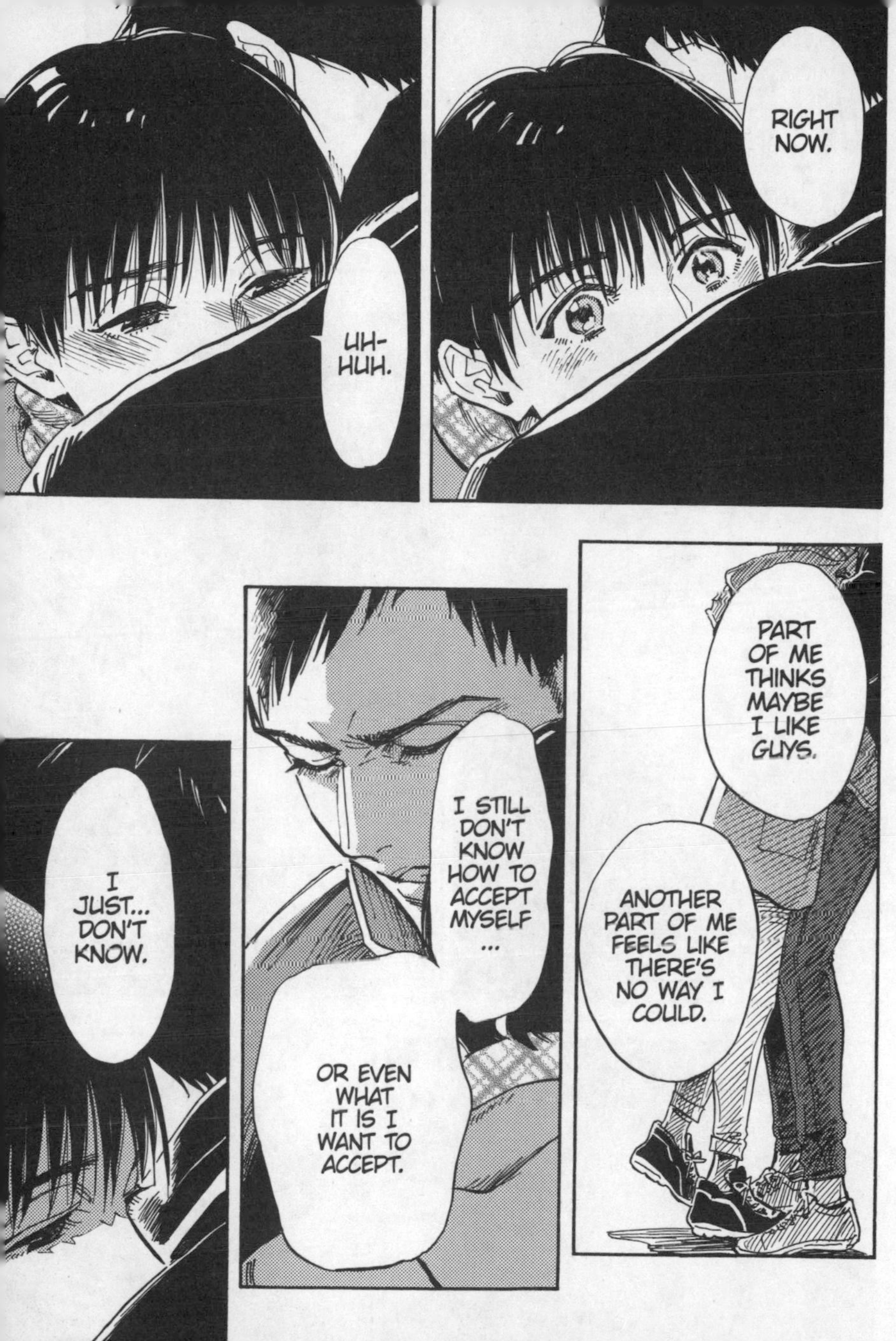
RIGHT NOW.
UH-HUH.
PART OF ME THINKS MAYBE I LIKE GUYS.
ANOTHER PART OF ME FEELS LIKE THERE'S NO WAY I COULD.
I STILL DON'T KNOW HOW TO ACCEPT MYSELF...
OR EVEN WHAT IT IS I WANT TO ACCEPT.
I JUST... DON'T KNOW.

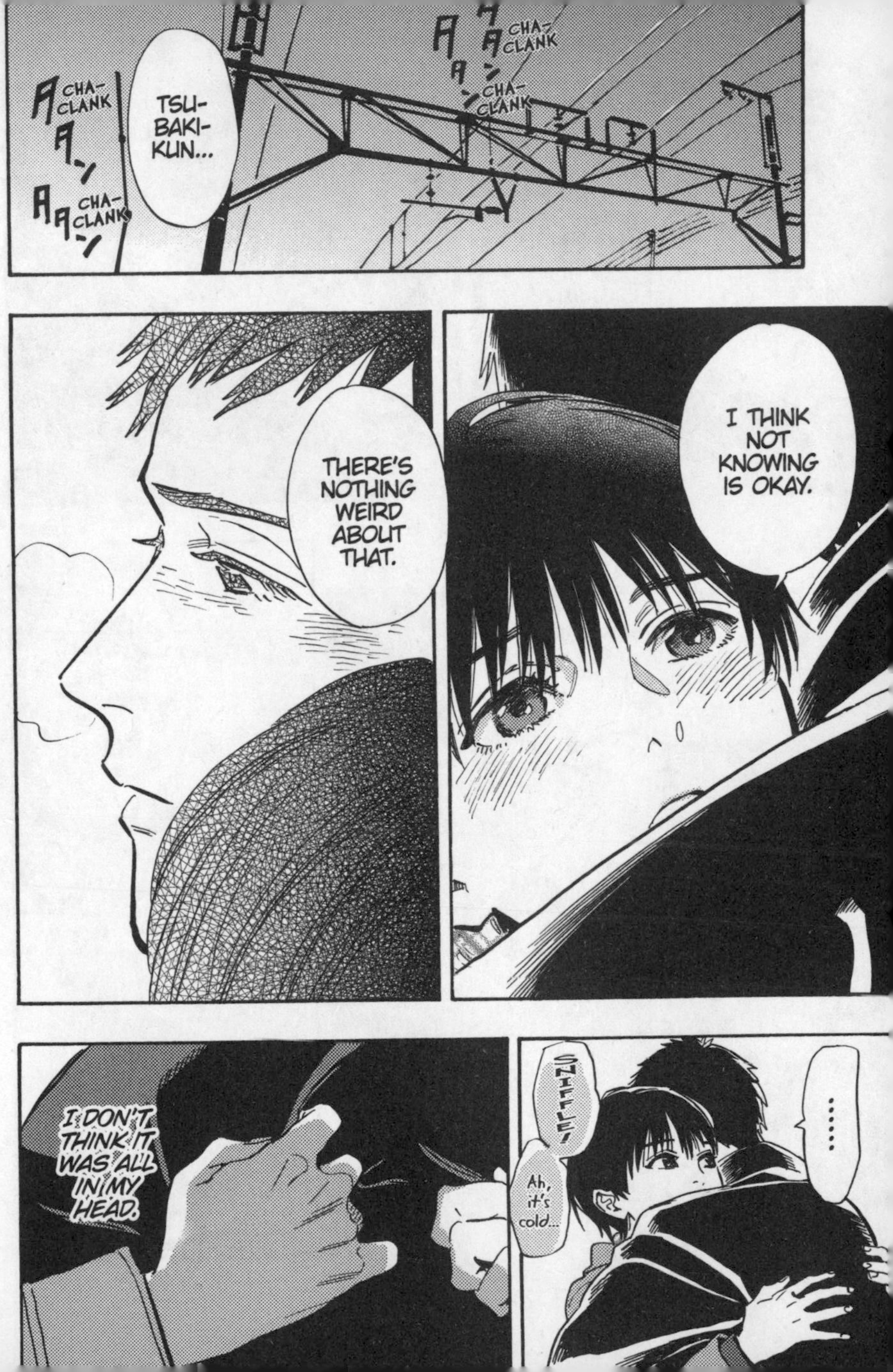
CHA-CLANK
CHA-CLANK
TSU-BAKI-KUN...
CHA-CLANK
CHA-CLANK
I THINK NOT KNOWING IS OKAY.
THERE'S NOTHING WEIRD ABOUT THAT.
......
SNIFFLE!
Ah, it's cold...
I DON'T THINK IT WAS ALL IN MY HEAD.

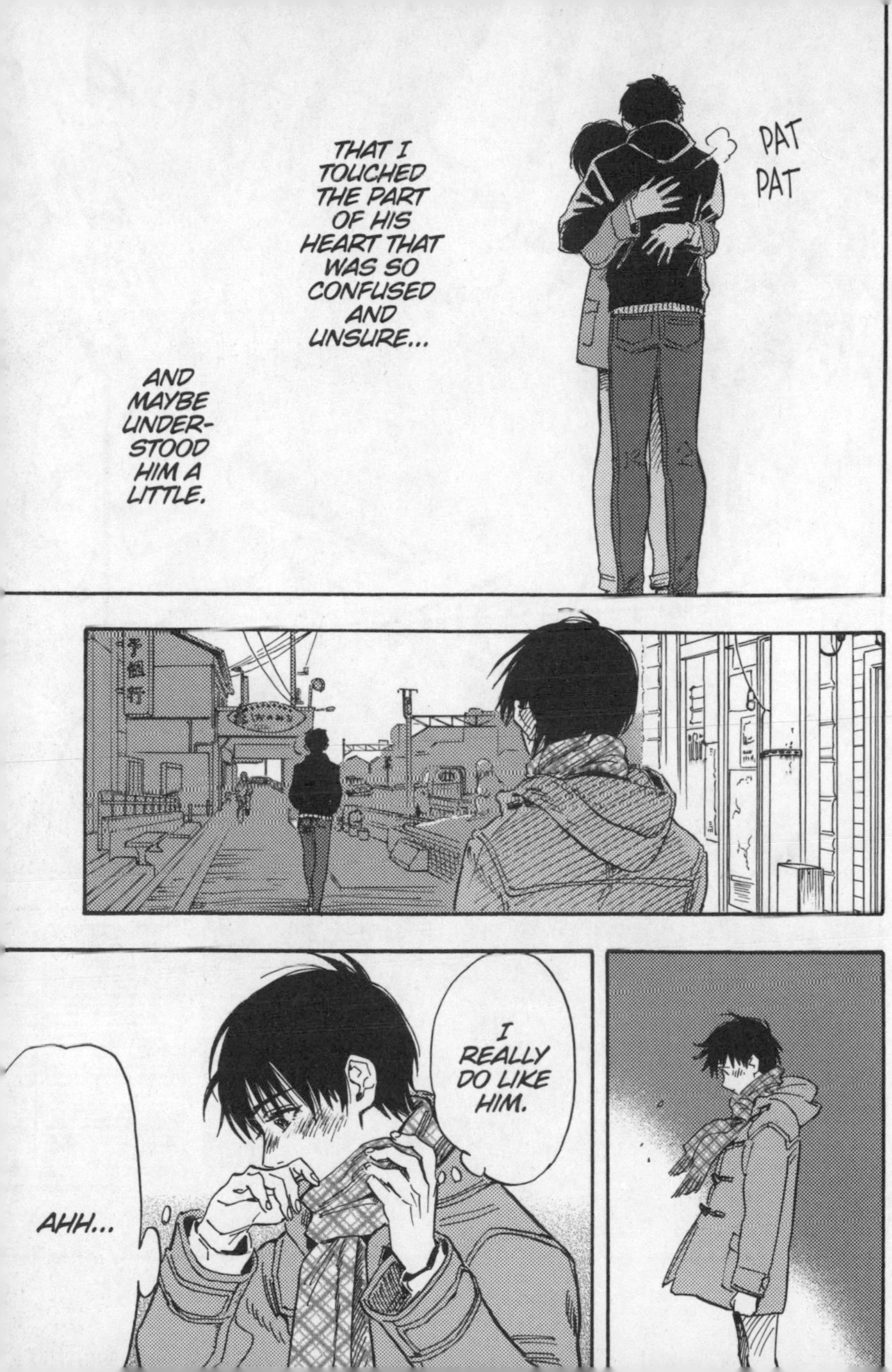
PAT PAT
THAT I TOUCHED THE PART OF HIS HEART THAT WAS SO CONFUSED AND UNSURE...
AND MAYBE UNDER-STOOD HIM A LITTLE.
I REALLY DO LIKE HIM.
AHH...

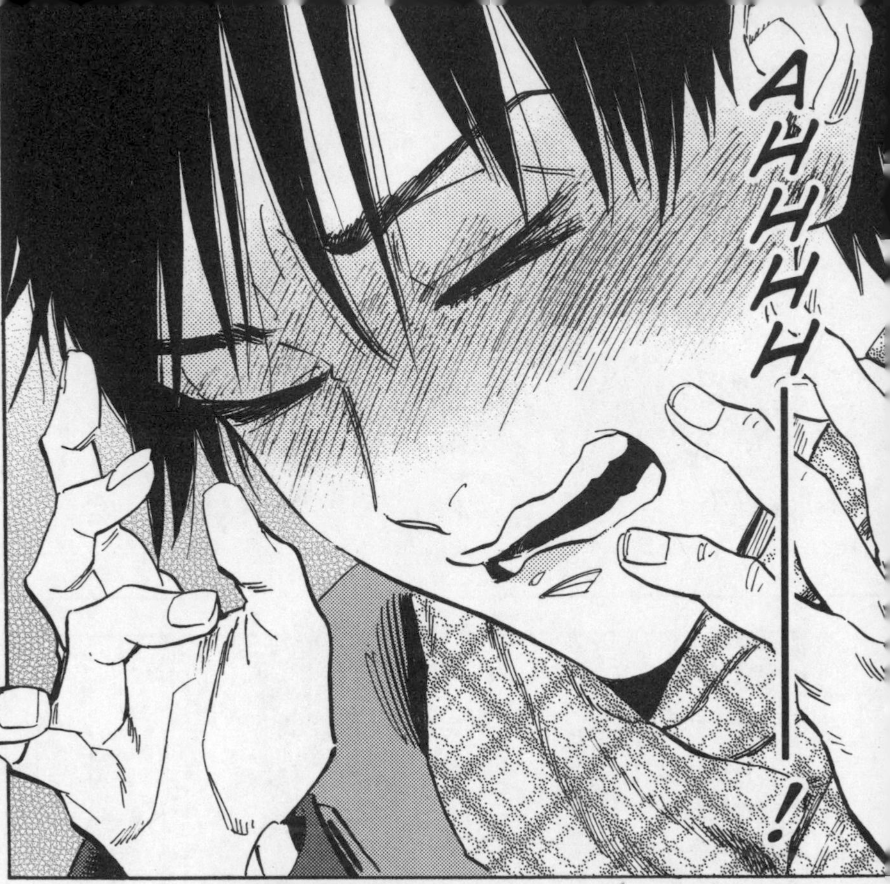
AHHHH—!
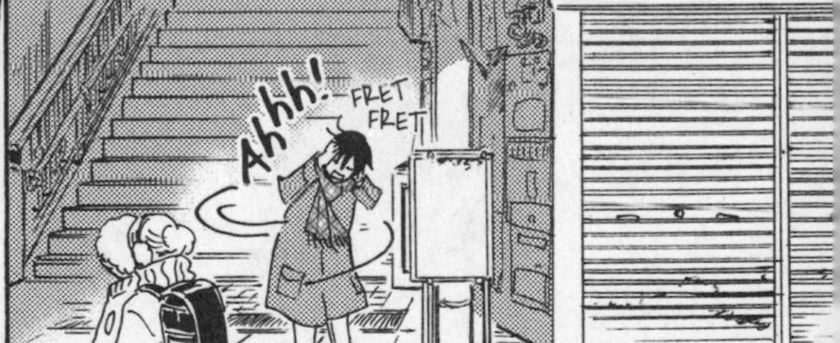
Ahhh!
FRET FRET
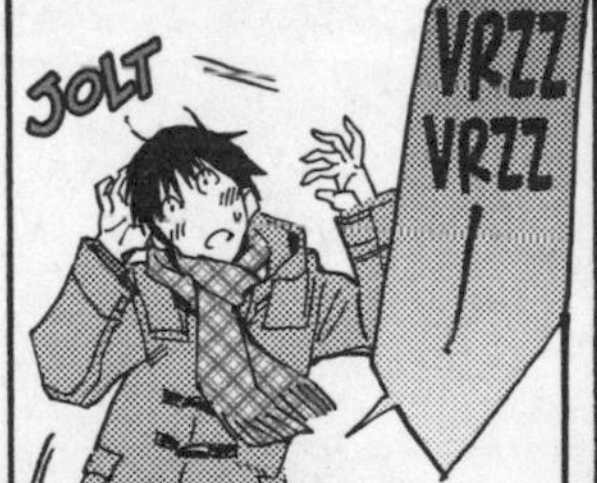
JOLT
VRZZ VRZZ

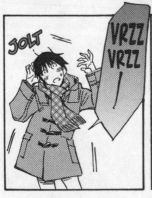

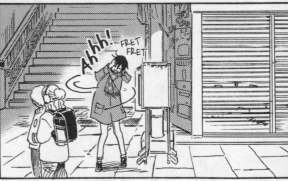

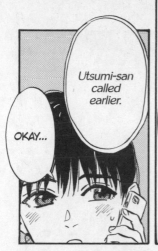

Tasukun? You got a sec?
DAICHI-SAN!
SURE. WHAT'S UP?
Utsumi-san called earlier.
OKAY...
He told me about what happened over there.
Sorry you got dragged into this.
HOLIDAY HOURS
OH...NO, DON'T WORRY ABOUT ME.
I mean, what matters is...
is Saki-san okay...?
SUUU-UUPER GOOD. SHE'S CHOWING DOWN ON DRIED SQUID AS WE SPEAK.
MNCH MNCH
Dried squid?

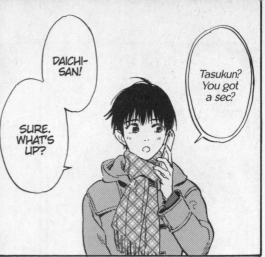

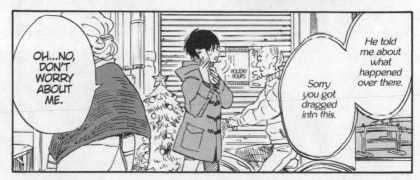

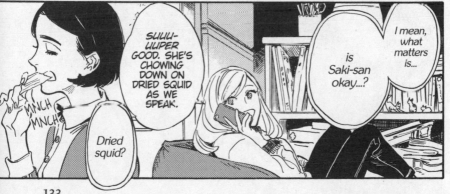

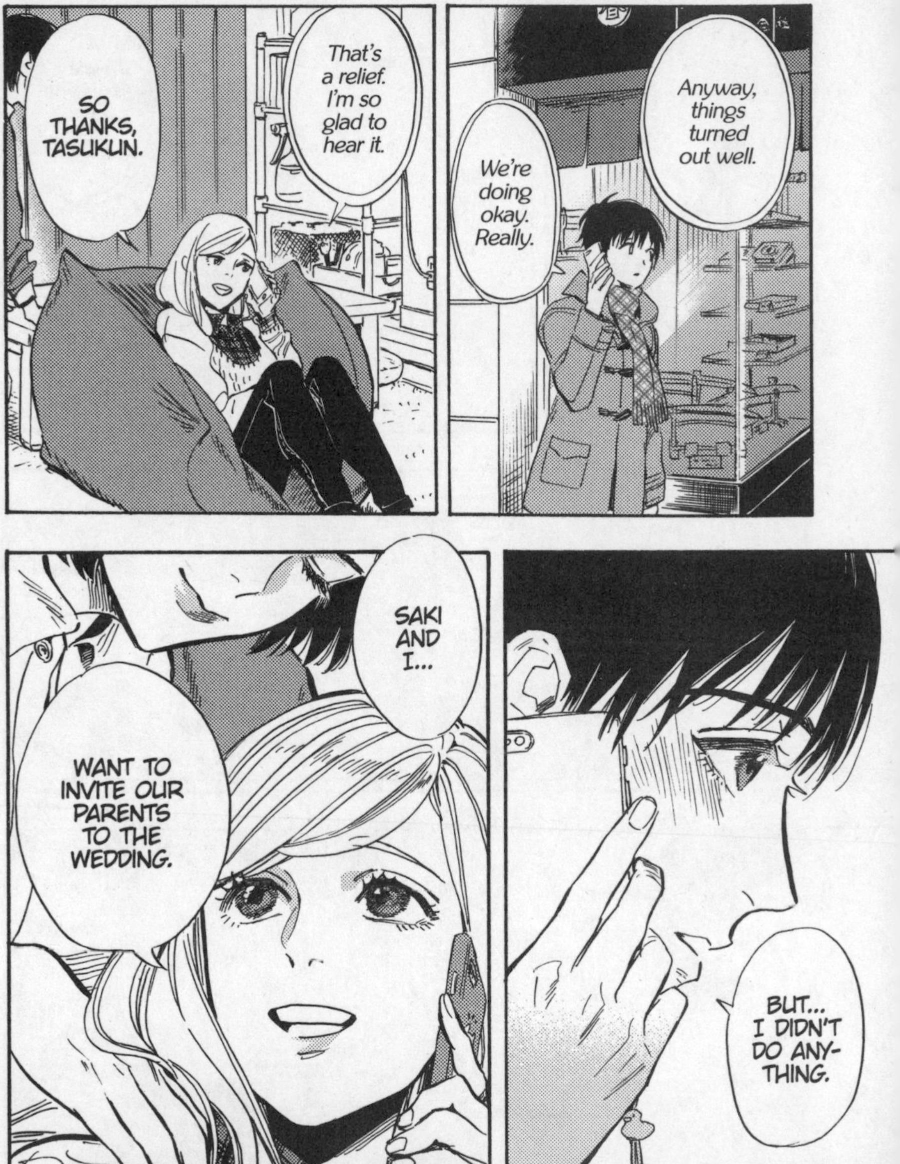
Anyway, things turned out well.
We're doing okay. Really.
That's a relief. I'm so glad to hear it.
SO THANKS, TASUKUN.
BUT... I DIDN'T DO ANY-THING.
SAKI AND I...
WANT TO INVITE OUR PARENTS TO THE WEDDING.

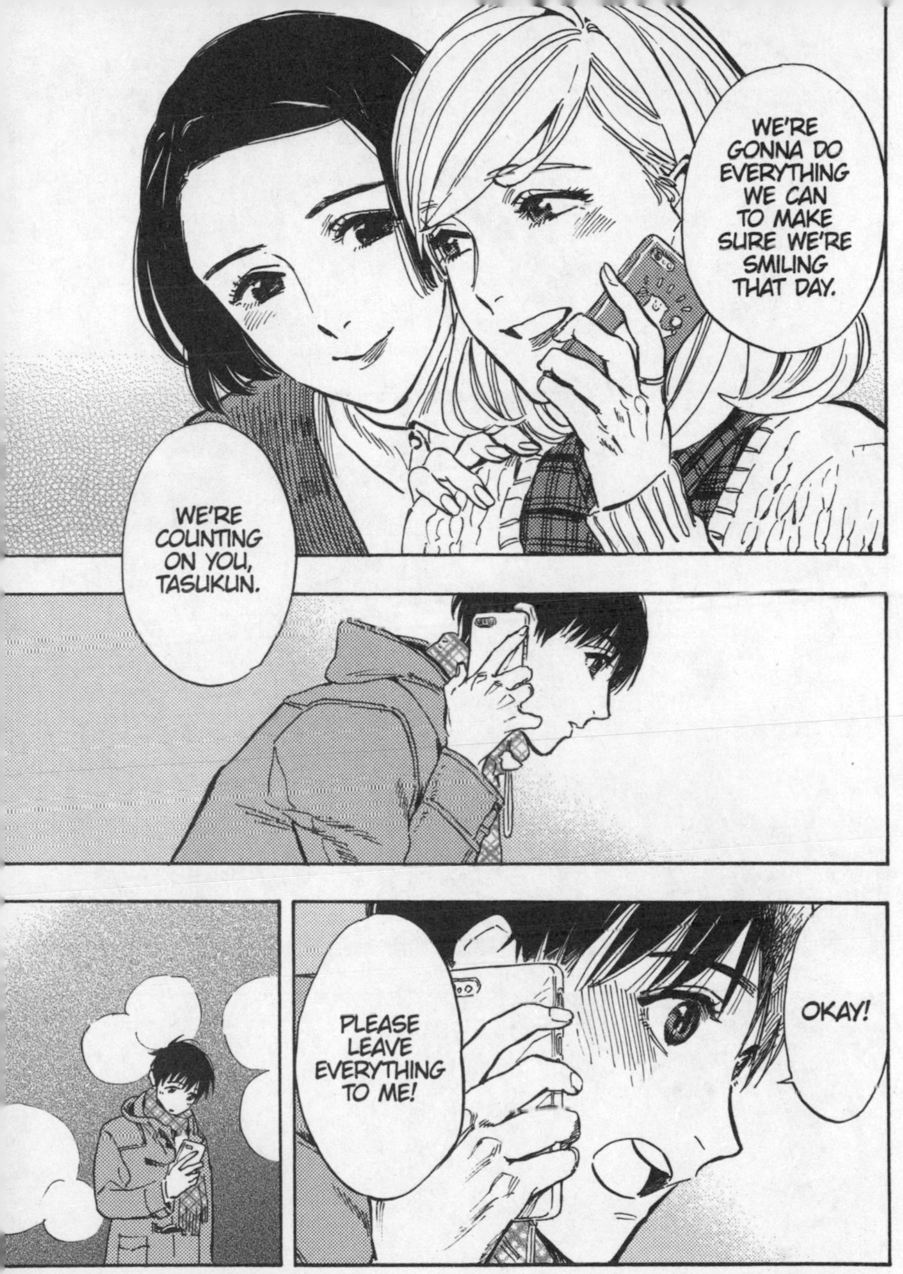
WE'RE GONNA DO EVERYTHING WE CAN TO MAKE SURE WE'RE SMILING THAT DAY.
WE'RE COUNTING ON YOU, TASUKUN.
OKAY!
PLEASE LEAVE EVERYTHING TO ME!

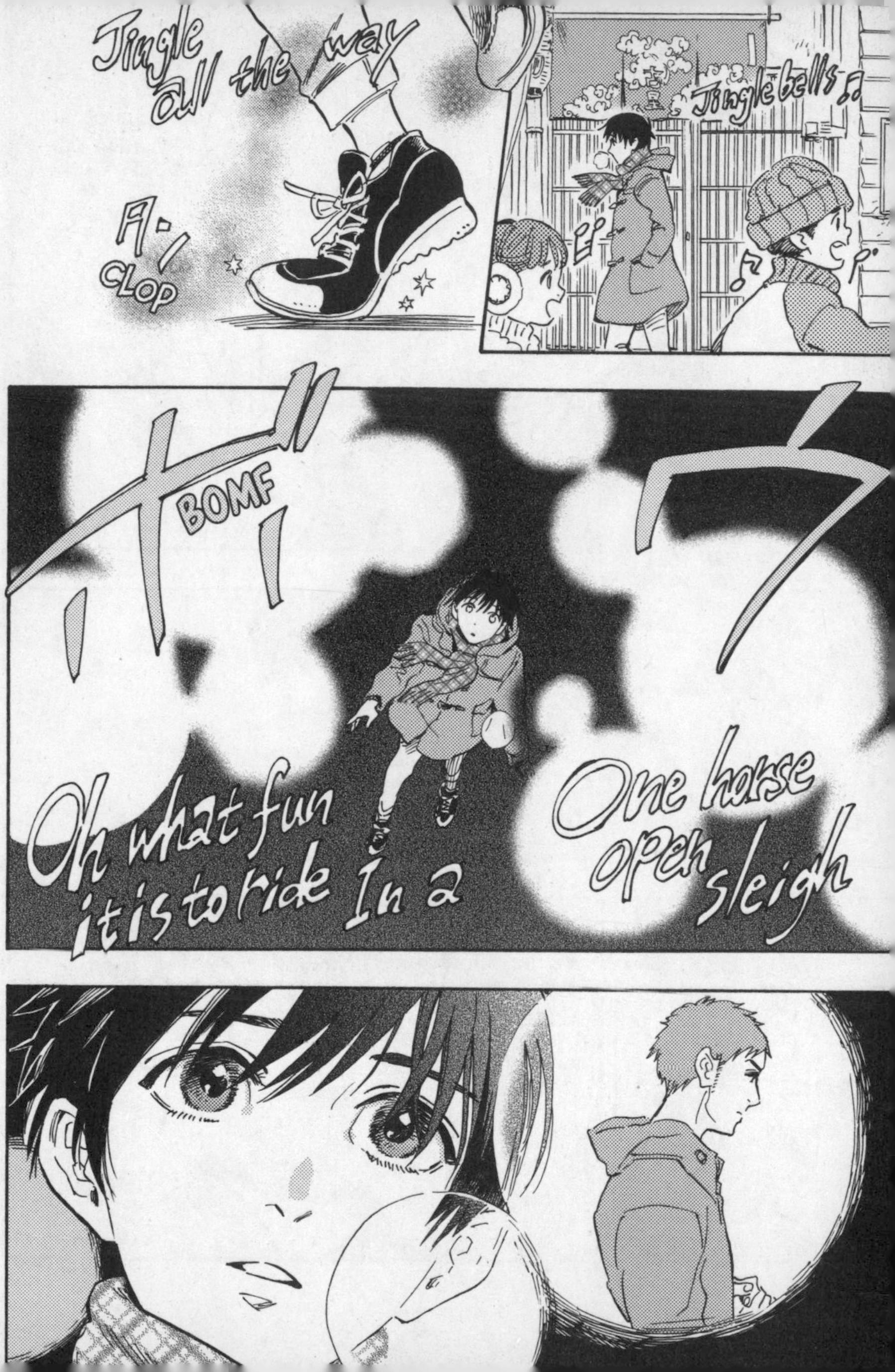
Jingle bells ♫
Jingle all the way
CLOP
BOMF
Oh what fun it is to ride In a
One horse open sleigh

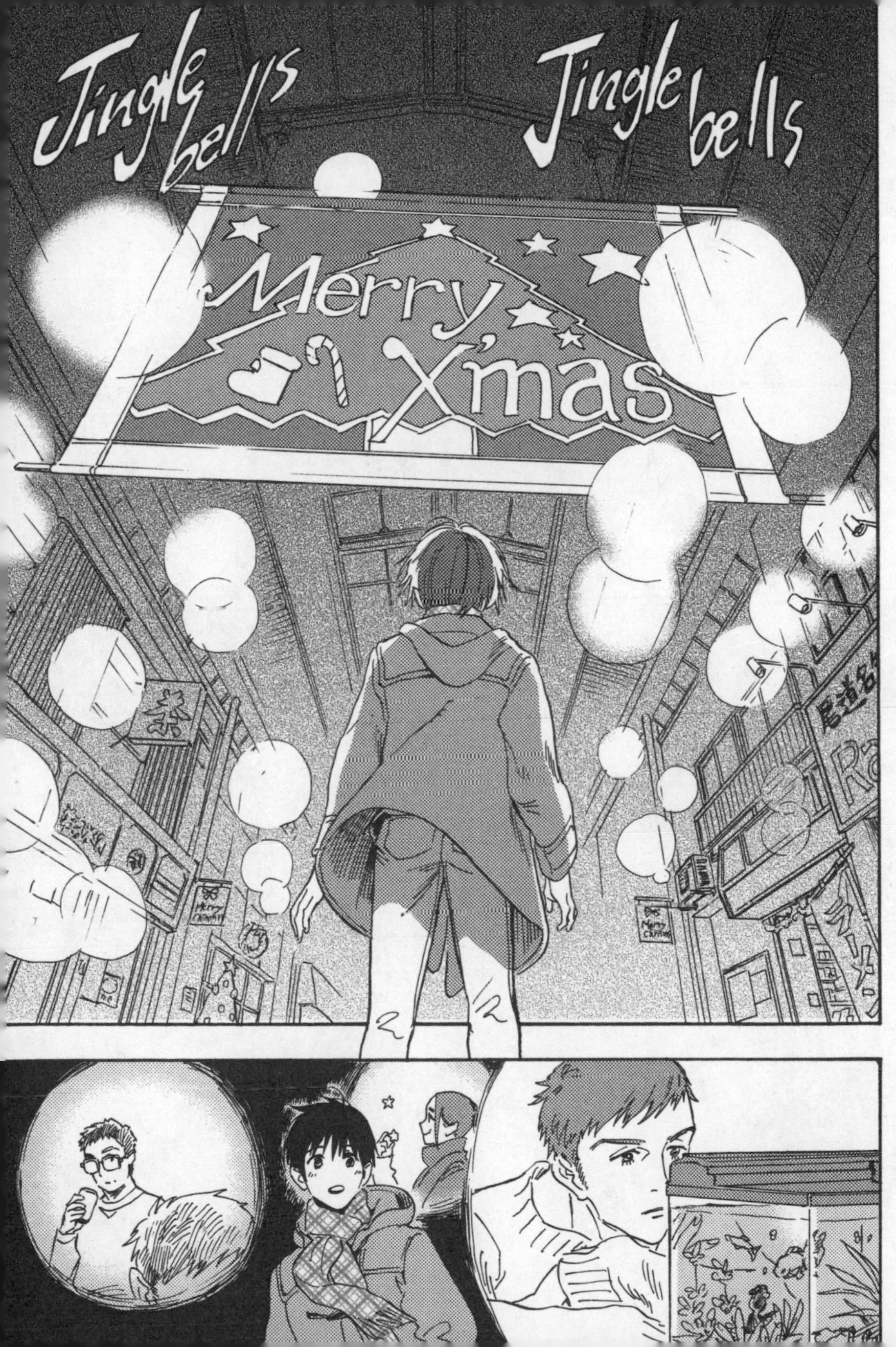
Jingle bells
Jingle bells
Merry X'mas

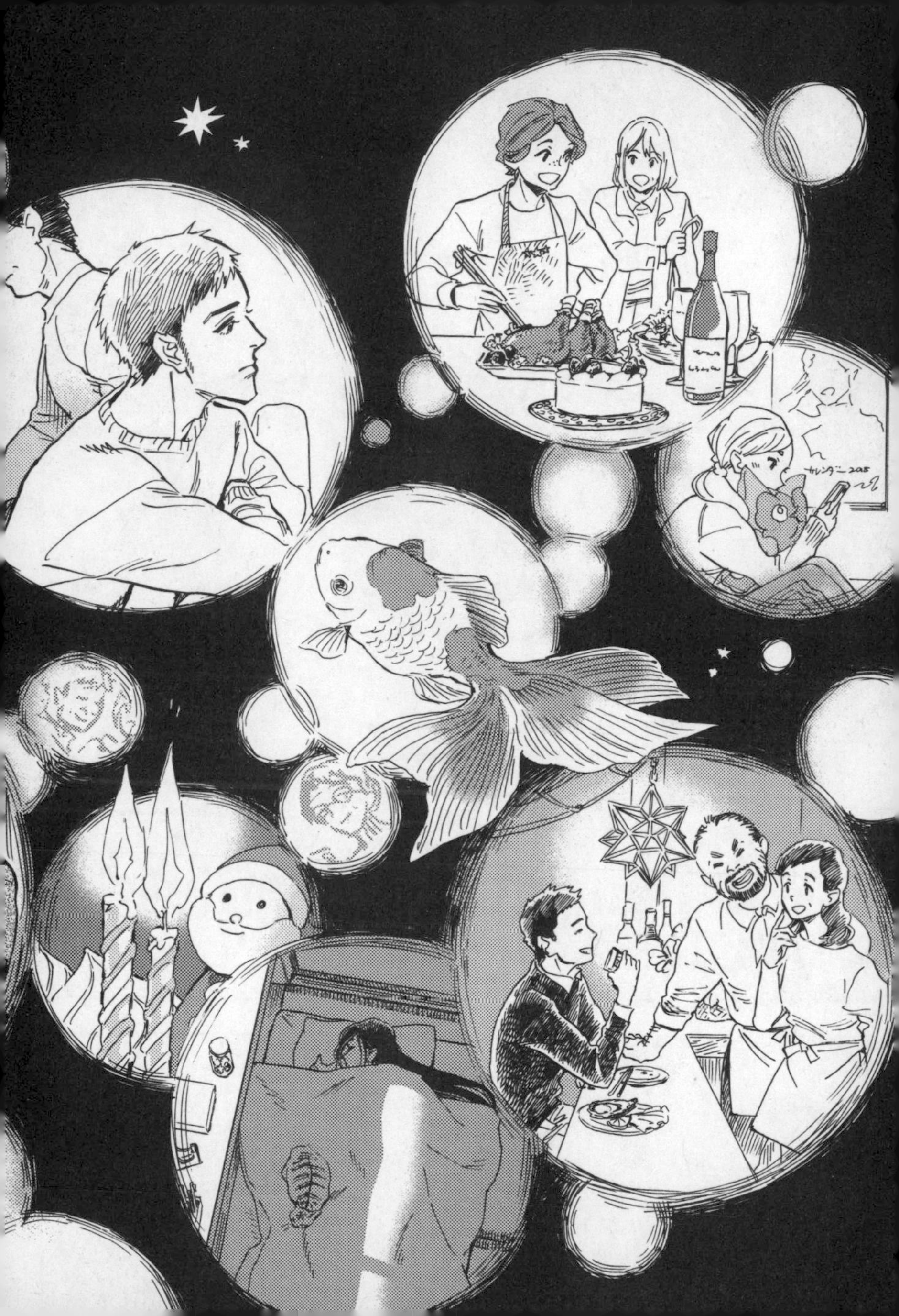

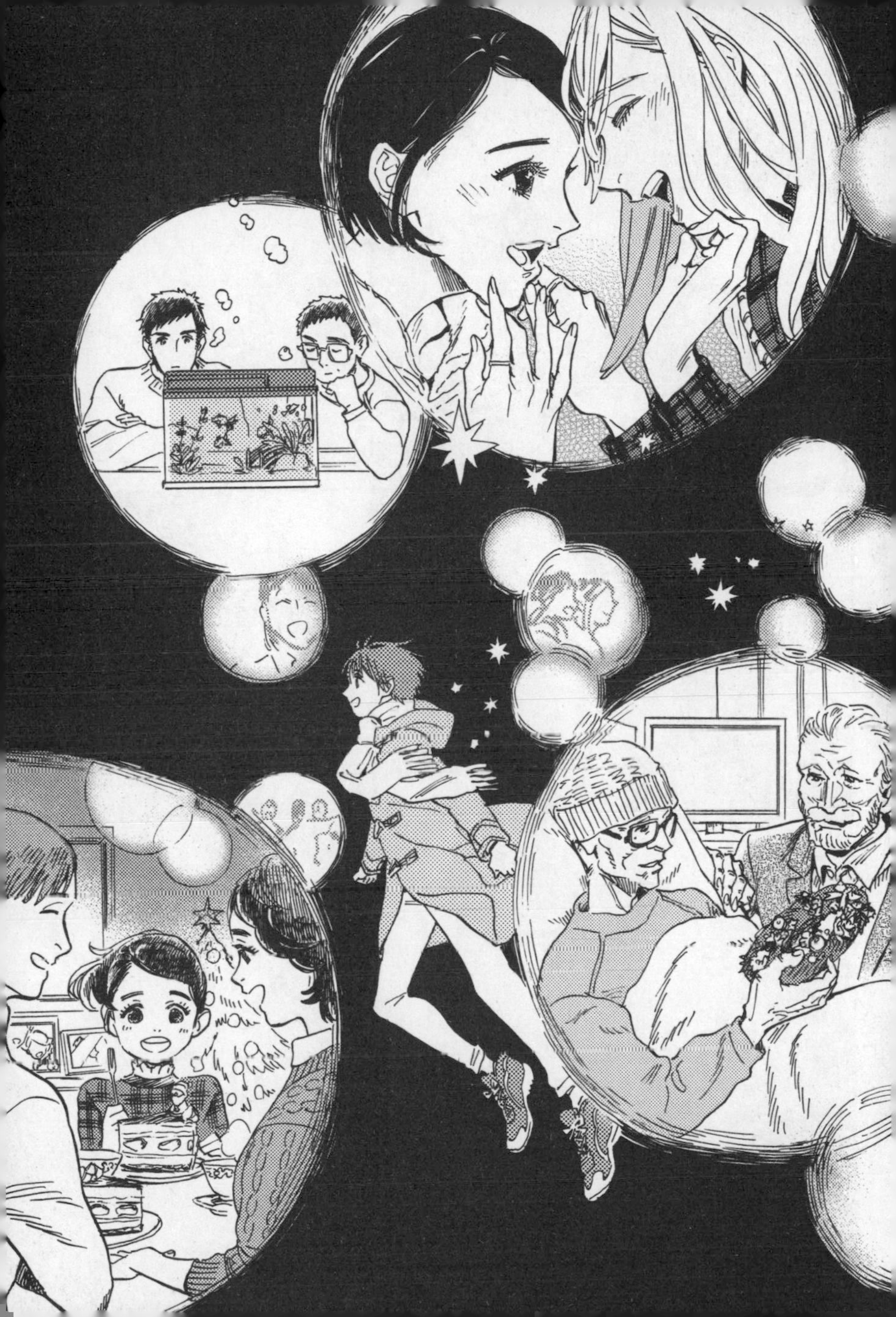

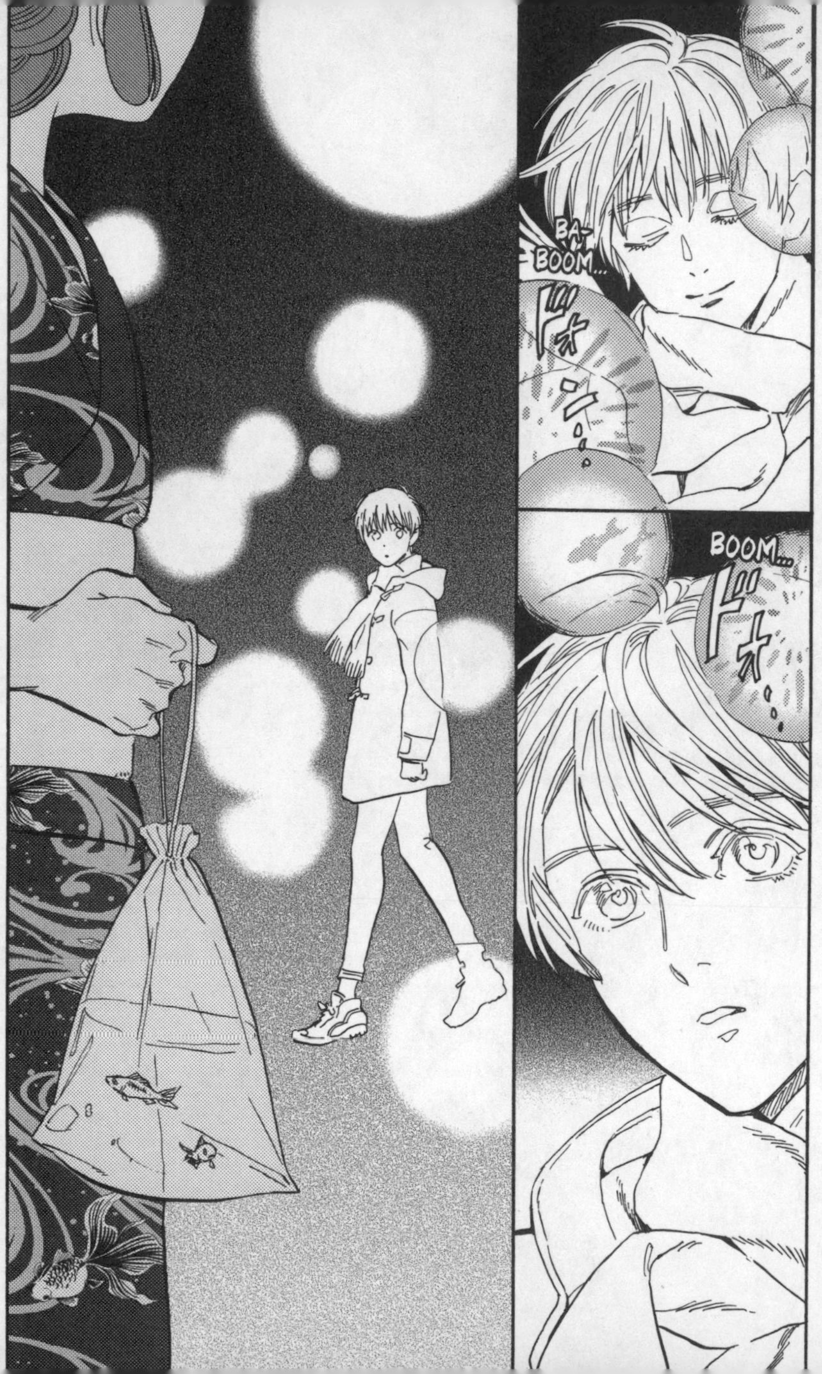
BA-BOOM...
ドォン
BOOM...
ドォ

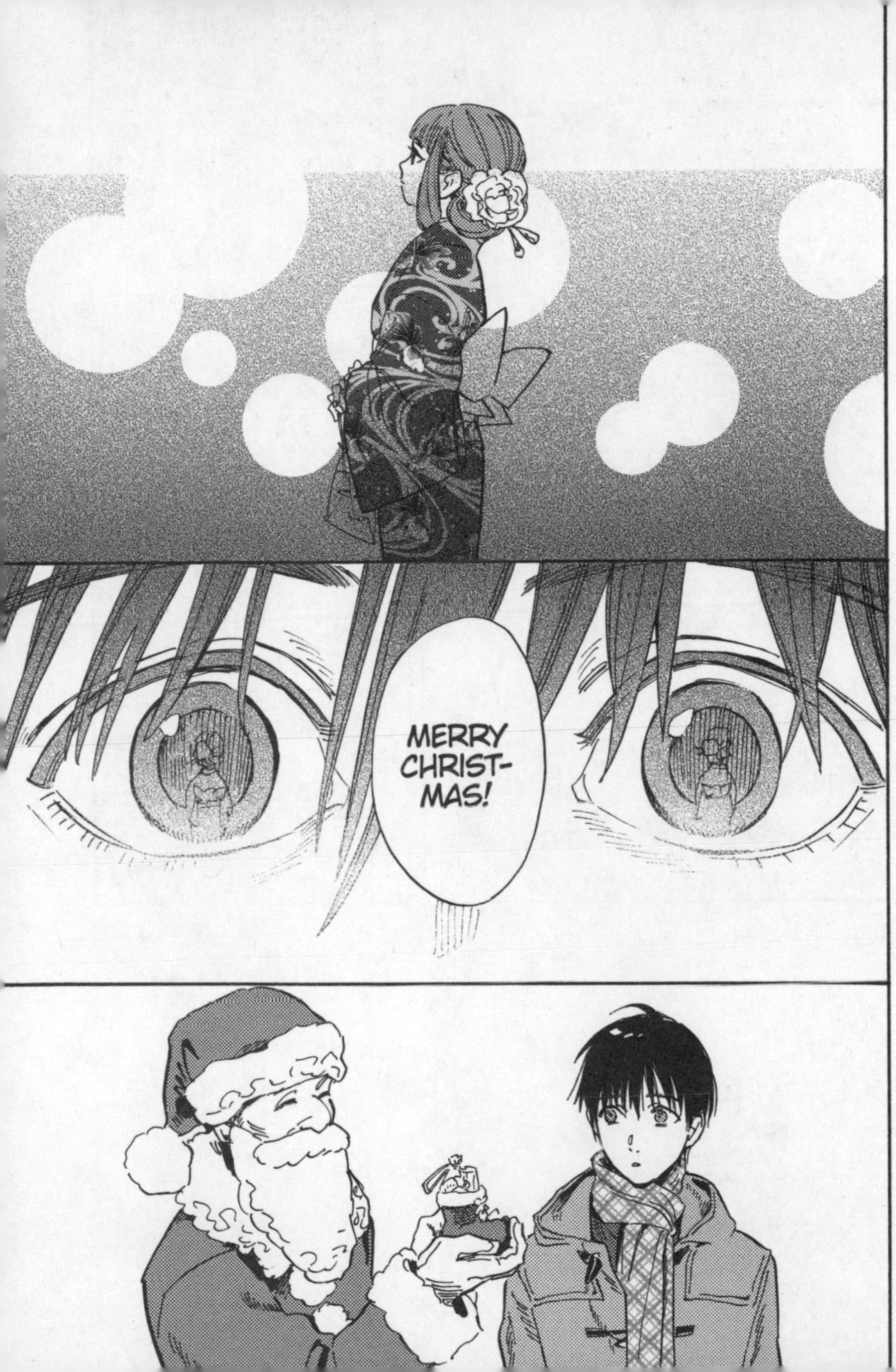
MERRY CHRIST-MAS!

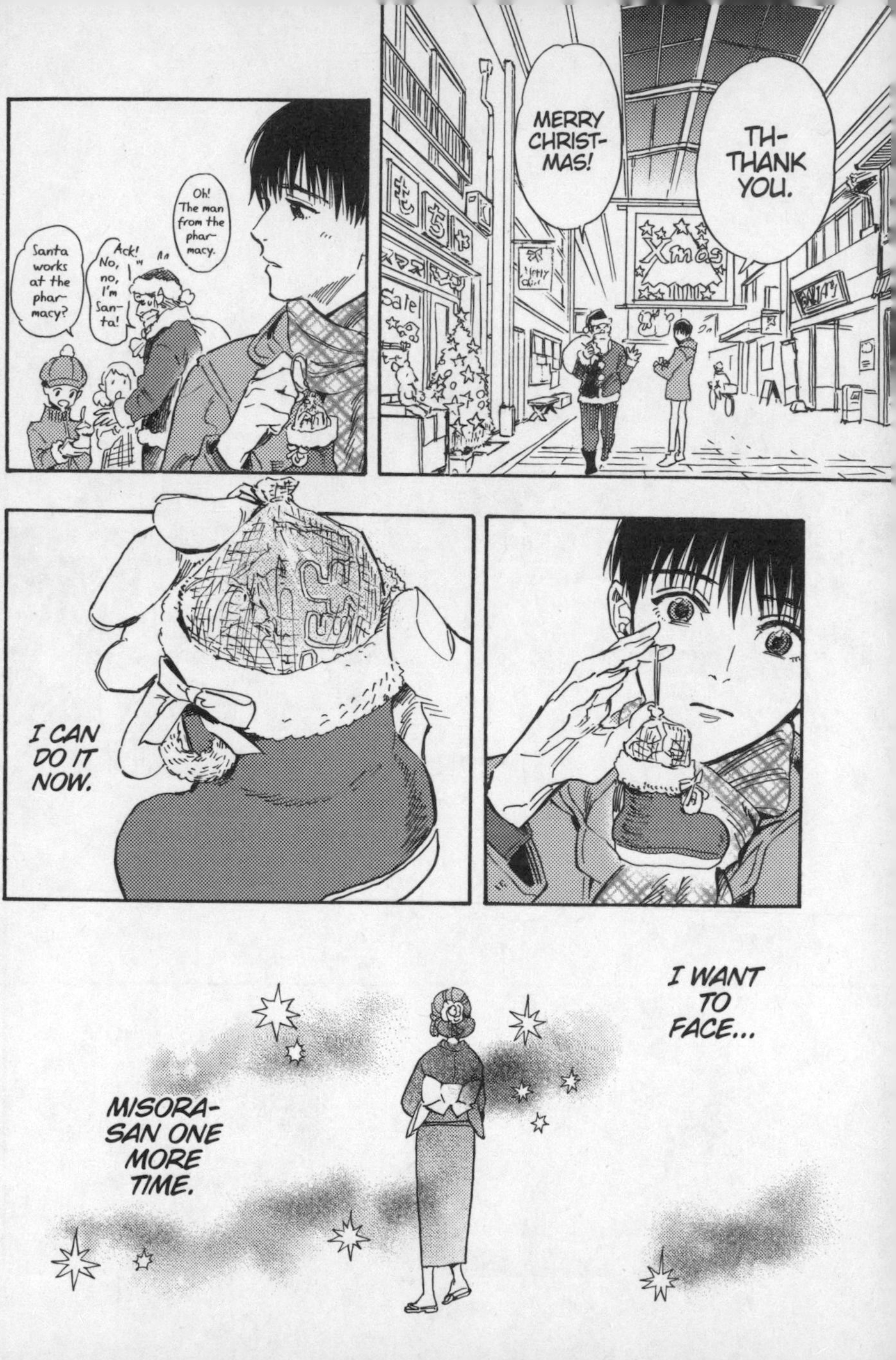
MERRY CHRIST-MAS!
TH-THANK YOU.
Xmas
Sale
Oh! The man from the phar-macy.
Santa works at the phar-macy?
Ack! No, no, I'm San-ta!
I CAN DO IT NOW.
I WANT TO FACE...
MISORA-SAN ONE MORE TIME.

Our Dreams at Dusk
SHIMANAMI **TASOGARE**

PON PON ROCK

There's a rock that makes a "pon pon" sound when you hit it.

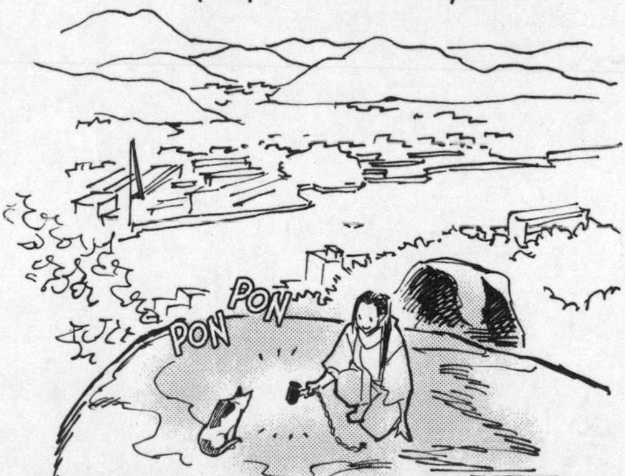
PON
PON

Chapter 21

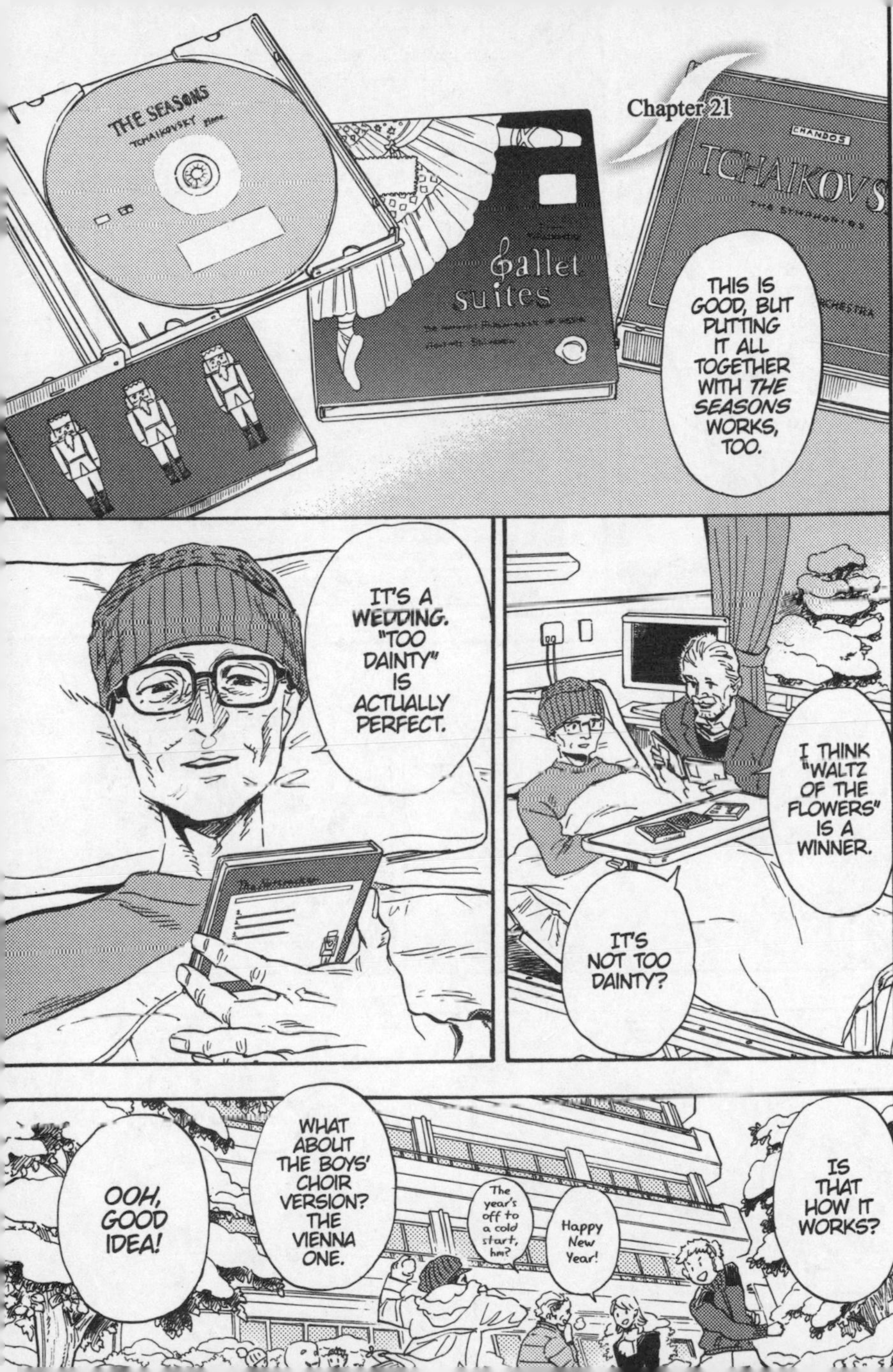
THE SEASONS
TCHAIKOVSKY piano
Ballet suites
CHANDOS
TCHAIKOVS
THE SYMPHONIES
ORCHESTRA
THIS IS GOOD, BUT PUTTING IT ALL TOGETHER WITH *THE SEASONS* WORKS, TOO.
I THINK "WALTZ OF THE FLOWERS" IS A WINNER.
IT'S NOT TOO DAINTY?
IT'S A WEDDING. "TOO DAINTY" IS ACTUALLY PERFECT.
IS THAT HOW IT WORKS?
Happy New Year!
The year's off to a cold start, hm?
WHAT ABOUT THE BOYS' CHOIR VERSION? THE VIENNA ONE.
OOH, GOOD IDEA!

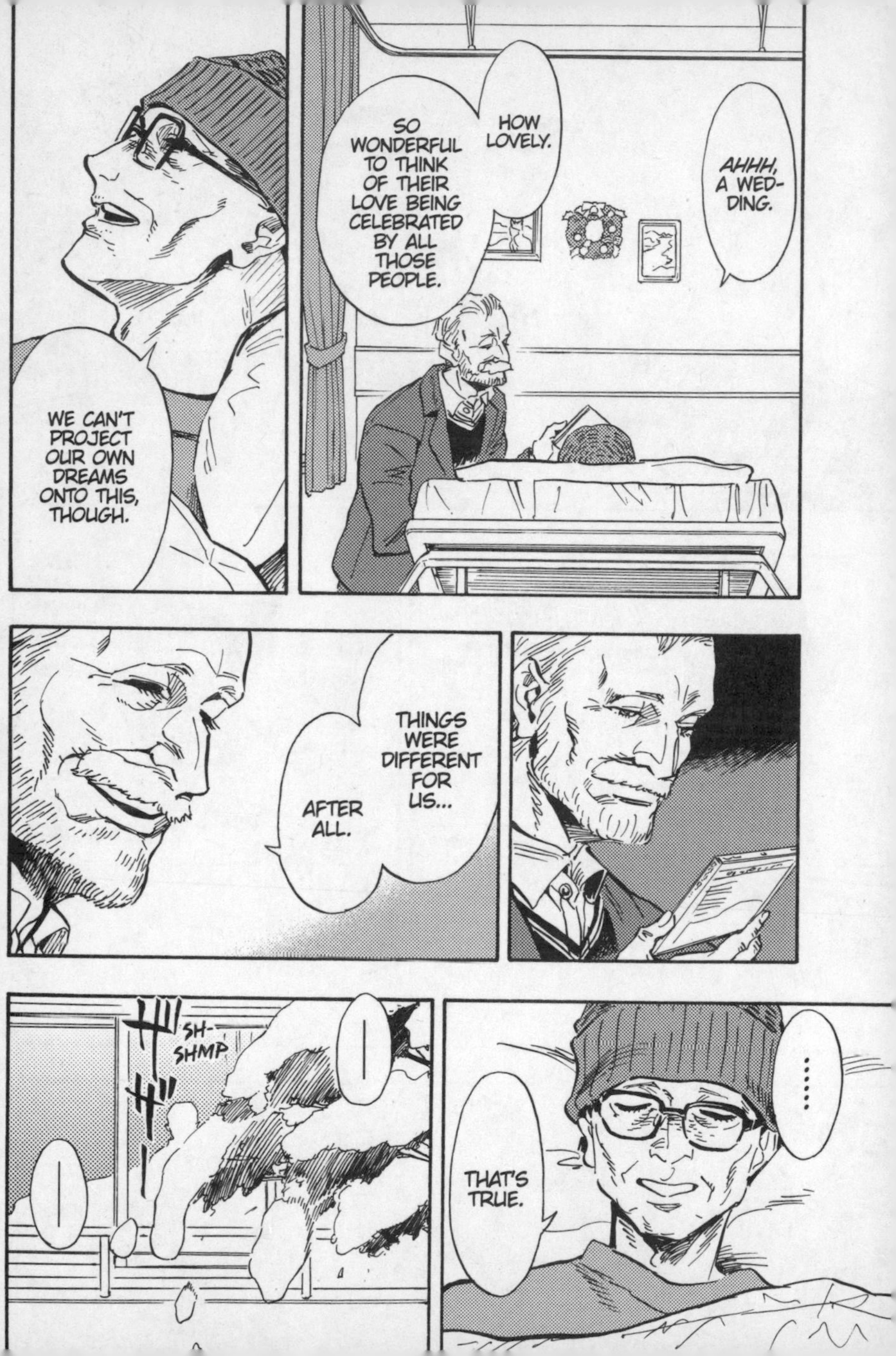
AHHH, A WED-DING.
HOW LOVELY.
SO WONDERFUL TO THINK OF THEIR LOVE BEING CELEBRATED BY ALL THOSE PEOPLE.
WE CAN'T PROJECT OUR OWN DREAMS ONTO THIS, THOUGH.
THINGS WERE DIFFERENT FOR US...
AFTER ALL.
......
THAT'S TRUE.
SH-SHMP

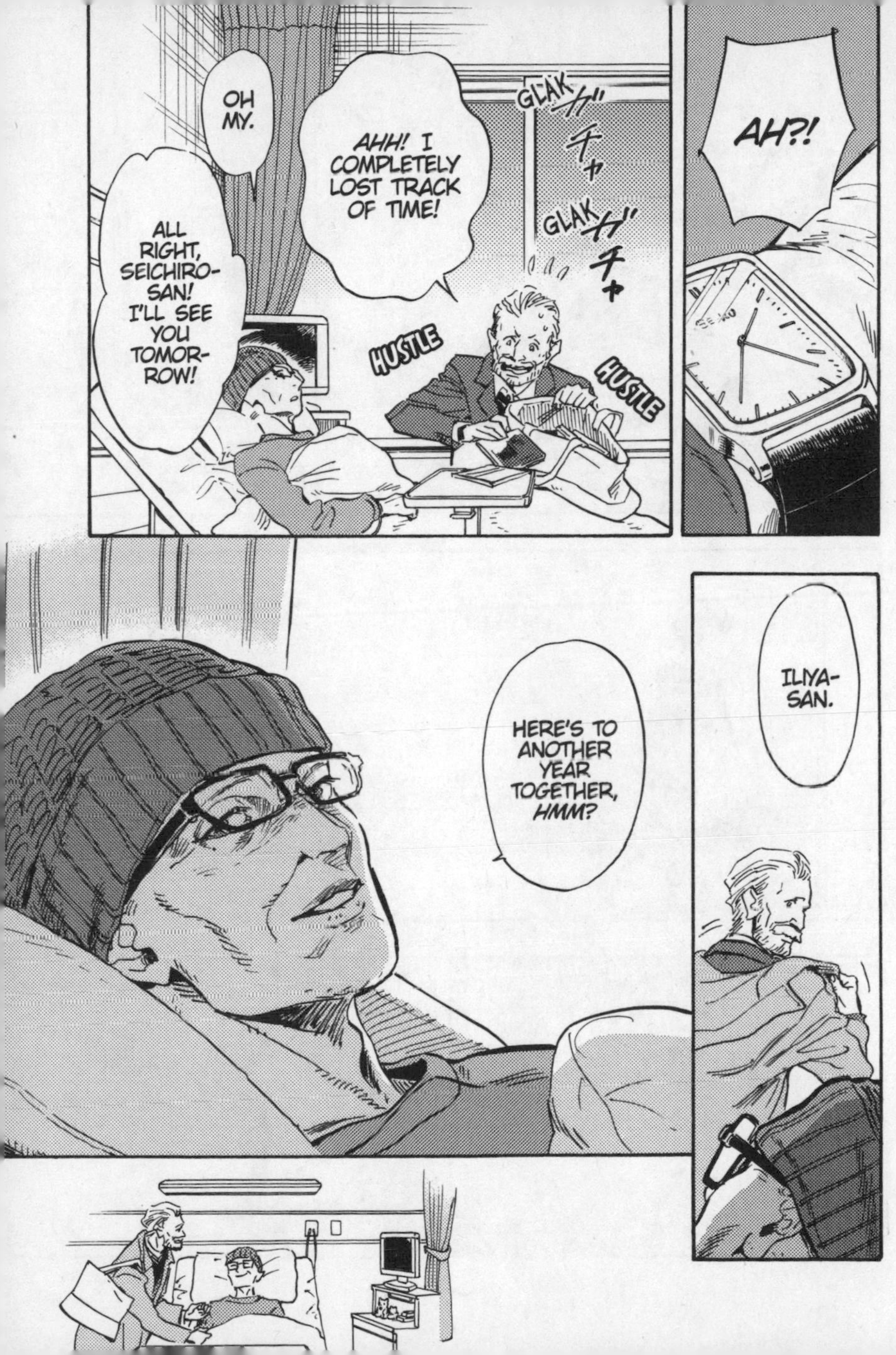
AH?!
AHH! I COMPLETELY LOST TRACK OF TIME!
GLAK ガチャ
GLAK ガチャ
HUSTLE
HUSTLE
OH MY.
ALL RIGHT, SEICHIRO-SAN! I'LL SEE YOU TOMOR-ROW!
ILIYA-SAN.
HERE'S TO ANOTHER YEAR TOGETHER, HMM?

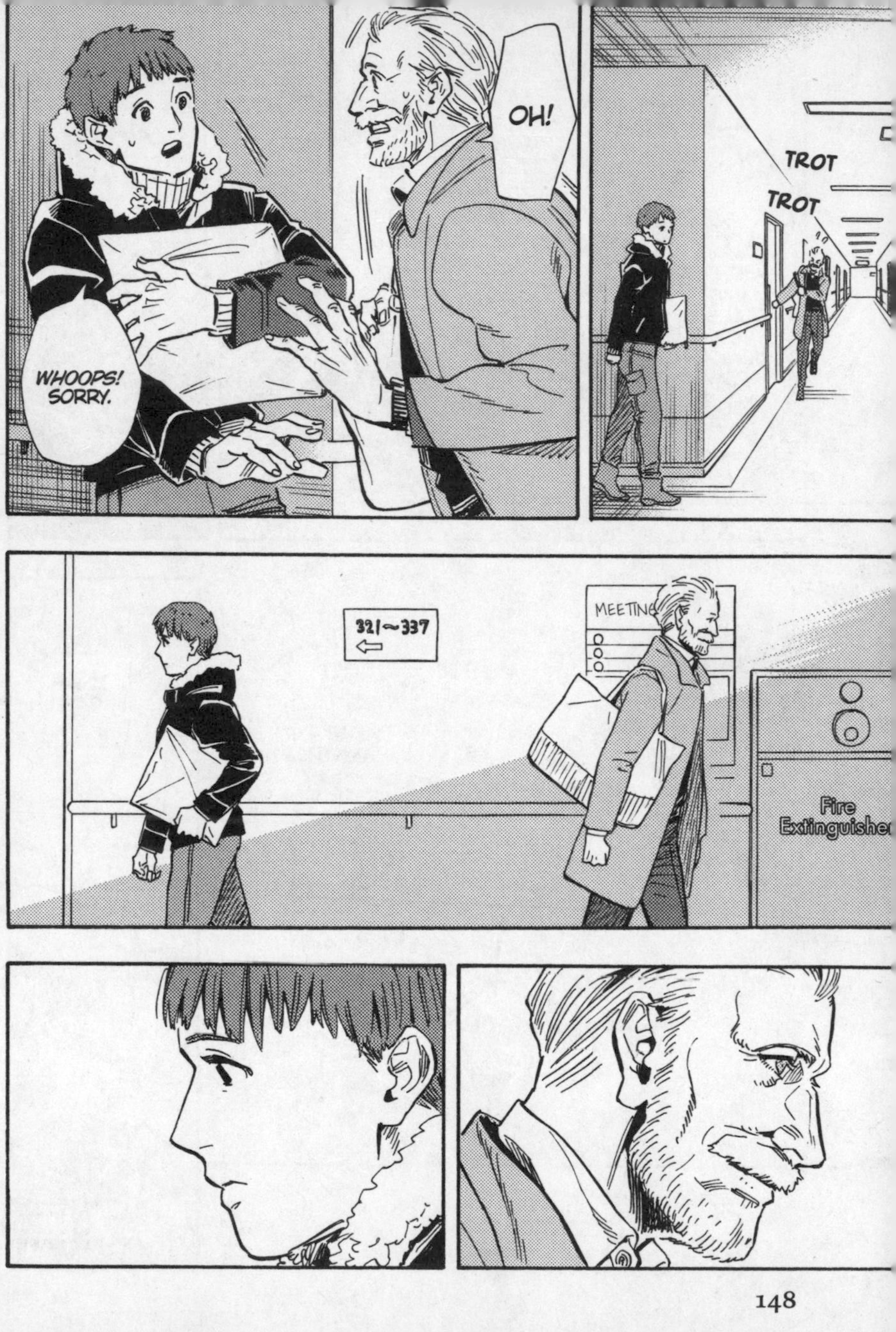
TROT
TROT
OH!
WHOOPS! SORRY.
MEETIN
321~337
Fire Extinguishe

Chapter 21

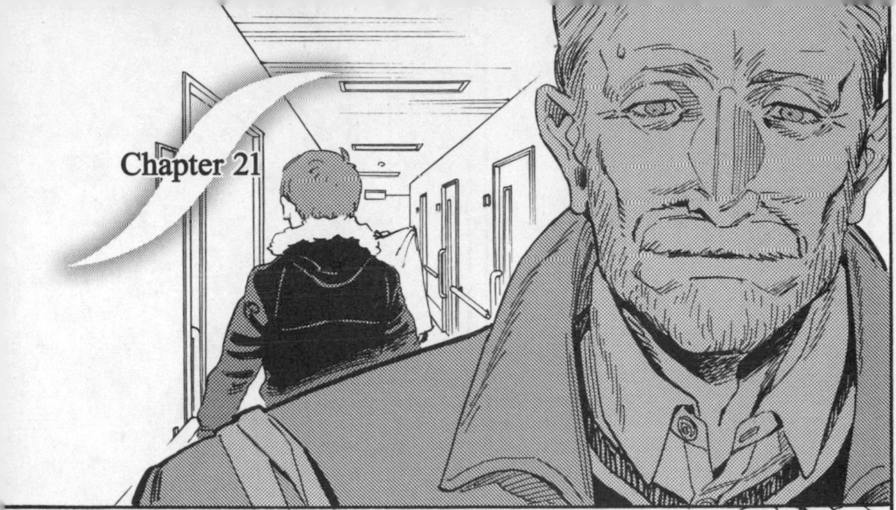

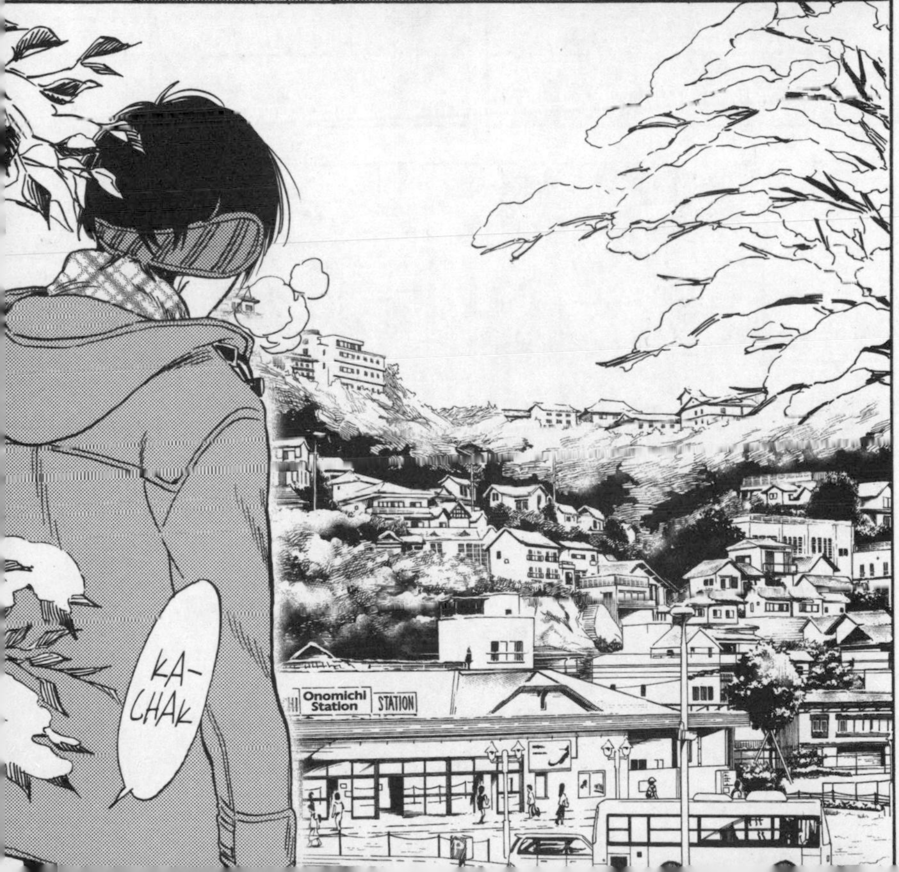
Onomichi Station
STATION
KA-CHAK

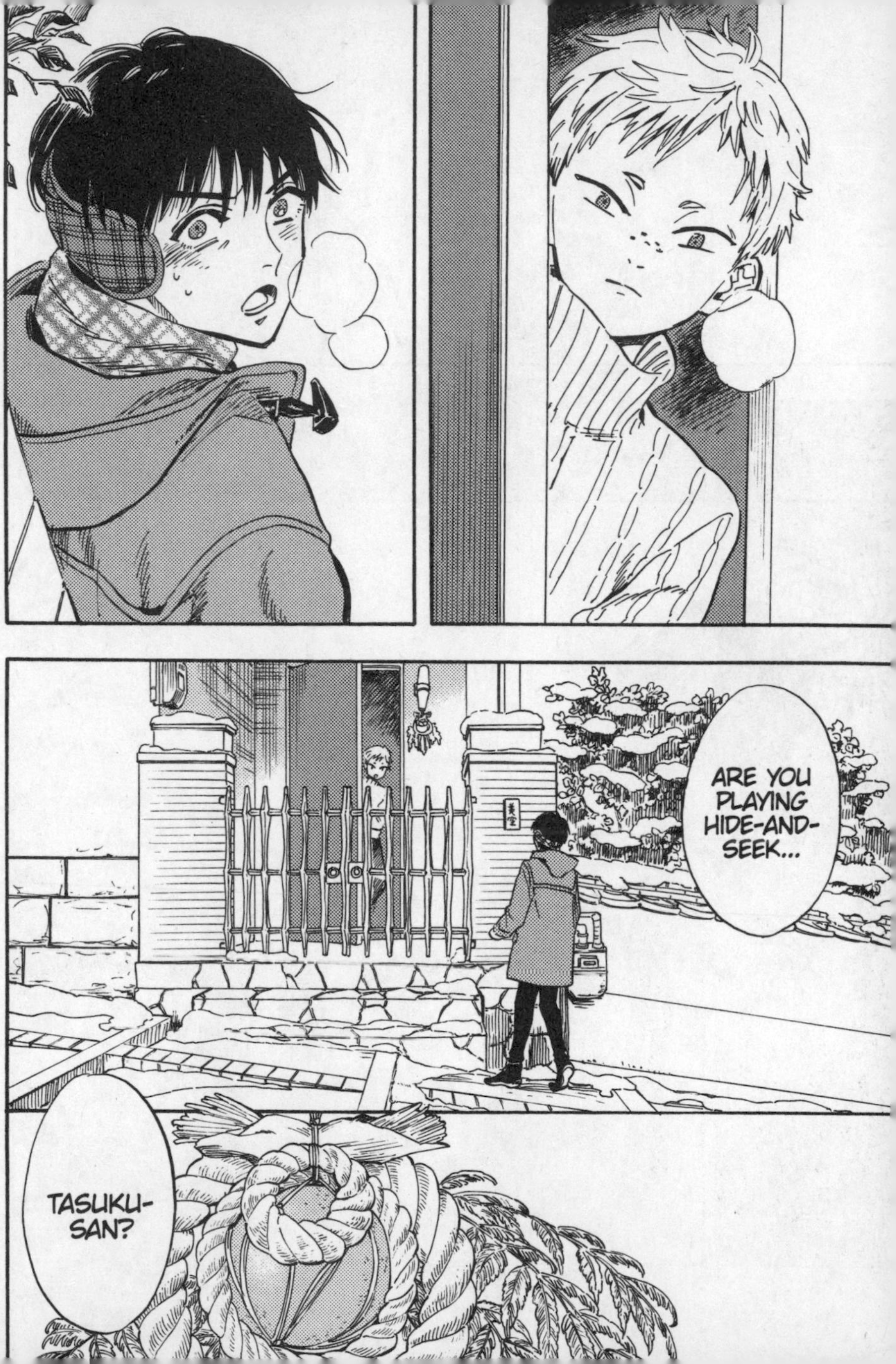
ARE YOU PLAYING HIDE-AND-SEEK...
TASUKU-SAN?

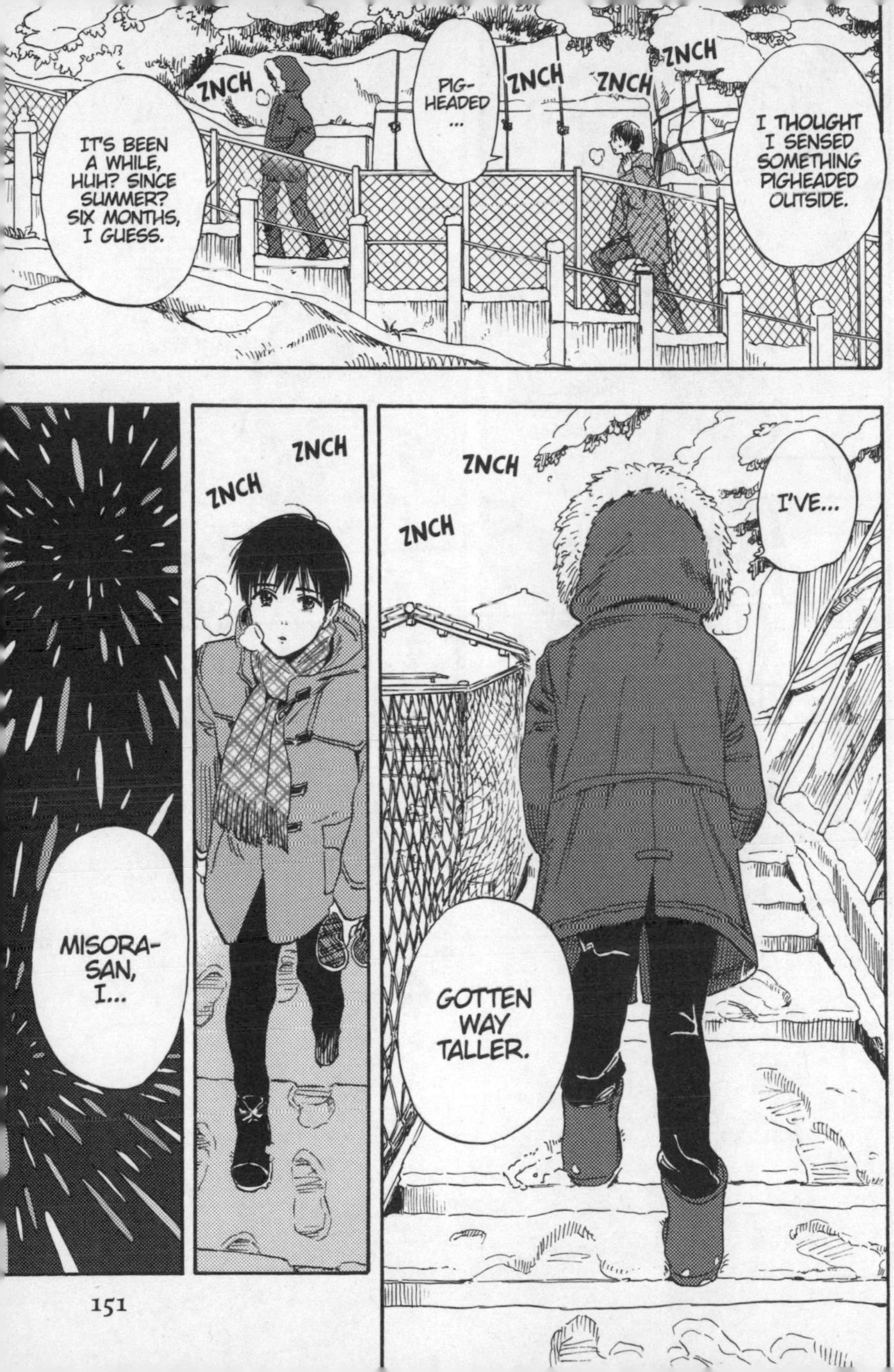
ZNCH
I THOUGHT I SENSED SOMETHING PIGHEADED OUTSIDE.
ZNCH
ZNCH
PIG-HEADED ...
ZNCH
IT'S BEEN A WHILE, HUH? SINCE SUMMER? SIX MONTHS, I GUESS.
ZNCH
I'VE...
ZNCH
GOTTEN WAY TALLER.
ZNCH
ZNCH
MISORA-SAN, I...

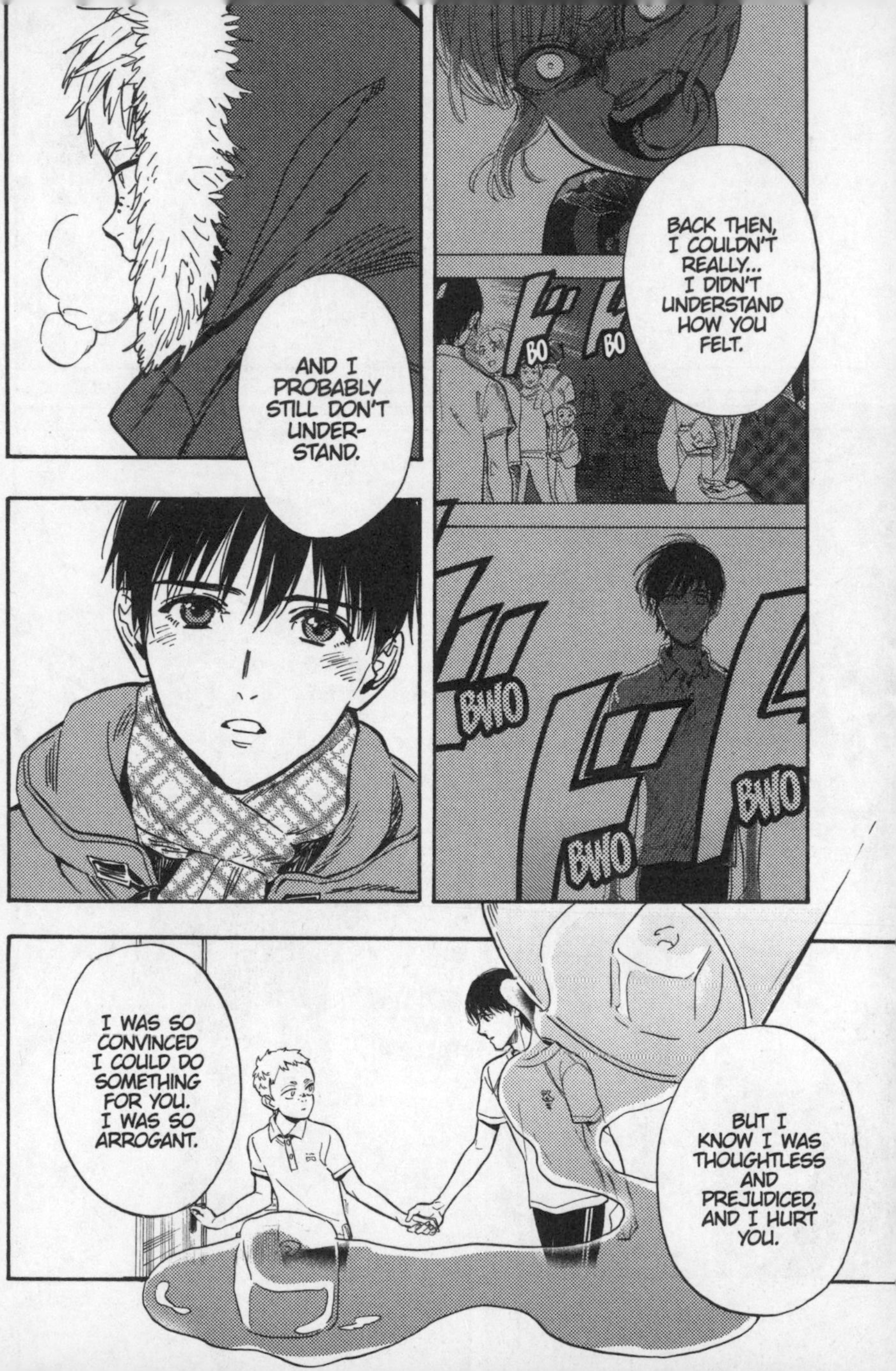
BACK THEN, I COULDN'T REALLY... I DIDN'T UNDERSTAND HOW YOU FELT.
BO
BO
AND I PROBABLY STILL DON'T UNDER-STAND.
BWO
BWO
BWO
BUT I KNOW I WAS THOUGHTLESS AND PREJUDICED, AND I HURT YOU.
I WAS SO CONVINCED I COULD DO SOMETHING FOR YOU. I WAS SO ARROGANT.

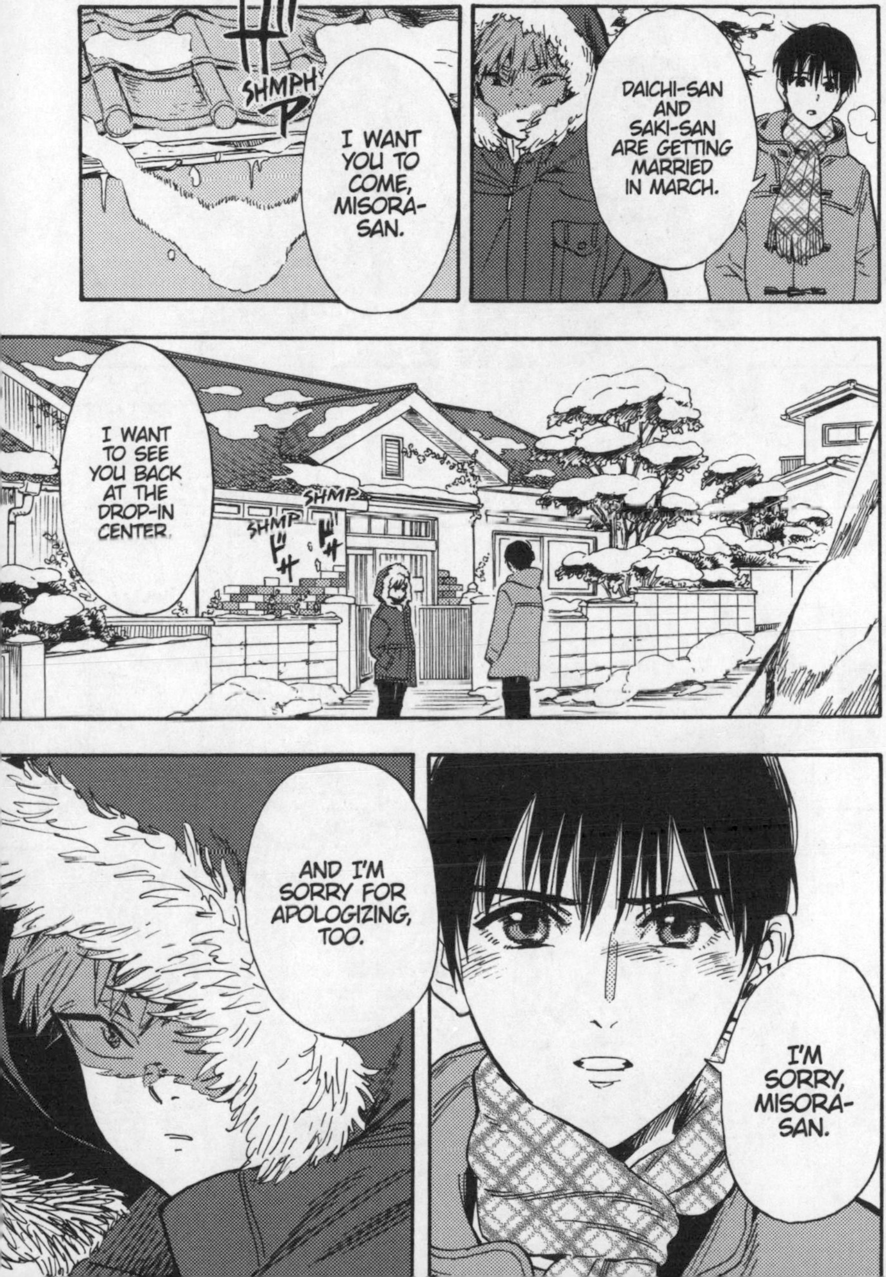
DAICHI-SAN AND SAKI-SAN ARE GETTING MARRIED IN MARCH.
SHMPH
I WANT YOU TO COME, MISORA-SAN.
I WANT TO SEE YOU BACK AT THE DROP-IN CENTER.
SHMP
SHMP
I'M SORRY, MISORA-SAN.
AND I'M SORRY FOR APOLOGIZING, TOO.

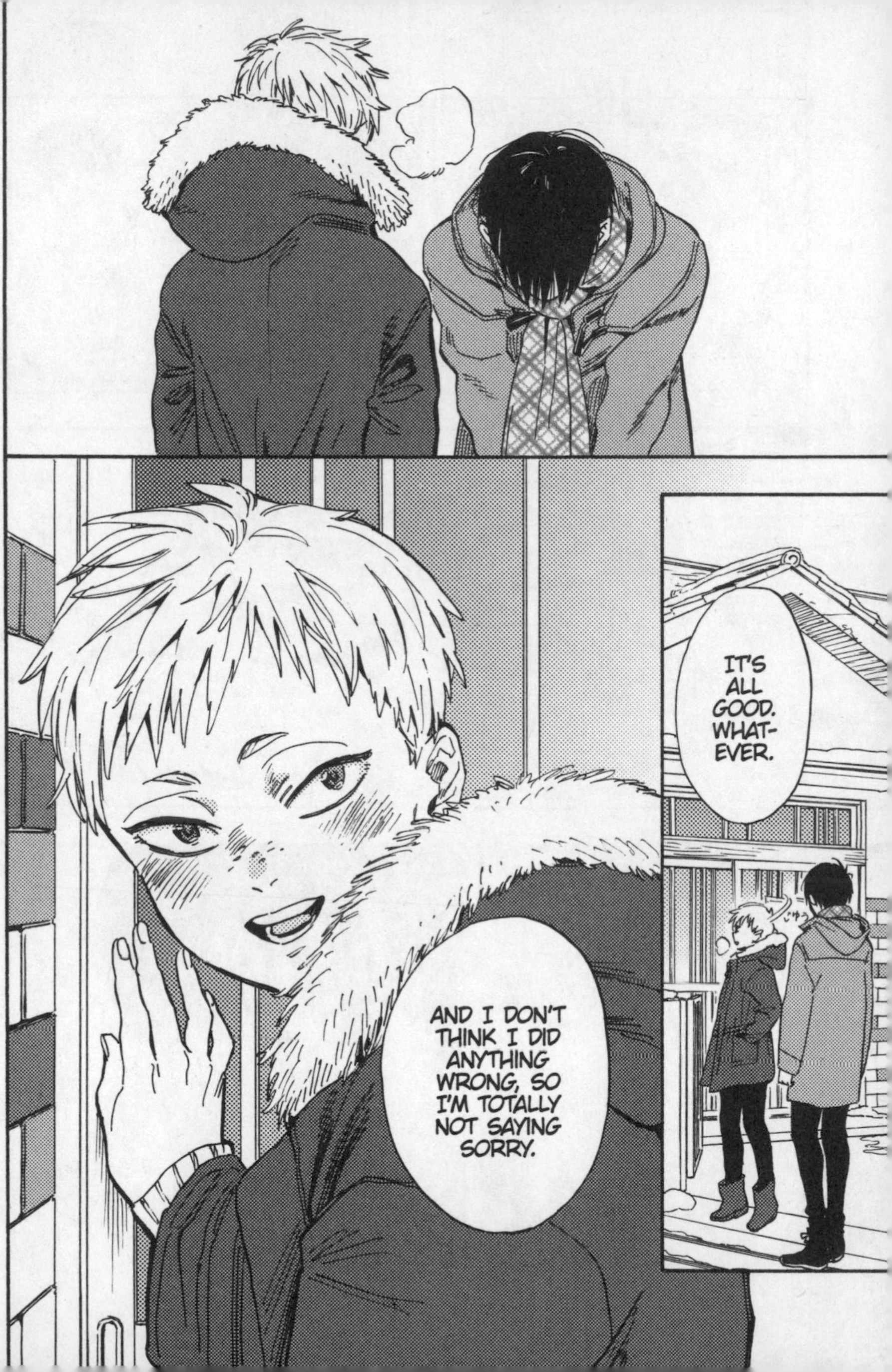
IT'S ALL GOOD. WHAT-EVER.
AND I DON'T THINK I DID ANYTHING WRONG, SO I'M TOTALLY NOT SAYING SORRY.

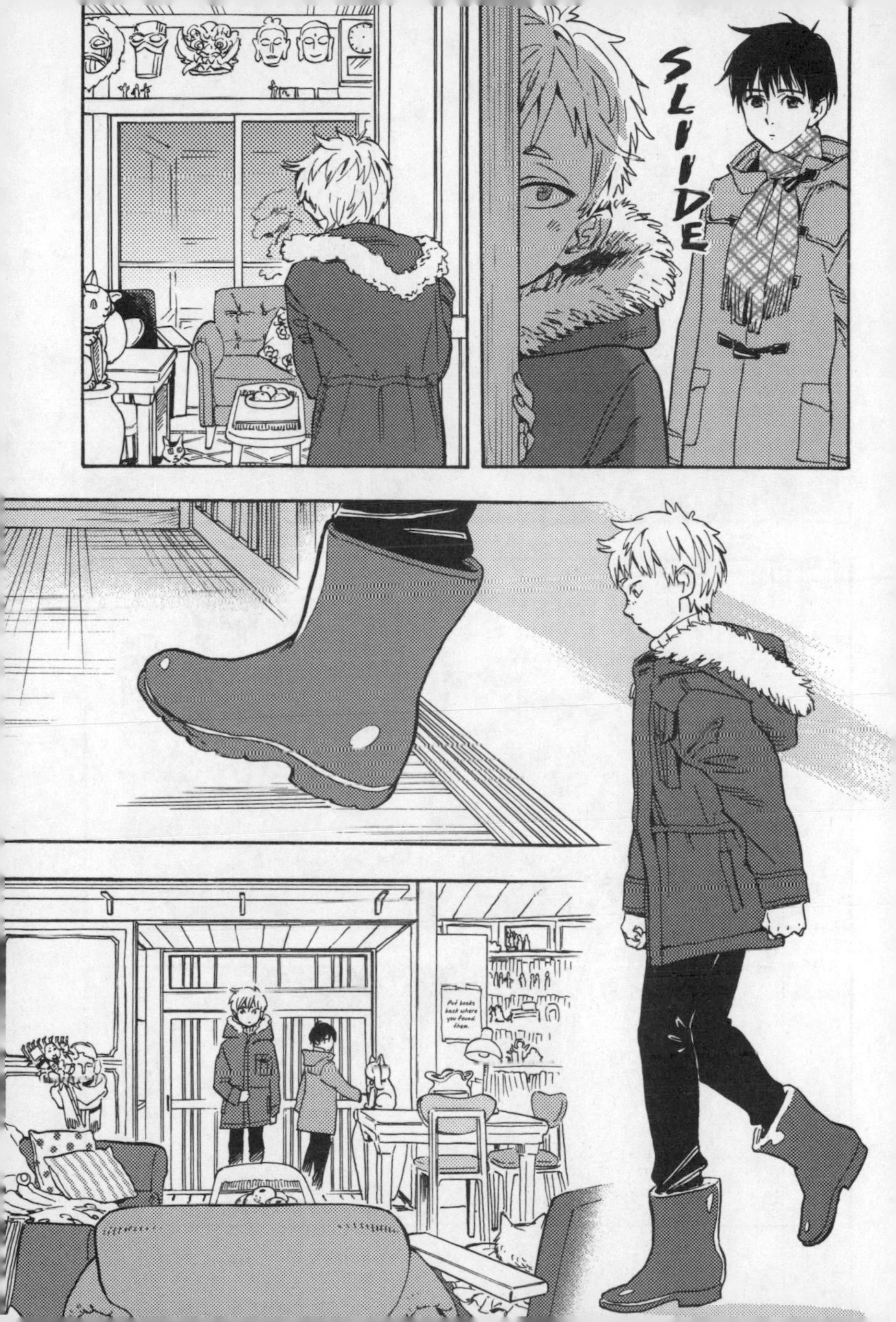
SLIIDE
Put books back where you found them.

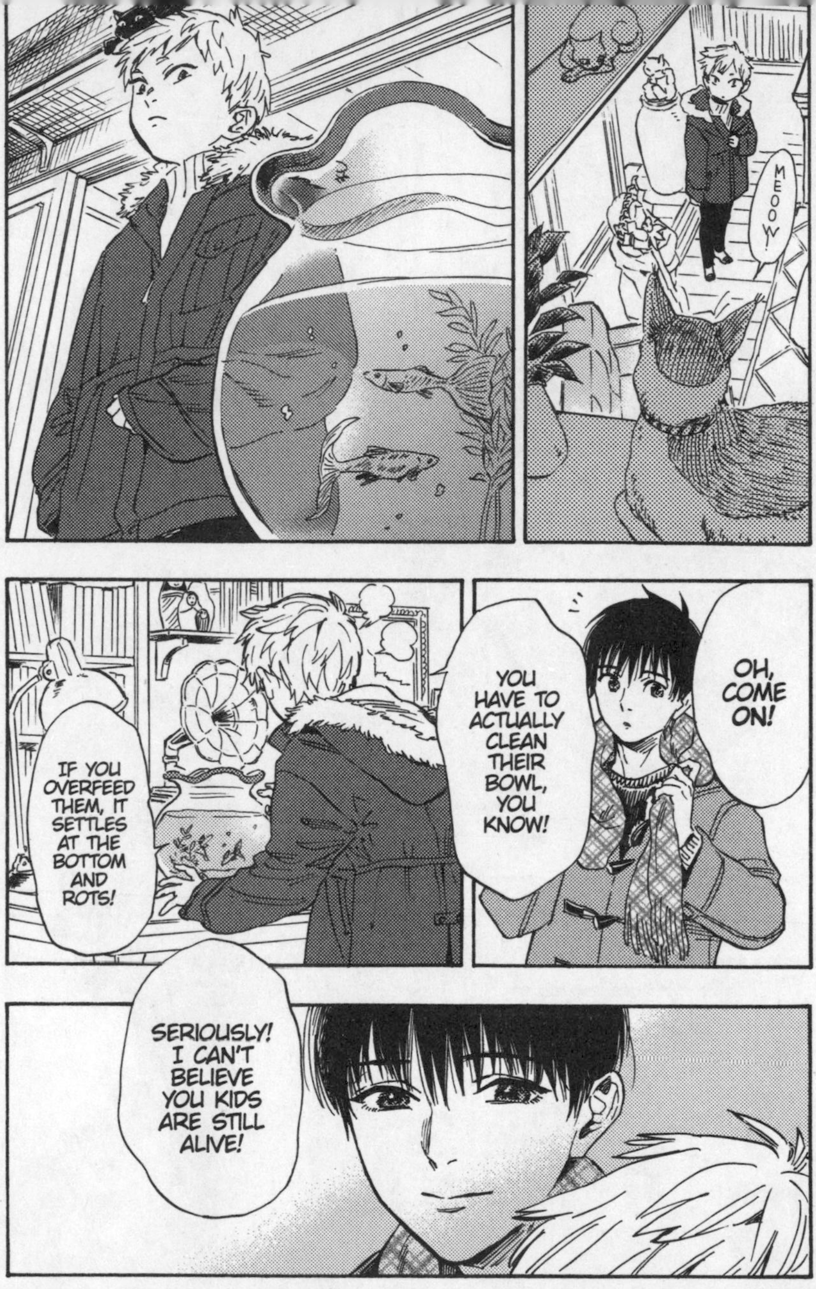
MEOOW!
OH, COME ON!
YOU HAVE TO ACTUALLY CLEAN THEIR BOWL, YOU KNOW!
IF YOU OVERFEED THEM, IT SETTLES AT THE BOTTOM AND ROTS!
SERIOUSLY! I CAN'T BELIEVE YOU KIDS ARE STILL ALIVE!

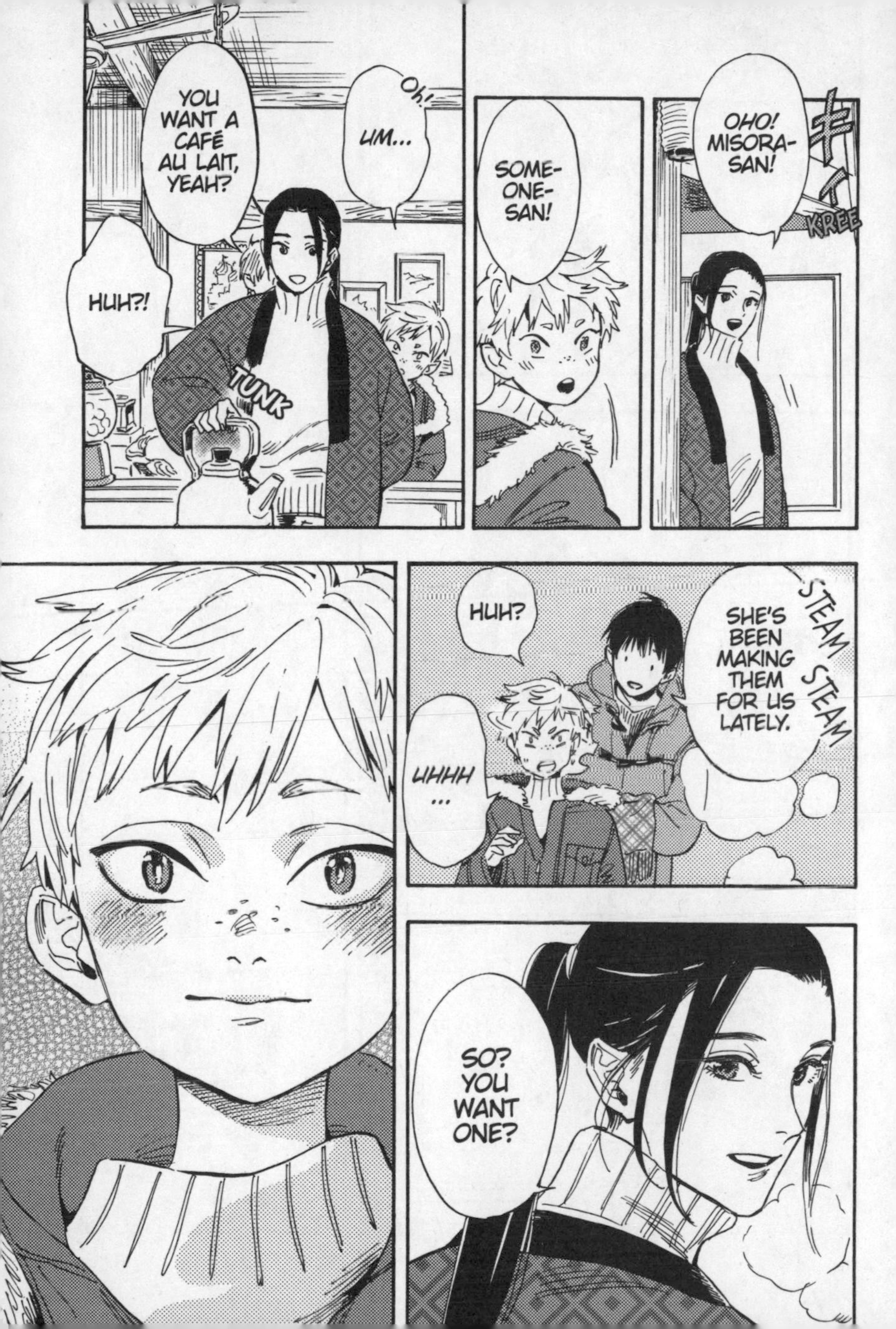
キィ
KREE
OHO! MISORA-SAN!
SOME-ONE-SAN!
Oh!
UM...
YOU WANT A CAFÉ AU LAIT, YEAH?
HUH?!
TUNK
STEAM STEAM
SHE'S BEEN MAKING THEM FOR US LATELY.
HUH?
UHHH ...
SO? YOU WANT ONE?

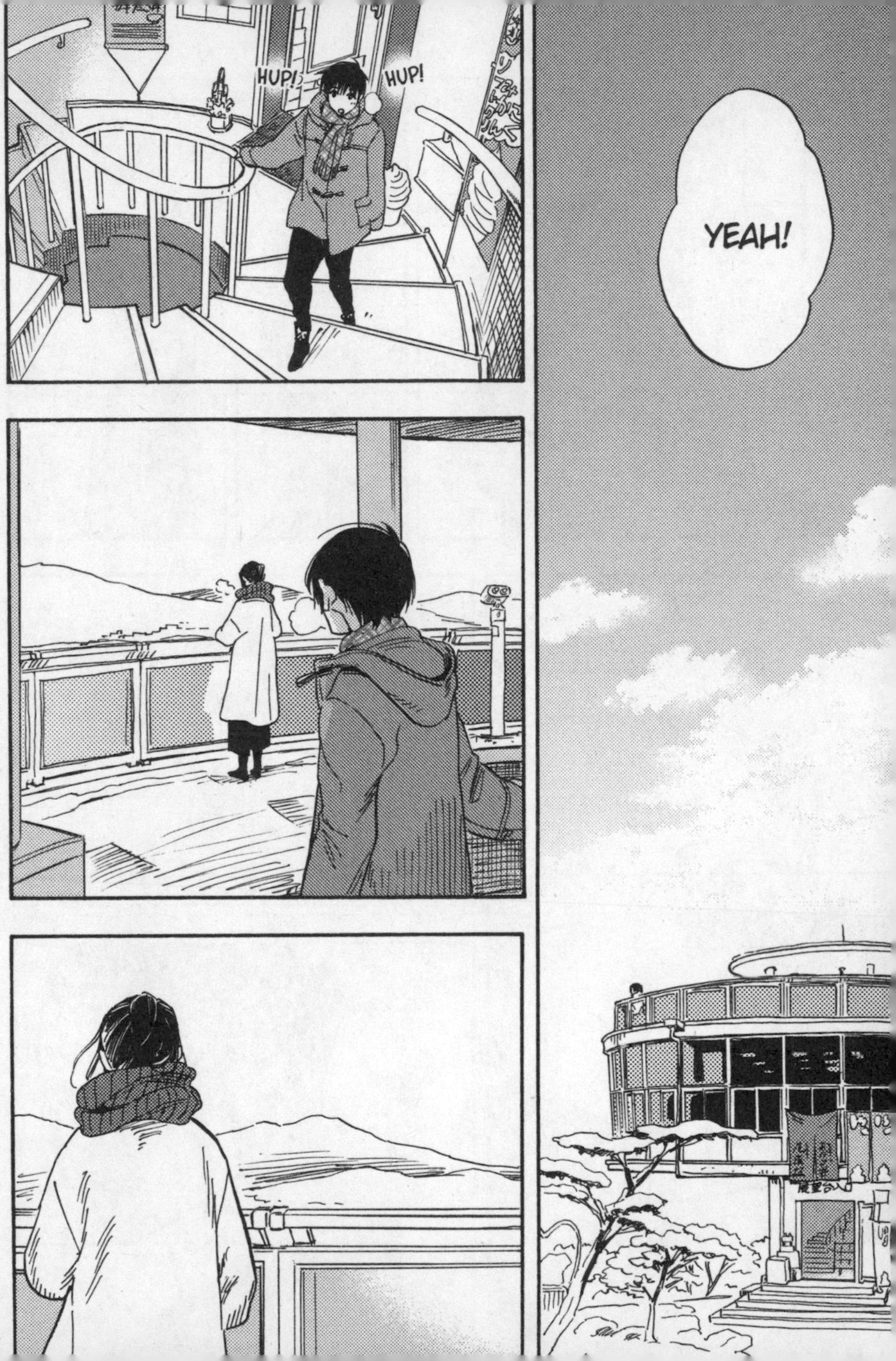
YEAH!
HUP!
HUP!

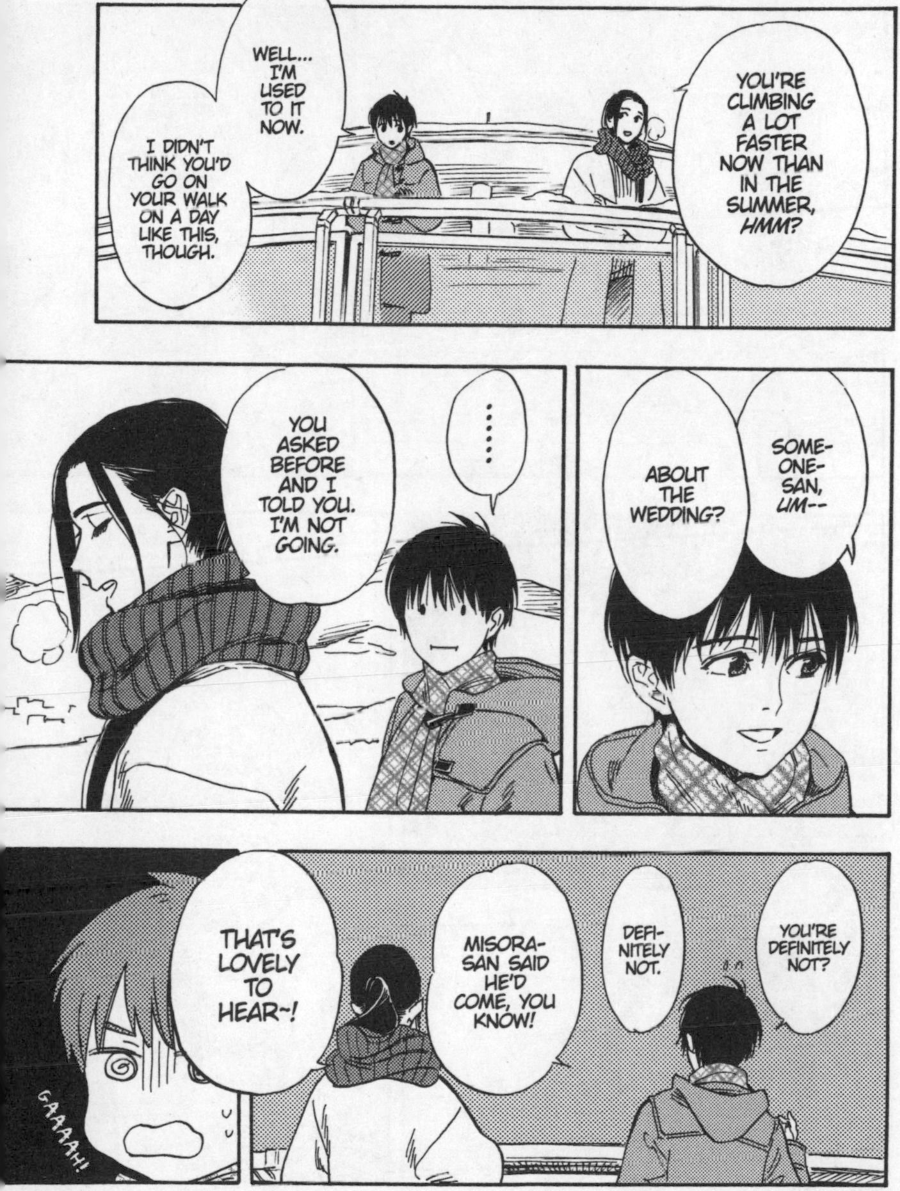
YOU'RE CLIMBING A LOT FASTER NOW THAN IN THE SUMMER, *HMM?*
WELL... I'M USED TO IT NOW.
I DIDN'T THINK YOU'D GO ON YOUR WALK ON A DAY LIKE THIS, THOUGH.
SOME-ONE-SAN, *UM--*
ABOUT THE WEDDING?
......
YOU ASKED BEFORE AND I TOLD YOU. I'M NOT GOING.
YOU'RE DEFINITELY NOT?
DEFI-NITELY NOT.
MISORA-SAN SAID HE'D COME, YOU KNOW!
THAT'S LOVELY TO HEAR~!
GAAAAH!

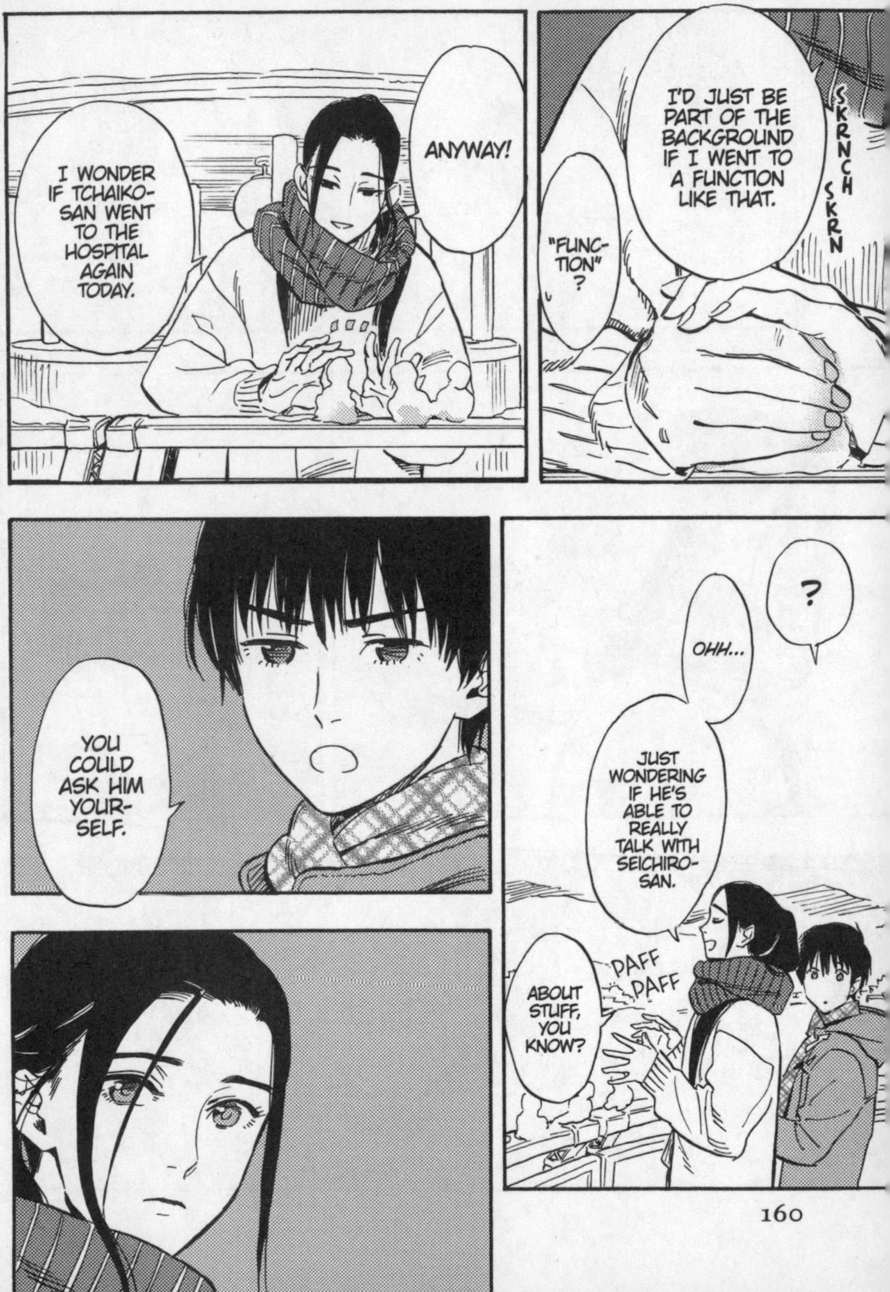
SKRNCH SKRN
I'D JUST BE PART OF THE BACKGROUND IF I WENT TO A FUNCTION LIKE THAT.
"FUNCTION"?
ANYWAY!
I WONDER IF TCHAIKO-SAN WENT TO THE HOSPITAL AGAIN TODAY.
?
OHH...
JUST WONDERING IF HE'S ABLE TO REALLY TALK WITH SEICHIRO-SAN.
PAFF PAFF
ABOUT STUFF, YOU KNOW?
YOU COULD ASK HIM YOUR-SELF.

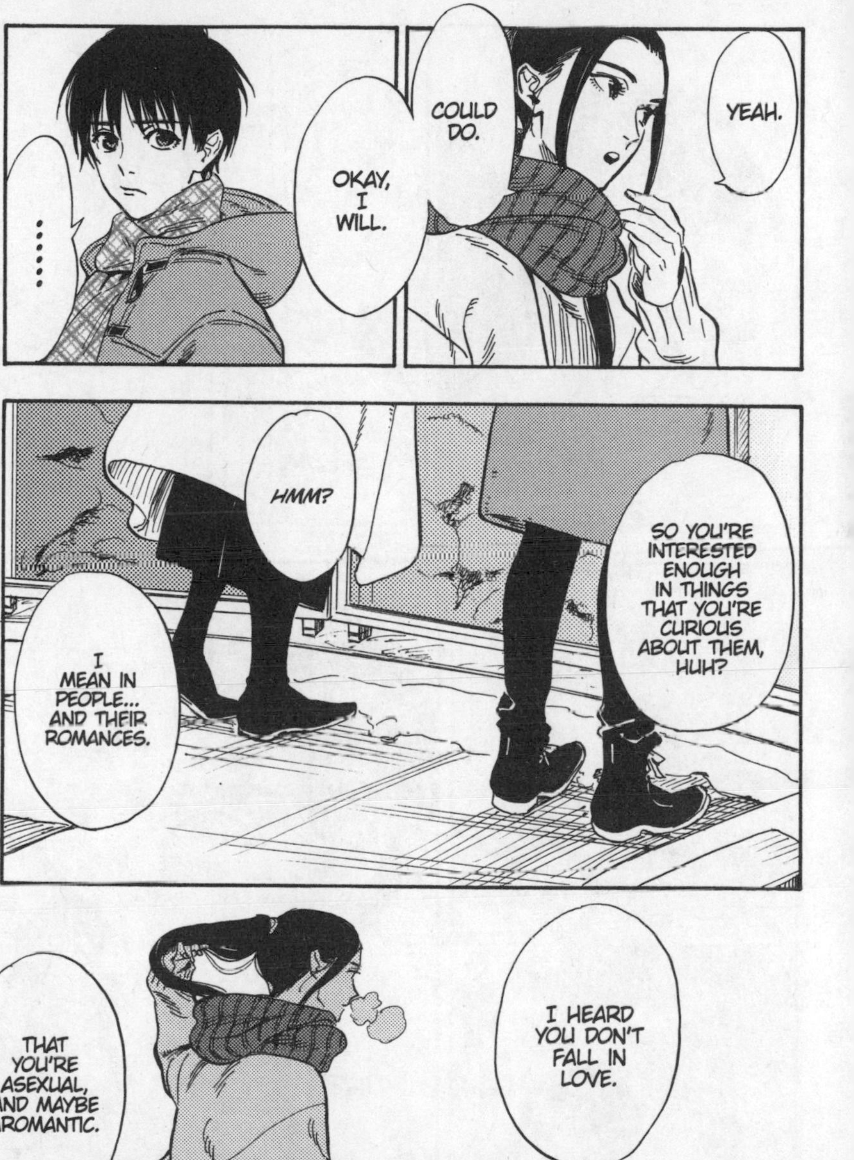
YEAH.
COULD DO.
OKAY, I WILL.
......
SO YOU'RE INTERESTED ENOUGH IN THINGS THAT YOU'RE CURIOUS ABOUT THEM, HUH?
HMM?
I MEAN IN PEOPLE... AND THEIR ROMANCES.
I HEARD YOU DON'T FALL IN LOVE.
THAT YOU'RE ASEXUAL, AND MAYBE AROMANTIC.

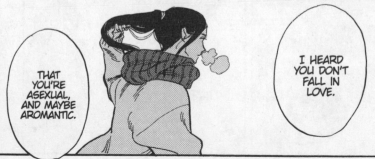

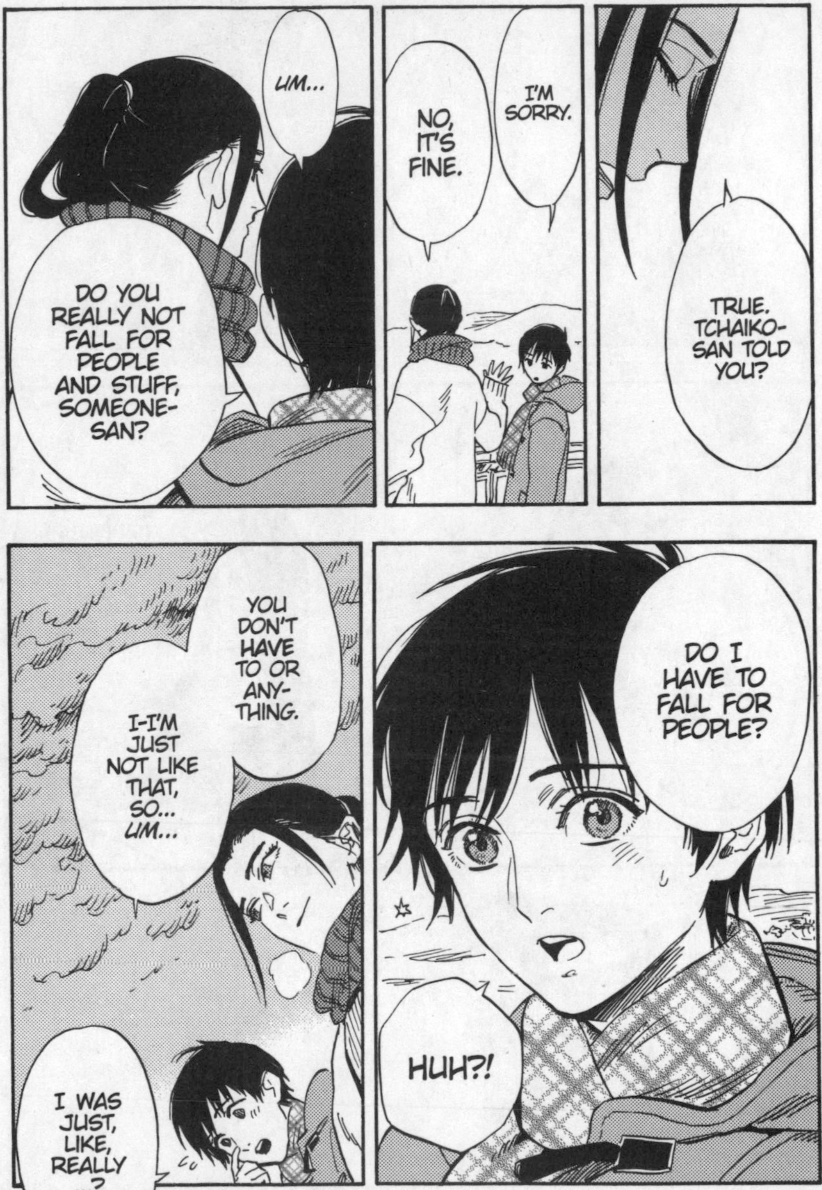
TRUE. TCHAIKO-SAN TOLD YOU?
I'M SORRY.
NO, IT'S FINE.
UM...
DO YOU REALLY NOT FALL FOR PEOPLE AND STUFF, SOMEONE-SAN?
DO I HAVE TO FALL FOR PEOPLE?
HUH?!
YOU DON'T HAVE TO OR ANYTHING.
I-I'M JUST NOT LIKE THAT, SO... UM...
I WAS JUST, LIKE, REALLY ...?

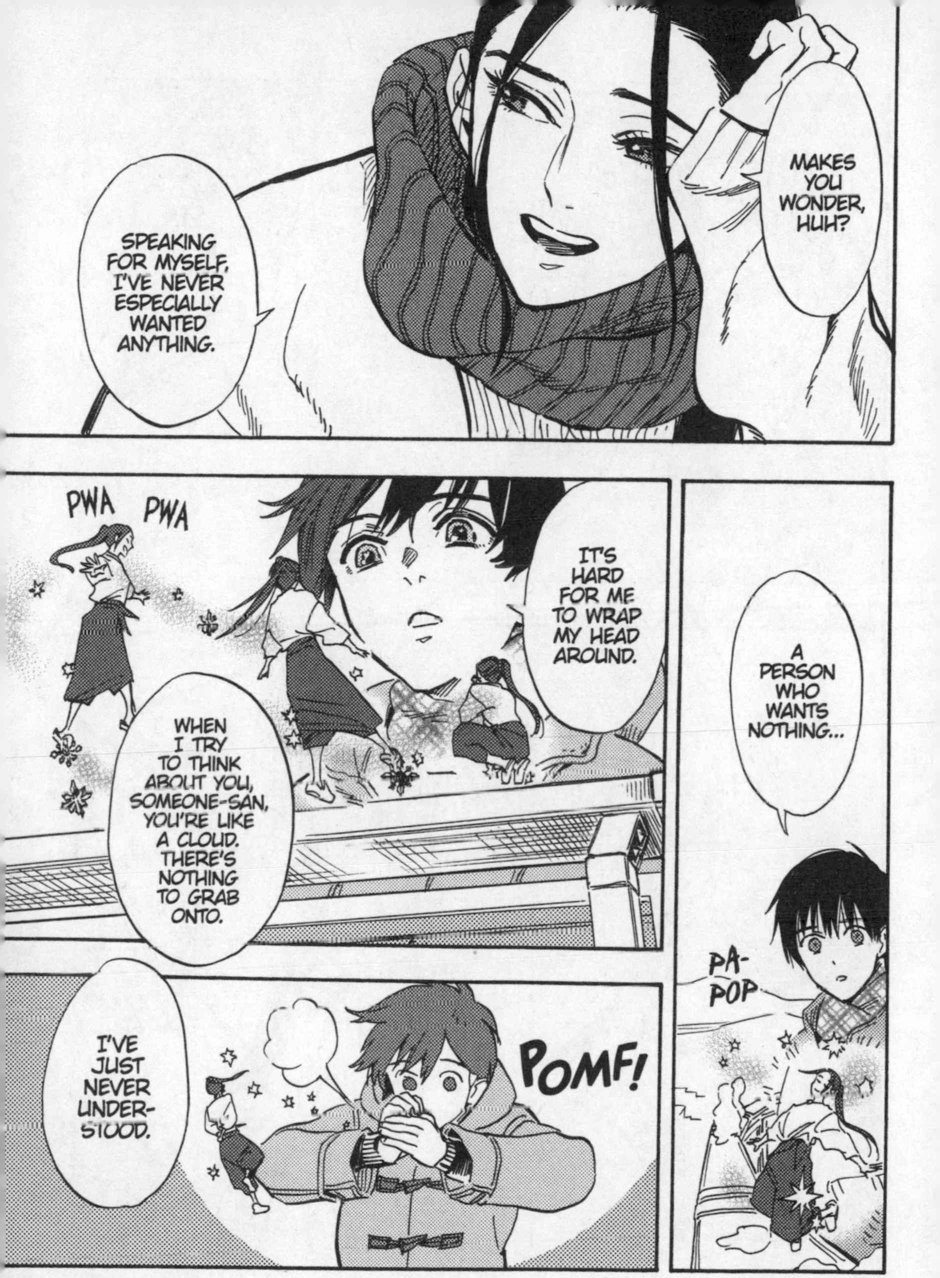
MAKES YOU WONDER, HUH?
SPEAKING FOR MYSELF, I'VE NEVER ESPECIALLY WANTED ANYTHING.
A PERSON WHO WANTS NOTHING...
PA-POP
IT'S HARD FOR ME TO WRAP MY HEAD AROUND.
PWA PWA
WHEN I TRY TO THINK ABOUT YOU, SOMEONE-SAN, YOU'RE LIKE A CLOUD. THERE'S NOTHING TO GRAB ONTO.
POMF!
I'VE JUST NEVER UNDER-STOOD.

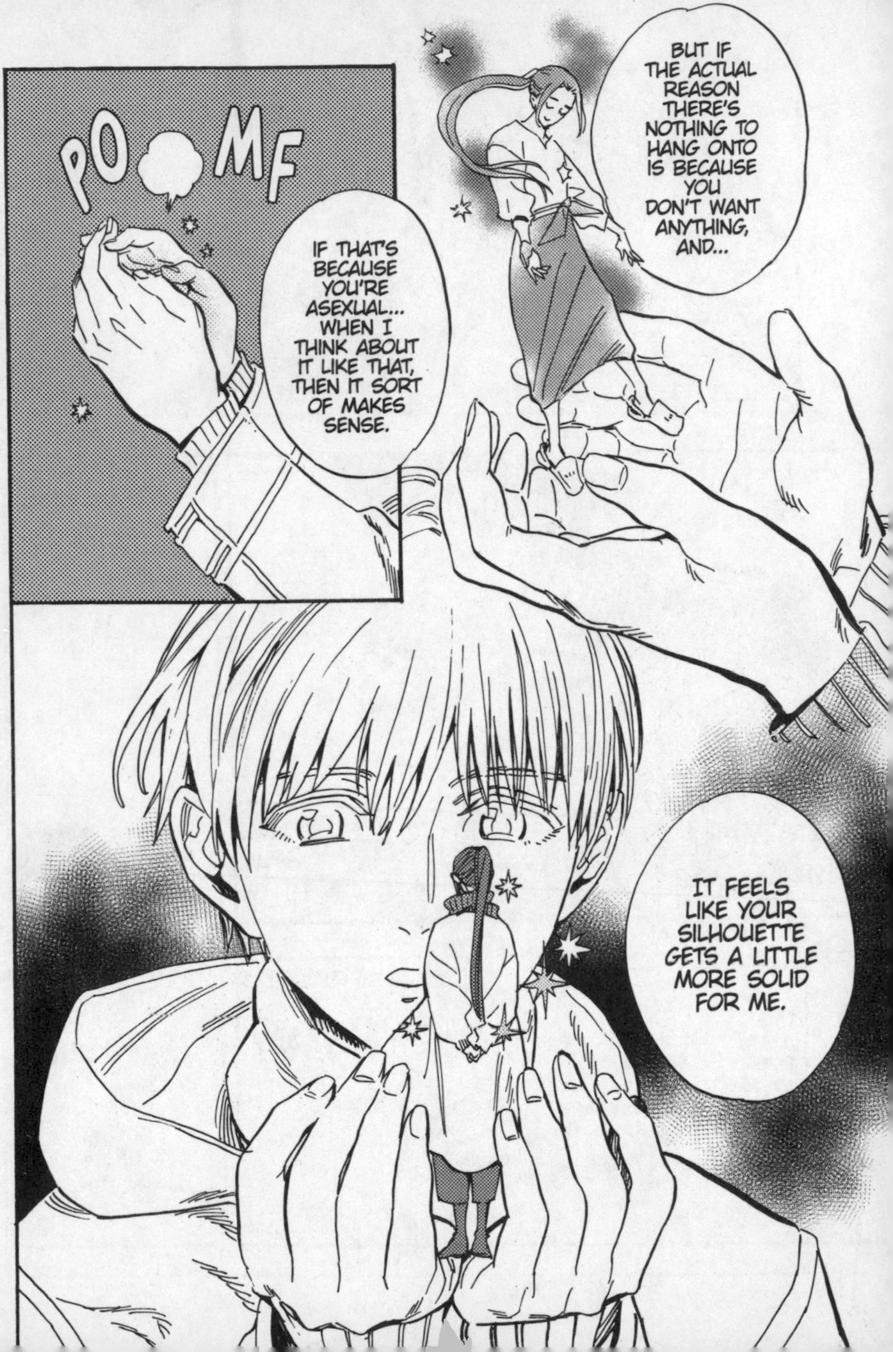
POOMF
IF THAT'S BECAUSE YOU'RE ASEXUAL... WHEN I THINK ABOUT IT LIKE THAT, THEN IT SORT OF MAKES SENSE.
BUT IF THE ACTUAL REASON THERE'S NOTHING TO HANG ONTO IS BECAUSE YOU DON'T WANT ANYTHING, AND...
IT FEELS LIKE YOUR SILHOUETTE GETS A LITTLE MORE SOLID FOR ME.

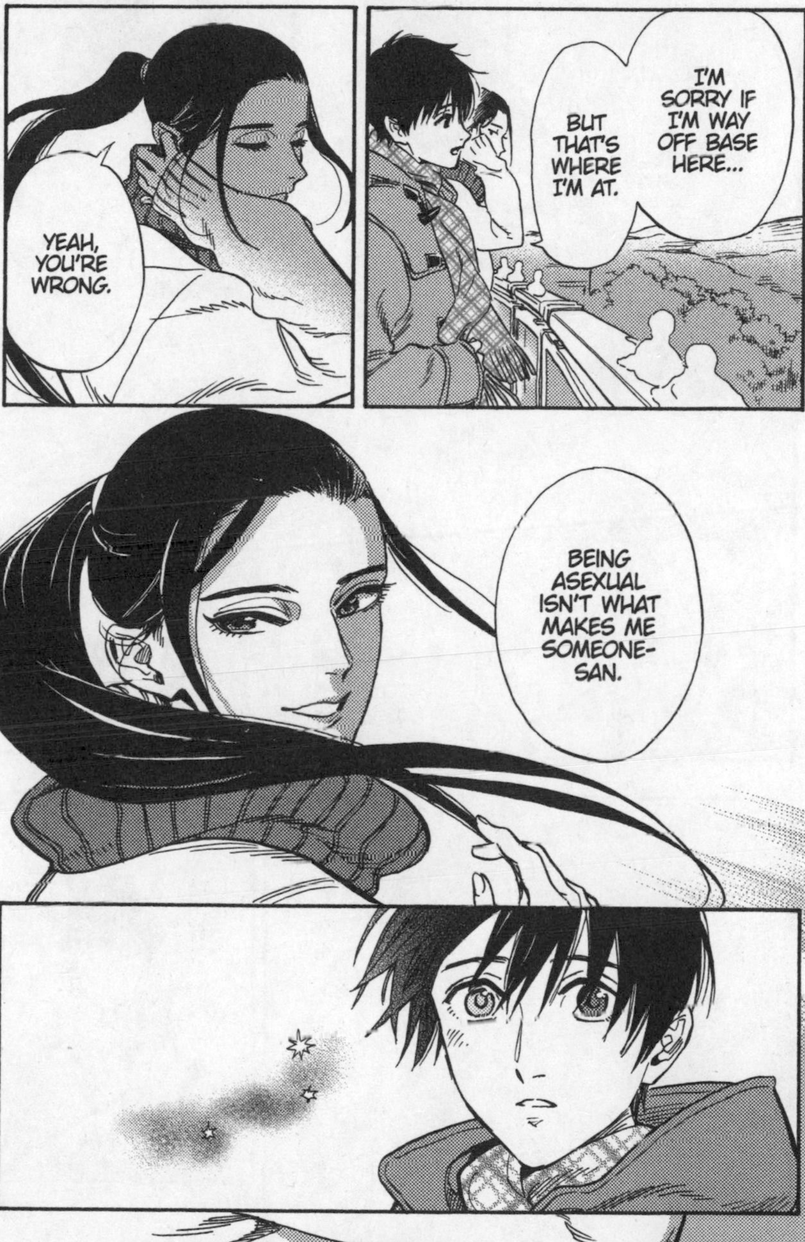
I'M SORRY IF I'M WAY OFF BASE HERE...
BUT THAT'S WHERE I'M AT.
YEAH, YOU'RE WRONG.
BEING ASEXUAL ISN'T WHAT MAKES ME SOMEONE-SAN.

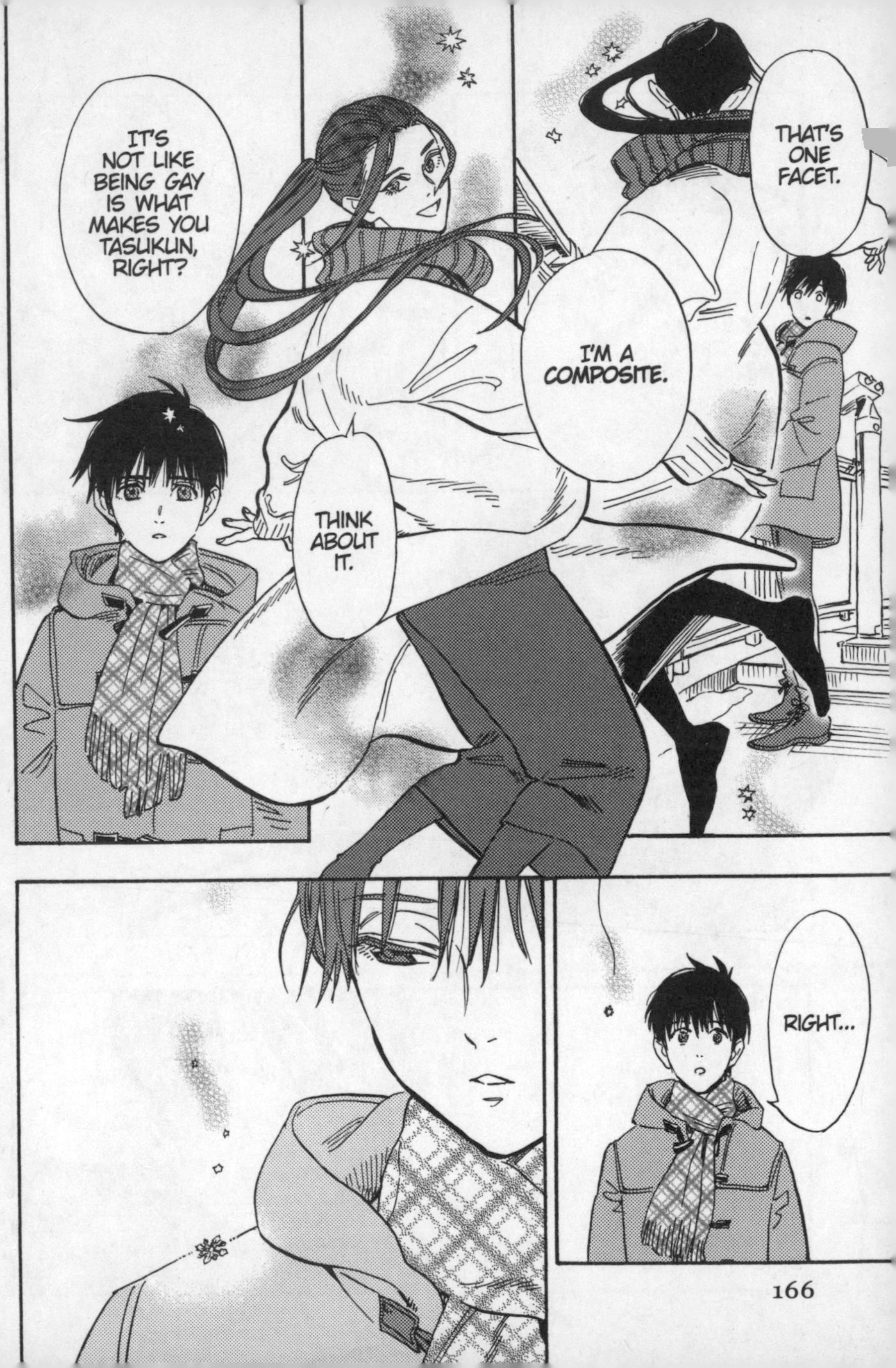
THAT'S ONE FACET.
I'M A COMPOSITE.
THINK ABOUT IT.
IT'S NOT LIKE BEING GAY IS WHAT MAKES YOU TASUKUN, RIGHT?
RIGHT...

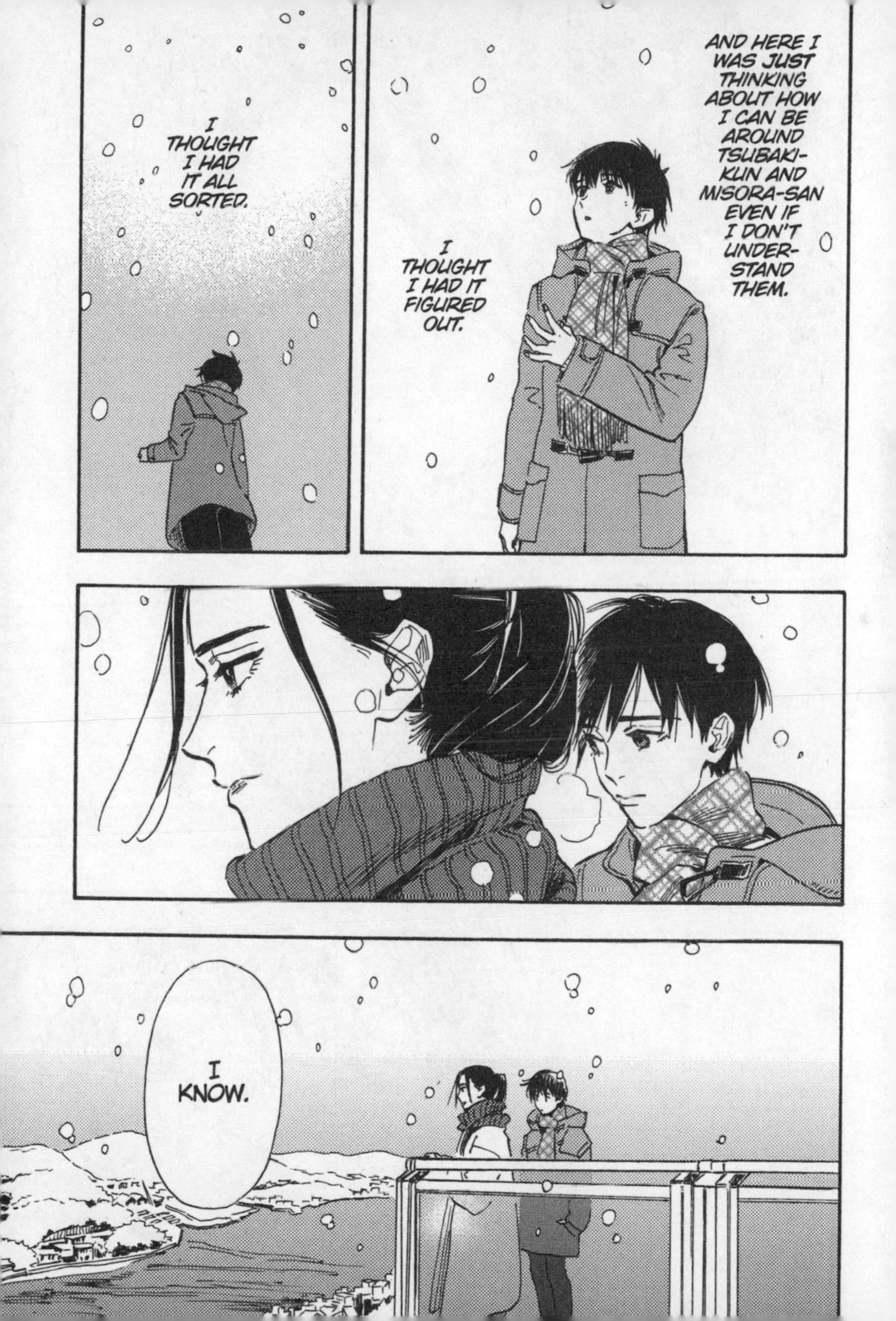
AND HERE I WAS JUST THINKING ABOUT HOW I CAN BE AROUND TSUBAKI-KUN AND MISORA-SAN EVEN IF I DON'T UNDER-STAND THEM.
I THOUGHT I HAD IT FIGURED OUT.
I THOUGHT I HAD IT ALL SORTED.
I KNOW.

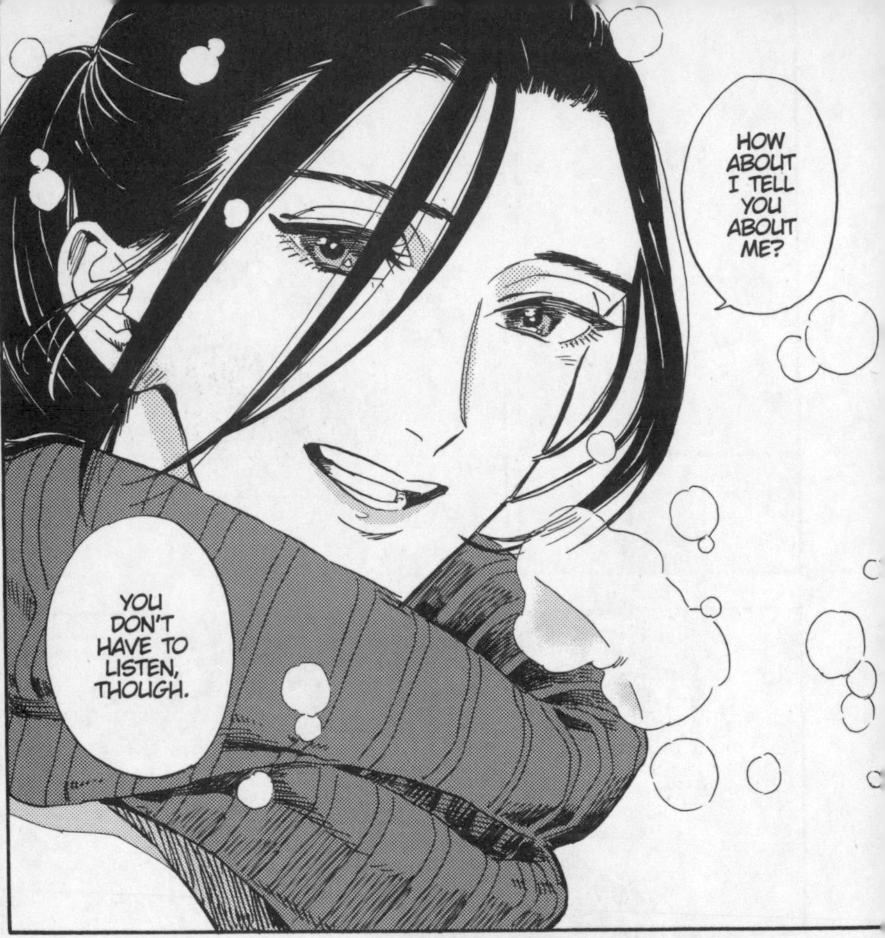
HOW ABOUT I TELL YOU ABOUT ME?
YOU DON'T HAVE TO LISTEN, THOUGH.
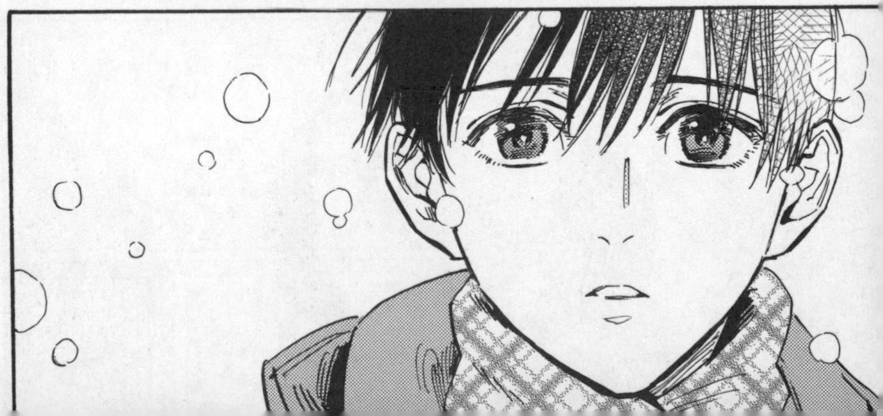

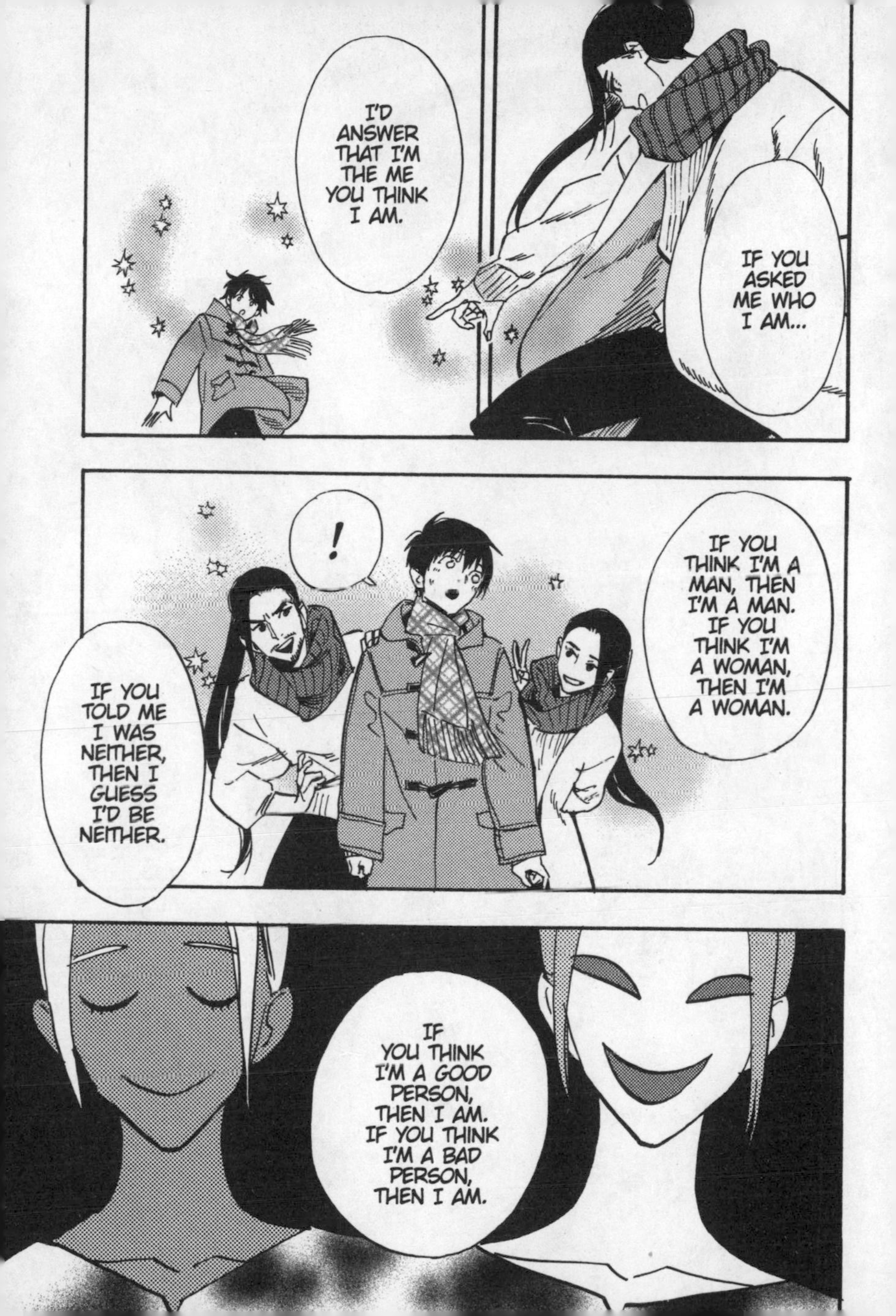
IF YOU ASKED ME WHO I AM...
I'D ANSWER THAT I'M THE ME YOU THINK I AM.
IF YOU THINK I'M A MAN, THEN I'M A MAN. IF YOU THINK I'M A WOMAN, THEN I'M A WOMAN.
!
IF YOU TOLD ME I WAS NEITHER, THEN I GUESS I'D BE NEITHER.
IF YOU THINK I'M A GOOD PERSON, THEN I AM. IF YOU THINK I'M A BAD PERSON, THEN I AM.

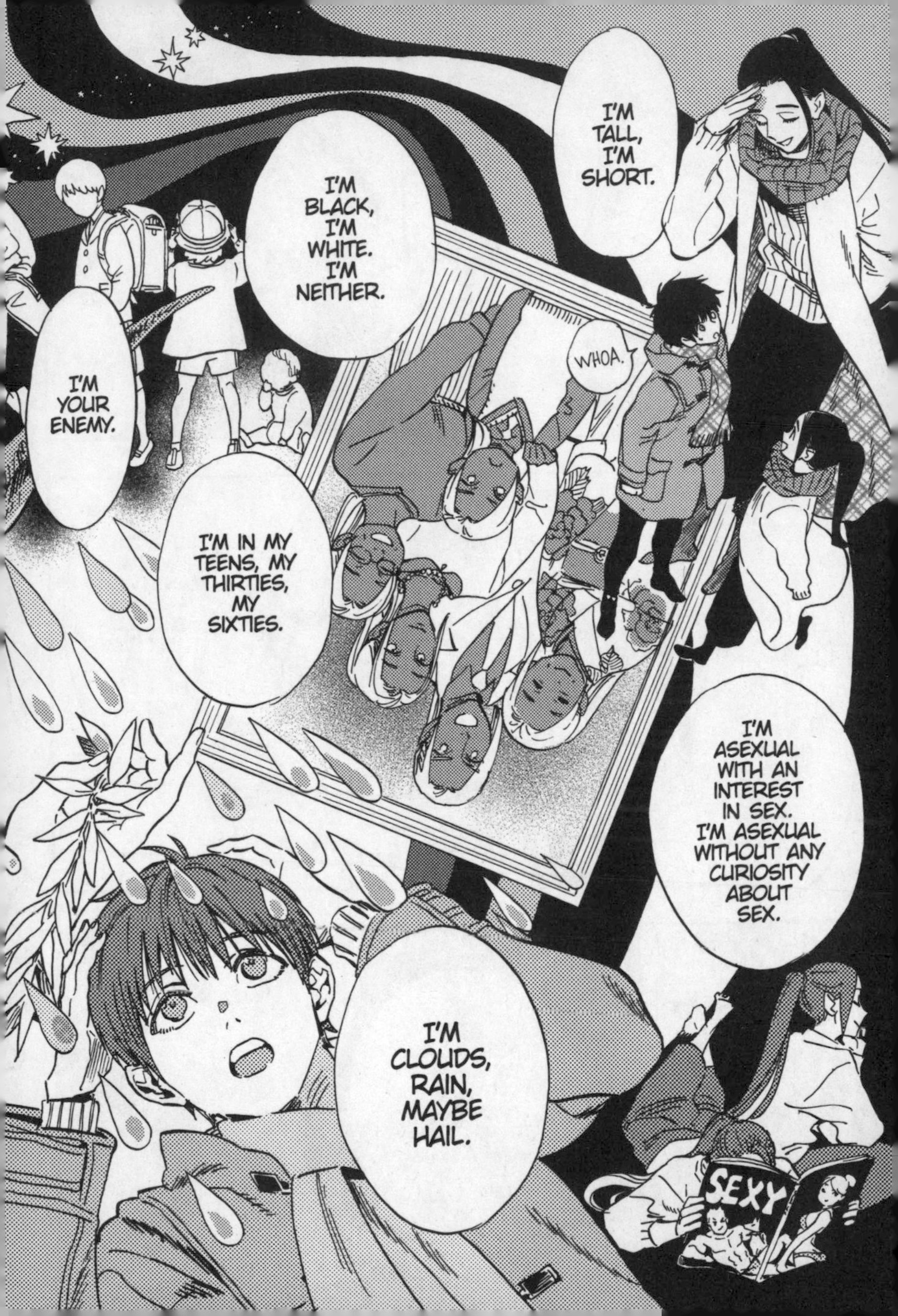
I'M TALL, I'M SHORT.
I'M BLACK, I'M WHITE. I'M NEITHER.
WHOA.
I'M YOUR ENEMY.
I'M IN MY TEENS, MY THIRTIES, MY SIXTIES.
I'M ASEXUAL WITH AN INTEREST IN SEX. I'M ASEXUAL WITHOUT ANY CURIOSITY ABOUT SEX.
I'M CLOUDS, RAIN, MAYBE HAIL.
SEXY

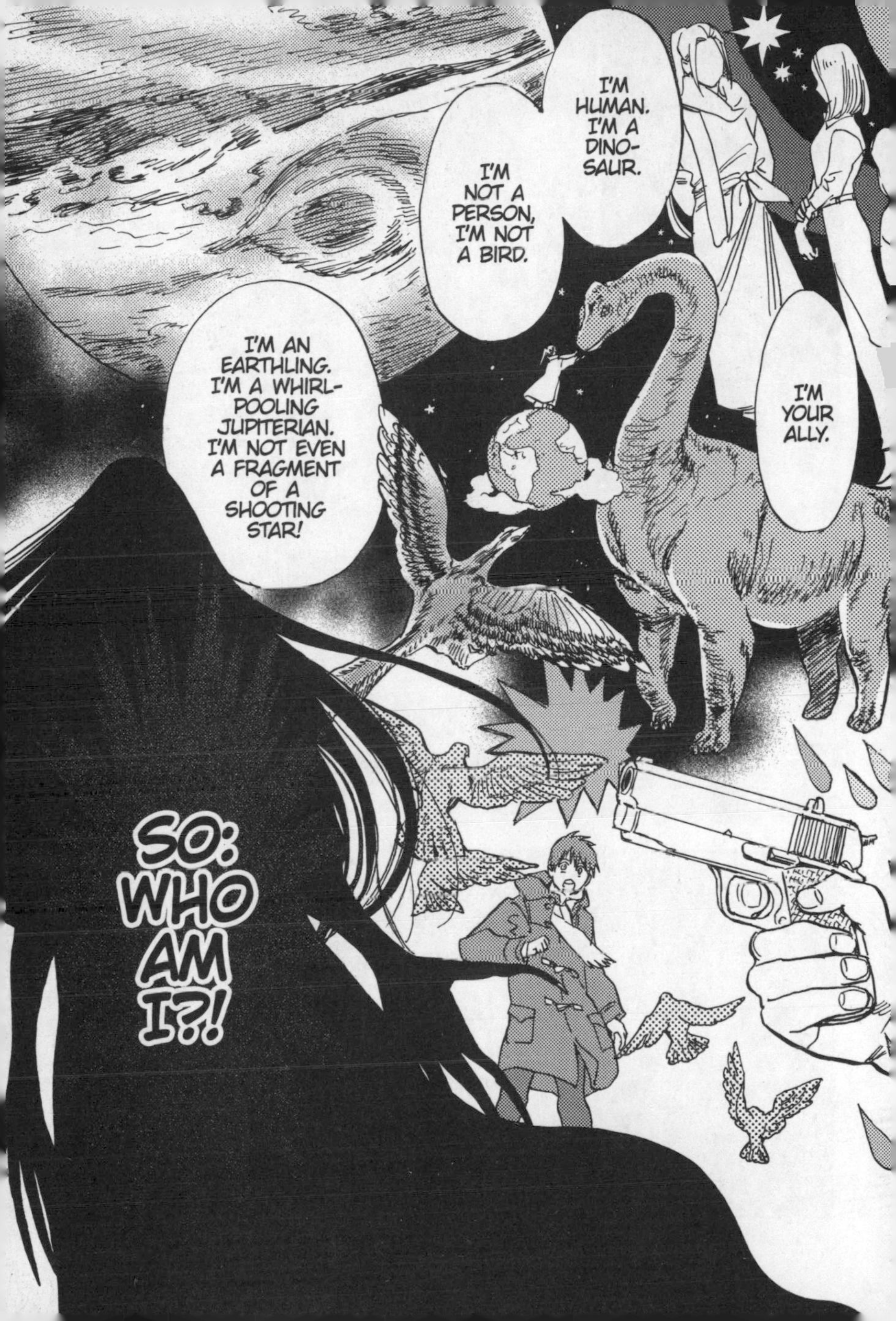
I'M YOUR ALLY.
I'M HUMAN. I'M A DINO-SAUR.
I'M NOT A PERSON, I'M NOT A BIRD.
I'M AN EARTHLING. I'M A WHIRL-POOLING JUPITERIAN. I'M NOT EVEN A FRAGMENT OF A SHOOTING STAR!
SO: WHO AM I?!

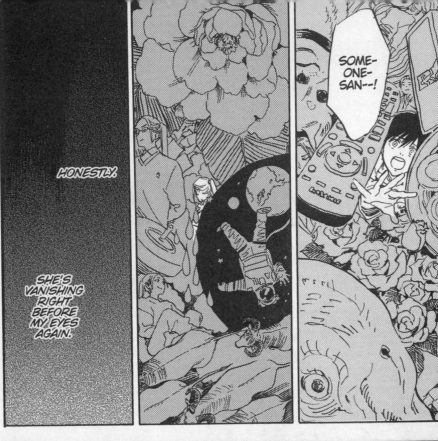

HONESTLY.

SHE'S VANISHING RIGHT BEFORE MY EYES AGAIN.

SOME-ONE-SAN--!

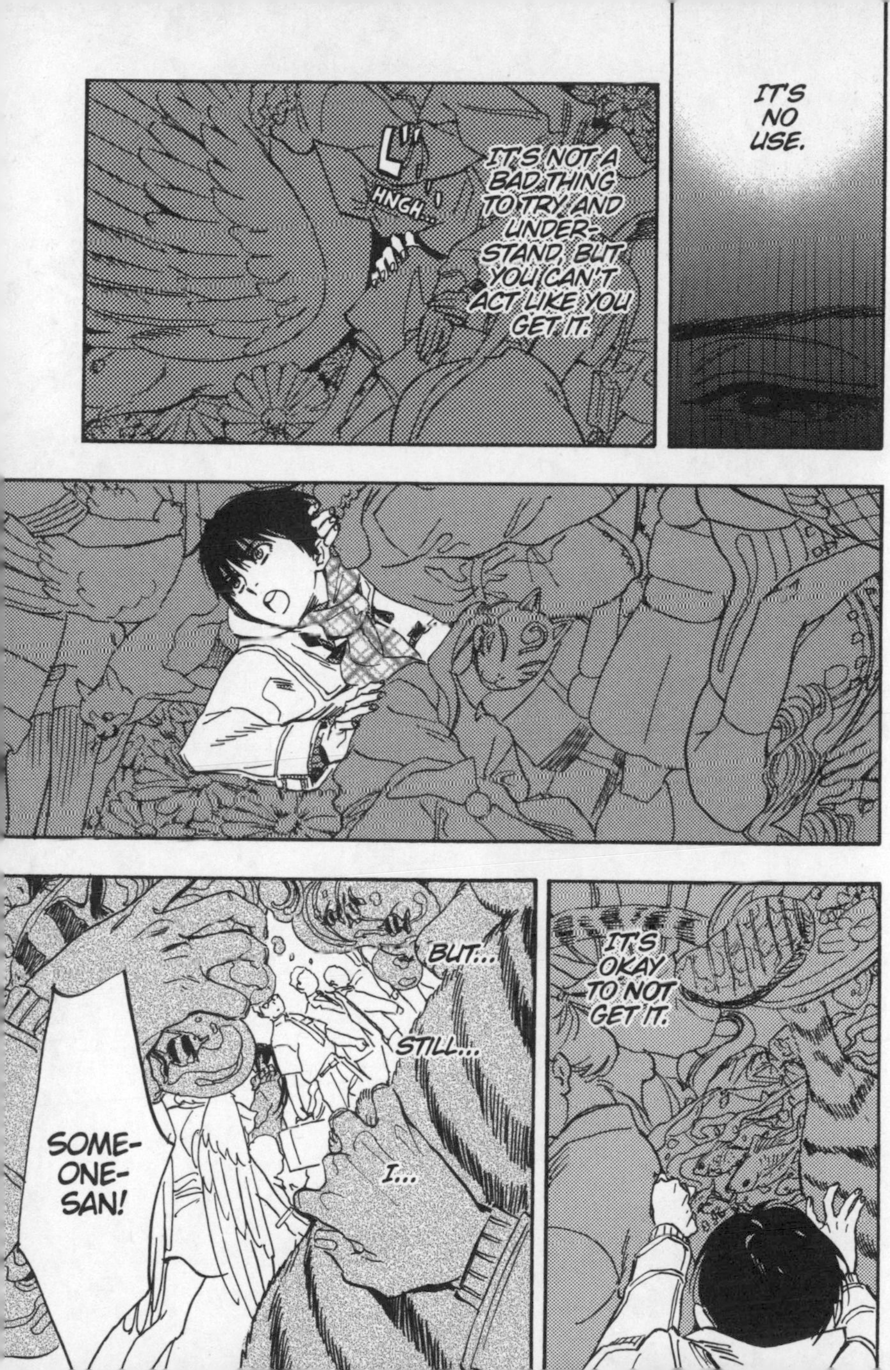
IT'S NO USE.
L''
HNGH...
IT'S NOT A BAD THING TO TRY AND UNDER-STAND, BUT YOU CAN'T ACT LIKE YOU GET IT.
IT'S OKAY TO NOT GET IT.
BUT...
STILL...
I...
SOME-ONE-SAN!

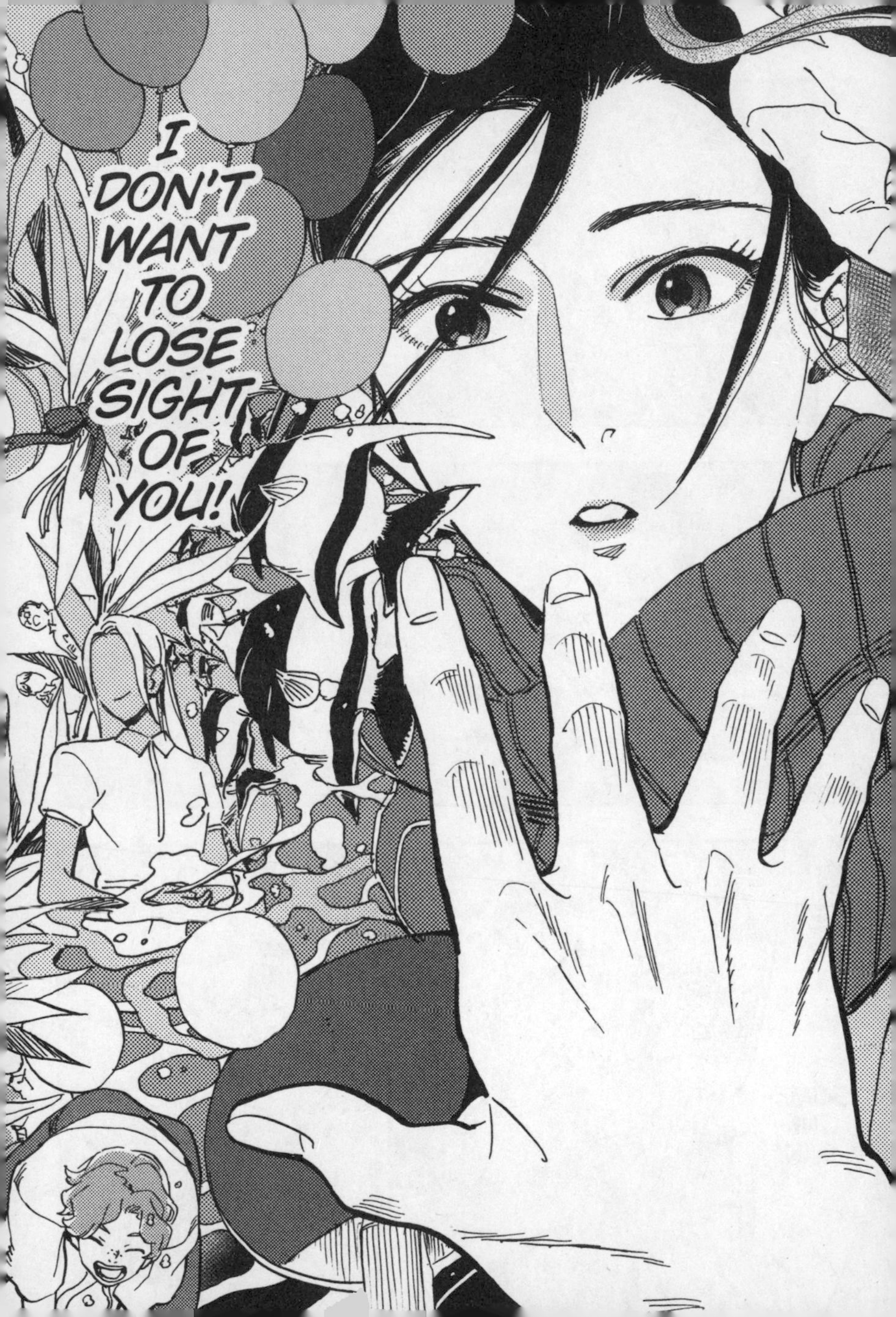
I DON'T WANT TO LOSE SIGHT OF YOU!

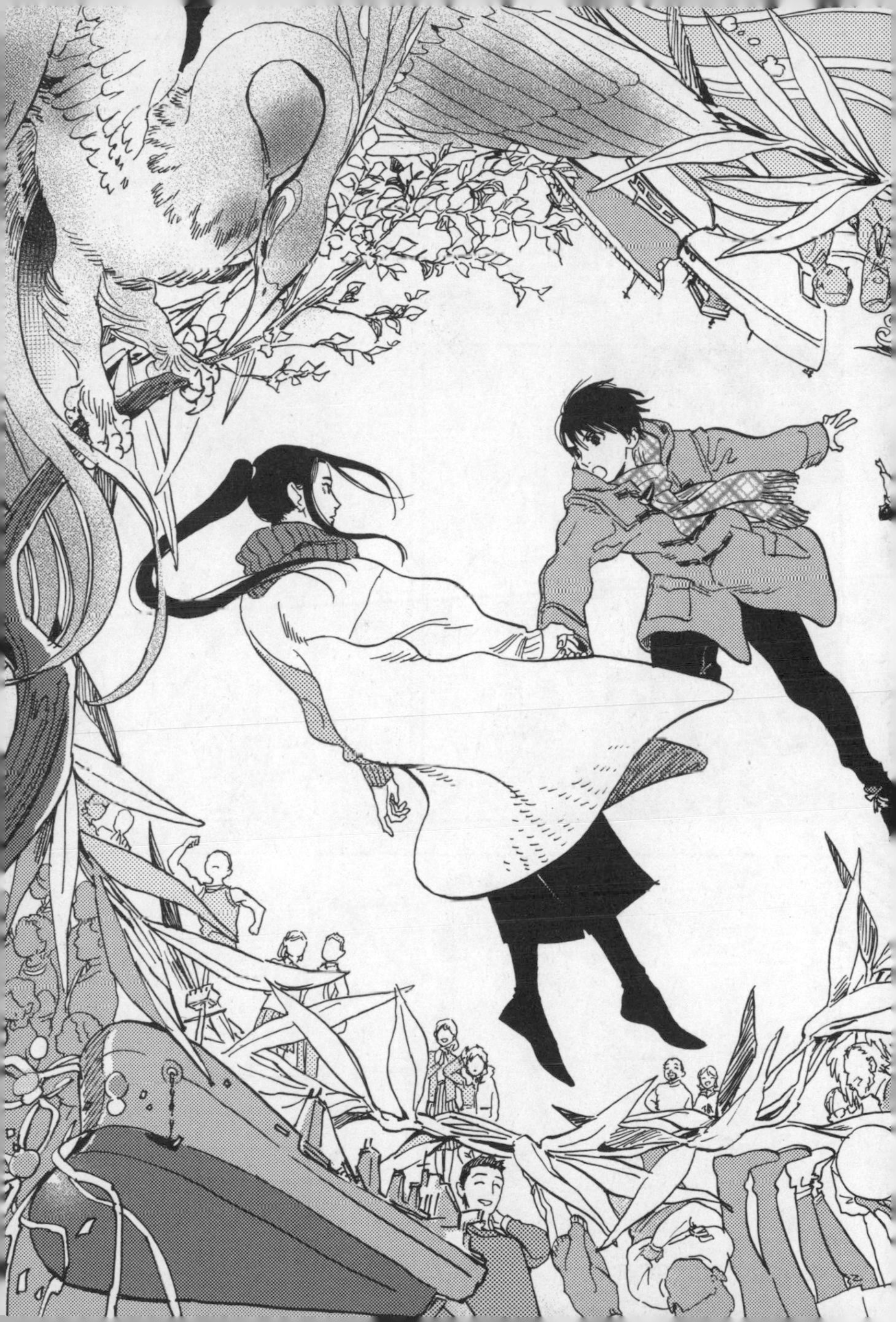

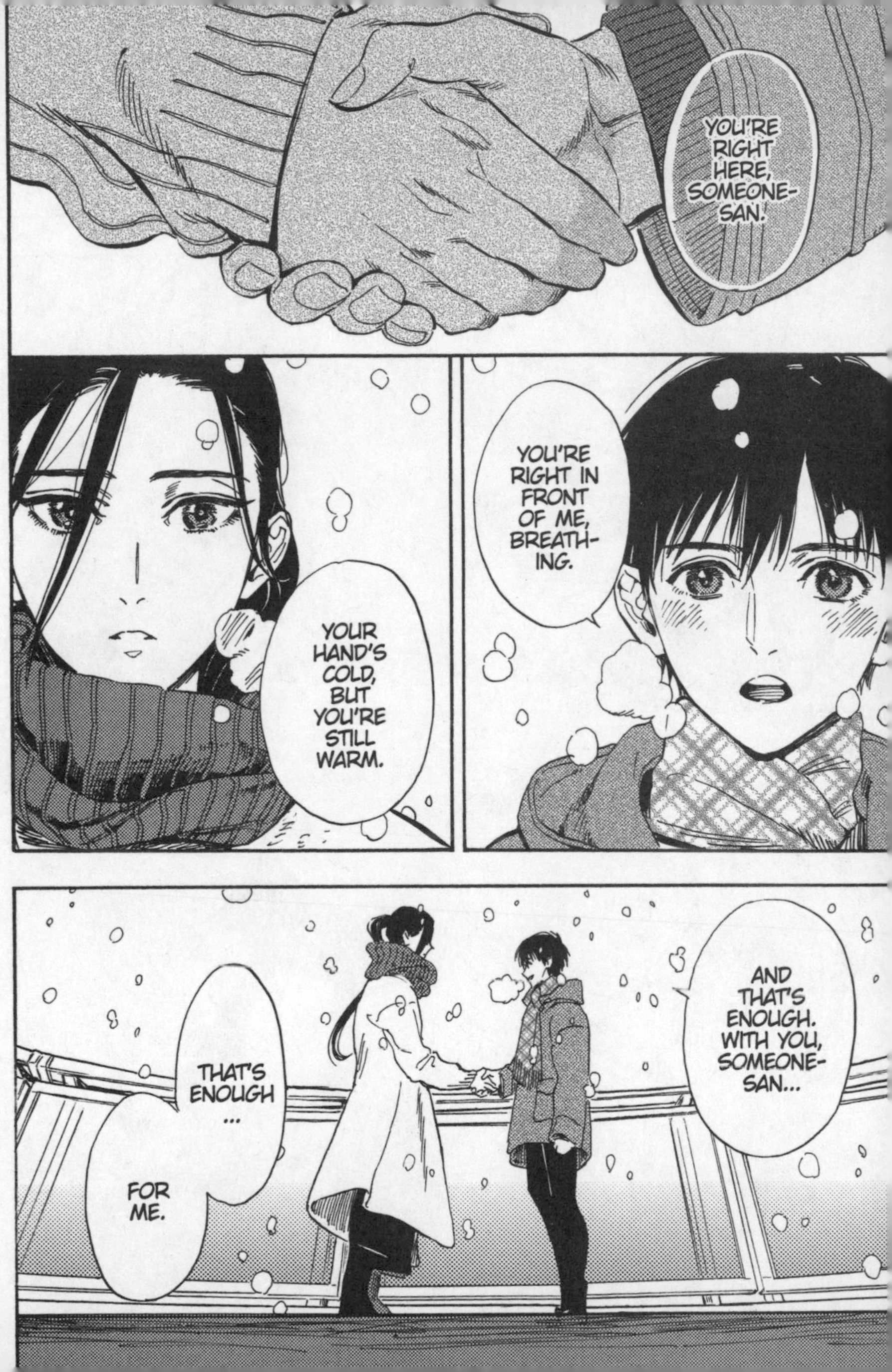
YOU'RE RIGHT HERE, SOMEONE-SAN!
YOU'RE RIGHT IN FRONT OF ME, BREATHING.
YOUR HAND'S COLD, BUT YOU'RE STILL WARM.
AND THAT'S ENOUGH. WITH YOU, SOMEONE-SAN...
THAT'S ENOUGH...
FOR ME.

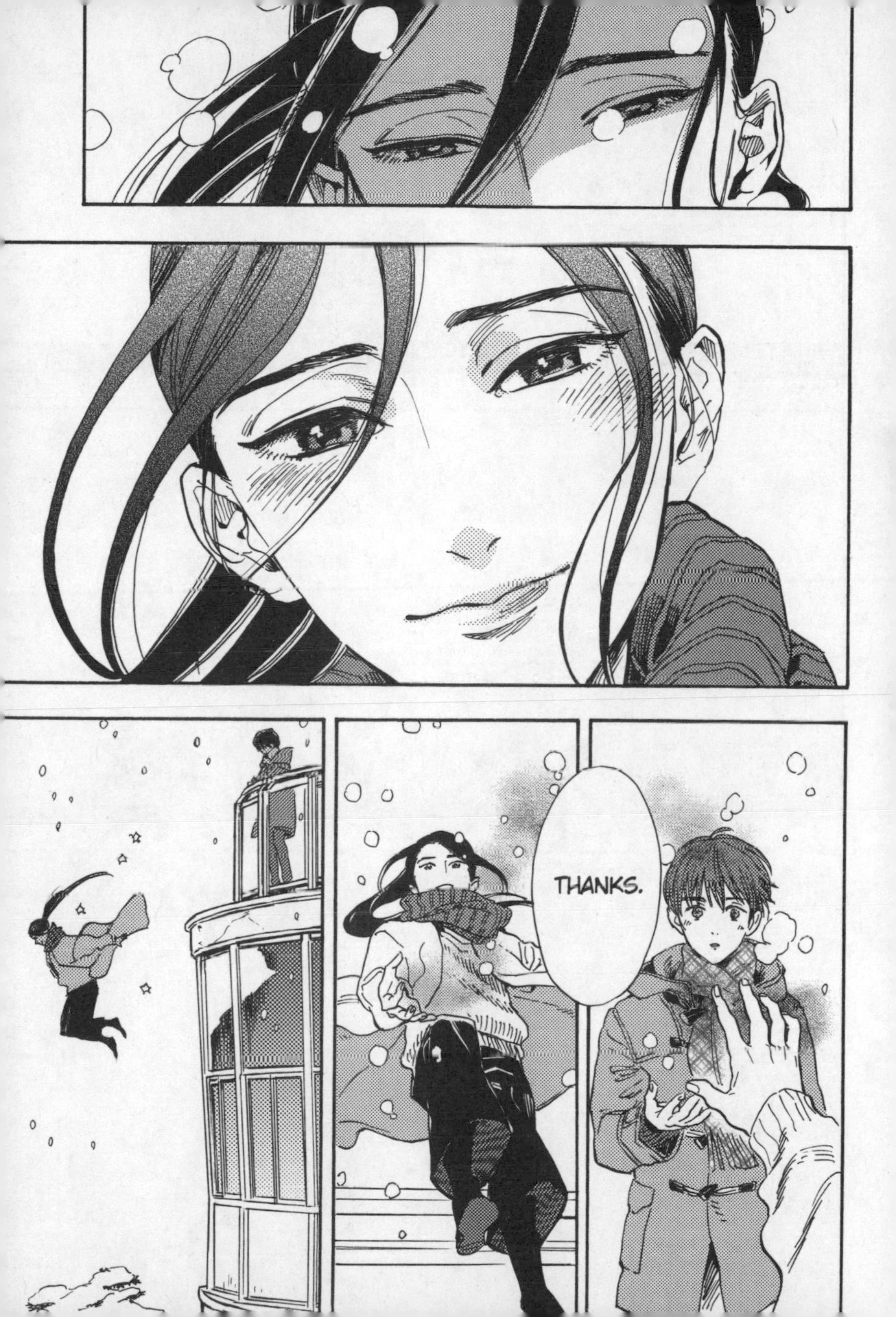
THANKS.

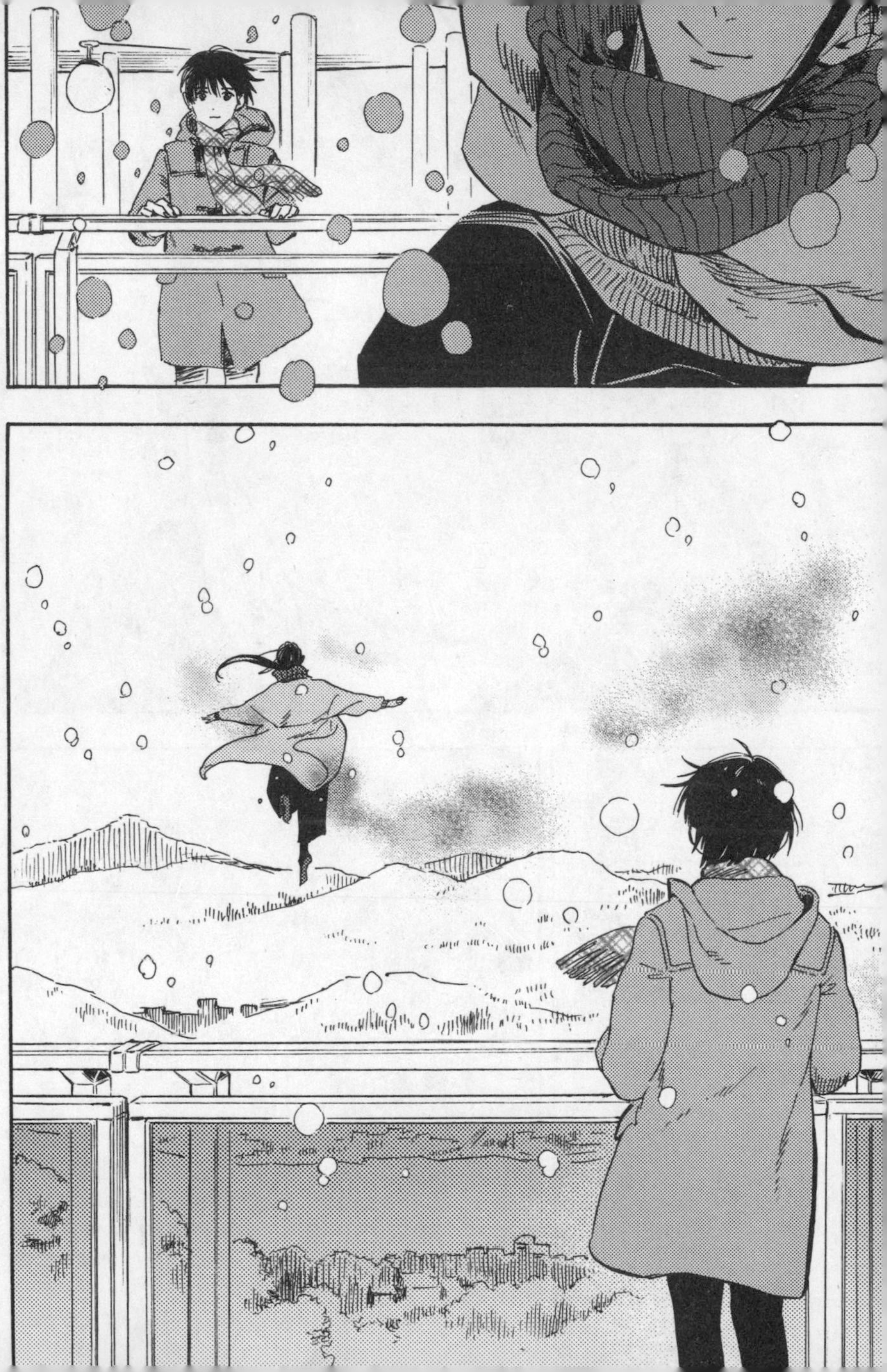

Our Dreams at Dusk

SHIMANAMI TASOGARE

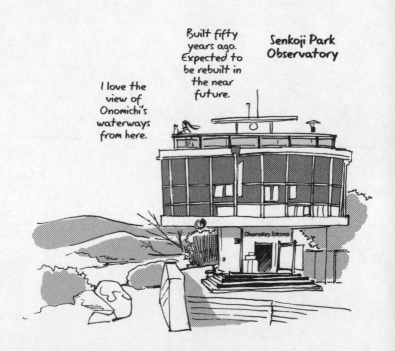

Senkoji Park Observatory
Built fifty years ago. Expected to be rebuilt in the near future.
I love the view of Onomichi's waterways from here.
Observatory Entrance

Chapter 22

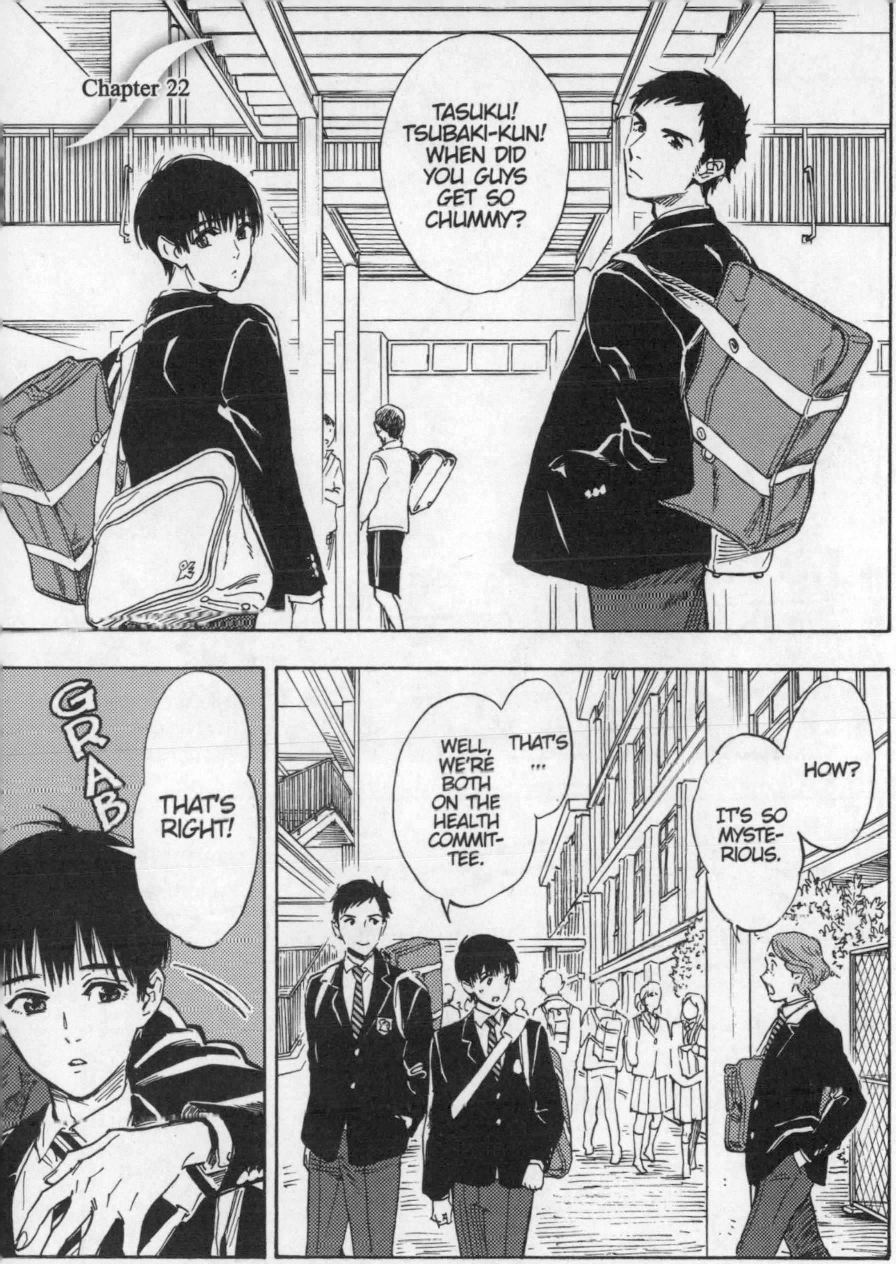
TASUKU! TSUBAKI-KUN! WHEN DID YOU GUYS GET SO CHUMMY?
HOW?
IT'S SO MYSTERIOUS.
THAT'S ...
WELL, WE'RE BOTH ON THE HEALTH COMMITTEE.
GRAB
THAT'S RIGHT!

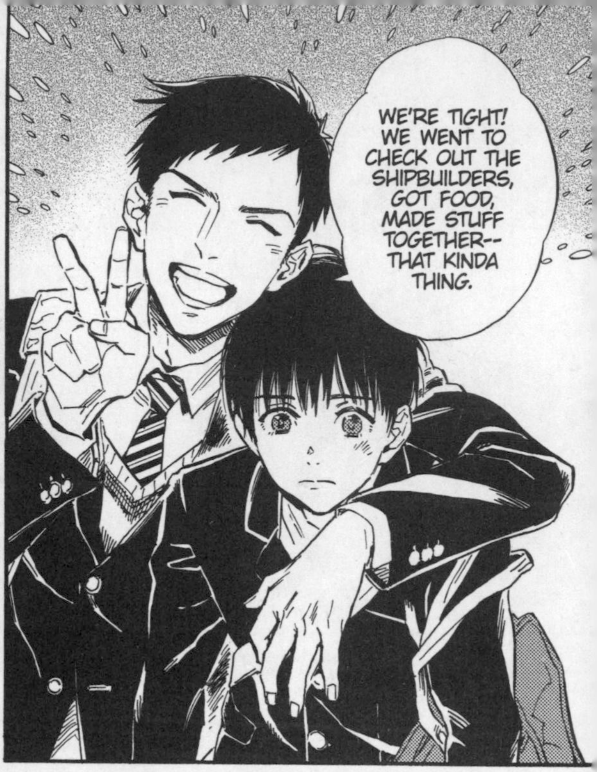
WE'RE TIGHT! WE WENT TO CHECK OUT THE SHIPBUILDERS, GOT FOOD, MADE STUFF TOGETHER-- THAT KINDA THING.

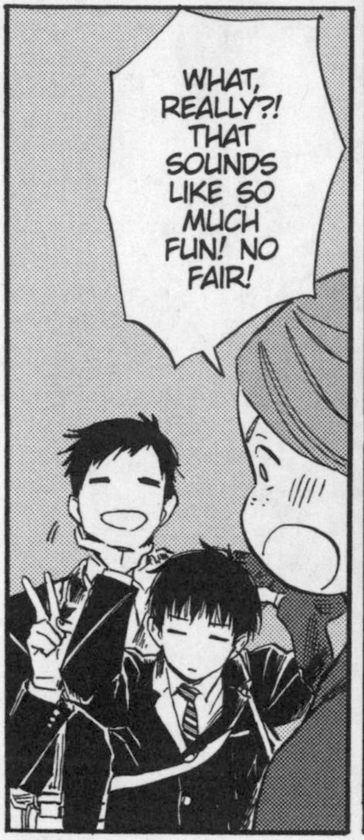
WHAT, REALLY?! THAT SOUNDS LIKE SO MUCH FUN! NO FAIR!

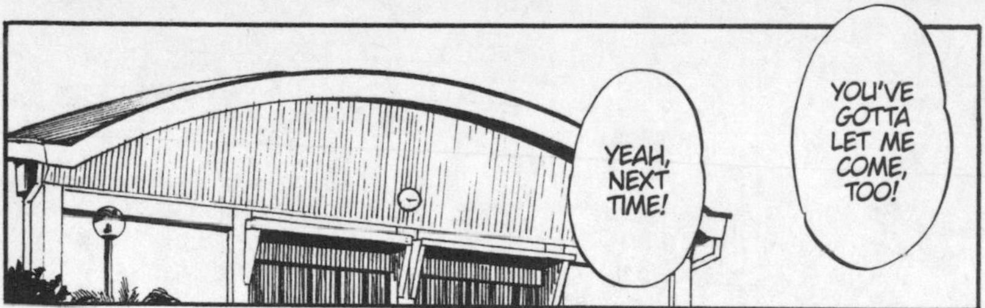
YOU'VE GOTTA LET ME COME, TOO!
YEAH, NEXT TIME!

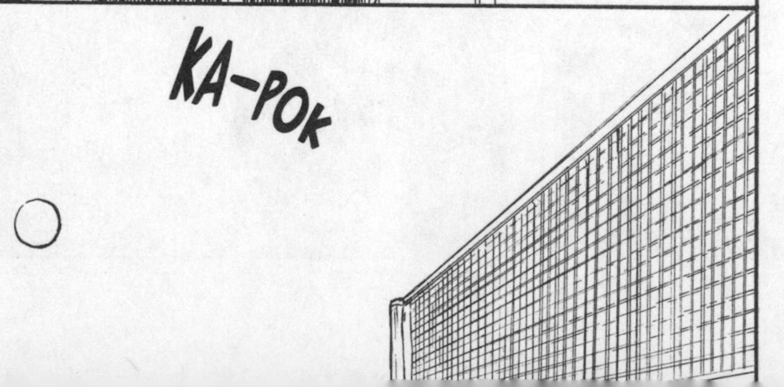
KA-POK

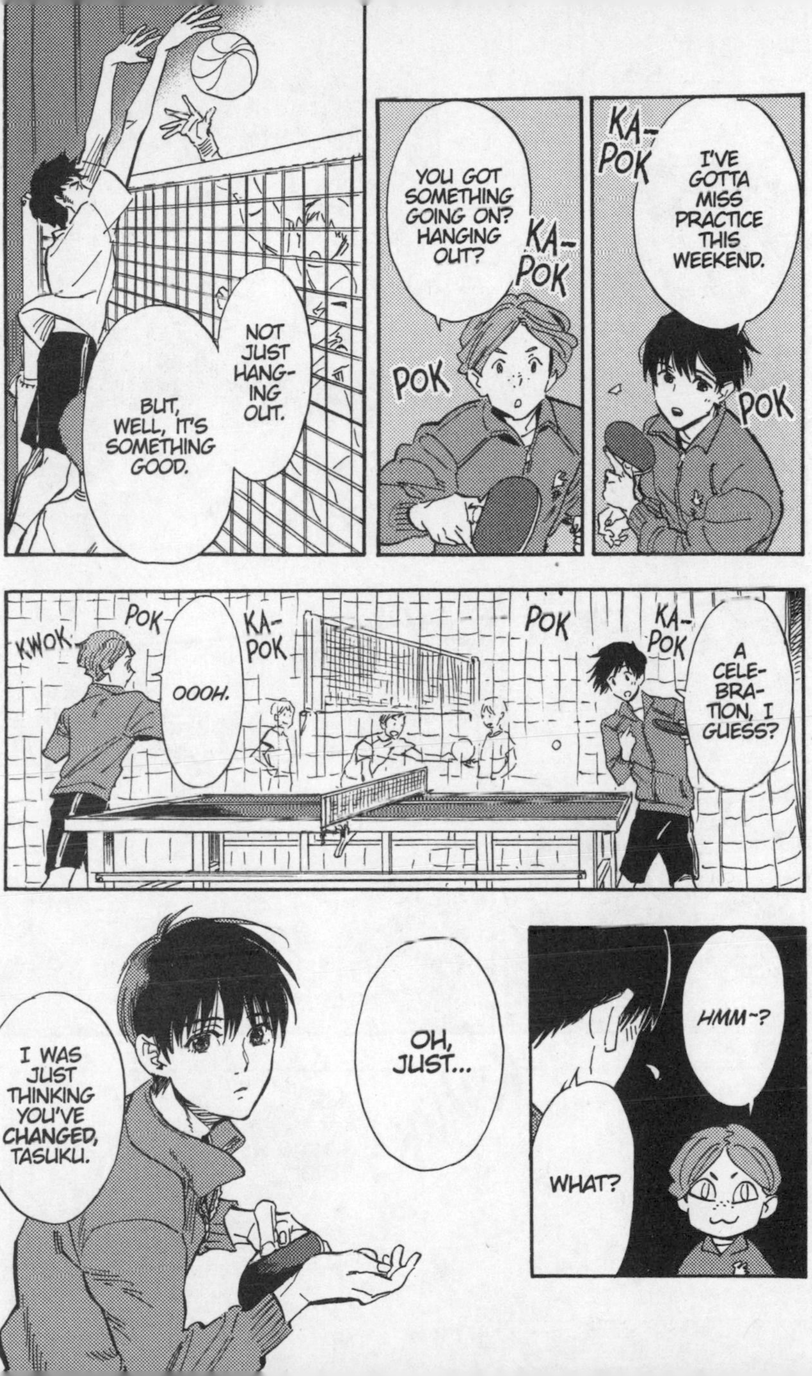
KA-POK
I'VE GOTTA MISS PRACTICE THIS WEEKEND.
POK
YOU GOT SOMETHING GOING ON? HANGING OUT?
KA-POK
POK
NOT JUST HANG-ING OUT.
BUT, WELL, IT'S SOMETHING GOOD.
KA-POK
A CELE-BRA-TION, I GUESS?
POK
KA-POK
OOOH.
POK
KWOK
HMM~?
WHAT?
OH, JUST...
I WAS JUST THINKING YOU'VE CHANGED, TASUKU.

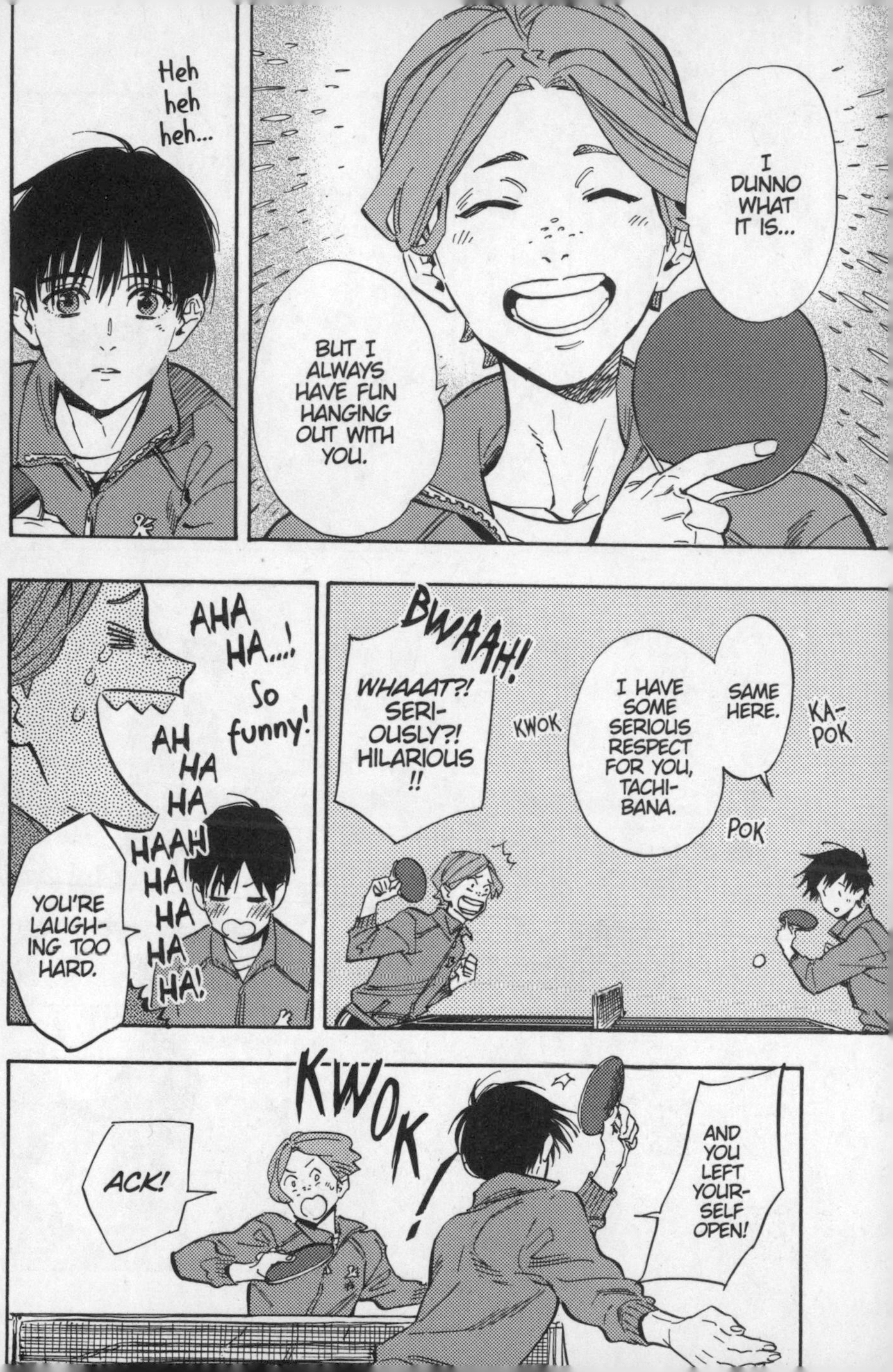
I DUNNO WHAT IT IS...
BUT I ALWAYS HAVE FUN HANGING OUT WITH YOU.
Heh heh heh...
KA-POK
SAME HERE.
I HAVE SOME SERIOUS RESPECT FOR YOU, TACHIBANA.
BWAAAH!
WHAAAT?! SERIOUSLY?! HILARIOUS!!
KWOK
POK
AHA HA...! So funny!
AH HA HA HAAH HA HA HA HA!
YOU'RE LAUGHING TOO HARD.
AND YOU LEFT YOURSELF OPEN!
KWOK!
ACK!

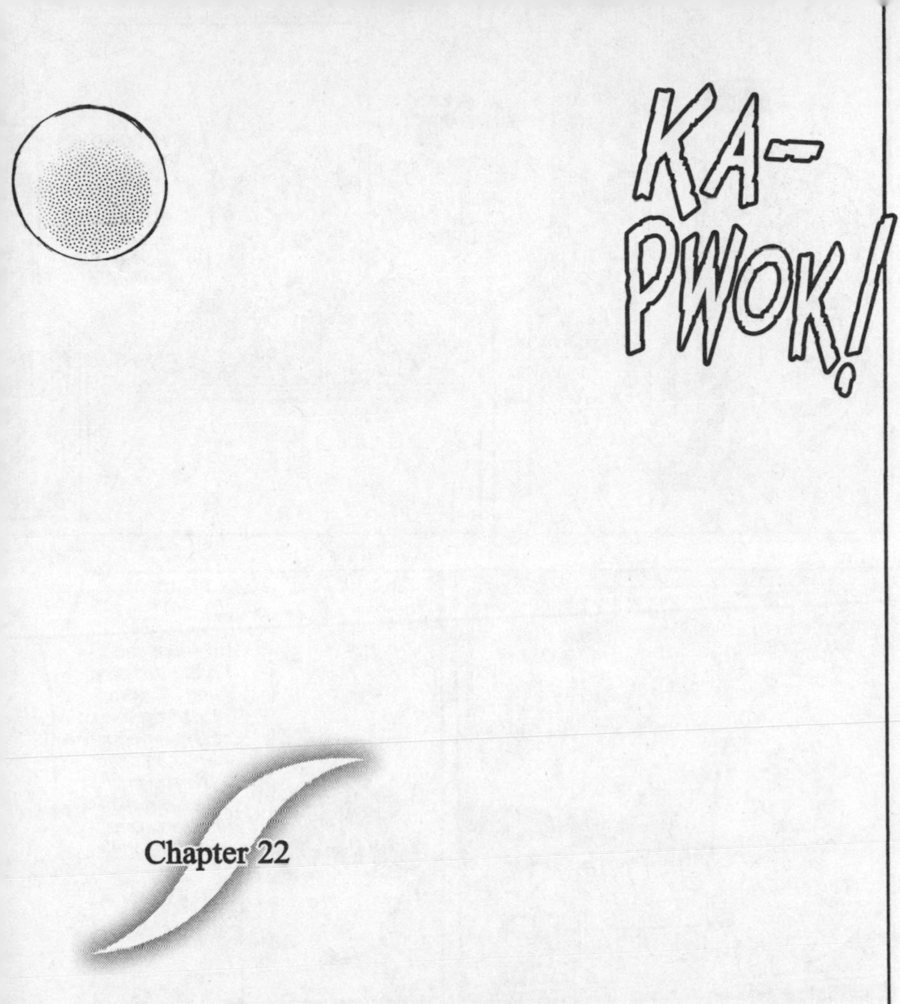
KA-PWOK!

Chapter 22

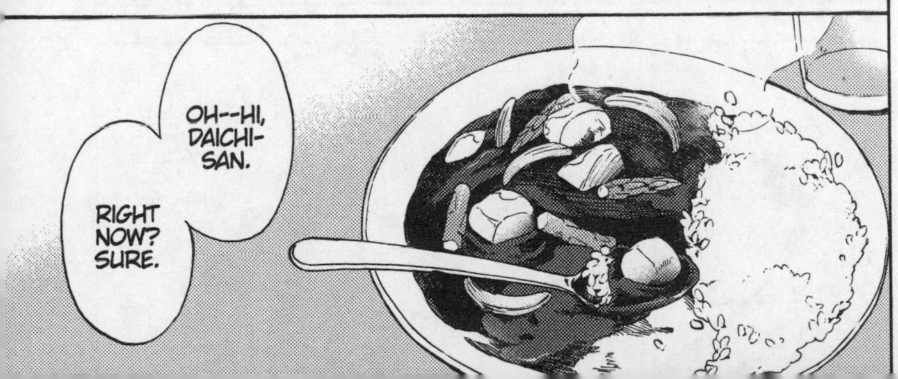
OH--HI, DAICHI-SAN.
RIGHT NOW? SURE.

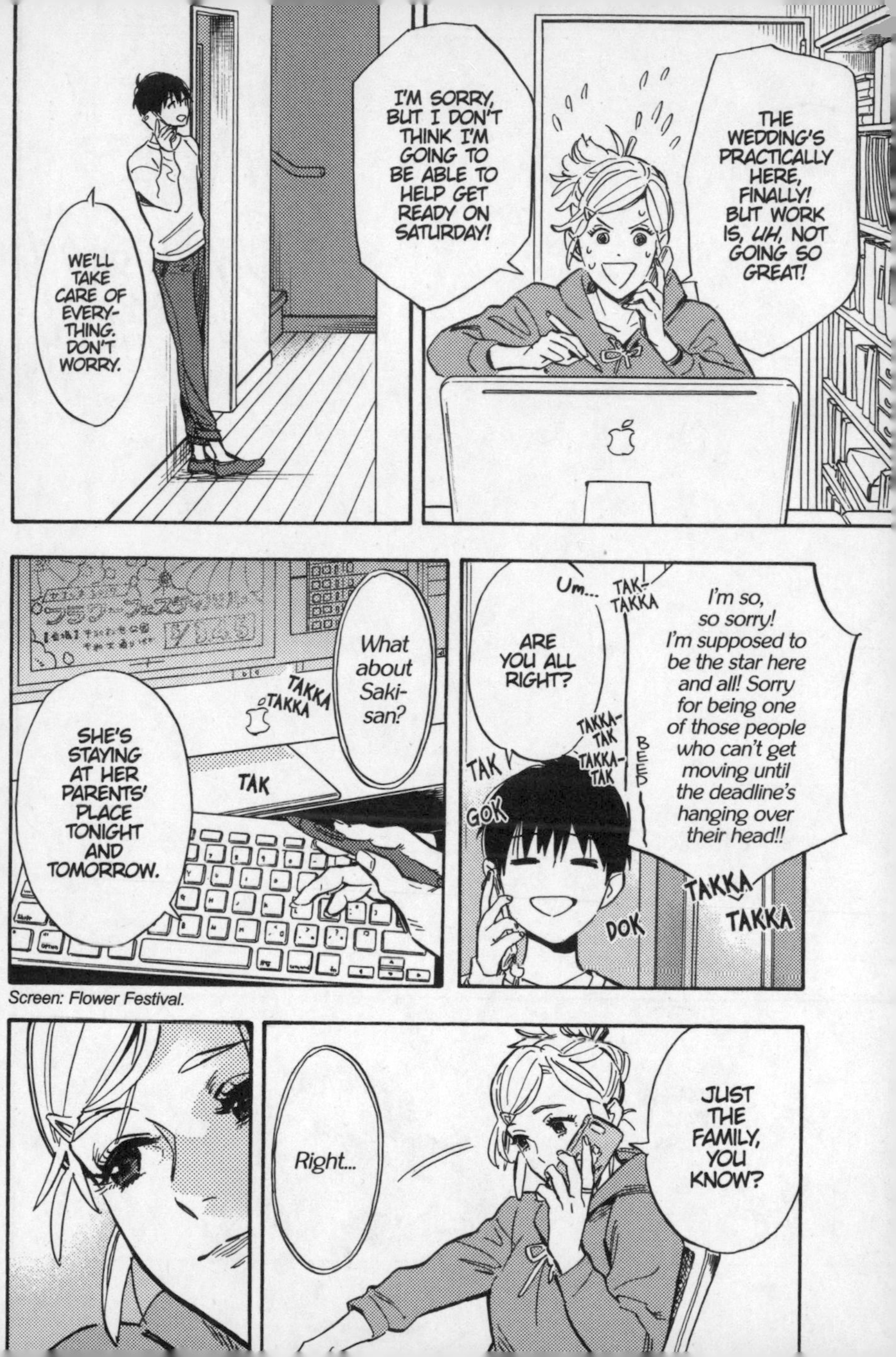
THE WEDDING'S PRACTICALLY HERE, FINALLY! BUT WORK IS, *UH*, NOT GOING SO GREAT!
I'M SORRY, BUT I DON'T THINK I'M GOING TO BE ABLE TO HELP GET READY ON SATURDAY!
WE'LL TAKE CARE OF EVERYTHING. DON'T WORRY.
I'm so, so sorry! I'm supposed to be the star here and all! Sorry for being one of those people who can't get moving until the deadline's hanging over their head!!
TAK-TAKKA
Um...
ARE YOU ALL RIGHT?
TAKKA-TAK
TAKKA-TAK
BEEP
TAK
GOK
TAKKA TAKKA
DOK
What about Saki-san?
TAKKA TAKKA
TAK
SHE'S STAYING AT HER PARENTS' PLACE TONIGHT AND TOMORROW.
JUST THE FAMILY, YOU KNOW?
Right...
Screen: Flower Festival.

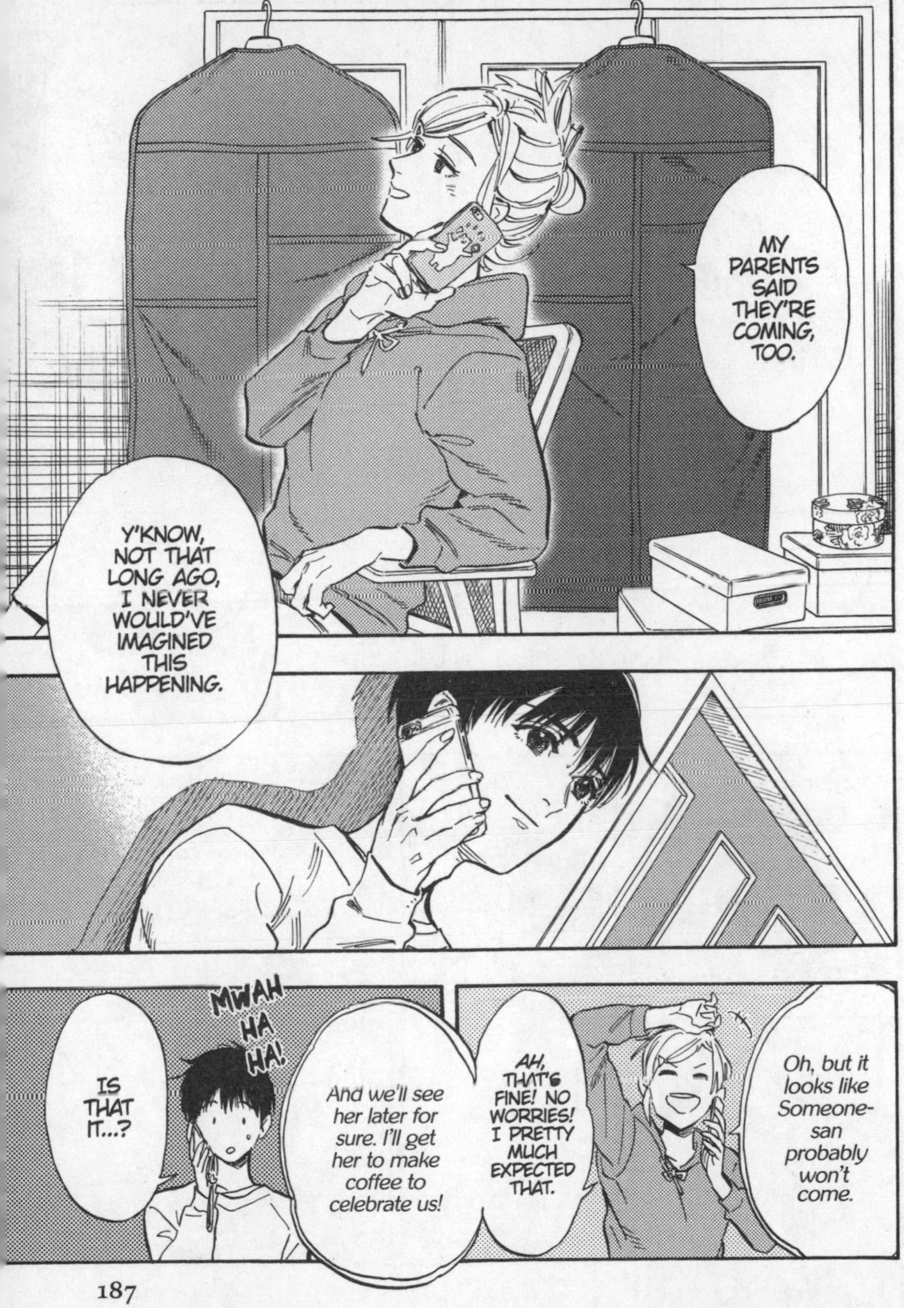
MY PARENTS SAID THEY'RE COMING, TOO.
Y'KNOW, NOT THAT LONG AGO, I NEVER WOULD'VE IMAGINED THIS HAPPENING.
Oh, but it looks like Someone-san probably won't come.
AH, THAT'S FINE! NO WORRIES! I PRETTY MUCH EXPECTED THAT.
And we'll see her later for sure. I'll get her to make coffee to celebrate us!
MWAH HA HA!
IS THAT IT...?

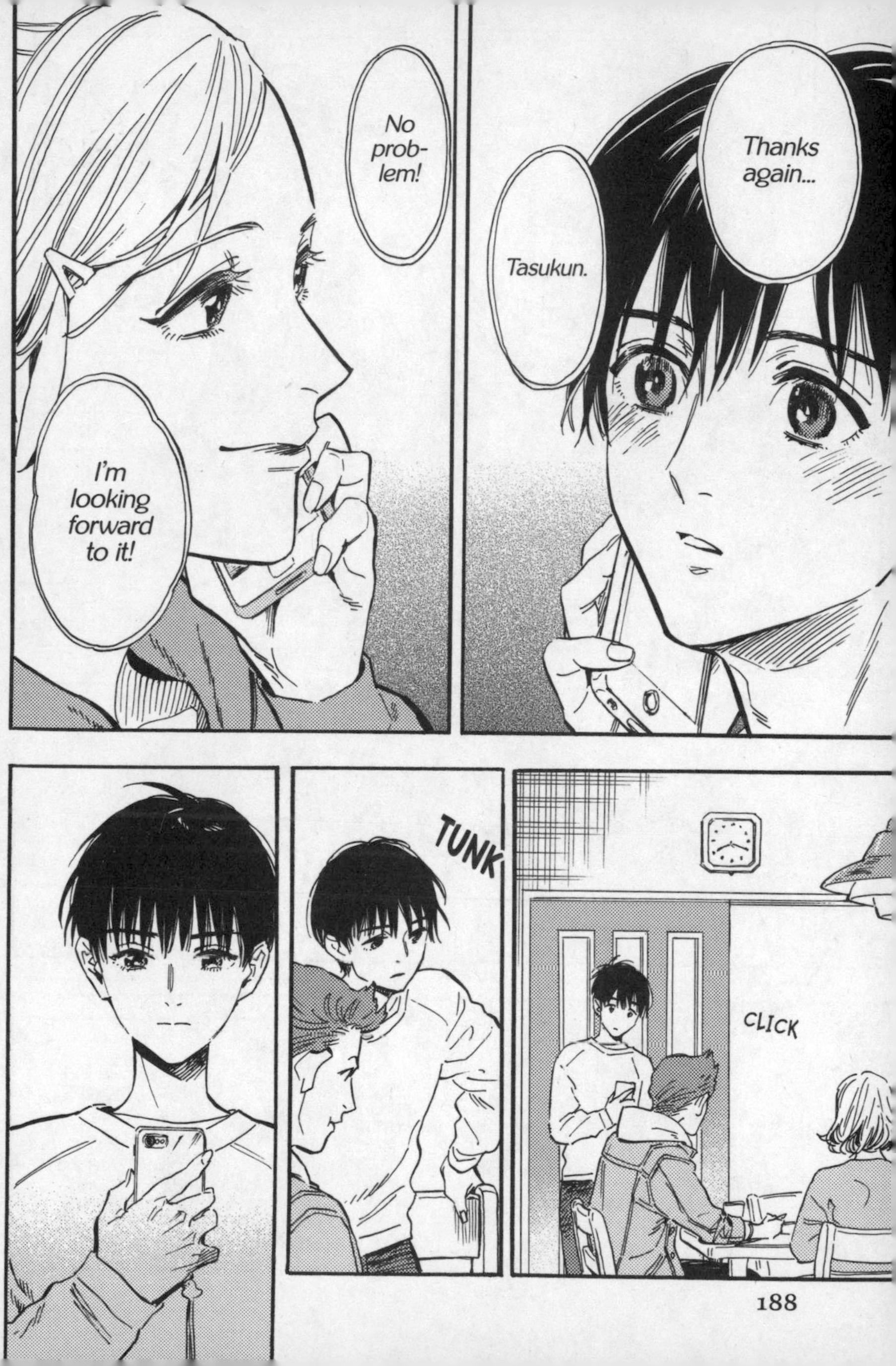
Thanks again...
Tasukun.
No prob-lem!
I'm looking forward to it!
CLICK
TUNK

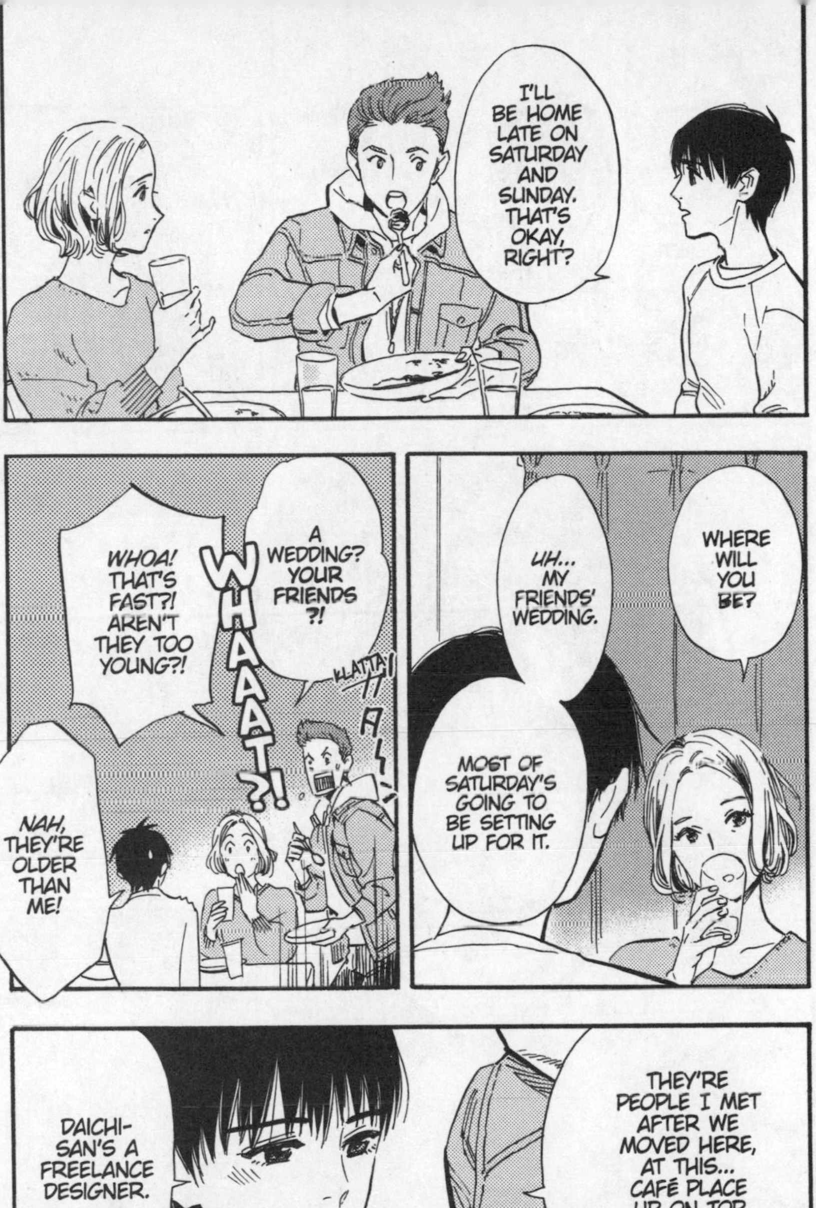
I'LL BE HOME LATE ON SATURDAY AND SUNDAY. THAT'S OKAY, RIGHT?
WHERE WILL YOU BE?
UH... MY FRIENDS' WEDDING.
MOST OF SATURDAY'S GOING TO BE SETTING UP FOR IT.
A WEDDING? YOUR FRIENDS?!
WHAAAT?!
KLATTA
WHOA! THAT'S FAST?! AREN'T THEY TOO YOUNG?!
NAH, THEY'RE OLDER THAN ME!
THEY'RE PEOPLE I MET AFTER WE MOVED HERE, AT THIS... CAFÉ PLACE UP ON TOP OF THE HILL.
DAICHI-SAN'S A FREELANCE DESIGNER.

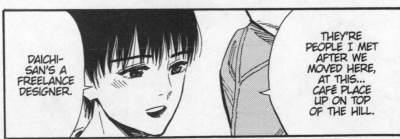

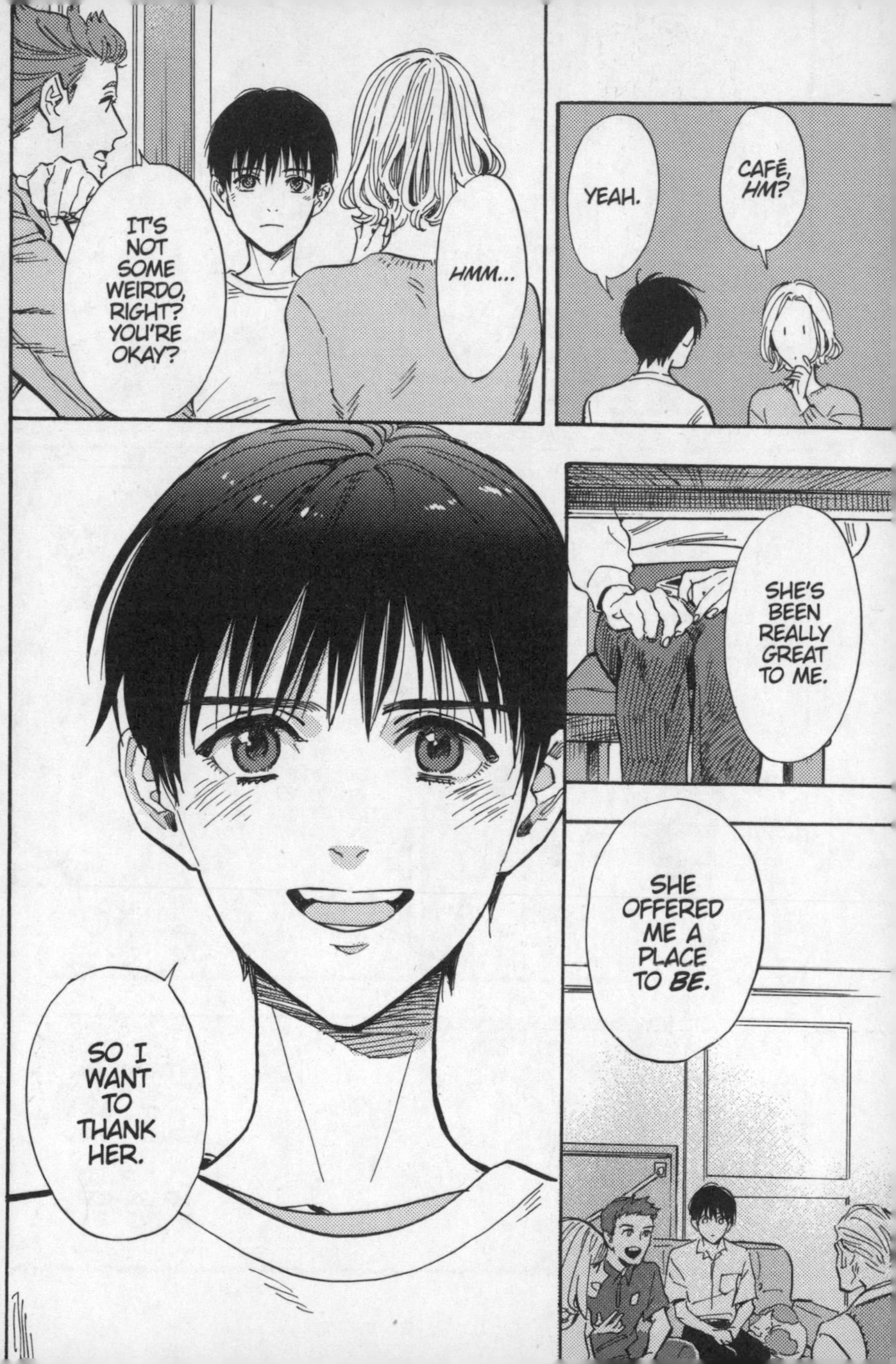
CAFÉ, HM?
YEAH.
HMM...
IT'S NOT SOME WEIRDO, RIGHT? YOU'RE OKAY?
SHE'S BEEN REALLY GREAT TO ME.
SHE OFFERED ME A PLACE TO BE.
SO I WANT TO THANK HER.

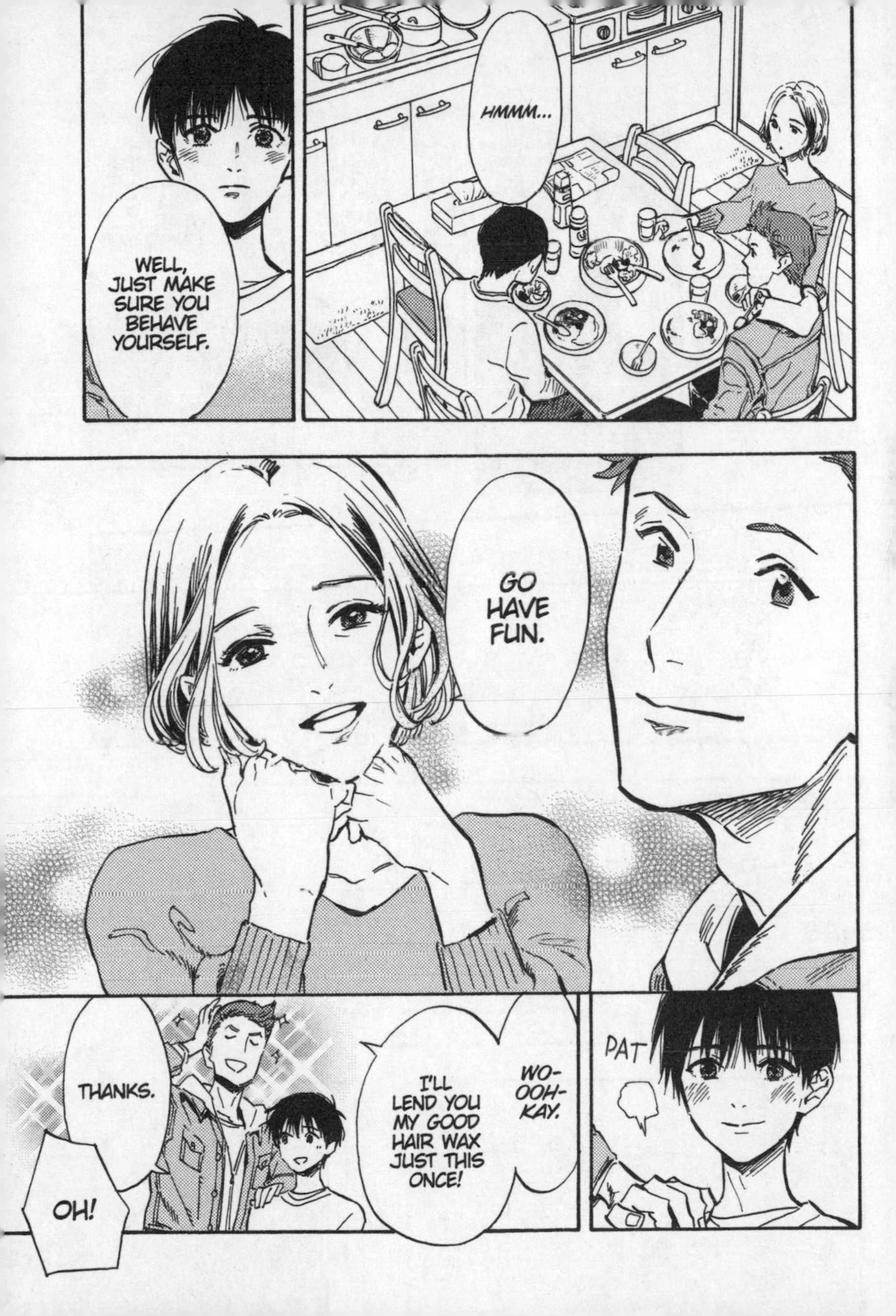
HMMM...
WELL, JUST MAKE SURE YOU BEHAVE YOURSELF.
GO HAVE FUN.
PAT
WO-OOH-KAY.
I'LL LEND YOU MY GOOD HAIR WAX JUST THIS ONCE!
THANKS.
OH!

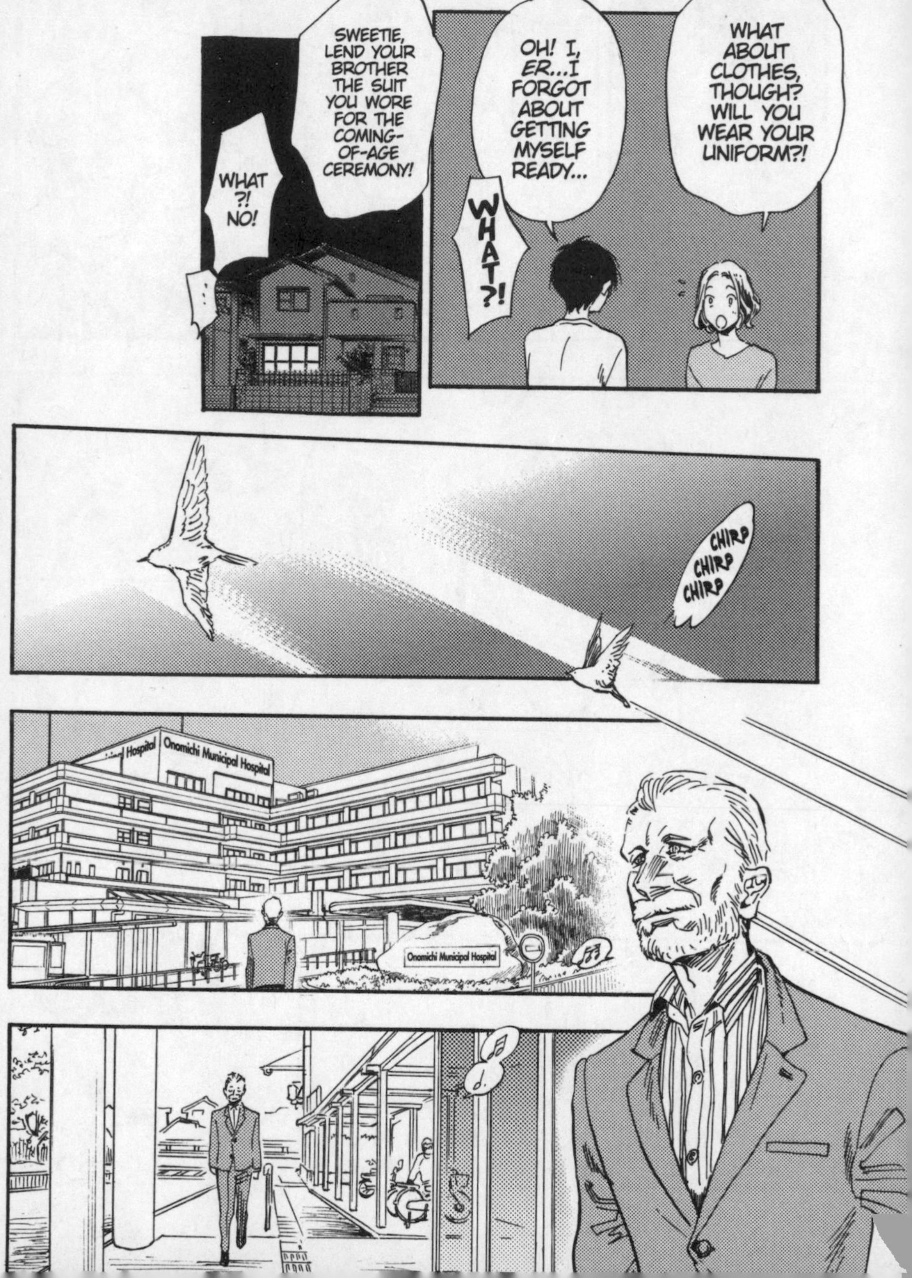
WHAT ABOUT CLOTHES, THOUGH? WILL YOU WEAR YOUR UNIFORM?!
OH! I, ER...I FORGOT ABOUT GETTING MYSELF READY...
WHAT?!
SWEETIE, LEND YOUR BROTHER THE SUIT YOU WORE FOR THE COMING-OF-AGE CEREMONY!
WHAT?! NO!
...
CHIRP CHIRP CHIRP
Onomichi Municipal Hospital
Onomichi Municipal Hospital

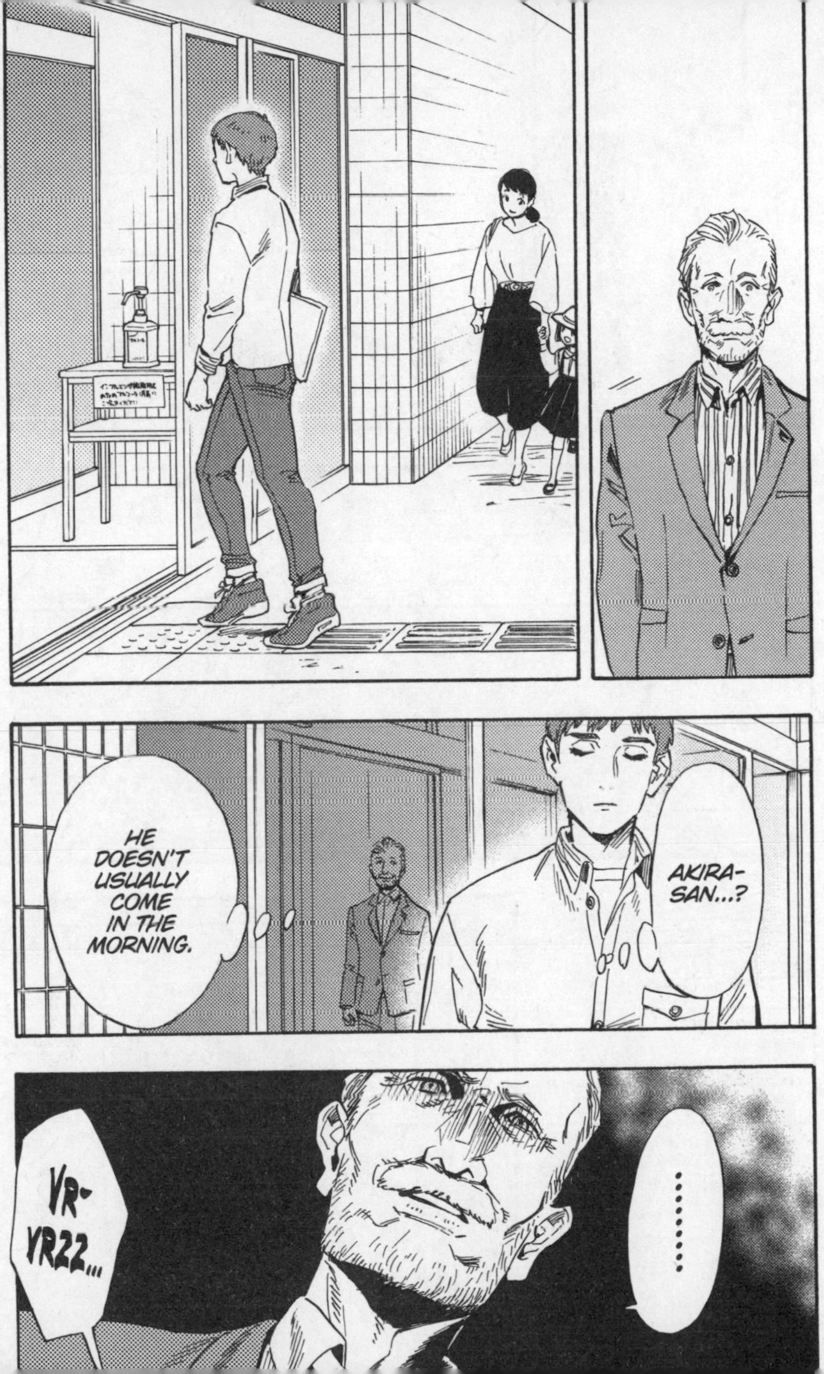
AKIRA-SAN...?
HE DOESN'T USUALLY COME IN THE MORNING.
......
VR- VRZZ...

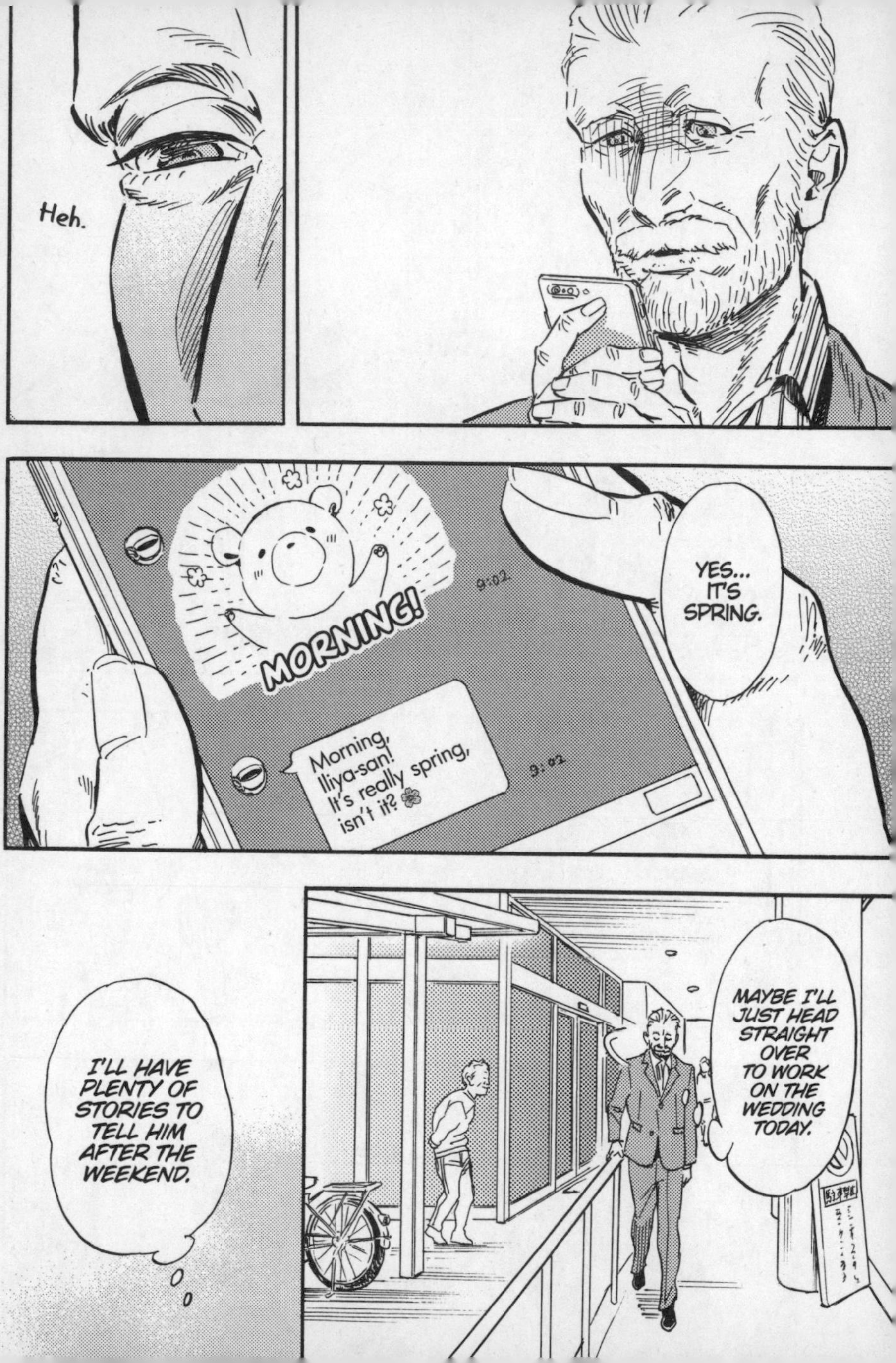

Heh.
YES... IT'S SPRING.
MORNING!
9:02
Morning, Iliya-san! It's really spring, isn't it?
9:02
MAYBE I'LL JUST HEAD STRAIGHT OVER TO WORK ON THE WEDDING TODAY.
I'LL HAVE PLENTY OF STORIES TO TELL HIM AFTER THE WEEKEND.

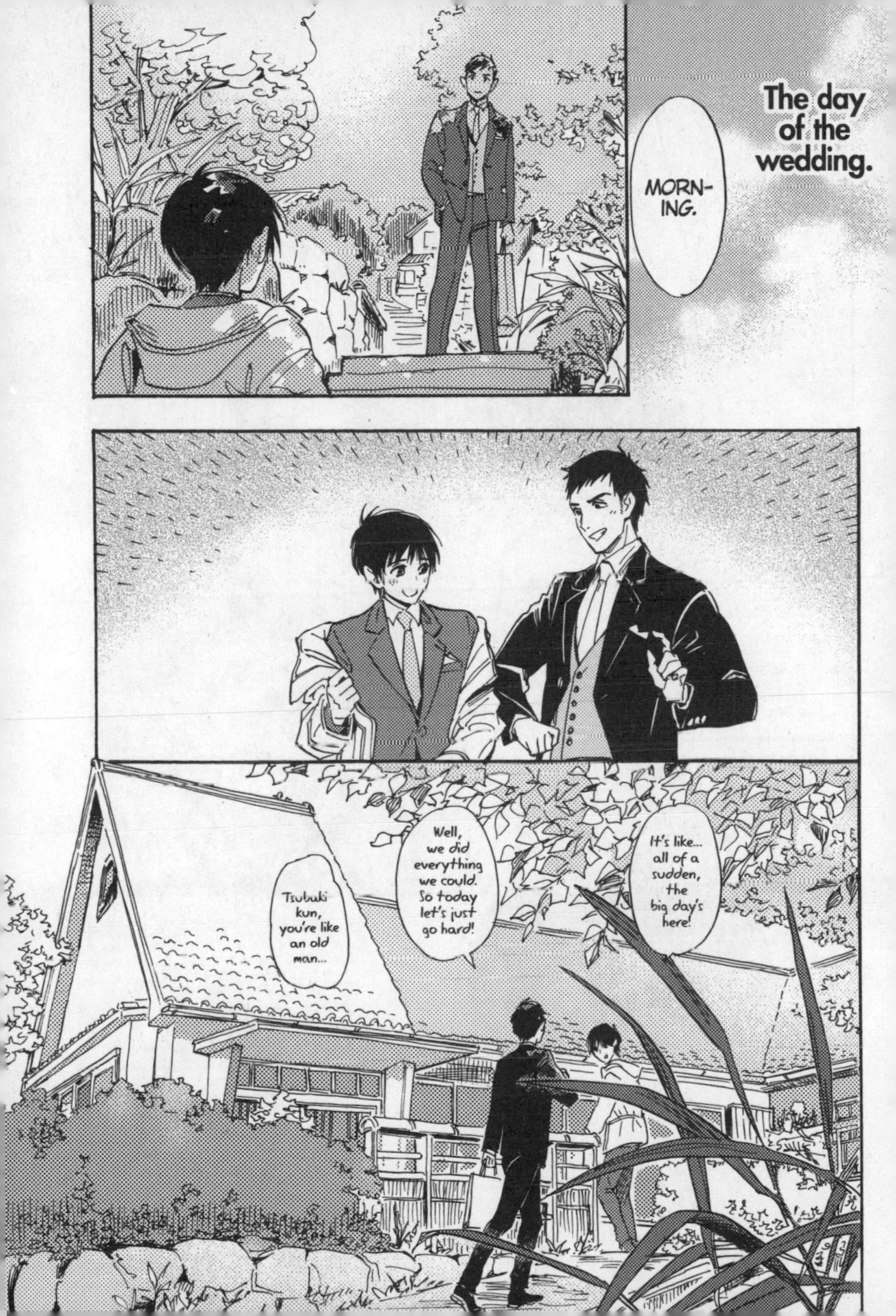
The day of the wedding.
MORN-ING.
It's like... all of a sudden, the big day's here!
Well, we did everything we could. So today let's just go hard!
Tsubaki kun, you're like an old man...

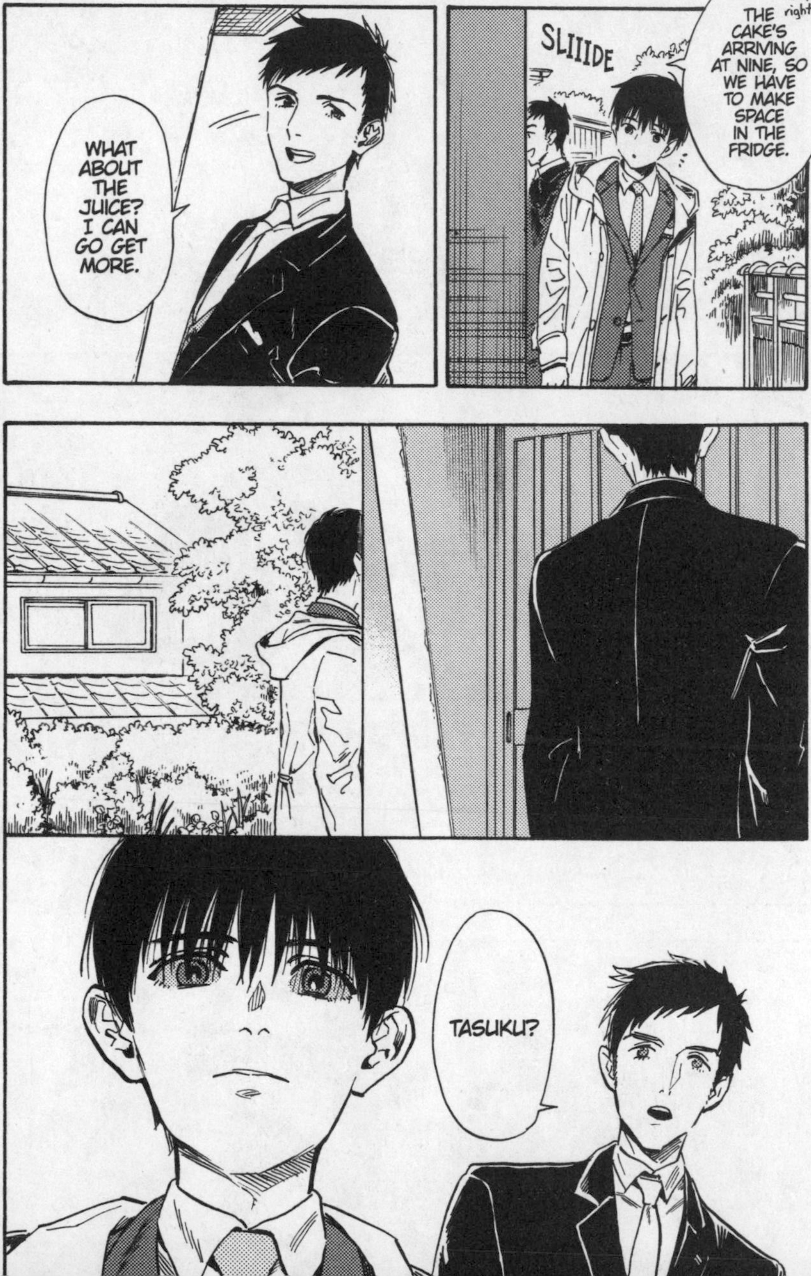
SLIIIDE
Oh, right. THE CAKE'S ARRIVING AT NINE, SO WE HAVE TO MAKE SPACE IN THE FRIDGE.
WHAT ABOUT THE JUICE? I CAN GO GET MORE.
TASUKU?

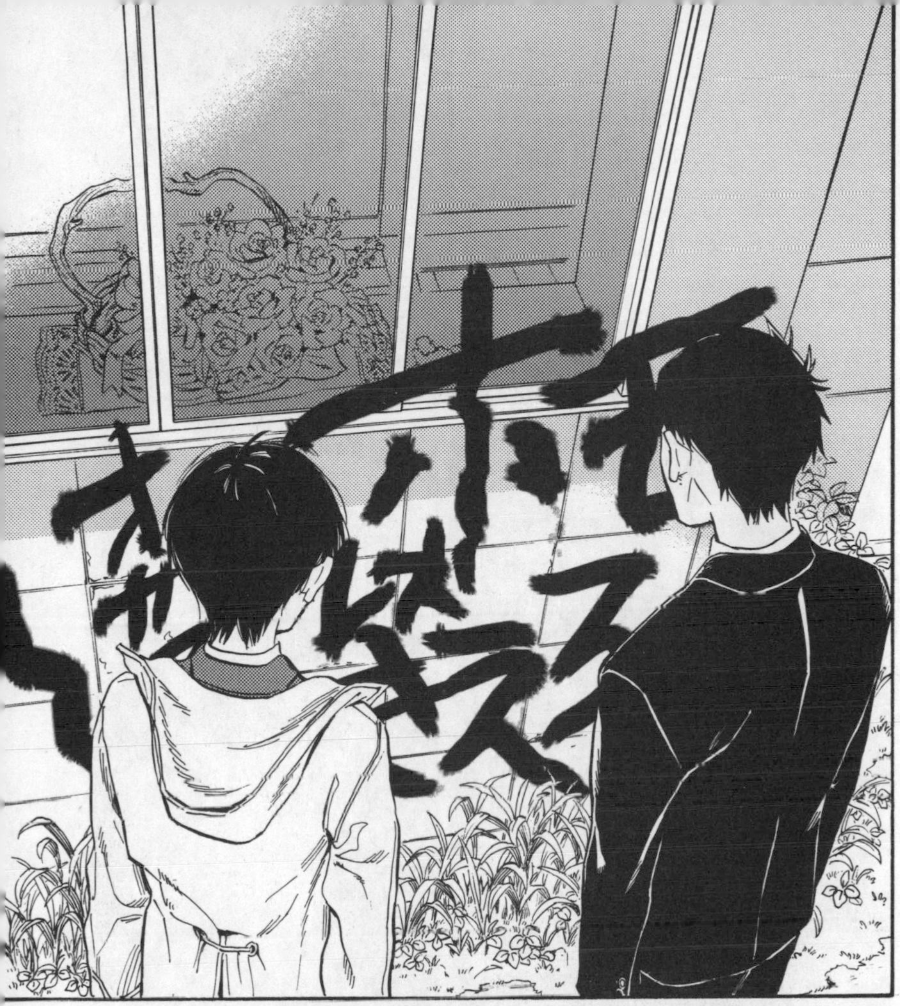

Graffiti: Go to Hell, Dykes & Homos!

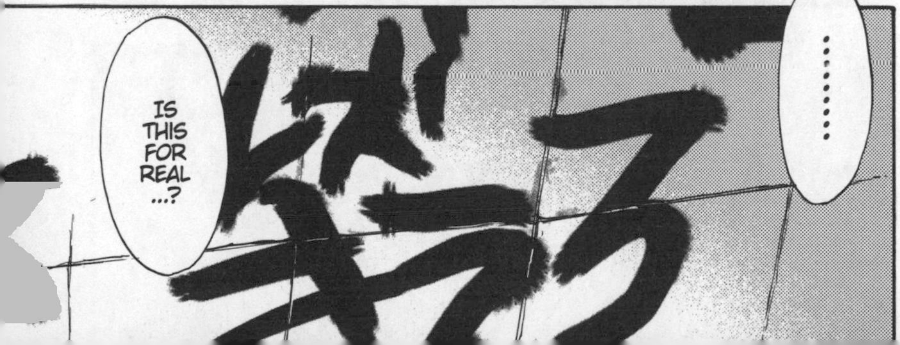
....
IS THIS FOR REAL ...?

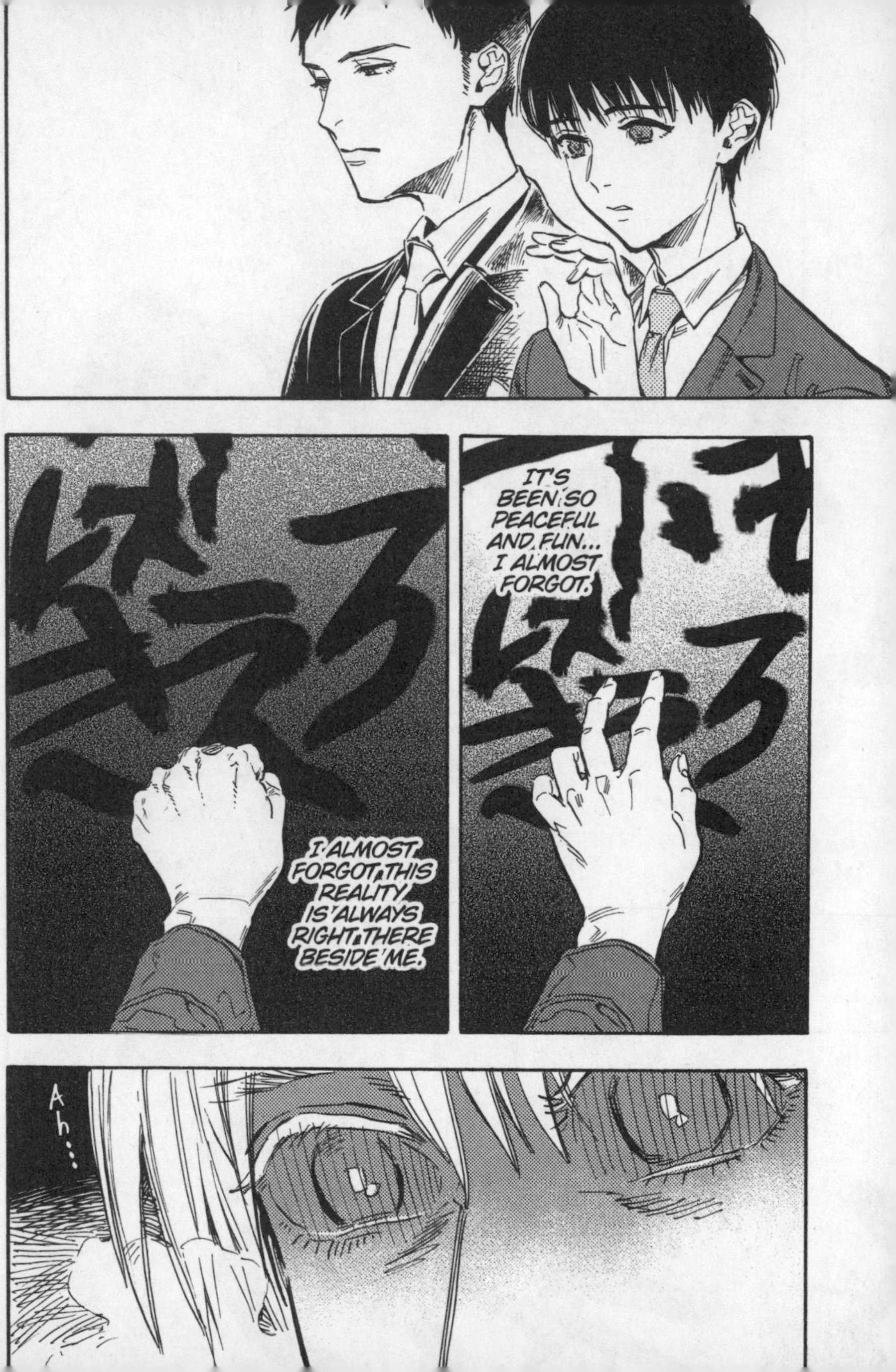
IT'S BEEN SO PEACEFUL AND FUN... I ALMOST FORGOT.
I ALMOST FORGOT THIS REALITY IS ALWAYS RIGHT THERE BESIDE ME.
Ah...

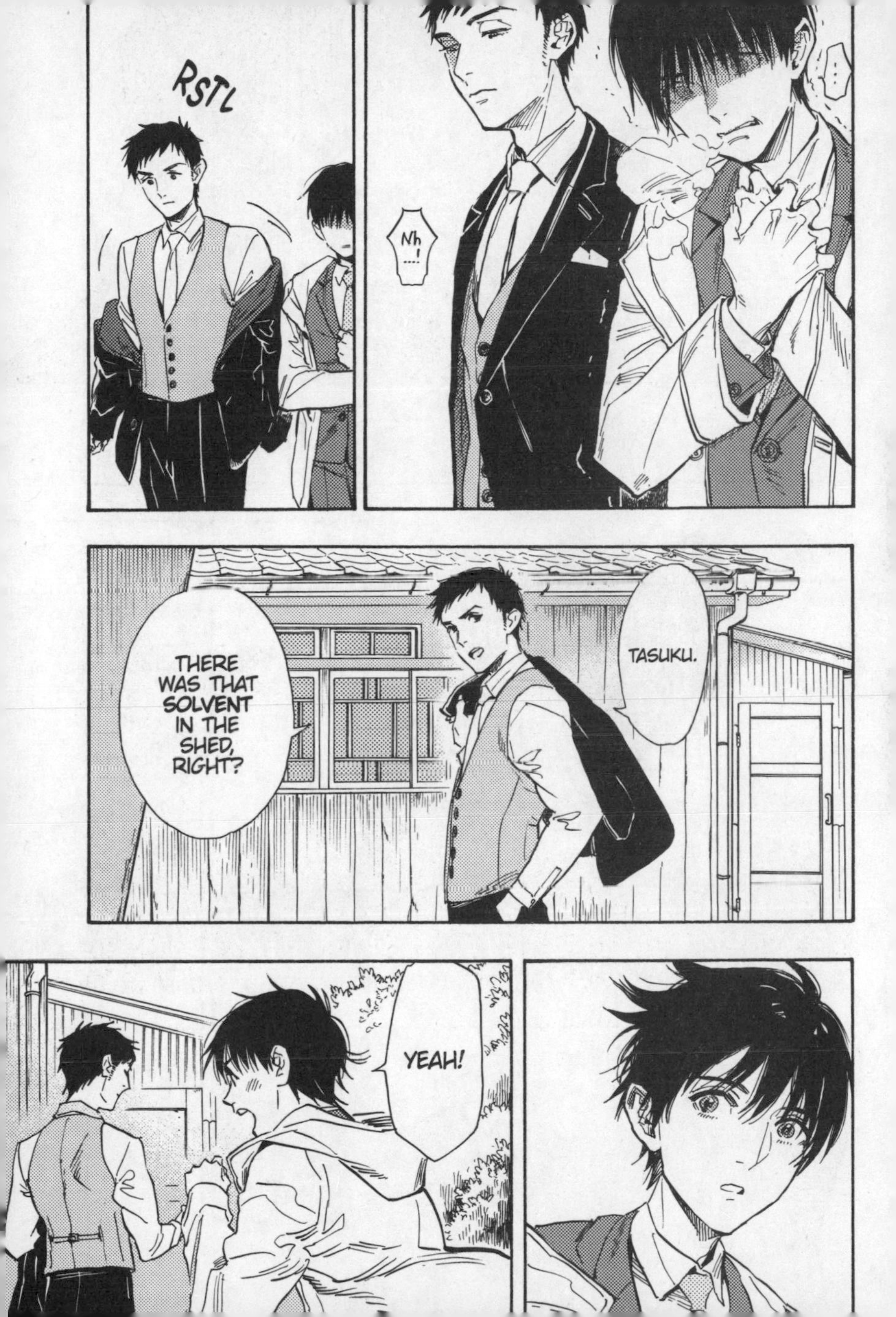
...!
Nh...!
RSTL
TASUKU.
THERE WAS THAT SOLVENT IN THE SHED, RIGHT?
YEAH!

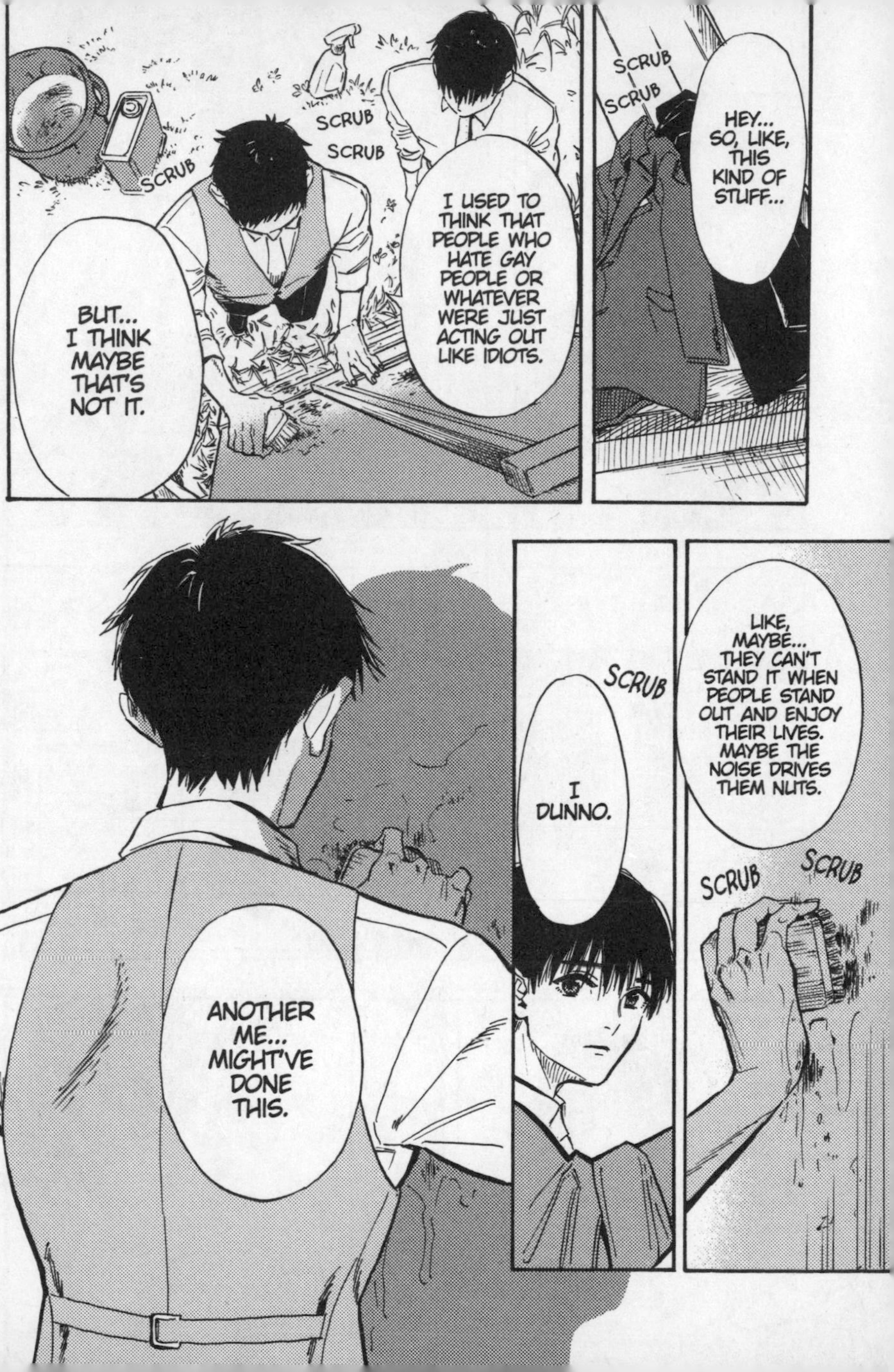

SCRUB
SCRUB
HEY... SO, LIKE, THIS KIND OF STUFF...
SCRUB
SCRUB
SCRUB
I USED TO THINK THAT PEOPLE WHO HATE GAY PEOPLE OR WHATEVER WERE JUST ACTING OUT LIKE IDIOTS.
BUT... I THINK MAYBE THAT'S NOT IT.
LIKE, MAYBE... THEY CAN'T STAND IT WHEN PEOPLE STAND OUT AND ENJOY THEIR LIVES. MAYBE THE NOISE DRIVES THEM NUTS.
SCRUB
SCRUB
SCRUB
I DUNNO.
ANOTHER ME... MIGHT'VE DONE THIS.

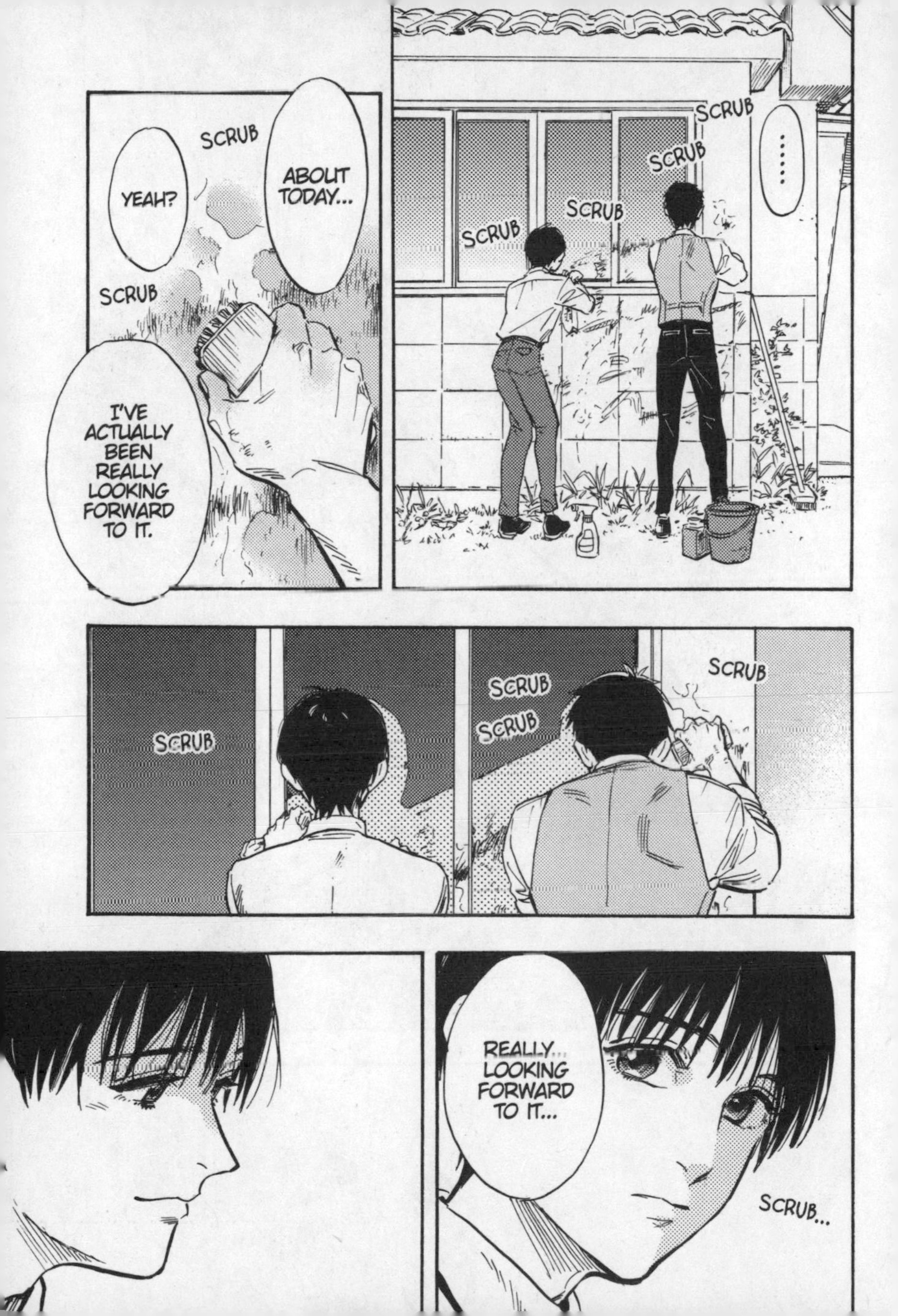
SCRUB
SCRUB
SCRUB
SCRUB
……
ABOUT TODAY...
SCRUB
YEAH?
SCRUB
I'VE ACTUALLY BEEN REALLY LOOKING FORWARD TO IT.
SCRUB
SCRUB
SCRUB
SCRUB
REALLY... LOOKING FORWARD TO IT...
SCRUB...

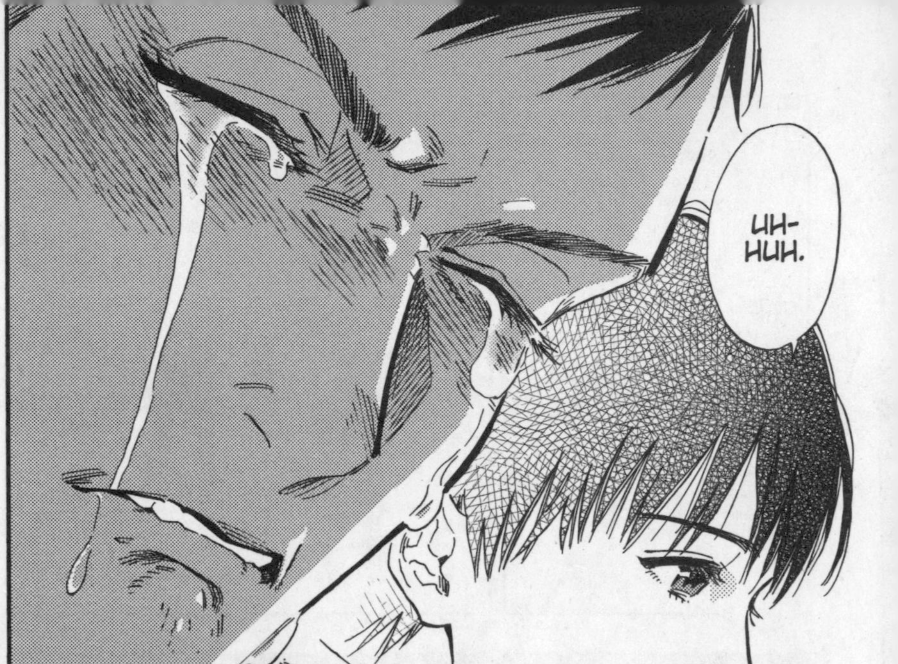
UH-
HUH.
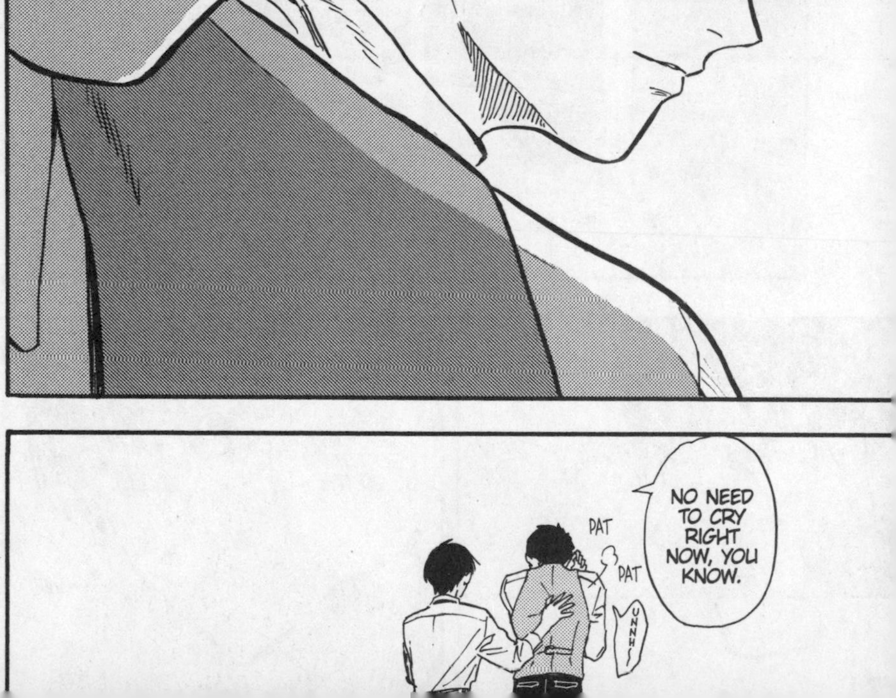
NO NEED TO CRY RIGHT NOW, YOU KNOW.
PAT
PAT
UNNH

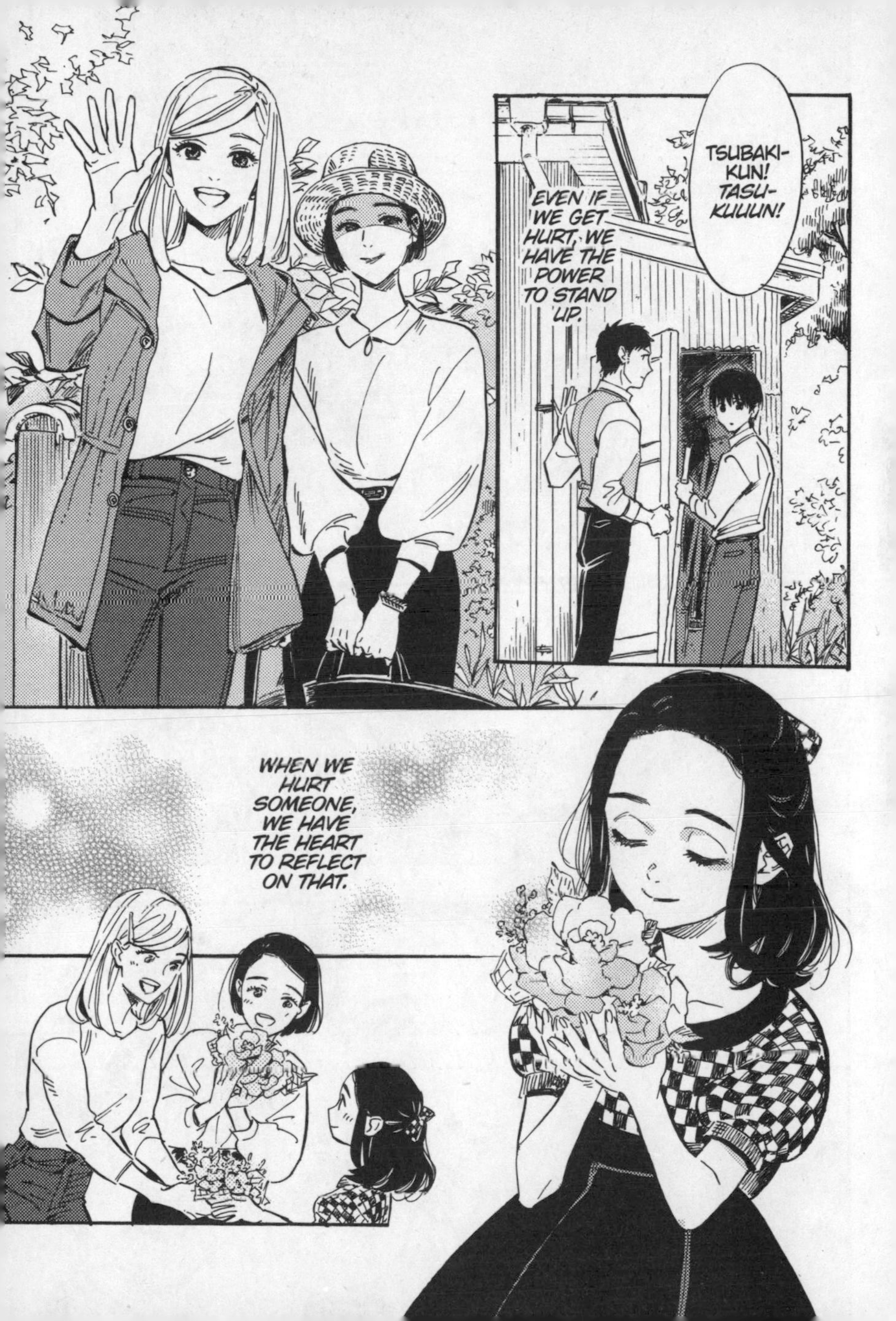
TSUBAKI-KUN! TASU-KUUUN!
EVEN IF WE GET HURT, WE HAVE THE POWER TO STAND UP.
WHEN WE HURT SOMEONE, WE HAVE THE HEART TO REFLECT ON THAT.

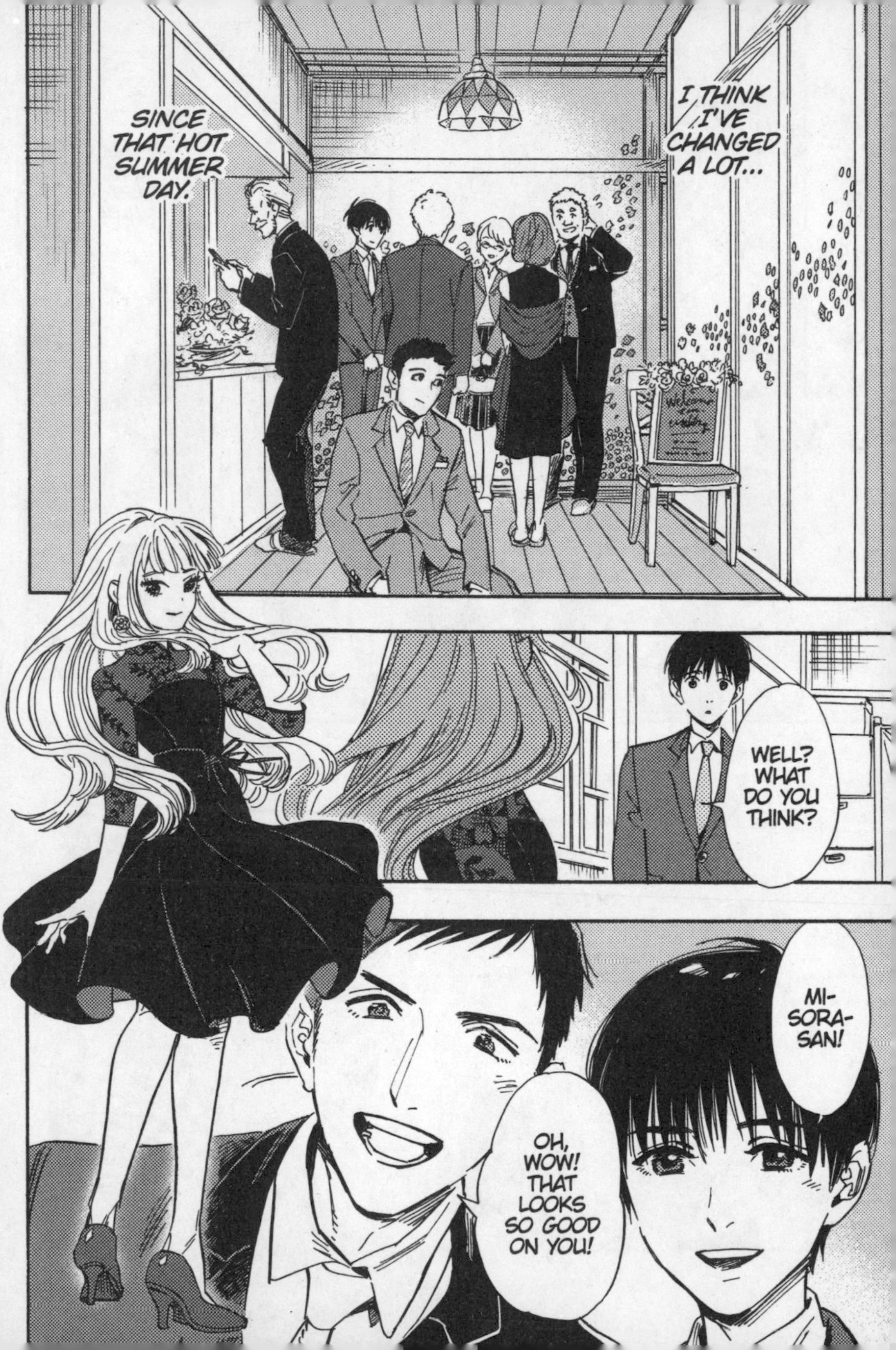
I THINK I'VE CHANGED A LOT...
SINCE THAT HOT SUMMER DAY.
WELL? WHAT DO YOU THINK?
MI-SORA-SAN!
OH, WOW! THAT LOOKS SO GOOD ON YOU!

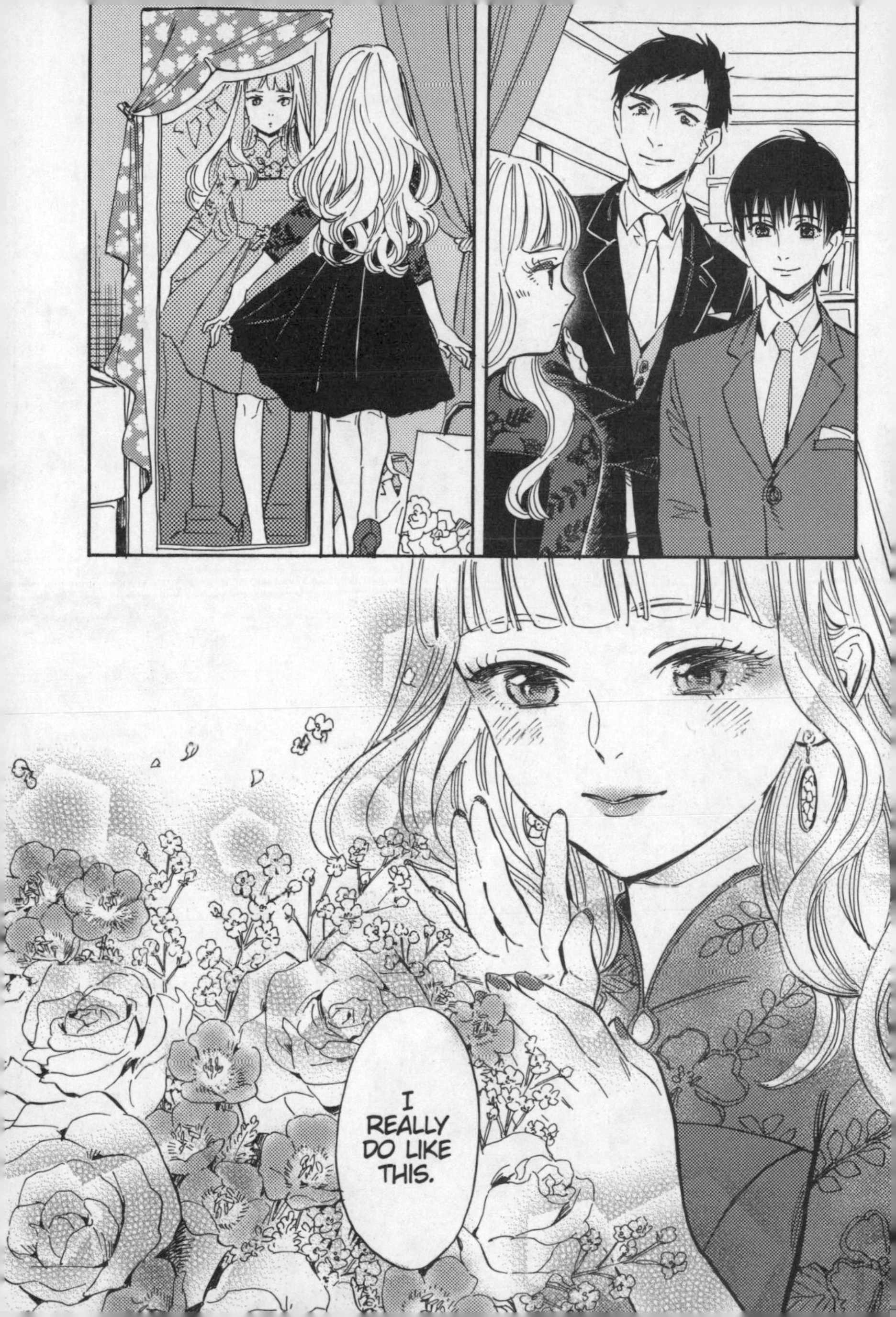
I REALLY DO LIKE THIS.

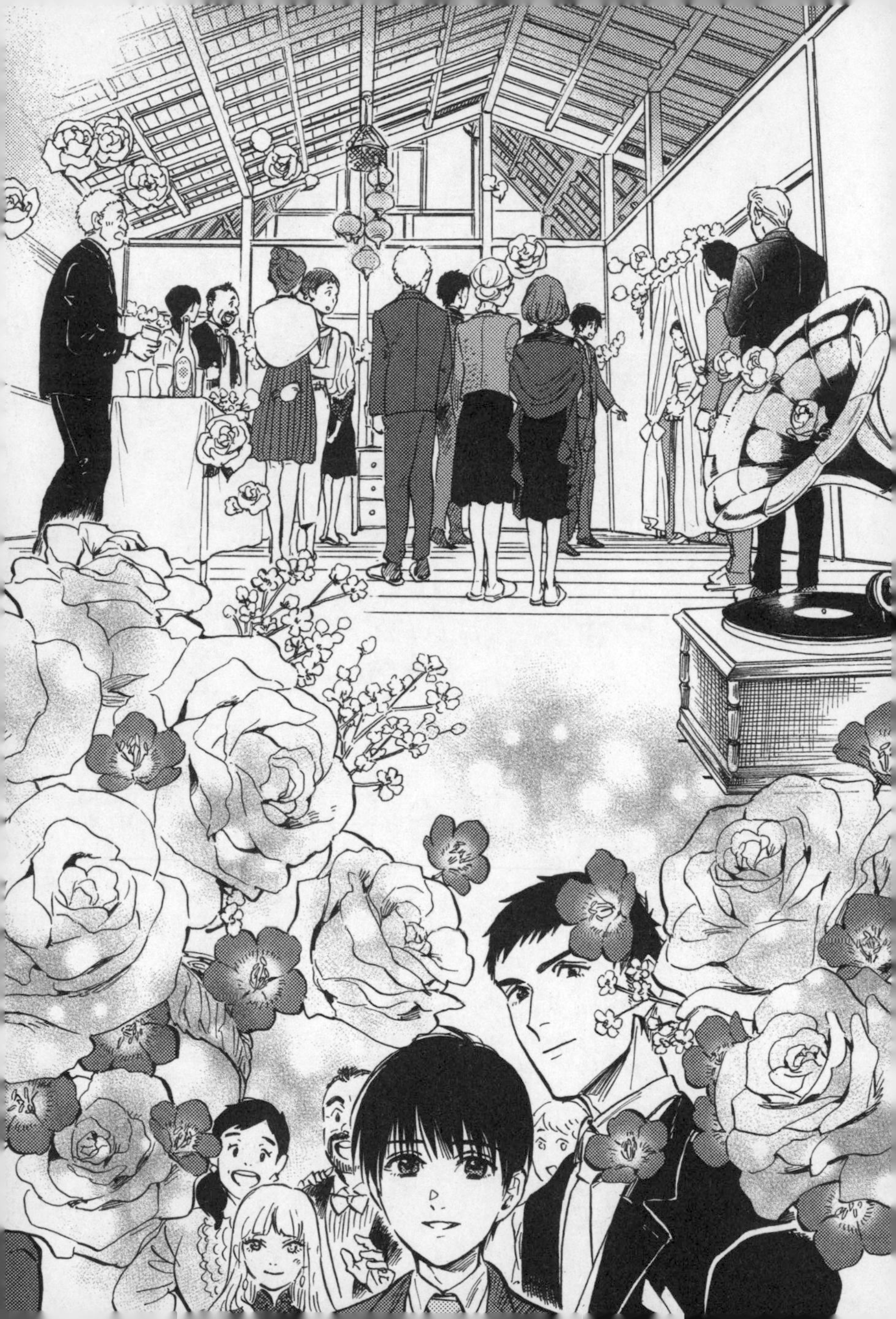

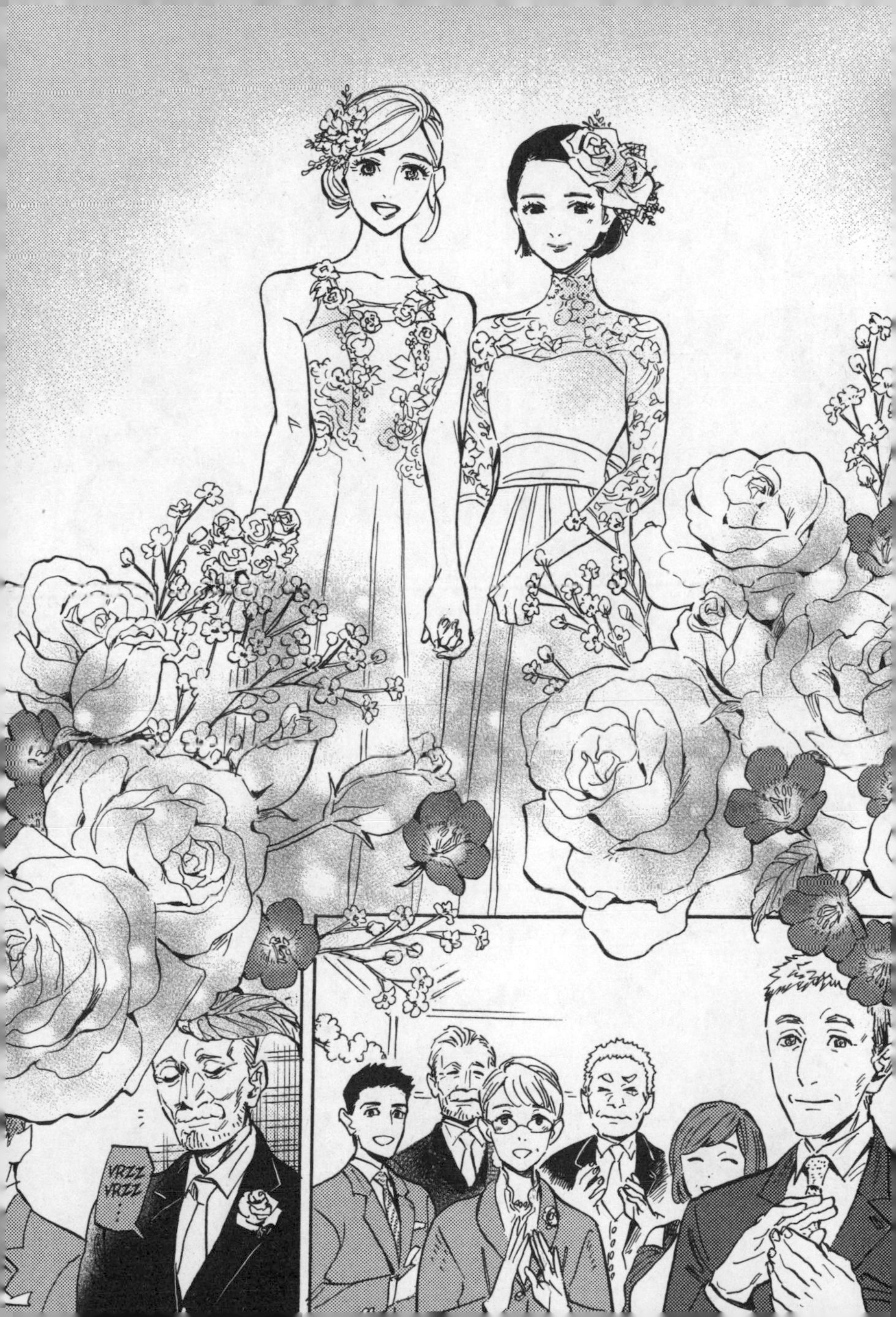
VRZZ
VRZZ

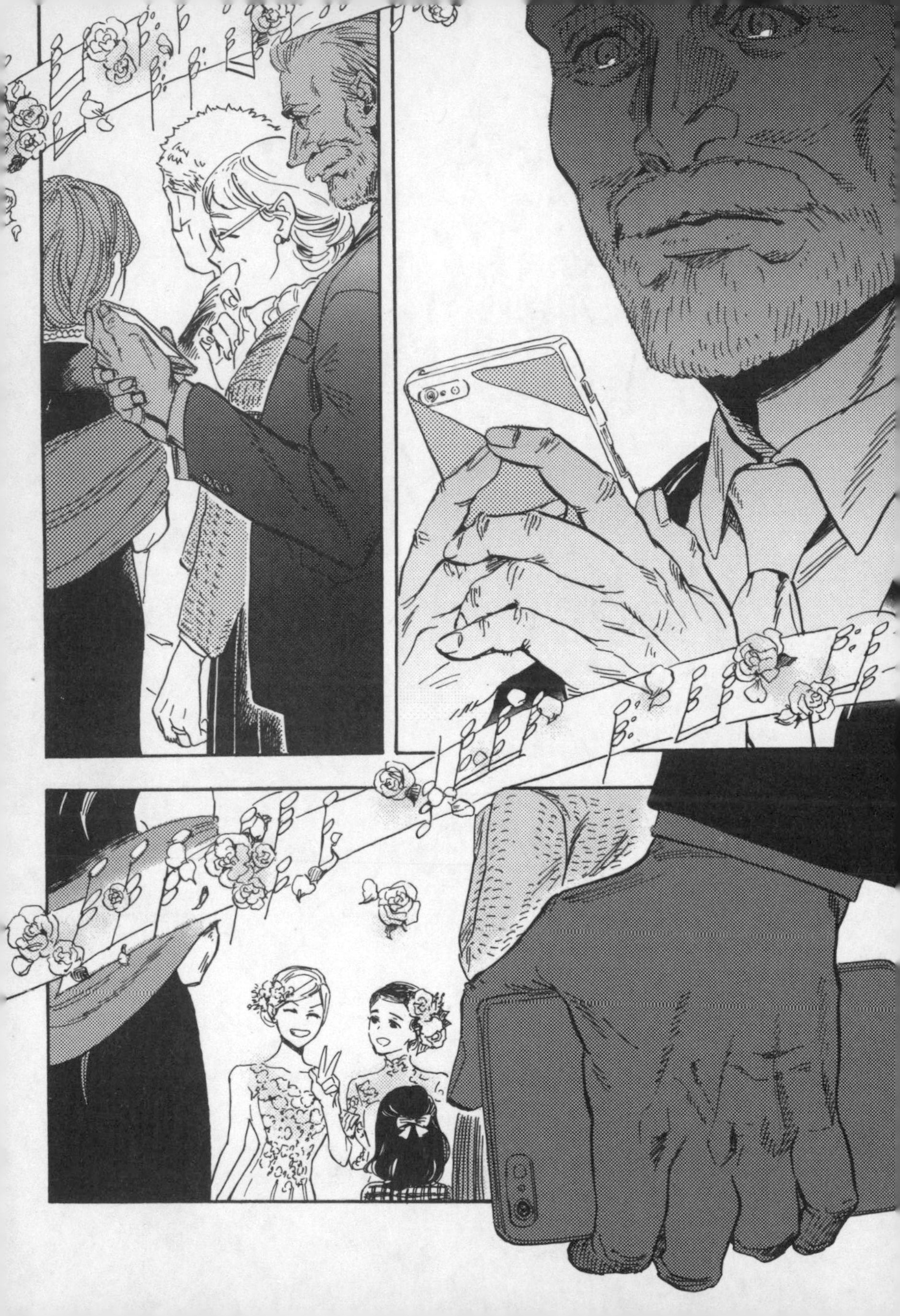

Our Dreams at Dusk
SHIMANAMI **TASOGARE**

Come visit Onomichi!

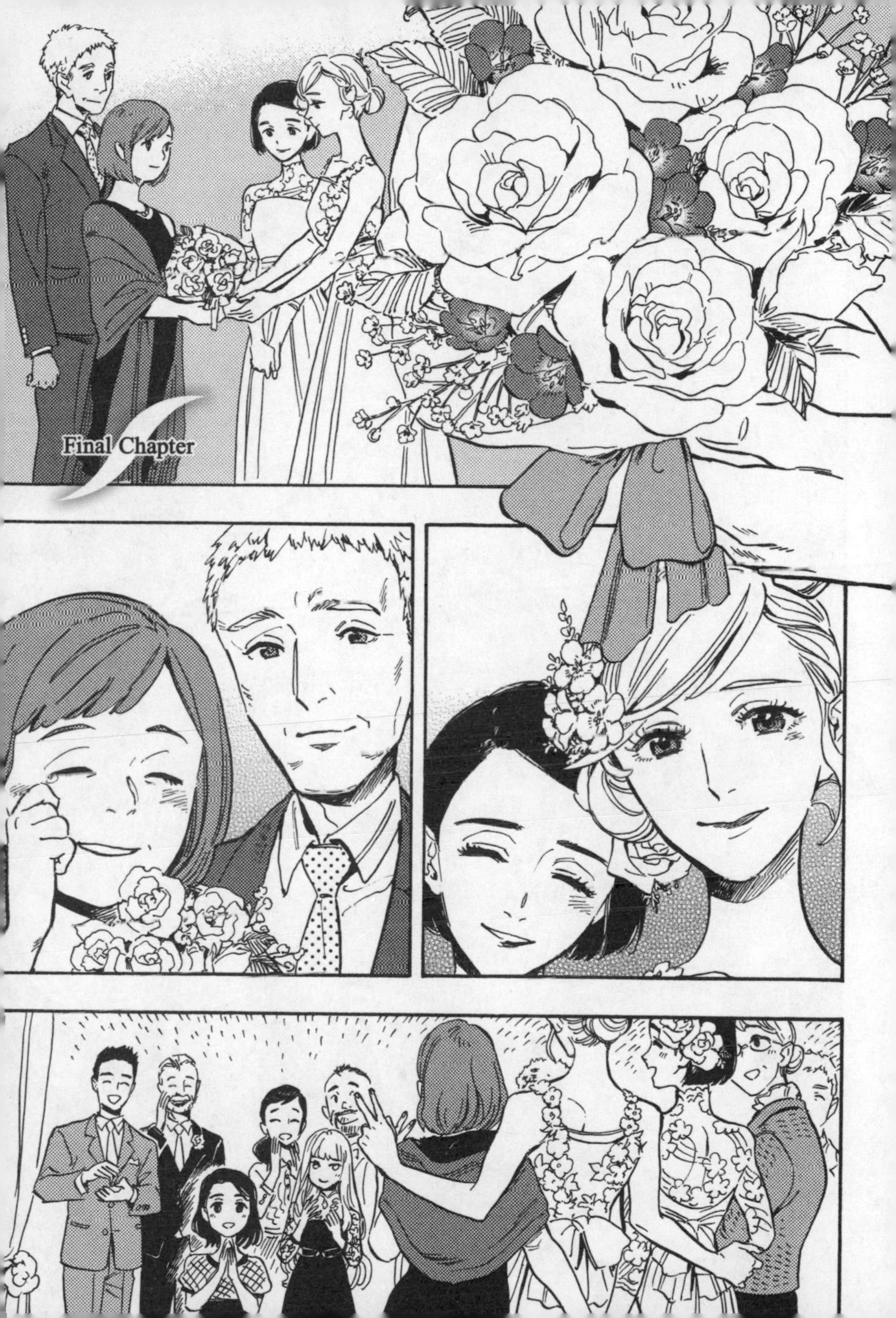
Final Chapter

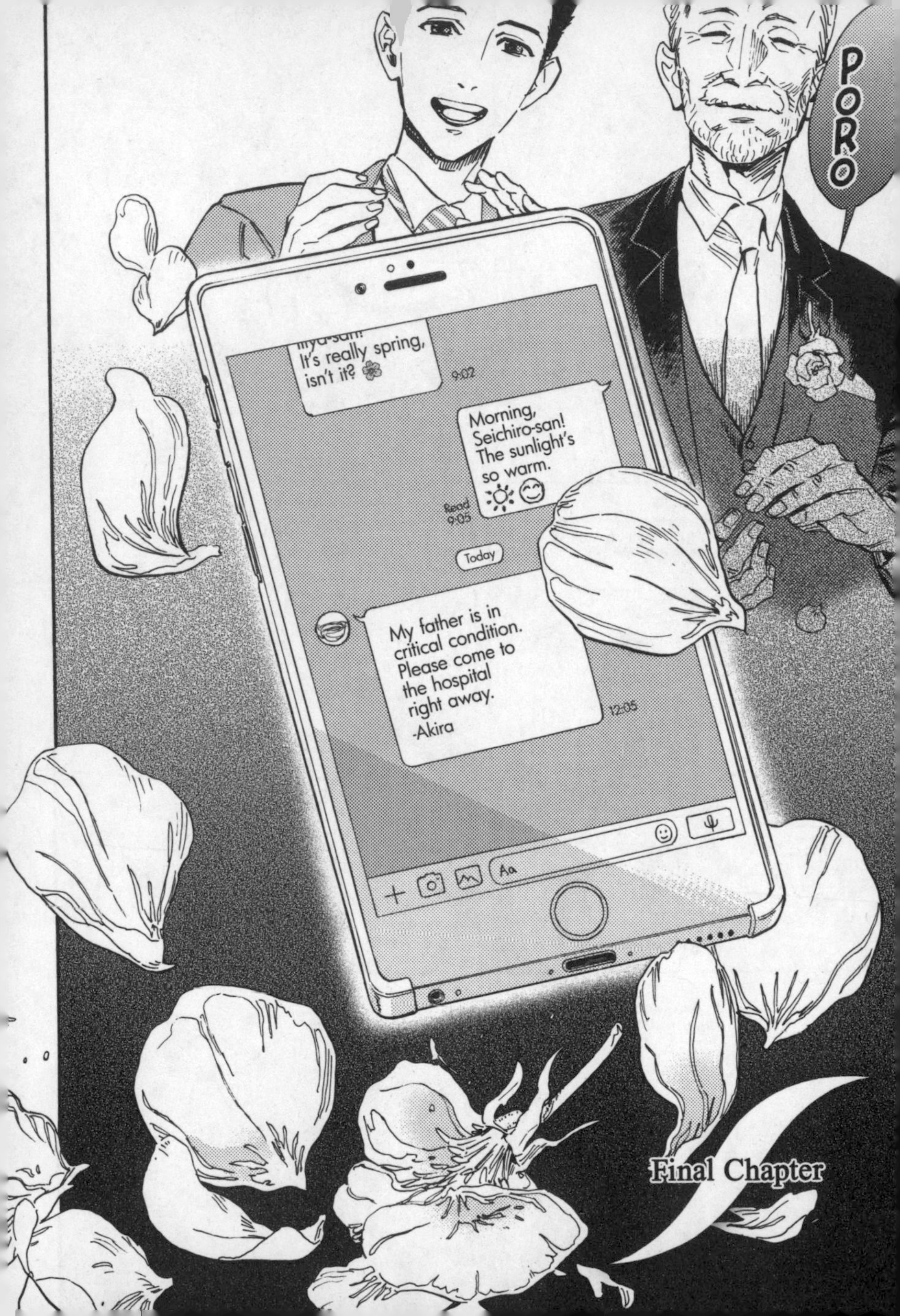
PORO
It's really spring, isn't it?
9:02
Morning, Seichiro-san! The sunlight's so warm.
Read 9:05
Today
My father is in critical condition. Please come to the hospital right away. -Akira
12:05
Aa
Final Chapter

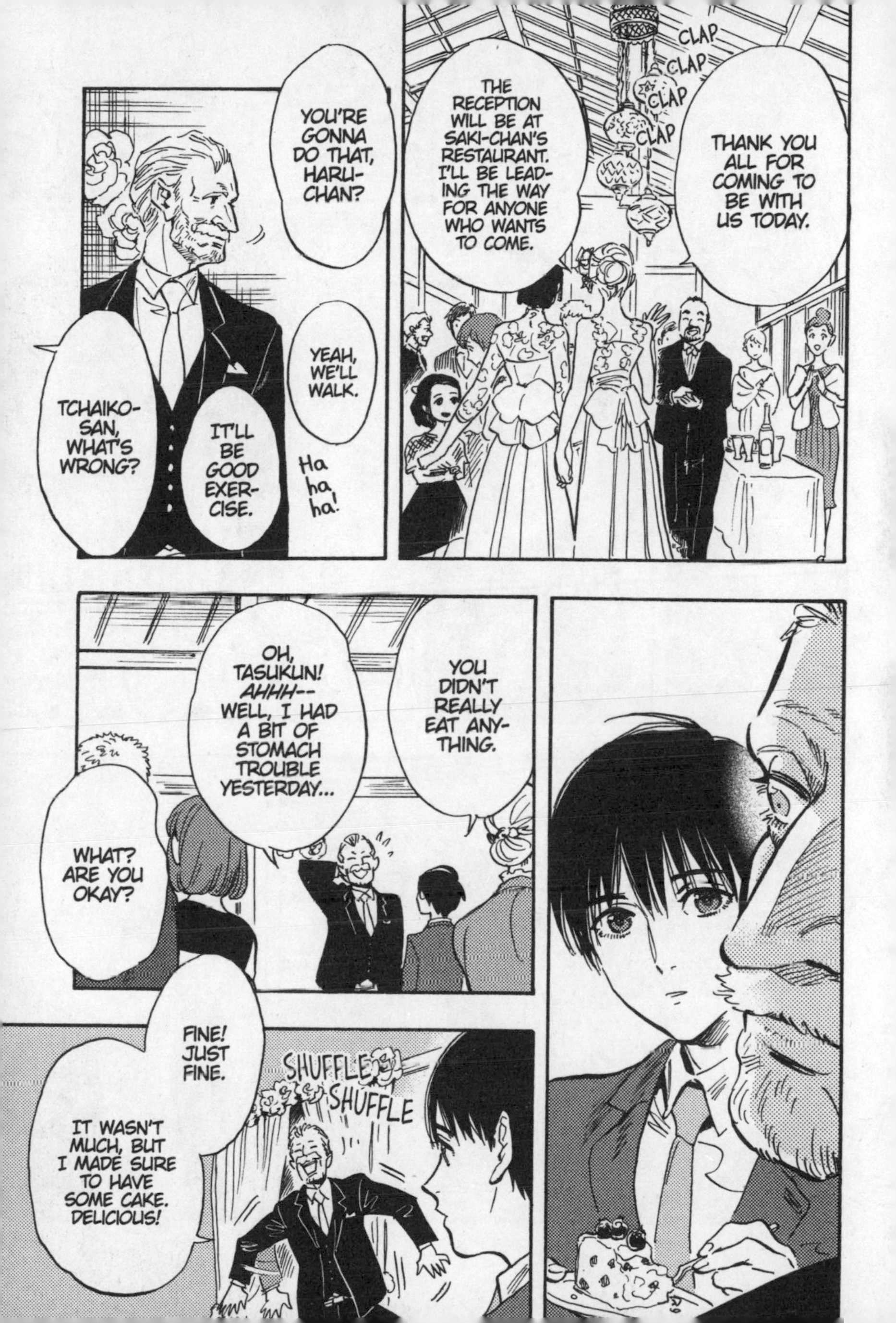
CLAP
CLAP
CLAP
CLAP
THANK YOU ALL FOR COMING TO BE WITH US TODAY.
THE RECEPTION WILL BE AT SAKI-CHAN'S RESTAURANT. I'LL BE LEADING THE WAY FOR ANYONE WHO WANTS TO COME.
YOU'RE GONNA DO THAT, HARU-CHAN?
YEAH, WE'LL WALK.
IT'LL BE GOOD EXERCISE.
Ha ha ha!
TCHAIKO-SAN, WHAT'S WRONG?
YOU DIDN'T REALLY EAT ANYTHING.
OH, TASUKUN! *AHHH--* WELL, I HAD A BIT OF STOMACH TROUBLE YESTERDAY...
WHAT? ARE YOU OKAY?
FINE! JUST FINE.
SHUFFLE
SHUFFLE
IT WASN'T MUCH, BUT I MADE SURE TO HAVE SOME CAKE. DELICIOUS!

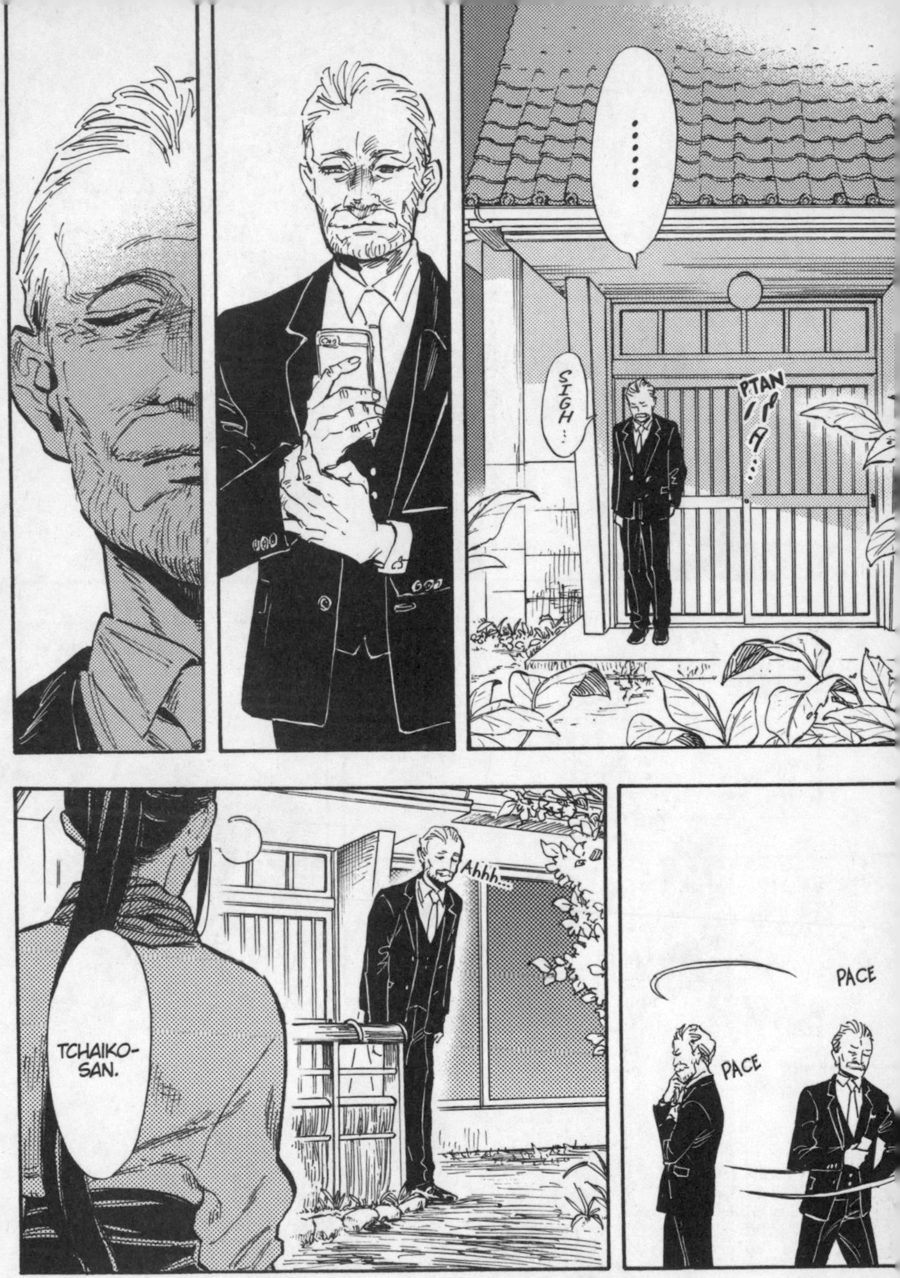
......
SIGH...
PTAN
PACE
PACE
Ahhh...
TCHAIKO-SAN.

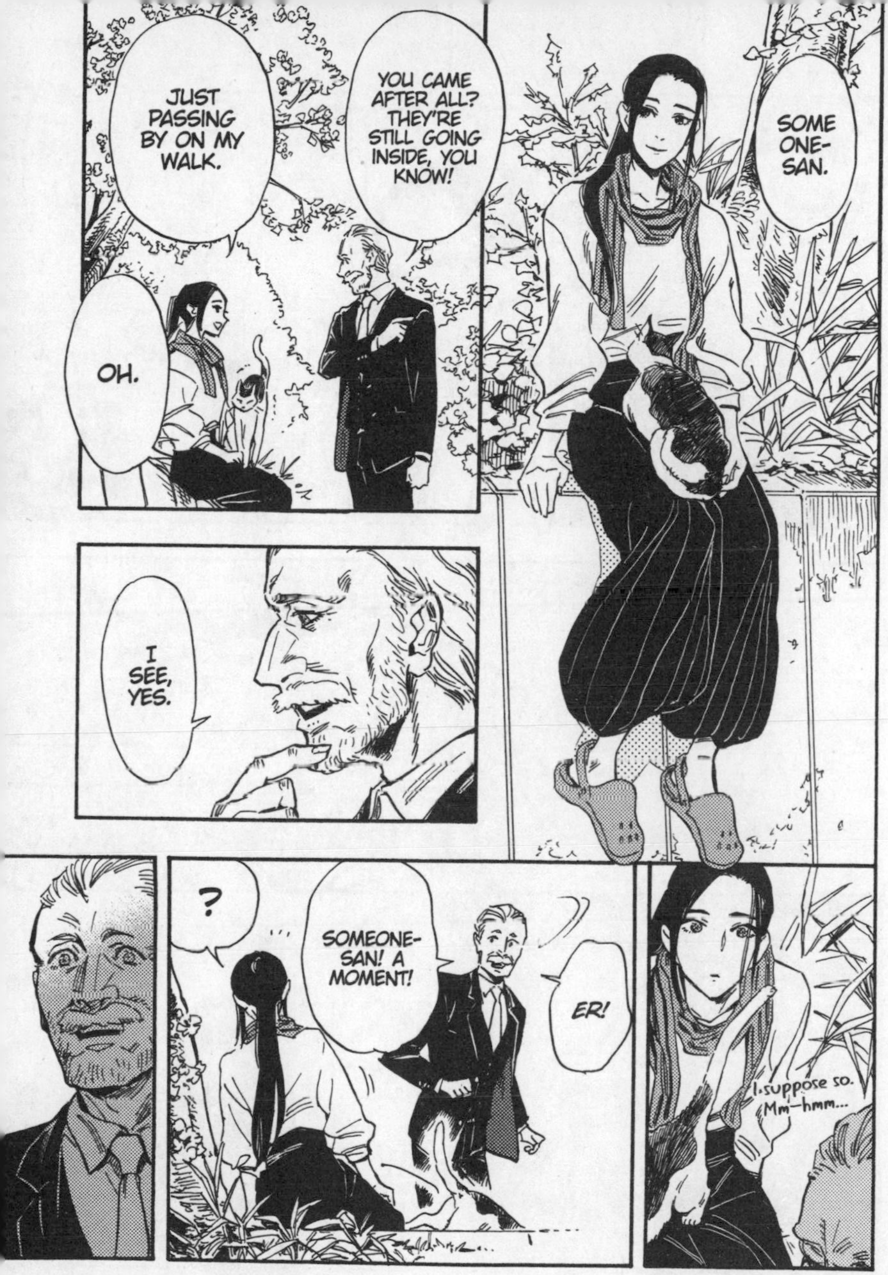
SOME ONE-SAN.
YOU CAME AFTER ALL? THEY'RE STILL GOING INSIDE, YOU KNOW!
JUST PASSING BY ON MY WALK.
OH.
I SEE, YES.
I suppose so. Mm-hmm...
ER!
SOMEONE-SAN! A MOMENT!
?

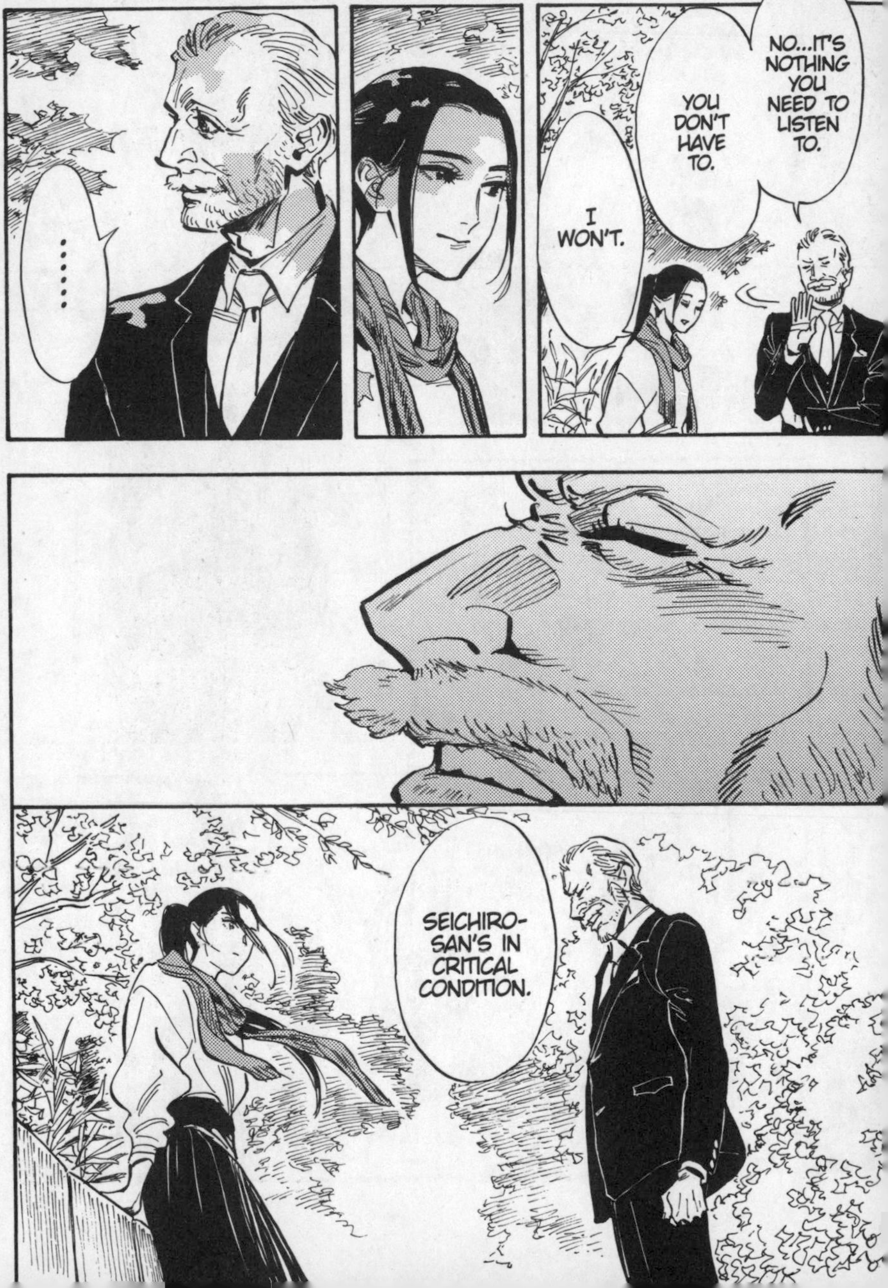
NO...IT'S NOTHING YOU NEED TO LISTEN TO.
YOU DON'T HAVE TO.
I WON'T.
......
SEICHIRO-SAN'S IN CRITICAL CONDITION.

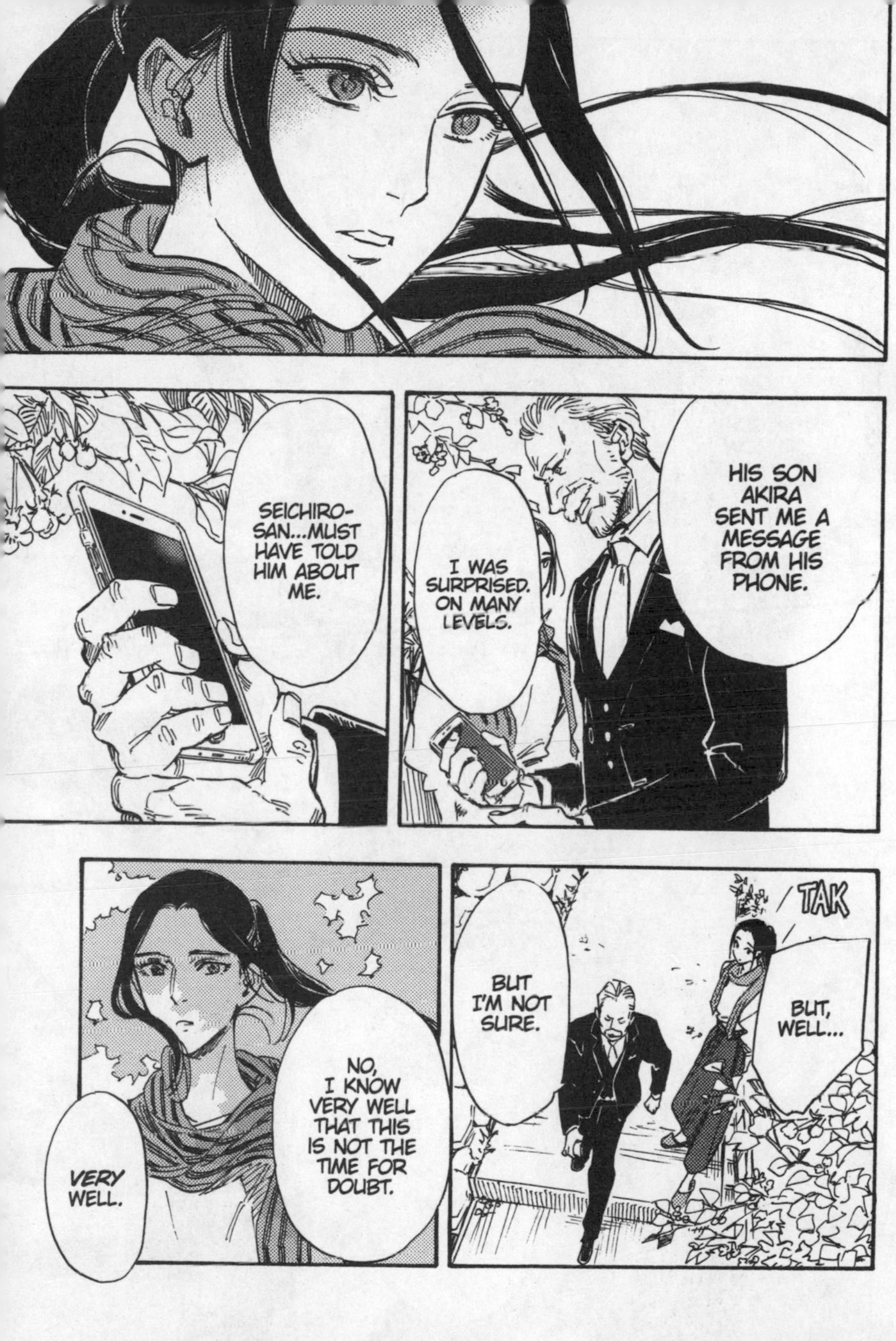
HIS SON AKIRA SENT ME A MESSAGE FROM HIS PHONE.
I WAS SURPRISED. ON MANY LEVELS.
SEICHIRO-SAN...MUST HAVE TOLD HIM ABOUT ME.
TAK
BUT, WELL...
BUT I'M NOT SURE.
NO, I KNOW VERY WELL THAT THIS IS NOT THE TIME FOR DOUBT.
VERY WELL.

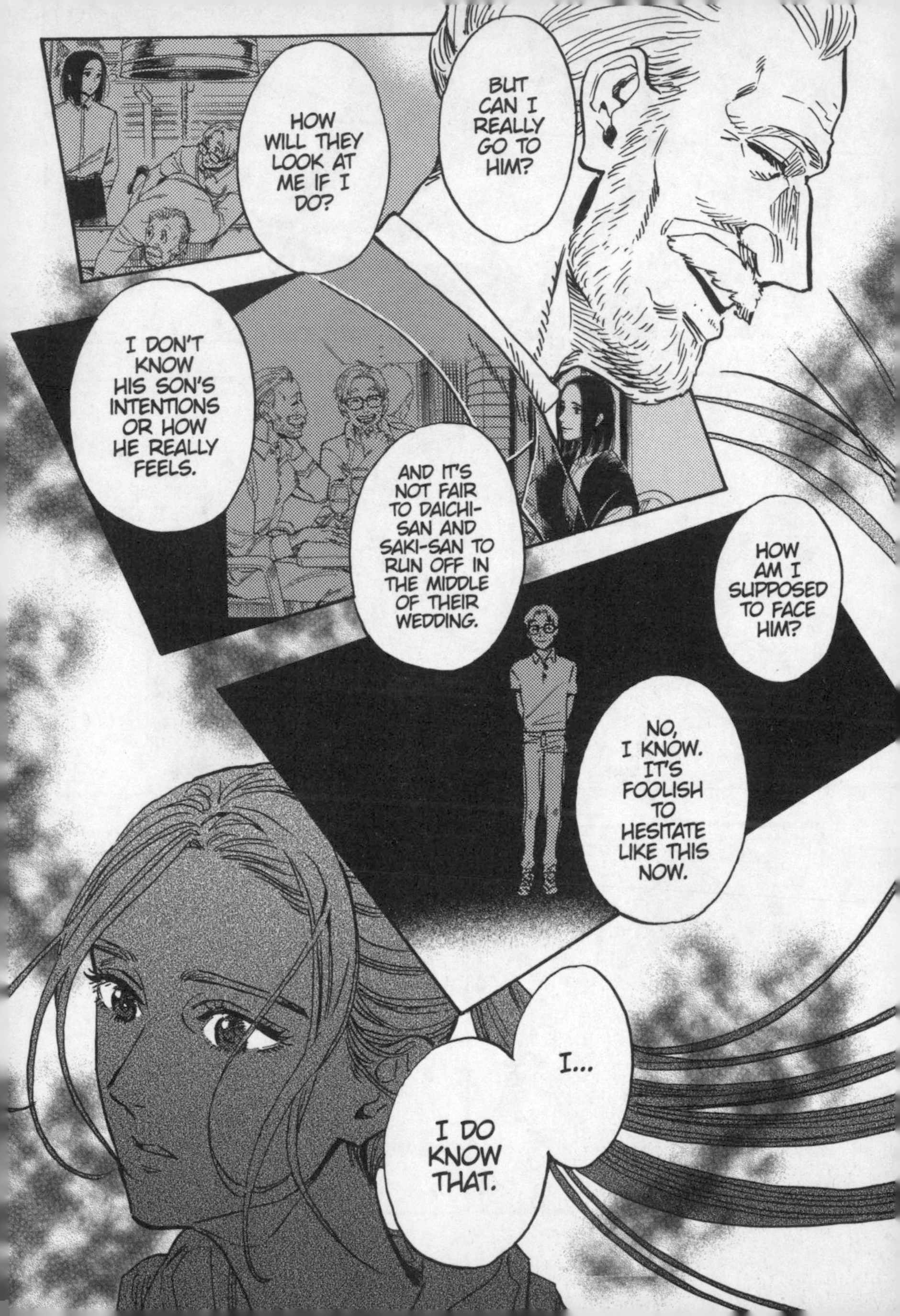
BUT CAN I REALLY GO TO HIM?
HOW WILL THEY LOOK AT ME IF I DO?
I DON'T KNOW HIS SON'S INTENTIONS OR HOW HE REALLY FEELS.
AND IT'S NOT FAIR TO DAICHI-SAN AND SAKI-SAN TO RUN OFF IN THE MIDDLE OF THEIR WEDDING.
HOW AM I SUPPOSED TO FACE HIM?
NO, I KNOW. IT'S FOOLISH TO HESITATE LIKE THIS NOW.
I...
I DO KNOW THAT.

PERHAPS IT'S SIMPLY...

THAT I'M AFRAID TO SEE HIM OFF.

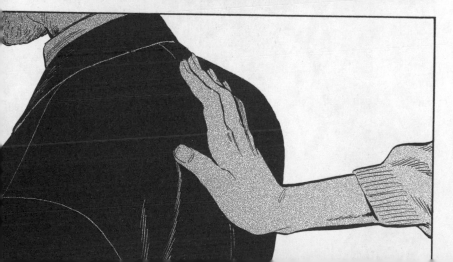

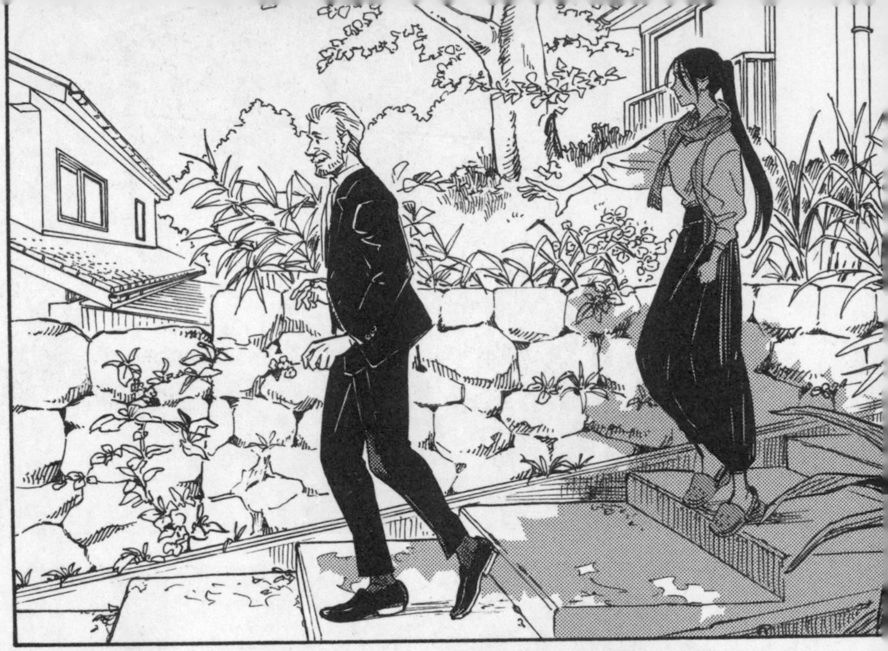

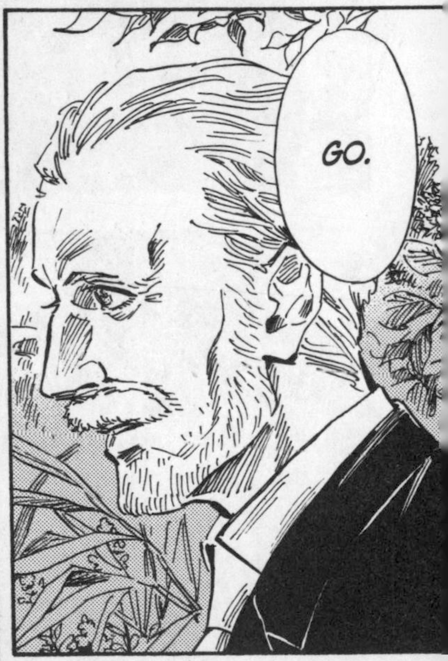
GO.

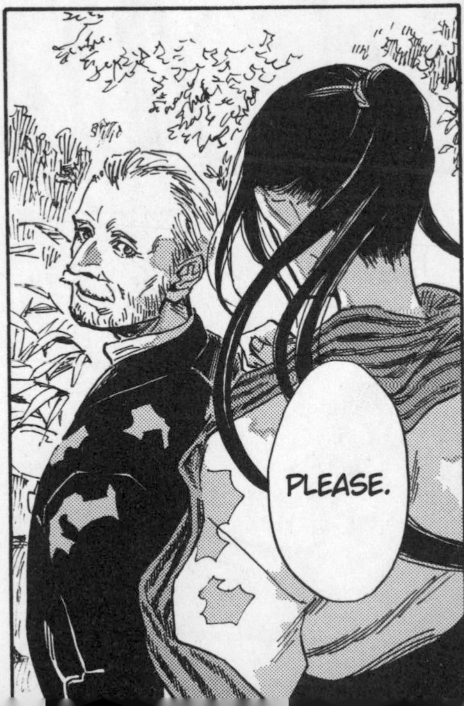
PLEASE.

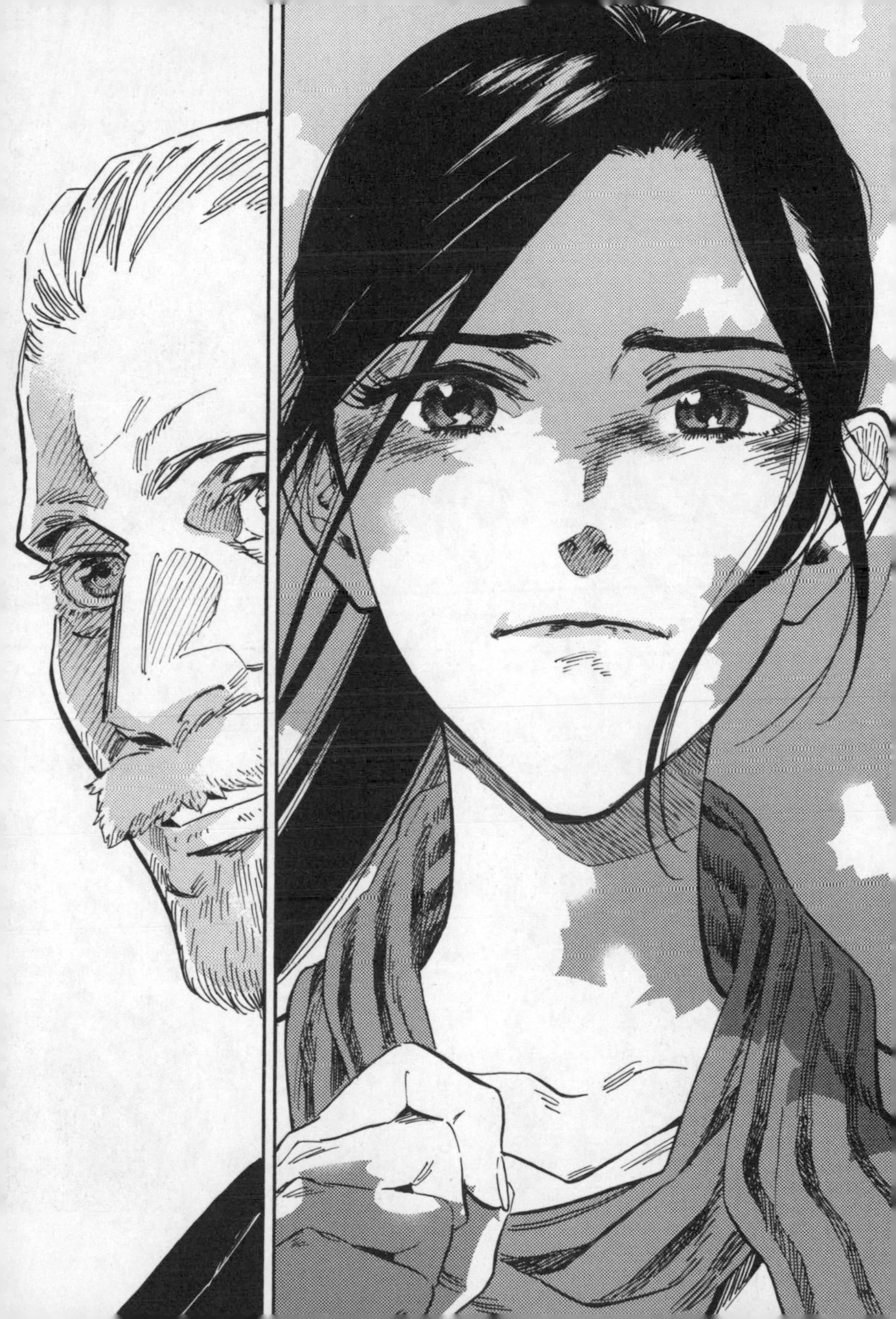

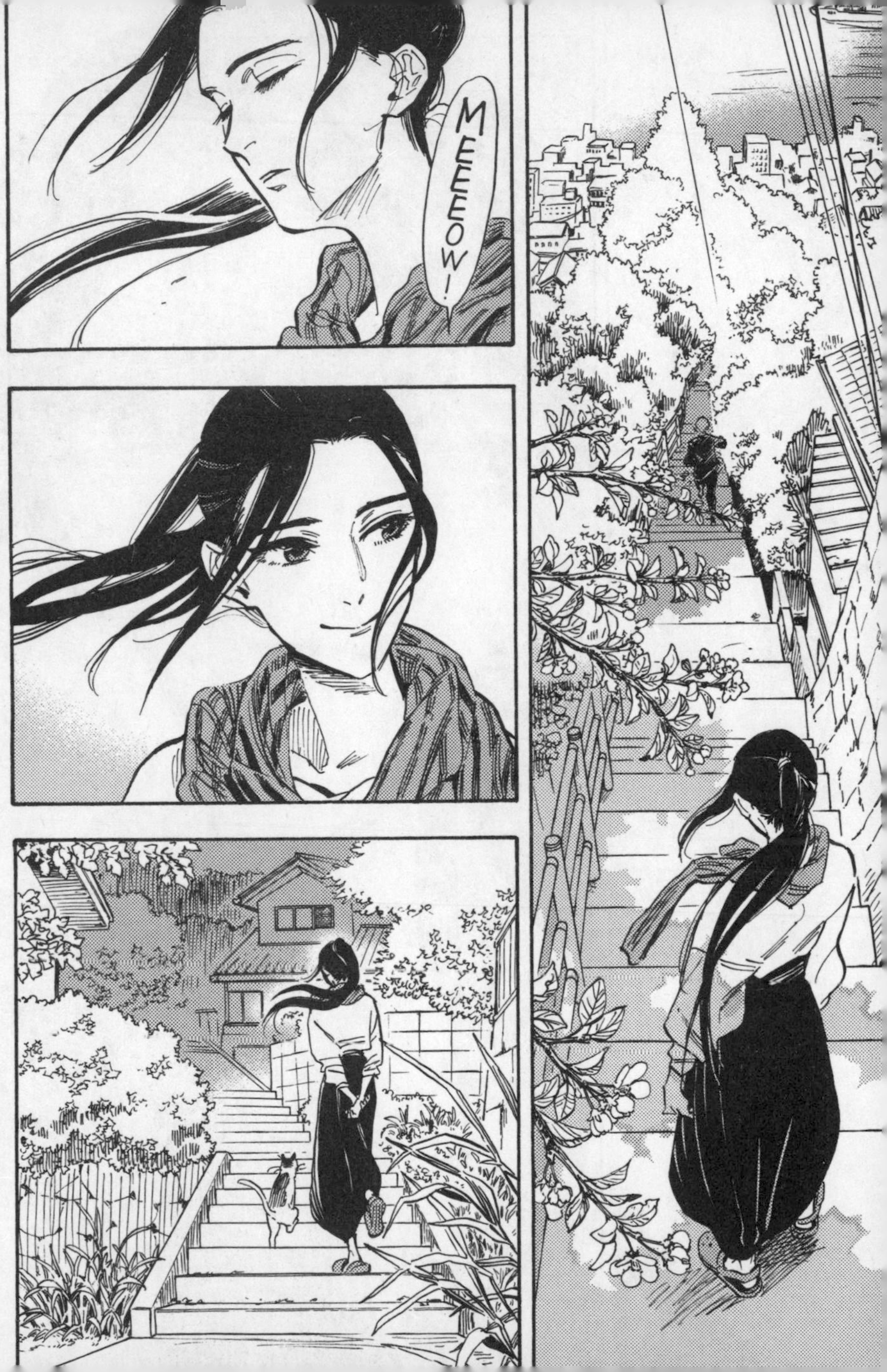
MEEEOW!

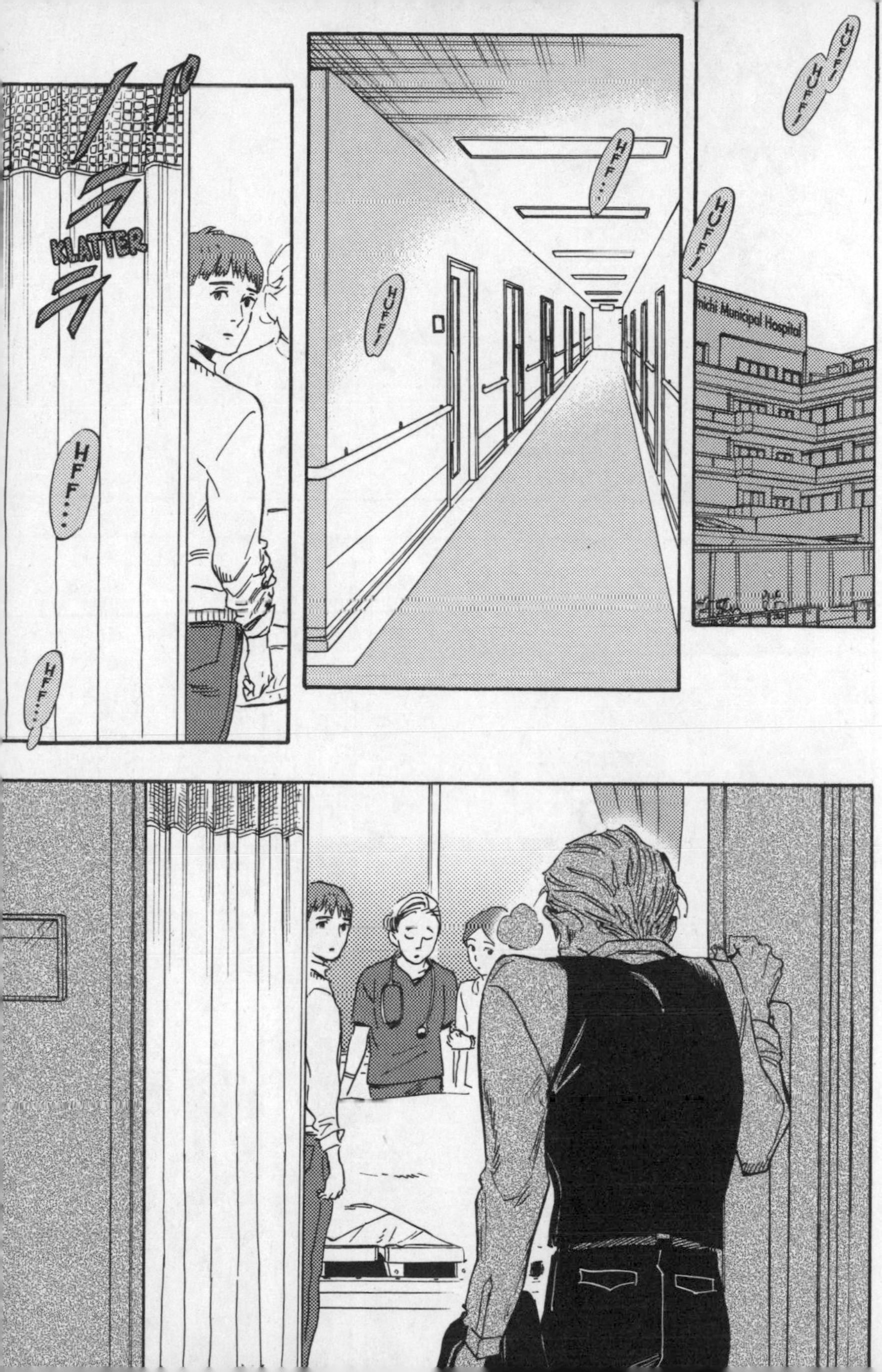

HUFF!
HUFF!
HUFF!
Municipal Hospital
HFF...
HUFF!
KLATTER
HFF...
HFF...

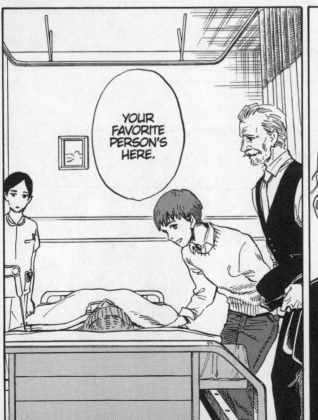

YOUR FAVORITE PERSON'S HERE.

LOOK, DAD.

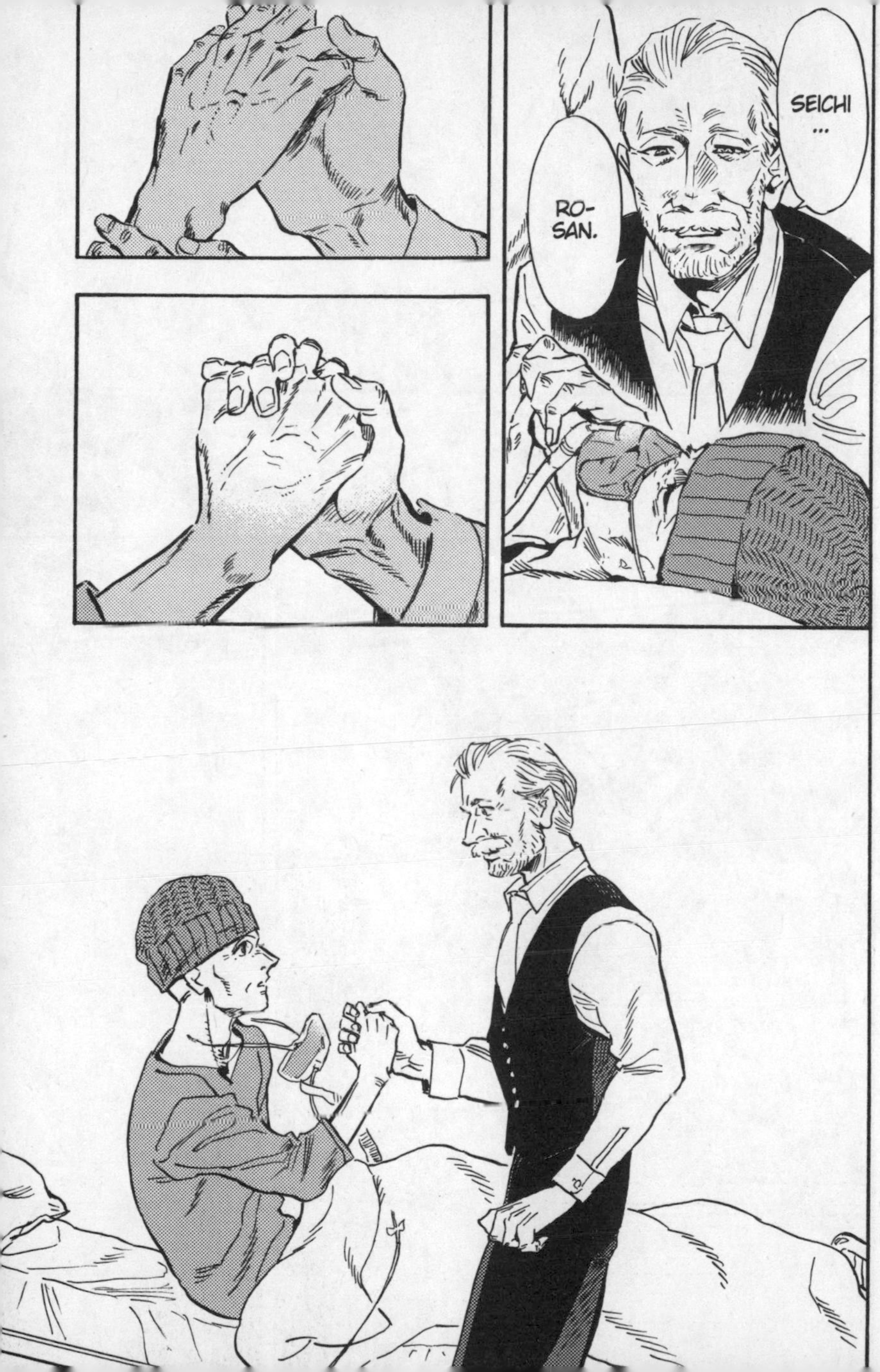
SEICHI ...
RO-SAN.

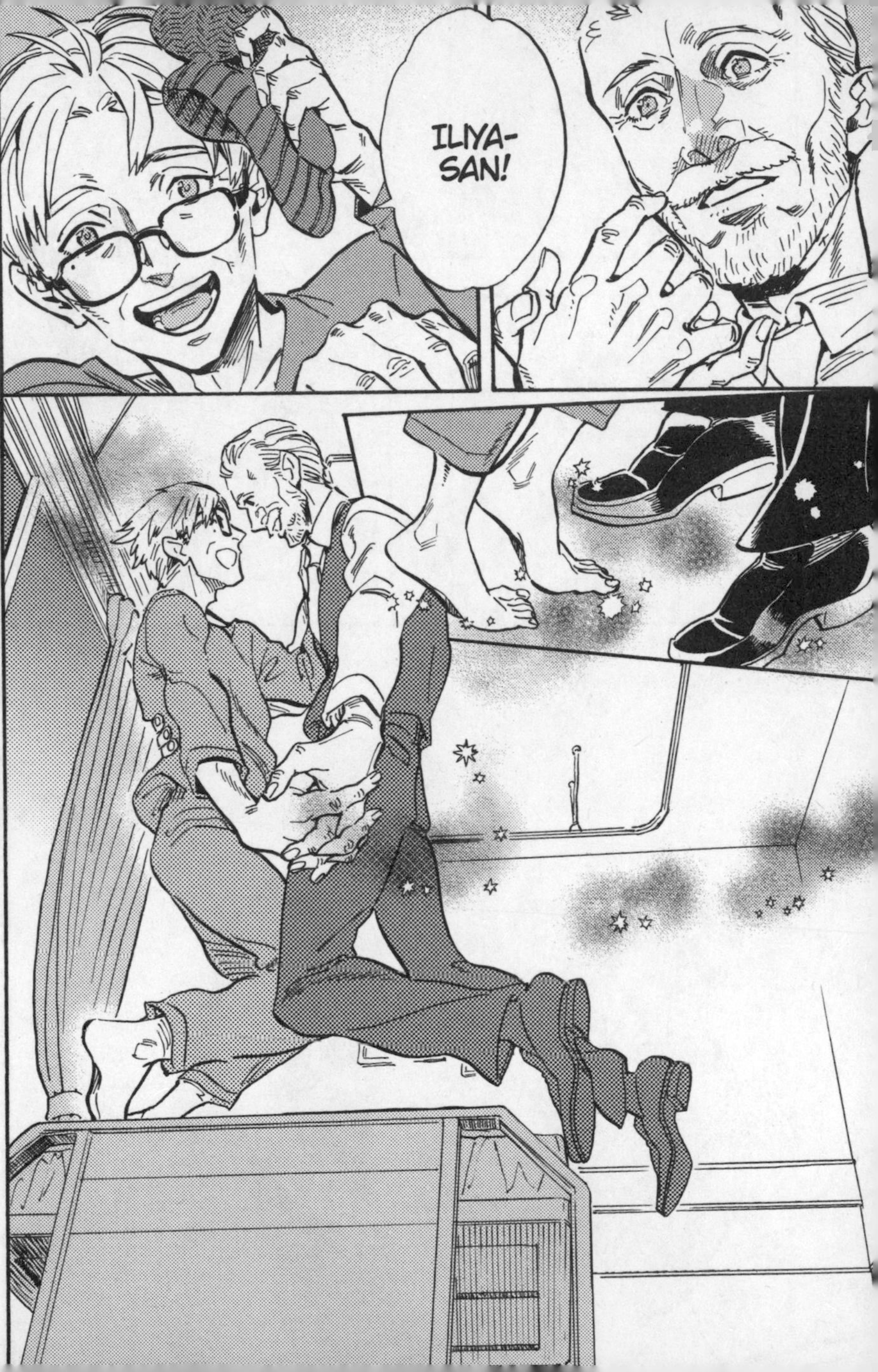
ILIYA-SAN!

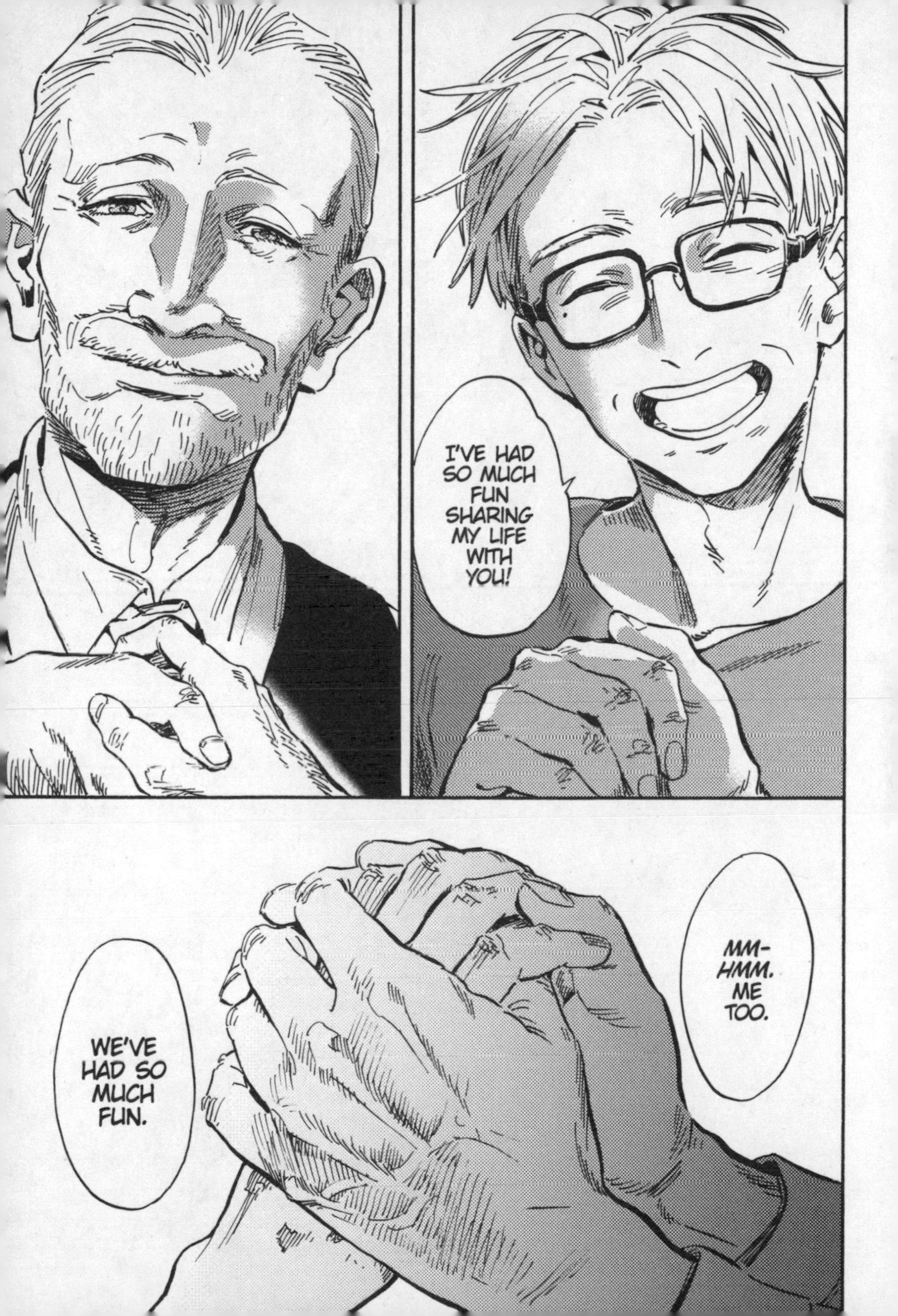
I'VE HAD SO MUCH FUN SHARING MY LIFE WITH YOU!
MM-HMM. ME TOO.
WE'VE HAD SO MUCH FUN.

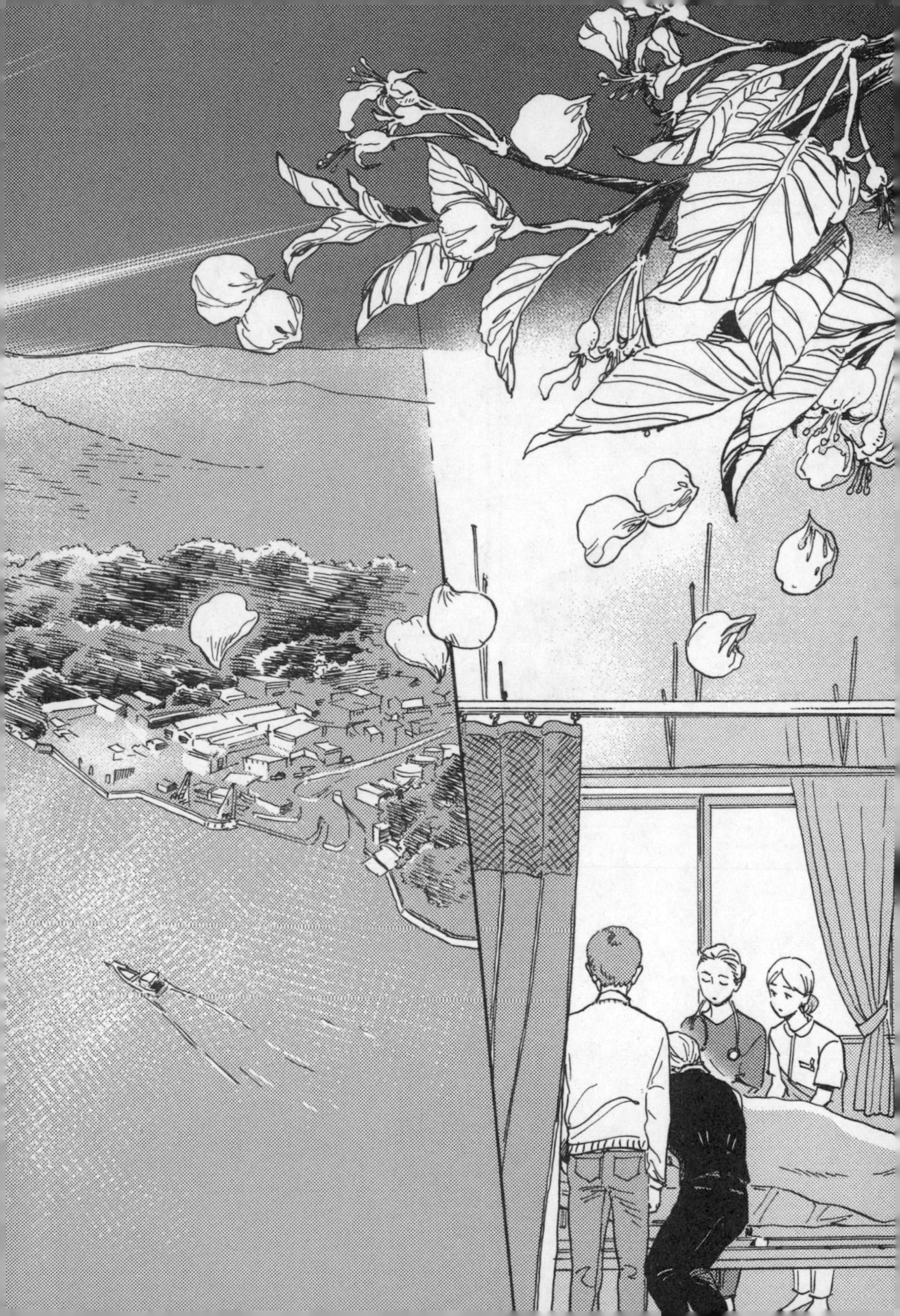

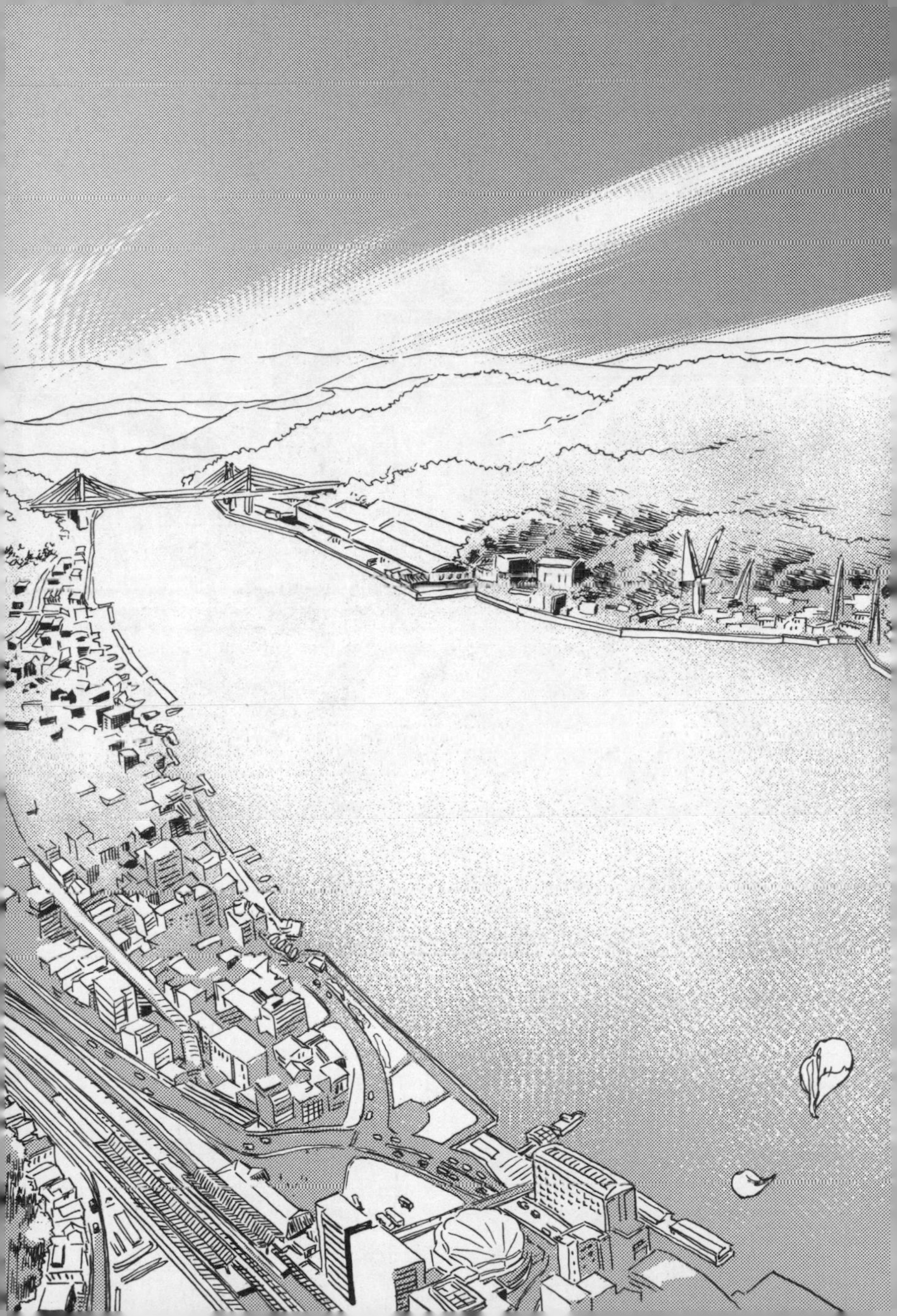

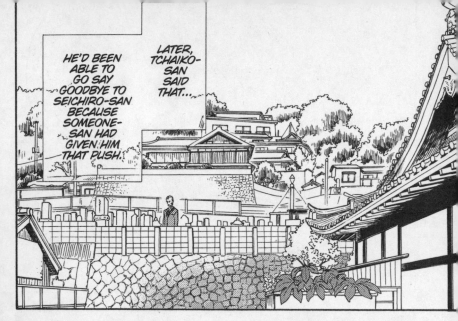

LATER,
TCHAIKO-
SAN
SAID
THAT...

HE'D BEEN
ABLE TO
GO SAY
GOODBYE TO
SEICHIRO-SAN
BECAUSE
SOMEONE-
SAN HAD
GIVEN HIM
THAT PUSH.

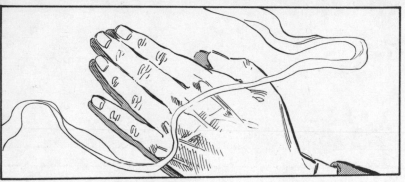

Gravestone: Seichiro.

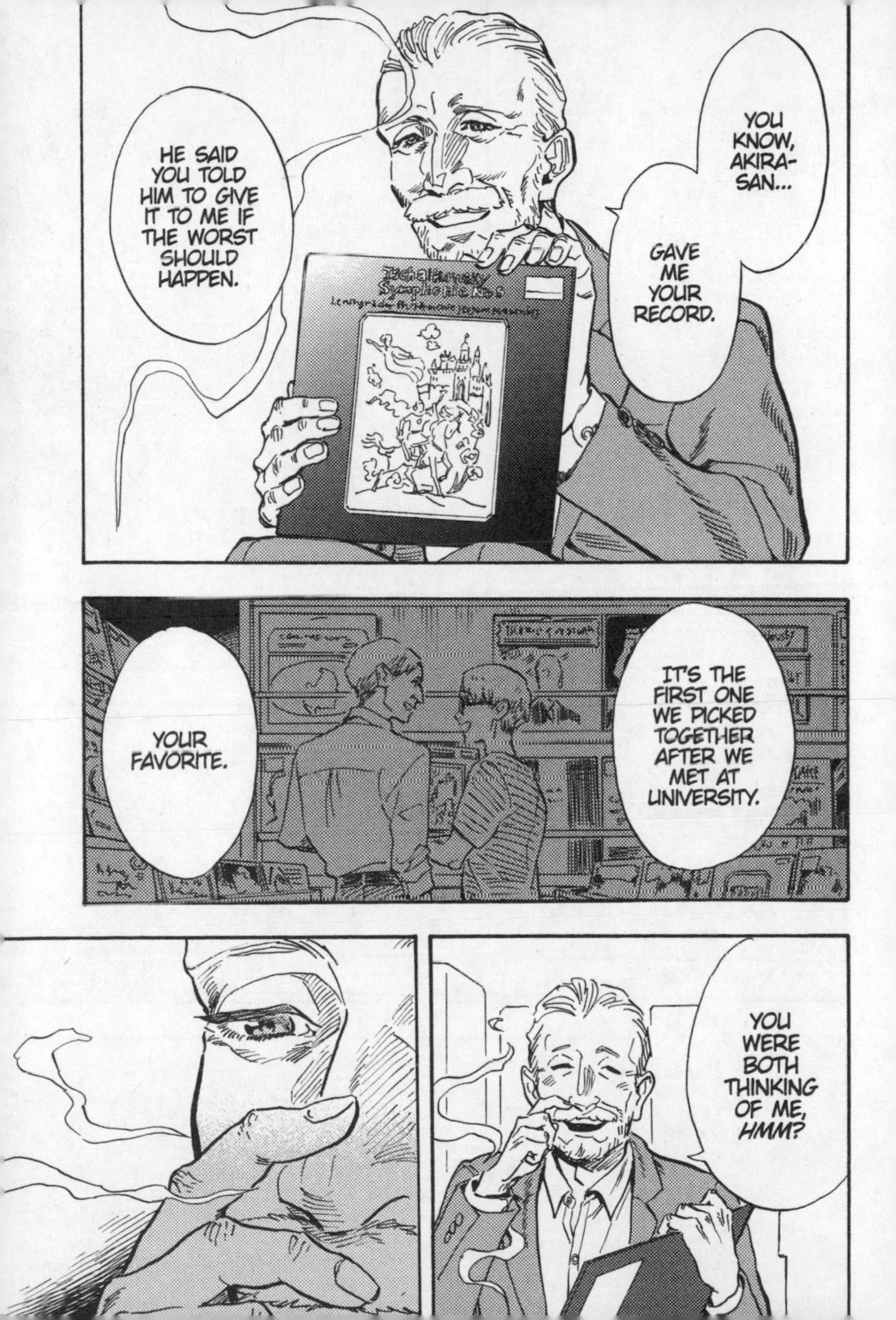
YOU KNOW, AKIRA-SAN...
GAVE ME YOUR RECORD.
HE SAID YOU TOLD HIM TO GIVE IT TO ME IF THE WORST SHOULD HAPPEN.
IT'S THE FIRST ONE WE PICKED TOGETHER AFTER WE MET AT UNIVERSITY.
YOUR FAVORITE.
YOU WERE BOTH THINKING OF ME, *HMM?*

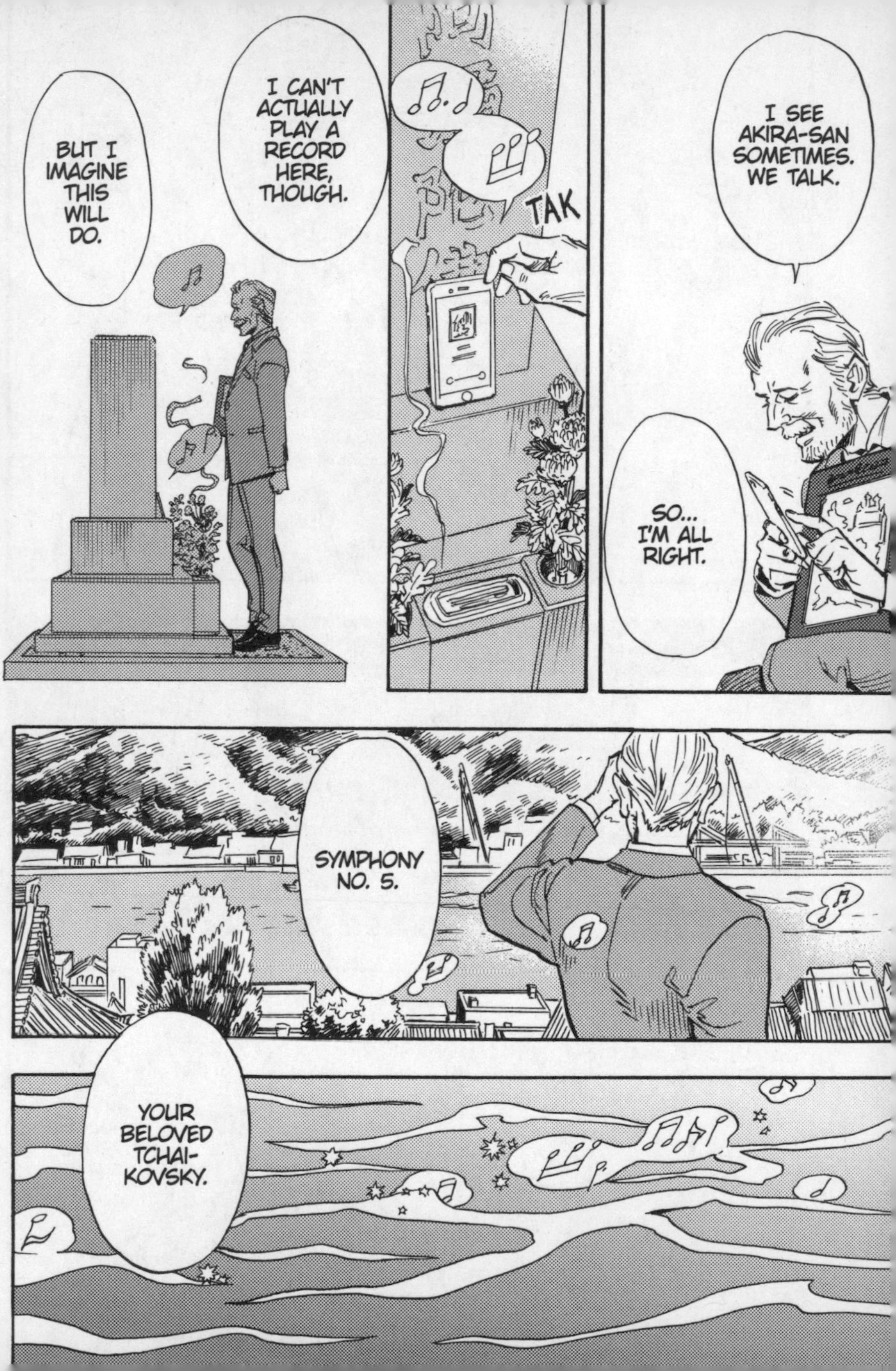
I SEE AKIRA-SAN SOMETIMES. WE TALK.
SO... I'M ALL RIGHT.
TAK
I CAN'T ACTUALLY PLAY A RECORD HERE, THOUGH.
BUT I IMAGINE THIS WILL DO.
SYMPHONY NO. 5.
YOUR BELOVED TCHAI-KOVSKY.

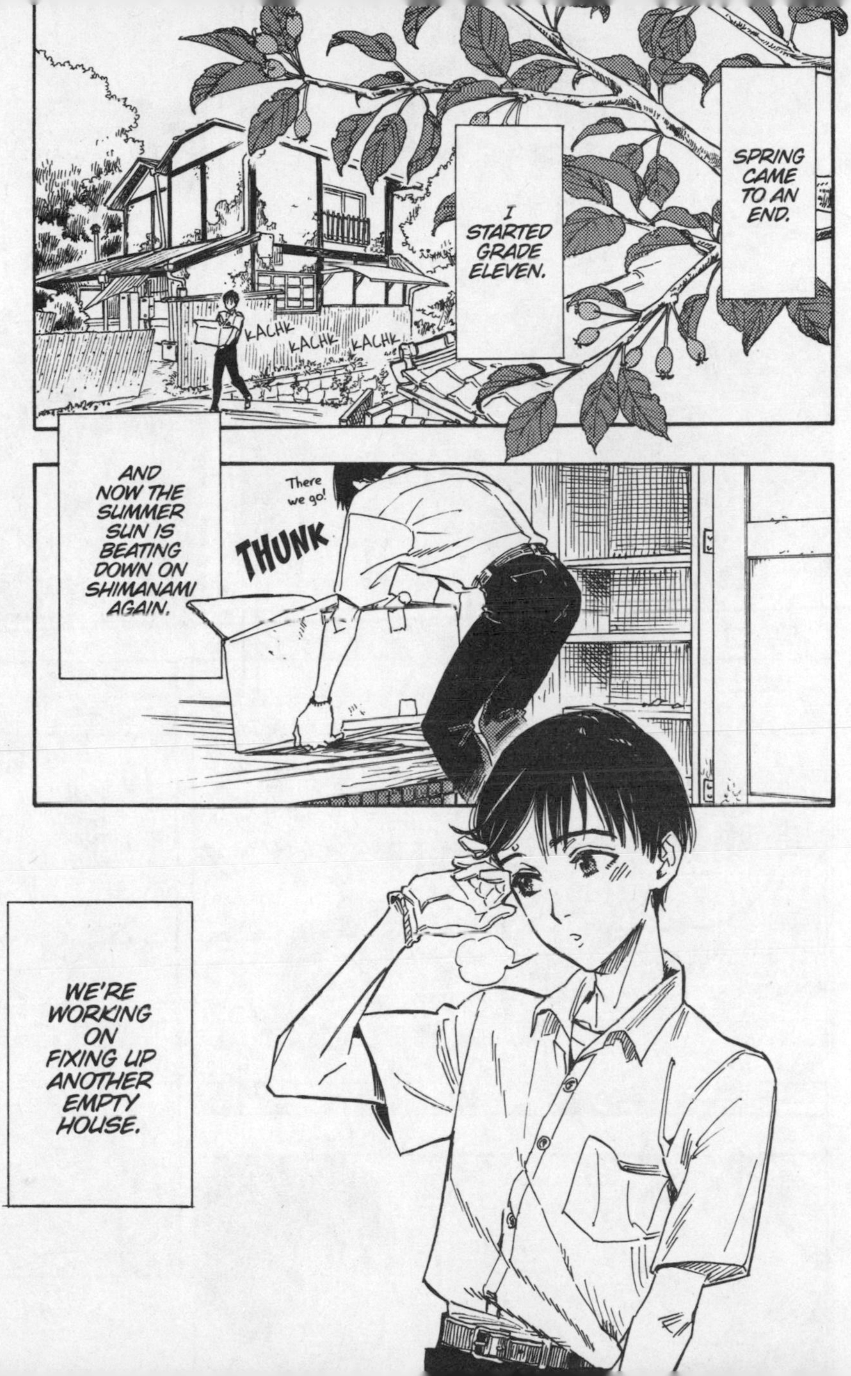
SPRING CAME TO AN END.
I STARTED GRADE ELEVEN.
KACHK
KACHK
KACHK
AND NOW THE SUMMER SUN IS BEATING DOWN ON SHIMANAMI AGAIN.
There we go!
THUNK
WE'RE WORKING ON FIXING UP ANOTHER EMPTY HOUSE.

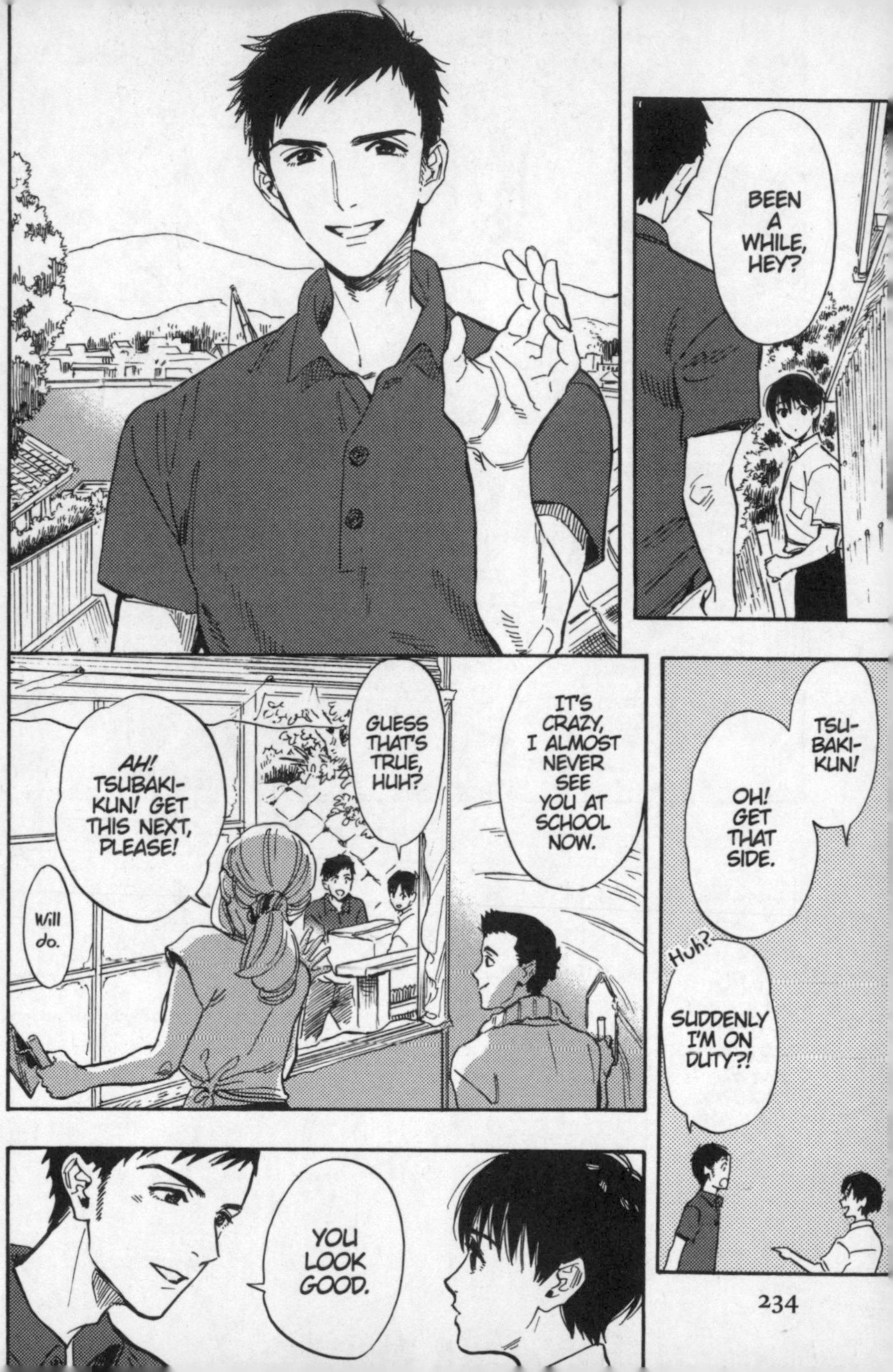
BEEN A WHILE, HEY?
TSUBAKI-KUN!
OH! GET THAT SIDE.
Huh?
SUDDENLY I'M ON DUTY?!
IT'S CRAZY, I ALMOST NEVER SEE YOU AT SCHOOL NOW.
GUESS THAT'S TRUE, HUH?
AH! TSUBAKI-KUN! GET THIS NEXT, PLEASE!
Will do.
YOU LOOK GOOD.

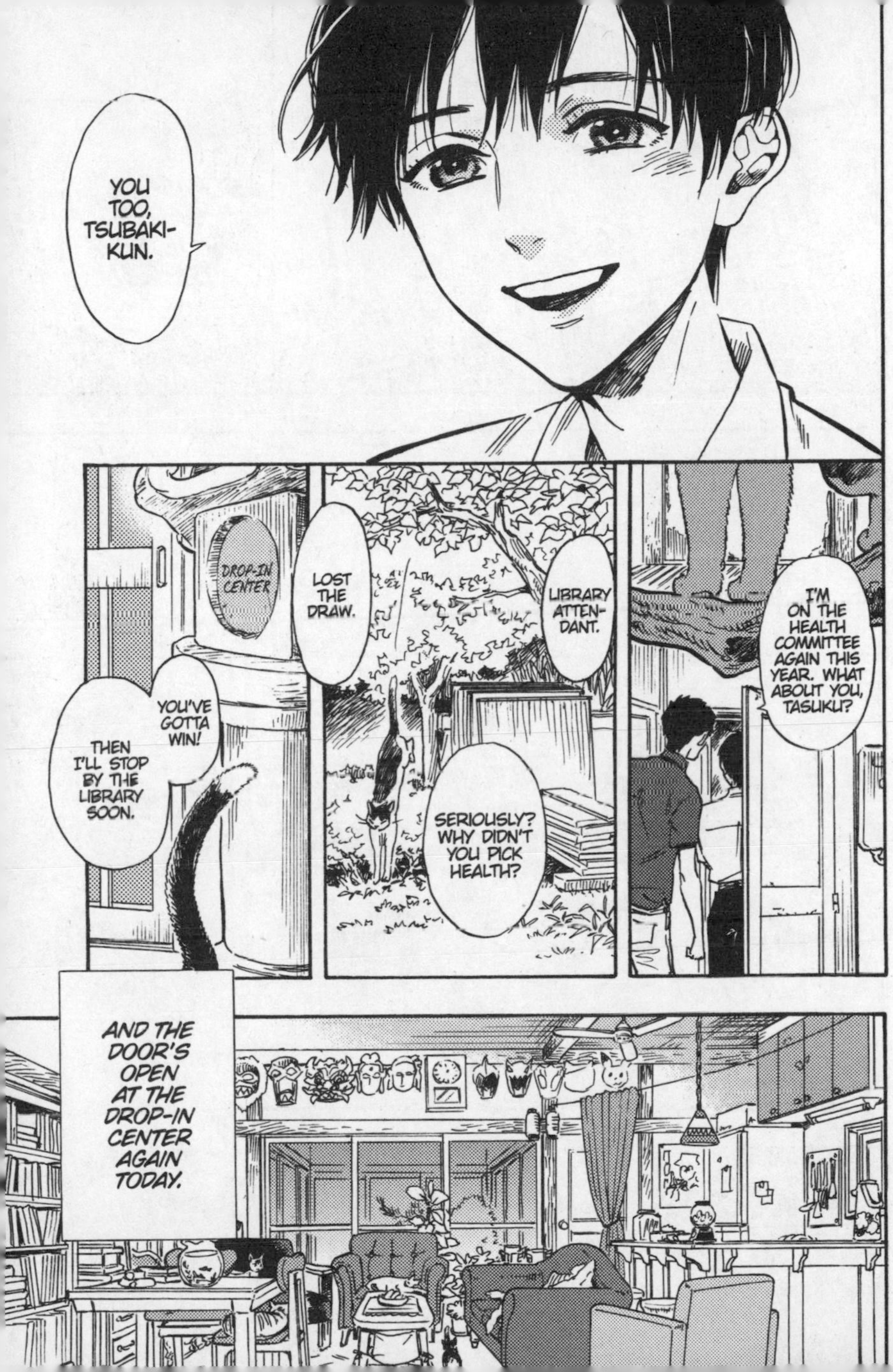
YOU TOO, TSUBAKI-KUN.
I'M ON THE HEALTH COMMITTEE AGAIN THIS YEAR. WHAT ABOUT YOU, TASUKU?
LIBRARY ATTENDANT.
SERIOUSLY? WHY DIDN'T YOU PICK HEALTH?
LOST THE DRAW.
DROP-IN CENTER
YOU'VE GOTTA WIN!
THEN I'LL STOP BY THE LIBRARY SOON.
AND THE DOOR'S OPEN AT THE DROP-IN CENTER AGAIN TODAY.

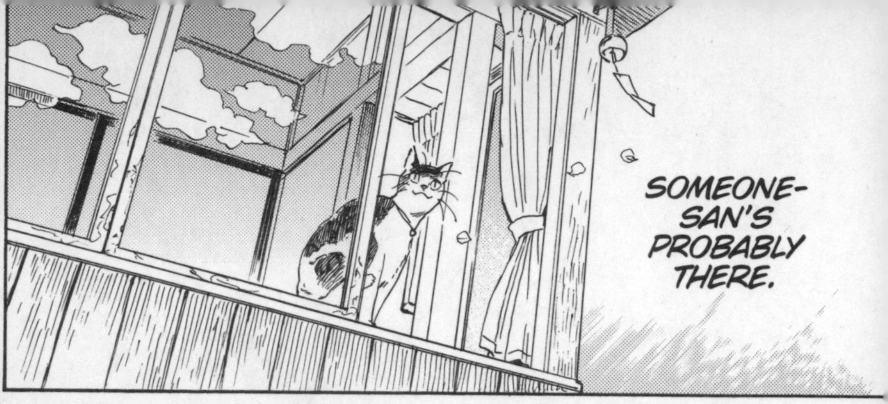
SOMEONE-SAN'S PROBABLY THERE.
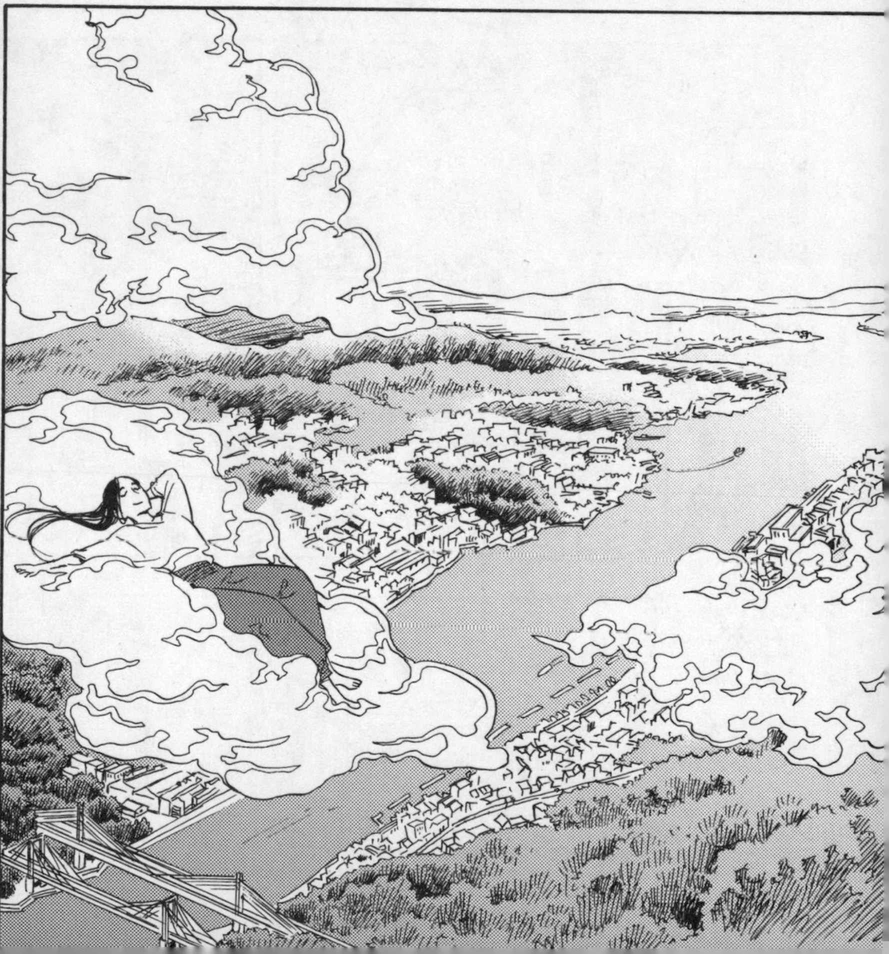

[Research Assistance]

NPO Onomichi Akiya Saisei Project
Masako Toyota

Trois Couleurs Co., Ltd.
Hiroko Masahara
Koyuki Higashi

Kentaro Tsuru
Mizuki Kunigi

Onomichi Municipal Tourism Department

[Manga Staff]

Ichijo Chinatsu
Hitani Yu
Shindai Kii

SHIMANAMI **TASOGARE**

Our Dreams at Dusk end

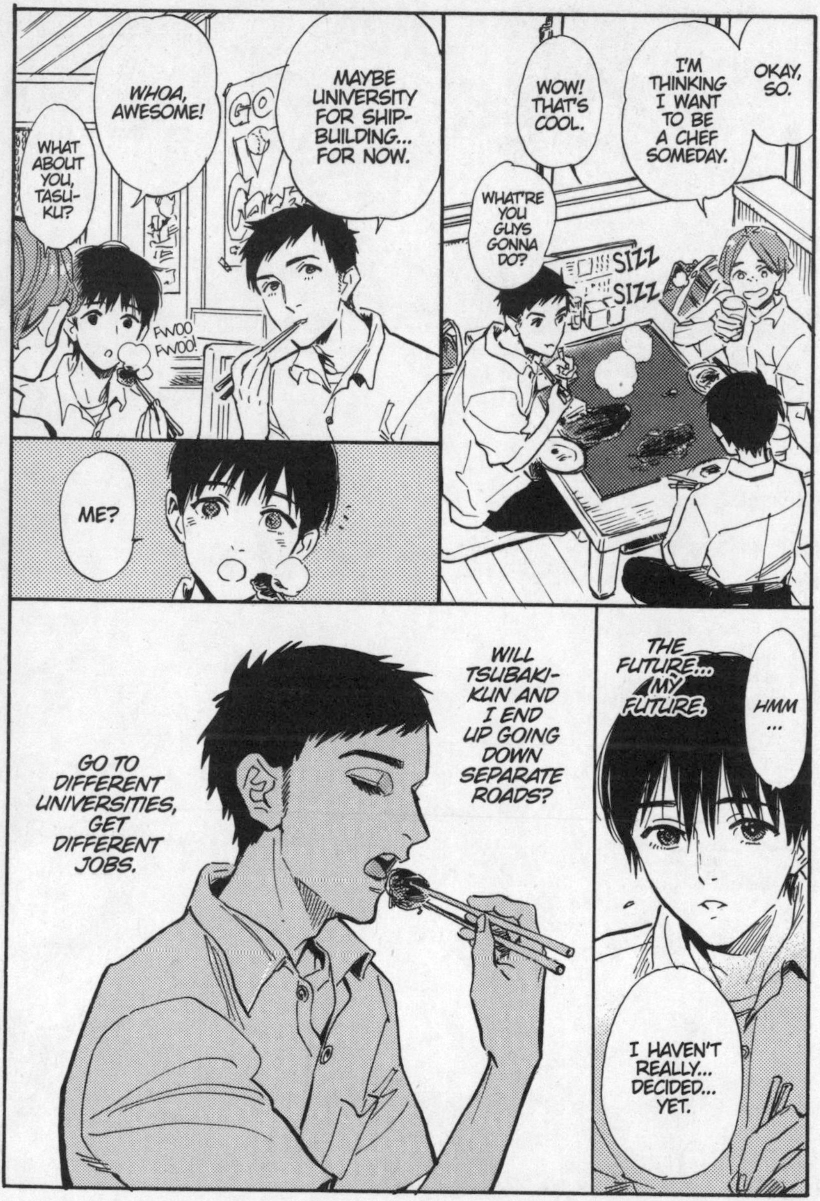
OKAY, SO.
I'M THINKING I WANT TO BE A CHEF SOMEDAY.
WOW! THAT'S COOL.
WHAT'RE YOU GUYS GONNA DO?
SIZZ SIZZ
MAYBE UNIVERSITY FOR SHIP-BUILDING... FOR NOW.
WHOA, AWESOME!
WHAT ABOUT YOU, TASUKU?
FWOO FWOO!
ME?
HMM...
THE FUTURE... MY FUTURE.
I HAVEN'T REALLY... DECIDED... YET.
WILL TSUBAKI-KUN AND I END UP GOING DOWN SEPARATE ROADS?
GO TO DIFFERENT UNIVERSITIES, GET DIFFERENT JOBS.

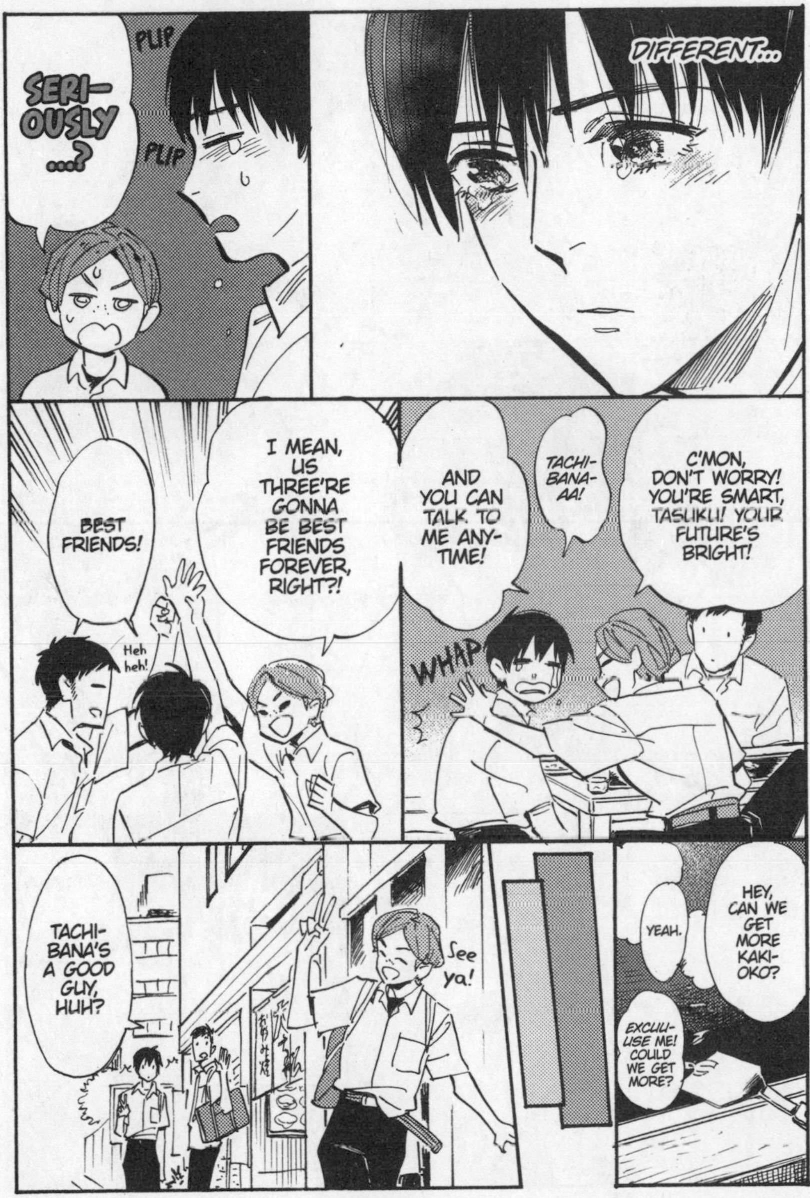
DIFFERENT...
PLIP
PLIP
SERI-OUSLY ...?
C'MON, DON'T WORRY! YOU'RE SMART, TASUKU! YOUR FUTURE'S BRIGHT!
TACHI-BANAA!
AND YOU CAN TALK TO ME ANY-TIME!
WHAP
I MEAN, US THREE'RE GONNA BE BEST FRIENDS FOREVER, RIGHT?!
BEST FRIENDS!
Heh heh!
HEY, CAN WE GET MORE KAKI-OKO?
YEAH.
EXCUU-USE ME! COULD WE GET MORE?
See ya!
TACHI-BANA'S A GOOD GUY, HUH?

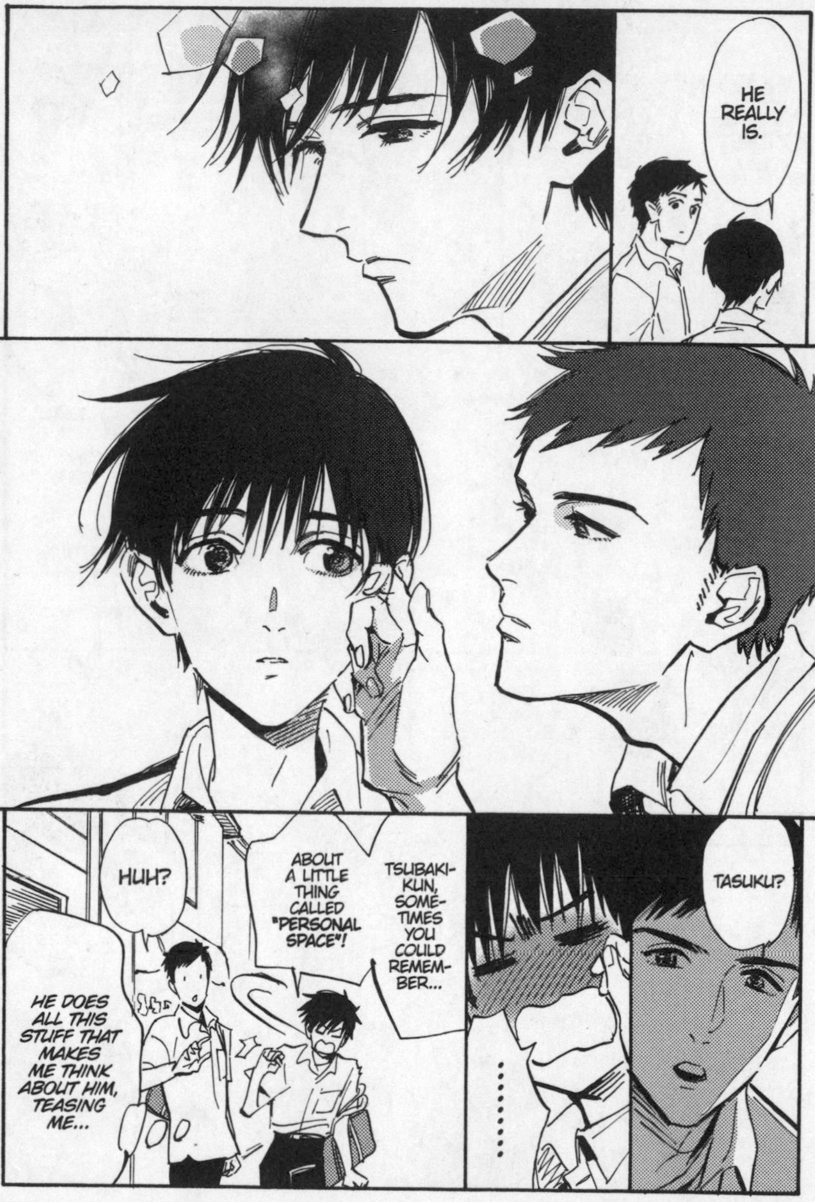
HE REALLY IS.
TASUKU?
......
TSUBAKI-KUN, SOMETIMES YOU COULD REMEMBER...
ABOUT A LITTLE THING CALLED "PERSONAL SPACE"!
HUH?
HE DOES ALL THIS STUFF THAT MAKES ME THINK ABOUT HIM, TEASING ME...

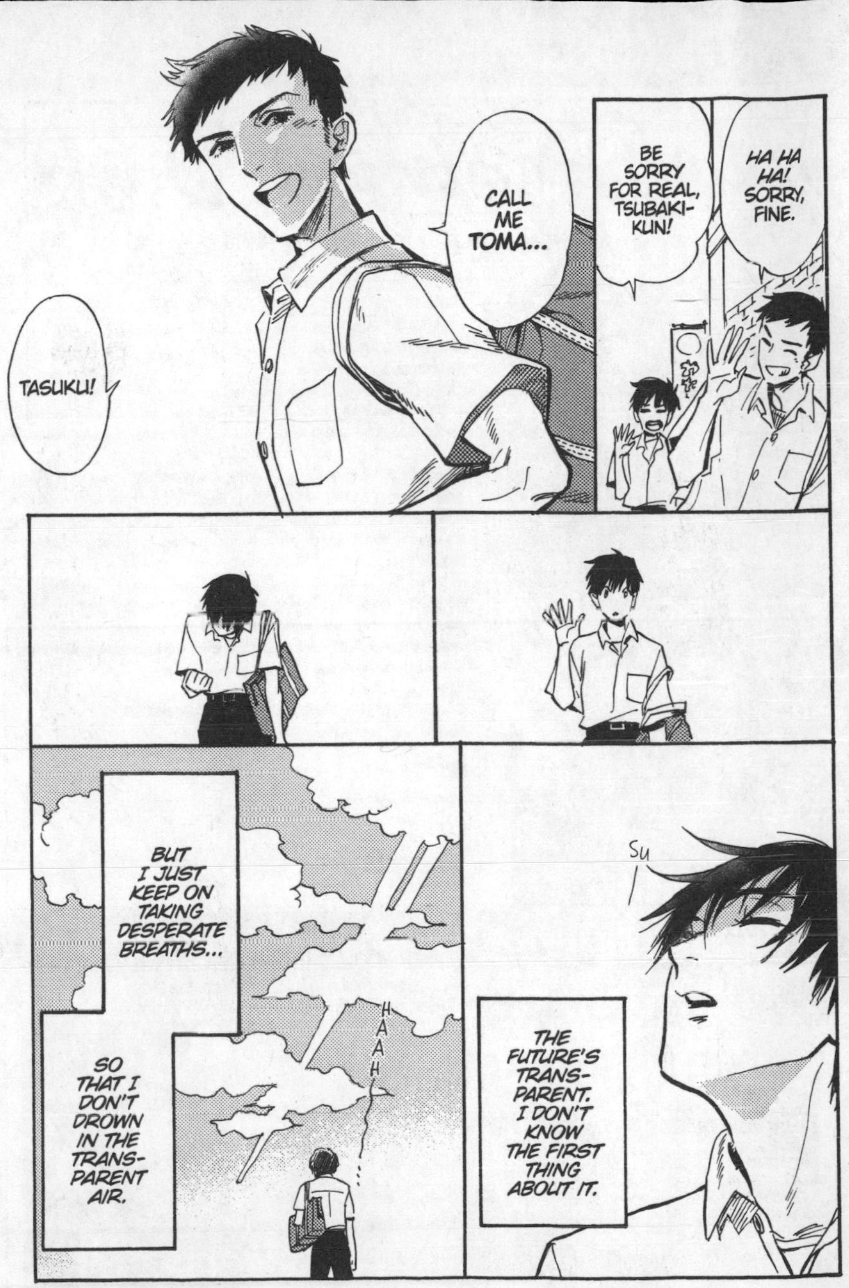
HA HA HA! SORRY, FINE.
BE SORRY FOR REAL, TSUBAKI-KUN!
CALL ME TOMA...
TASUKU!
Su
THE FUTURE'S TRANSPARENT. I DON'T KNOW THE FIRST THING ABOUT IT.
BUT I JUST KEEP ON TAKING DESPERATE BREATHS...
HAAAH
SO THAT I DON'T DROWN IN THE TRANSPARENT AIR.

SEVEN SEAS ENTERTAINMENT PRESENTS

Our Dreams at Dusk

SHIMANAMI TASOGARE

story and art by YUHKI KAMATANI　VOL. 4

TRANSLATION
Jocelyne Allen

ADAPTATION
Ysabet MacFarlane

LETTERING AND RETOUCH
Kaitlyn Wiley

COVER DESIGN
KC Fabellon

ORIGINAL EDITION DESIGNER
Hiroshi NIIGAMI (NARTI ; S)

PROOFREADER
**Kurestin Armada
Danielle King**

EDITOR
Jenn Grunigen

PRODUCTION MANAGER
Lissa Pattillo

EDITOR-IN-CHIEF
Adam Arnold

PUBLISHER
Jason DeAngelis

SHIMANAMI TASOGARE Vol. 4 by Yuhki KAMATANI
© 2015 Yuhki KAMATANI
All rights reserved.
Original Japanese edition published by SHOGAKUKAN.
English translation rights in the United States of America, Canada, and the
United Kingdom arranged with SHOGAKUKAN through Tuttle-Mori Agency, Inc.

Seven Seas press and purchase enquiries can be sent to Marketing Manager
Lianne Sentar at press@gomanga.com. Information regarding the distribution
and purchase of digital editions is available from Digital Manager CK Russell
at digital@gomanga.com.

Seven Seas and the Seven Seas logo are trademarks of
Seven Seas Entertainment. All rights reserved.

ISBN: 978-1-64275-063-8

Printed in Canada

First Printing: December 2019

10 9 8 7 6 5 4 3 2 1

FOLLOW US ONLINE: *www.sevenseasentertainment.com*

READING DIRECTIONS

This book reads from **right to left**, Japanese style. If this is your first time reading manga, you start reading from the top right panel on each page and take it from there. If you get lost, just follow the numbered diagram here. It may seem backwards at first, but you'll get the hang of it! Have fun!!

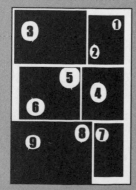